D1593785

Blasphemy, Immorality, and Anarchy

By the author:

The Most Ancient Testimony:
Sixteenth Century Christian Hebraica
in the Age of Renaissance Nostalgia

Michael Servetus: A Case Study
in Total Heresy

The Crisis of Reformation:
Confrontation and Conciliation

Blasphemy, Immorality, and Anarchy:

The Ranters and
the English Revolution

 Jerome Friedman

Ohio University Press
Athens, Ohio   London

Library of Congress Cataloging-in-Publication

Friedman, Jerome.
  Blasphemy, immorality, and anarchy.

  Bibliography: p.
  Includes index.
  1. Ranters. 2. Great Britain—History—Puritan
Revolution, 1642-1660. 3. England—Church history—
17th century. I. Title.
BX9375.R3F75 1987   284   86-23819
ISBN 0-8214-0861-5

For Phillip Bebb;
best of friends, best of colleagues.

Contents

PART TWO: THE ANTI-RANTERS

Acknowledgements

I owe much to many people for their help and support in preparing this book. Dr. Lawrence Buck, Provost of Widener College, first proposed this topic to me in 1981 over coffee at 7:30 A.M. in Iowa City at a meeting of the Sixteenth Century Studies Conference. Professor Phillip Bebb of Ohio University, to whom this volume is dedicated, was the first to read the manuscript and, as in the past, his advice was as eagerly incorporated as it was originally sought. Special thanks to Janet L. Kronenberg who took valuable time from her law practice to read and edit the original draft of the volume. Her critical opinion on matters of legal procedure, logic, syntax and style demonstrates the benefit of having intelligent friends.

I am indebted to many institutions and agencies for their generous financial support during the years this book was written. Dr. Eugene P. Wenninger, Dean of Research and Sponsored Programs at Kent State University, provided financial aid, travel grants and authorized leaves of absence. A generous travel grant from the American Philosophical Society permitted me to visit archives and acquire source material otherwise beyond my reach.

The librarians and staffs of several libraries were very helpful. In Great Britain, I received excellent service at the British Museum, the Bodleian Library, the John Rylands Library and the Library of the Society of Friends. Similarly, special thanks to the Huntington and Folger Libraries and the library of Union Theological Seminary in the United States. Mr. Michael Cole, Associate Director of the Interlibrary Loan Services at Kent State University, was especially helpful in arranging for the photoduplication of many thousands of pages of source materials. This project, consisting entirely of materials unavailable in Ohio, would have been largely impossible without his help.

Finally, my deep thanks and personal appreciation to Ms. Helen Gawthrop of the Ohio University Press. Her efforts in producing this volume demonstrate the skill, competence, sensitivity and attention required to turn typed pages into a published book.

Preface

There can be no doubt that the Ranters were the most radical and the most peculiar sect of the Cromwellian interregnum. Coming into prominence about 1649, the Ranters captivated the minds of many Englishmen for the next decade. They were the incarnation of the Hobbesian nightmare of masses running wild in the streets, and even Gerard Winstanley, the leader of the equally detestable and feared Diggers, considered the Ranters an abomination. Other contemporaries and subsequent authorities have been no more friendly. The 1911 edition of the *Encyclopaedia Britannica* wrote that the Ranters were the dregs of the Seeker movement.[1] Rufus Jones, the mild mannered and tolerant historian of mystical sectarianism, concluded "The Ranters got a bad name from everybody who came into contact with them, and there is no question that it was a degenerate movement."[2] In their own day, George Fox fumed about the immorality of those Ranters he met in prison. He observed how they drank, smoked, derided common concepts of God and, worst of all, "they sang, whistled and danced."[3]

Despite such disagreeable statements, the Ranters were important for a variety of reasons. For a few crucial years Ranter leaders found a large following in London's urban poor, though Ranter activity was also reported in virtually every corner of England as well. The Ranters' appeal was to the lowest strata of English society: the urban poor and the landless rural population, street people, criminals, and prostitutes. The Ranter message was varied. Religious institutions were a sham and God was within you. There was no heaven, no hell, and, hence, no need to live as if there were. All governance and property were theft, corruption, and extortion. All institutions emanated from and fostered class dominance and were thus of no significance to the poor Englishman. There were neither licit nor illicit forms of behavior, just deeds. In a word, the Ranters were the first recognizable movement expounding ideas that might be called class conscious anarchism. Tame and civil Ranters wanted merely to destroy all religious institutions. More radical Ranters called for the abolition of all government and private property, and the most extreme of all hoped for a universal conflagration to destroy everything.

The Ranters were more than mere malcontents feeding upon the inability of a revolutionary society in turmoil to reach political and religious

PREFACE

consensus. They were also the heirs of the long and wonderful traditions of ancient and medieval heretical dualism found in the Brethren of the Free Spirit and in the Cathari, Bogomils, Messalians, Paulicians and Gnostics before them.[4] Much as the Gnostics were considered a plague by early Christians, and the Cathari and Bogomils and Paulicians in later centuries, the Ranters, too, were thought by their contemporaries to be an infection and social disease. Ranters were neither polite nor modest and caused a good deal of trouble, but they were not dismissed by their contemporaries as they have been ignored by historians. The Blasphemy Act of 1650 was aimed exclusively at prosecuting and persecuting the Ranters, and almost every Ranter treated in these pages was tried, found guilty in a court of law and sent to jail. Some, like Bauthumley, were more unfortunate; for speaking blasphemy his tongue was bored through with a hot poker.

It is difficult to make too many generalizations about the Ranters for most were fierce individualists who found no need for common confessions or lists of dogmas. Some, like Coppe and Robins, were probably insane, and Tany was absolutely mad. Freeman and Norwood were upstanding gentlemen dreaming of a free England, while others such as Coppin were theologians of high caliber. Bauthumley was a spokesman for a religious quietism lost in the din and drumming of Presbyterian politics and intolerance. Foster was a political arsonist ready to pitch England into a worldwide bonfire in which all would be destroyed so that a new society, Phoenix-like, could emerge from the ashes. All the while, Clarkson preached redemption through sin as the surest path to salvation. The Ranters were a varied and fascinating lot, and yet, up to this time, not a single adequate treatment can be found describing and analyzing what Ranters actually believed and wrote. Indeed, not a single Ranter has been the subject of serious scholarly scrutiny. It is true that many Ranter treatises were destroyed by Parliament or through the passage of time, but there is no lack of original source material, as the many treatises analyzed in this volume will indicate. Indeed, considering the number of works dealing with the Cathari, the Paulicians and the Brethren of the Free Spirit, whose views are largely known only through the records of the courts of Inquisition, neglect of the far more fruitful Ranters is difficult to comprehend. Perhaps students of medieval heresy have been studying the wrong period, or students of English history have missed an entire world of thought. I am indebted to both groups of scholars, for through their negligence I have been left with a world to describe.

It is unusual for readers to open a volume concerning a subject about which they know very little; yet, few readers can claim familiarity with

xii

Ranter thought or their antecedents. Chapter 1 will present a short general background of the events and sectarianism of the times, and nature of the Ranter family tree. The remainder of the first part of this volume is pure Ranter dualism and consists of an analysis of every Ranter author and treatise extant. The division of Ranters into various categories is arbitrary to the extent that Ranters themselves recognized no strict lines of demarcation and got along quite well with one another despite their differences. These categories are not mutually exclusive, and more than one author might fit into more than one category. The division was created to permit the reader to appreciate the fundamental differences or plethora of orientations expressed by these thinkers. Philosophical Ranters, for instance, more than other Ranters were concerned with the religious, conceptual, and intellectual implications of dualism and its meaning for creation, good and evil. They were the premier religious thinkers of the movement, and both Bauthumley and Coppin were required reading among Ranters. The Sexual Libertines accepted the philosophical foundations of dualism but were more concerned with how mankind should live life on earth while awaiting death and the merger of the soul with God. That they are called Sexual Libertines tells us something about the conclusions they drew. Thus, whereas philosophical Ranters were overwhelmed by the dualism of matter and spirit, good and evil, and were often very ascetic, the Libertines accepted the same dichotomy but decided to make the best of their temporary sojourn in this corrupt world of physical matter. The Libertines Coppe and Clarkson were many things, but no one called them ascetic.

Revolutionary Ranters were philosophical dualists who drew social implications from their thought. Hence, most were concerned with the religious, political and economic institutions all of which were understood to be Satan's tools for the control of mankind in this evil world. To be a revolutionary Ranter simply meant that one wished to put an end to Satan's control of the world by any means possible. Where Parliament wished to use the army against the King, the Ranters wished to use the army against everyone starting with the King and then Parliament, and then the nobility and then. . . . Gentlemen Ranters were a branch of the revolutionists but with one important difference; they were officers in the army and enthusiastic about the army's ability to hasten the destruction of England.

Divine Ranters were individuals considered Ranters by contemporaries and by their followers as well; but they differed somewhat from other Ranters in that they believed they were the actual living God. To an extent these Ranters represented the Free Spirit wing of Ranter antecedents rather than the influence of medieval dualism. Additionally, some were insane. Tho-

PREFACE

mas Tany, or Theauraujohn His Aurora, as he preferred to be called, was the consummate Ranter, combining all Ranter elements into a bizarre and fascinating intellectual system which included his own language, logic, grammar and sources. Some might point out that Tany was stark raving mad, but then Nietzsche was not well balanced and Schopenhauer was very depressed and finally he commited suicide.

Tales of Two Parsons concerns the lives, loves and writings of two notorious Ranters, John Pordage and Thomas Webb. Alone among Ranters, these two gentlemen held appointments as pastors until, for a variety of incredible offenses, they were thrown out of their positions.

The second part of this volume concerns anti-Ranter literature and materials. This is the lightest section of the book containing as it does all of the most outrageous poems, pictures, plays and slanderous treatises written against the Ranters. Serious religious polemics from a variety of orthodox and sectarian sources are also presented. To the best of my knowledge, every existent piece of anti-Ranter literature has been included.

A few words are necessary concerning the use of texts cited in this book. In the case of Ranter authors, all the writings have been analyzed. This involves some measure of repetition, but so little has been written about the Ranters and so many of these treatises are not readily available, that complete treatment demands as complete coverage as possible. It is hoped that increased familiarity with the remarkable writings of the Ranters will stimulate further study of this unusual sect.

Because this volume makes little use of secondary literature but intensive use of primary sources, footnoting has been streamlined to benefit both reader and publisher. All primary source information including author, title, and year of publication is located in the first page of each chapter with page number of each citation from each individual treatise within the body of the text itself. Place of publication in all cases is London. Secondary sources are noted in the traditional fashion at the end of the volume. Other than in titles, spelling has been modernized to improve readability. Where possible, sentence structure has been left intact to transmit the author's true intent.

Introduction

Only recently have historians expressed interest in the sectarianism of the civil war years. Until the last two generations, most historians concentrated upon the political history of the conflict or the mass of orthodox religious literature generated by the "Puritan Revolution." These orientations, predicated upon the large quantities of available published orthodox religious writings, political documents and state papers, suited the late nineteenth-century intellectual emphasis upon the state as the proper area of historical concern and the belief that only the governing social elite merited investigation. More recently, economic and social historians have widened our perspective about the conditions of life and the motives of governmental and class action, and growing numbers of historians have found in the sectarian radicals a great well of untapped material about the life and beliefs of commoners during this tumultuous age. Even so, the study of sectarian radicalism, like everything else, has its own traditions to be understood.

Reasonably, the first radicals studied were those with a modern constituency. Hence, Quaker historians, if at first only for the gratification of their own members, wrote about their history and created libraries and journals much as Mennonites and other radical churches of the sixteenth century have also embarked upon scholarly pursuits in service of their own community.[5] In similar fashion, Unitarian historians have written about interregnum Socinianism and scholars from the Anabaptist tradition have published materials about the small gathered Anabaptist churches of this time.[6]

Though not a religious sect, the Levellers also attracted the attention of those who saw their own ideals fostered by this earlier community. Before and during the Second World War progressive historians identified the Levellers as seventeenth-century harbingers of the social ideals they themselves accepted. Like the Levellers, these scholars, then opposed to fascism and authoritarianism, also believed they knew something about civil wars, the claims of those who spoke in the name of religious, or in this case ideological, truth and the need for religious and social toleration. The election of progressive and labor governments in many western European countries and the general belief that Europe might be rebuilt around positive social values further accelerated the social-democratic desire to locate early modern precedents for post world war social policy.[7]

Those radicals having neither constituency nor historical great-grand-

1

children might have suffered a lack of twentieth-century interest but eventually these, too, attracted the efforts of scholars. Though there is no single chiliastic church, for instance, recent confessional interest in the apocalyptic tradition has led to the study of millenarianism of earlier ages. Scholars have written about such ideas from a medieval perspective, from the vantage point of the sixteenth-century Reformation and in light of a developing modern eschatology found in both Nazism and Leninist communism. Eventually, scholars also found England's Fifth Monarchy Men, apocalypticians with a vengeance for where others merely carried signs concerning the imminent end of the world, the Fifth Monarchists believed they were actually living through it. Indeed, they saw in Cromwell and the bloody conflict surrounding his efforts nothing but signs of God's presence.[8] Even those sects with almost no obvious modern following have been studied by scholars and several books have recently appeared about the Familists and the Muggletonians.[9]

And yet, despite the vast proportions of civil war period literature, modern historical scholarship has either neglected the Ranters entirely or has mouthed earlier nasty views of them without bothering to look into the Ranters themselves. Indeed, there are few areas where the secondary literature is of such poor quality. In his monumental work of 1909, Rufus Jones, the sure friend of so many unpopular and persecuted religious groups, had little good to write about the Ranters. He noted that "the Ranters got a bad name from everybody who came into contact with them, and there is no question that it was a degenerate movement, though," Jones added, "many of the so-called Ranters were honest sincere persons trying in their crude fashion to utter the profound truth of divine indwelling."[10]

As one continues to read Jones, it becomes obvious that the Ranters were degenerate primarily for not becoming Quakers. Indeed, Jones dealt with the Ranters only because of their importance to early Quakerism when the two movements were similar. Unlike the Quakers, however, Jones tells us the Ranters were led by "some unstable, ill balanced men and women, [who] were swept quite off the poise of sanity by it and large groups of common people (this was essentially a movement of common people) were carried into a cheap half-digested 'spiritualism' which bristled with dangers."

In making his evaluation, Jones cited several contemporary Quakers concerning Ranters and noted "these accounts for the most part show a horror of Ranterism and a hostility to its exponents. But these accounts are almost without exception vague and general, with few actual sins specified . . ." Despite the admitted vagueness of his sources, Jones cited the polemical treatises against the Ranters written by such eminent Quakers as Samuel Fisher, Richard Hickock, G. F. Thomas Curtis and others. In one instance, after citing a very long portion of a very venomous treatise by George Roulston, dealt with later in this volume, Jones noted "but it shows itself on its own face to be thoroughly unreliable and its account of the Ranter doctrine and doings is of little value." Despite his concession that few of his anti-Ranter sources were credible or specific, Jones observed "it is at any rate perfectly clear even when full allowance is made for sectarian misunderstanding and exaggeration, that the Ranter movement was a serious outbreak of mental and moral disorder. The movement furnishes much information on the widespread existence, in the period, of unstable mental conditions . . ." Concluding his treatment of the Ranters, Jones cited, as do all Quaker historians, the contemporary Quaker assessment that "had not the Quakers come, the Ranters [would] have overrun the nation." One wonders how this widespread insanity characterizing England accounts for the fact that so many Quakers were originally Ranters.

While it is not surprising that Jones, a Quaker historian, would cite partial Quaker sources against the Ranters, it is difficult to understand why he used so few Ranter sources in explaining what they believed. The materials, then as now, existed and might have been consulted. In fact, only a few snippets of Ranter thought are presented and only where they supported the overall contentions of Quaker authors. Jones can be forgiven his oversight, however, for the subject of his work was the history of Quakerism and only one half chapter was devoted to the Ranters. If it is true that every daughter religion must distance itself from the mother religion which is then conceived as the fullness of evil, Jones' evaluation is easily explained. Paul condemned the Pharisees and Martin Luther liberated Christianity from the bed of Catholic superstition. Jones sought to free Quakerism from its early Ranter origins.

A more balanced view of the Ranters is provided by Christopher Hill in his most important work, *The World Turned Up-side Down: Radical Ideas During the English Revolution*, first published in 1972.[11] This work has several advantages over Jones' treatment. Mr. Hill is certainly no proponent of any religious group finding its origin in those tumultuous days and perhaps for this reason is able to present much good information about England's extreme left and radical sects without drawing moral conclusions. The purpose of his volume was to treat the many strange and weird ideas circulating at the time; consequently the Ranters received far better treatment though they were still confined to a brief chapter. Mr. Hill was willing to accept all radicals on their own terms and present their views from their own perspective; hence this volume is fundamental in breaking the rigid mind-set that has developed over the centuries that all English Radicals were Levellers, Diggers, extreme Puritans or insane people. In this regard his volume serves the same valuable purpose as did George Williams' *The Radical Reformation*, which did so much to catalogue, explain and express what radicals a century earlier believed.[12] Yet, every silver lining has its cloud and Mr. Hill, understandably, could devote only a chapter or so to the Ranters. The anti-Ranter materials are put into a far better perspective but this melange of so many radical tendencies is able to present the reader with just a few choice pieces from Ranter sources. As a result, a few of Hill's conclusions are erroneous while others are not well supported. Still, Christopher Hill opened the door to the world of radical sectarianism for the scholar and student. All of us who walk through this door do so because of Hill's efforts.

Like Jones and many others, Hill places the Ranters at the tail end of the Seekers and leading to the Quakers. There is some historical accuracy to this assessment because many Seekers did become Ranters and many Ranters did become Quakers. It is also true that all were initially Church of England and wore socks. This assessment suffers from too linear an understanding of sectarian groups and may be predicated upon a slighting of what Ranters actually believed and therefore how they differed from both Seekers and Quakers. Moreover, neither Jones nor Hill nor others usually creating such neat categories actually made an in-depth investigation of the many different Ranter writings. In his monumental undertaking of treating so many others who were not Ranters and whose views may have been easier to describe, Hill did not consider Ranters as a separate group. Thus, when Hill writes, "It is very difficult to define what Ranters believed, as opposed to individuals who are called Ranters" one must not accept this statement too literally.

It is reasonable to suppose that books and articles devoted to the Ranters might do them greater justice than partial treatments where the Ranters are included in more general studies. In fact, this is not the case, for some authors have written about the Ranters but then only to make a point about some other historical phenomenon. In 1971 G. F. S. Ellens published a short article in *Church History* entitled, "The Ranters Ranting: Reflections on a Ranting Counter Culture,"[13] based upon his Columbia University dissertation of 1968 entitled "Case Studies in 17th century Enthusiasm, Especially the Ranters." The focus of the article is presented in the first paragraph. "The Ranter Counter Culture," we are informed "was a phenomenon of Puritan England." As we recall, everything in the late 1960s was analyzed in terms of the counter culture, and in this faddish vein Ellens noted "This was not a movement towards a goal; it was a movement of repulsion away from English society as represented by the Puritans. It implied a rejection of the Puritan Establishment, its ethics, its values and its goals." Hence, the Ranters, like the Hippies, are held to be similar phenomena despite the obvious difference that the Hippies did reject an established political orientation whereas the Ranters originated in revolutionary times when there was no "establishment" and where the king had been executed, Parliament disbanded, and the army was in disarray, and the organized Church of England disenfranchised from its monopoly. In order to prove that Ranters were a counter culture, and that Puritans were an establishment, Ellens relied upon the writings of M. Stubbs, who will be dealt with later in this volume. Stubbs is presented as an archetypical Puritan although there is no evidence to support this representation. Reading history through Stubbs' eyes the author noted "that the Ranters were almost all drawn from the lower classes probably points to a connection between their social and economic status and their depressed state of mind in religious matters. This stands in marked contrast to the stolid stability and confidence of the Puritan." In another example of the author's unwillingness to treat the Ranters on their own terms, Ellens incredibly noted that "pantheism robs individuals of their reality and deprives history of any powerful movement. When adopted by erstwhile Christians, it is sign of loss of hope and is a movement towards atheism." Despite Ellens' contentions, the Ranters were not pantheists, but his evaluation is hardly evidenced from a reading of Spinoza, Boehm, Zen and other pantheistic strains far removed from atheism or expressive of a loss of hope.

When Ellens is unable to rely upon pop-historical criticism, he depends upon the pop-psychology of the decade. The Ranters are compared to suburban middle class youngsters much like those portrayed in Jimmy Dean films, and as young people whose consciousness has been raised by Reich's *Greening of America*. Thus "we might come to see that after the rejection of a guilt and pain producing religious consciousness and system, relief might be sought in a simple religious condition, one that got back to nature, to a culture of warm brotherhood within a free community. It would be natural to seek to overthrow artificial religion with artificial society." Of course, had the Ranters become Puritans they would have replaced an artificial religion and society with one bursting with stolidity and confidence. They did not become Puritans, evidently, because they were depressed and repressed.

Toward the end of the article Ellens finally drew the conclusion he had labored to create. "From the study of the Ranter counter culture the reader may feel that some analogy between Ranters and Hippies could be made. The likenesses between these two groups of persons separated by 300 years of time are striking . . ." The next three pages are filled with descriptions of Hippie culture as fully convincing as earlier descriptions of Ranters and pantheism with the concluding paragraph noting "the definitive book about our modern social ills, of which the Hippies are a symptom, remains to be written."

Ellens' article had everything: Ranting Ranters, Puritan establishments, stolid and stable Puritans, repressed and depressed lower classes, a return to nature, atheistic and hopeless pantheists, misunderstood Hippies, pop psychology and the strangest description of the drug culture ever to appear in print. Only one thing was lacking in this eclectic work: extensive citation from Ranter sources beyond those pieced together from Jones and other authors. By carefully manipulating his citations from Jones' long list of anti-Ranters, Ellens was able to present a very partial view of Ranter life and thought and to draw an analogy to the present that would elude the most imaginative scholar. By setting up dubious postulates and maxims, as about pantheism and Puritanism, the author constructed an article with neither historical verification nor critical thought. And by avoiding Ranter writings Ellens was able to use anti-Ranter polemics and diatribes to assess what Ranters believed and how they lived. Perhaps worst of all, Ellens saw fit to explain a seventeenth-century phenomenon, which he neither investigated nor understood, by analogy to a subsequent twentieth-century phenomenon which he neither investigated nor understood.

More useful is Mr. Frank McGregor's Oxford University thesis entitled *The Ranters*. While not treating the Ranters individually in depth, it is an excellent general introduction to who the Ranters were and what beliefs characterized their movement. It is still useful as a general introduction. Mr. McGregor has also produced an interesting chapter about the Ranters in an edited volume concerning the radicalism of the day, though it does not seem to go past his original thesis.[14]

Most useful is A. L. Morton's book, *The World of the Ranters*, which is a fine general introduction to England's left sectarian environment. This volume, the only one specifically about Ranters, has seven chapters but only two deal with a general description of the Ranters with the remainder devoted to the *world* of the Ranters.[15] The author's true interest is Leveller democracy with the result that the volume is a very thoughtful description of the intellectual strains comprising that tendency. Ranter antecedents include only the Seekers, with Morton devoting the single largest chapter in the book to an analysis of Saltmarsh, who was not a Ranter. The author also devoted considerable attention to Walwyn, also not a Ranter, though both were part of the world of the Ranters. Ranter authors themselves received only fragmentary treatment with many not discussed at all. Morton's general assessment seems to be that the Ranters were degenerate Levellers rather than degenerate Seekers or Quakers. No connection with Hippies was pursued.

Two authors have done yeoman service in making thoughtful contributions to the study of Ranters. Norman Cohn's monumental work, *The Pursuit of the Millenium*, presented the first modern account of the Ranters, though in abbreviated form.[16] Because the seventeenth century was beyond the scope of his work, the Ranters could not be included as an integral chapter of his book. Yet, they were so reminiscent of the Brethren of the Free Spirit and other medieval illuminist sects that Cohn included large extracts from both Ranter and anti-Ranter writings in an appendix with just enough of his own text to indicate the importance of this unstudied group. The extracts presented were drawn from a select list of authors including Bauthumley, Salmon, Clarkson, and Coppe, and then only from a few of their treastises. The anti-Ranter materials cover a wide spectrum of thought and Cohn did not differentiate between the various sorts of materials constituting this literature. Nonetheless, Cohn was the first scholar to see the importance of the Ranters as the final chapter in a furious tradition with very, very old roots in western civilization.

Even more helpful is Nigel Smith's very recent volume entitled *A Collection of Ranter Writings from the 17th Century*.[17] This critical edition presents many of the works by Coppe, Clarkson, Salmon and Bauthumley along with a thoughtful introduction. If this volume does not represent all Ranter tendencies, it makes available some of the more essential texts of leading Ranter authors.

Of all these treatments, only the last two attempted honest appraisals of Ranter thought predicated upon the use of Ranter materials. Other than Cohn, Smith, and Hill, most authors seem far more interested in using the Ranters to make an argument about other groups or other times. In determining that Ranters were degenerate Seekers, degenerate Quakers, or degenerate Levellers or proto-Hippies, these authors do not distinguish between actual Ranter writings and anti-Ranter sources in determining the content of Ranter thought. It is doubtful that any of these authors would even briefly consider writing about blacks, Jews or socialists by using, often almost exclusively, segregationist, Nazi or Birch Society sources. Consequently, despite the existence of a small amount of secondary literature on the subject, the Ranters still demand complete and objective appraisal. It is to be hoped that this volume will fill that need.

Part One: The Ranters

1. The Civil War, Sectarianism and the Ranter Family Tree

Students of the civil war period are well aware of the mushroom-like proliferation of religious sects during the interregnum.[18] One could compose a list of these sects which would include, among others, Brownists and Barrowists, Grindletonians and Socinians, Seekers and Squatters, Diggers and Behmenists, Ranters and Muggletonians, Independents and Quakers, Antinomians, Anabaptists, Levellers, the Fifth Monarchists and, of course, the Blackloists. One might also include the Arminians, Apostles and Adamites, and still wonder whether the Proud Quakers merited a separate category. One should not exclude the Shakers, though they might be included as part of the Ranters, and there were several different types of Sabbatarians. Before we concentrate upon the Ranters, the most radical of these sects, it is necessary to devote a few words to explaining how and why these new groups came about during the interregnum and where within this sectarian thicket one might locate the Ranters. We might also see how traditions of scholars have treated sectarianism, and whether or not we might classify these different sects into categories. This process will enable us to appreciate sectarianism as a varied and unusual religious expression in a chaotic and competitive political and religious atmosphere.

However justified rebellion against Charles I may have seemed at the time, the architects of revolution were unable to create any semblance of orderly rule to replace the tyranny they so hated. In order to defeat King Charles, Parliament created the "New Model Army," a popular army consisting of lower class soldiers led by common class officers.[19] This new social institution did indeed defeat the king but also increasingly reflected a radical orientation and energy in its subsequent conflict with the conservative Parliament. It removed Presbyterian officers, dissolved the House of Lords, purged Parliament of its conservative members and executed Charles after finding him guilty of treason. Through 1647 and 1648 the new core of common, and increasingly radical, army officers debated the nature of governance and the way in which England's political institutions should be rebuilt. There was no question that power lay in the army's hands, and had Cromwell wished social revolution, he might have led these radical officers along new and experimental paths of governance. In fact,

9

Cromwell derided the king and had no patience with Parliament's conservatives, but he detested those radical officers seeking far-reaching social reform as well. Hence, at the same time that Parliament defeated monarchy and the army hobbled Parliament, Cromwell also purged the army leadership of its radical elements and executed those "Leveller" leaders willing to oppose him with the same fervor that had motivated them against the King, Parliament and Lords. In short, the English Revolution, like so many others since the seventeenth century, began to devour its own ranks as soon as the initial enemy was defeated. Each succeeding purge and conflict alienated yet another constituency of the English population, and the very deeds and events bringing the increasingly narrowly based ruling clique to another month of power made difficult any political consensus and compromise with the defeated. The conservative army leadership under Cromwell soon found that it would be forced to do what it had naively hoped defeat of the king would enable them to do: to create a totally new government.

The civil wars occasioned more than political anarchy: religious anarchy, too, was a product of these years. The fiscal and political abuses of the Church of England were hated, and after its leading bishop was executed, an aggressive Puritan Presbyterian party, full of revolutionary righteous indignation with previous "popish and Roman practices," hoped to create a new religious order. The Puritans outlawed the old Anglican Church, the old prayer book and service, and instituted a repressive and ascetic religious legislation more thorough than the alleged tyranny of the old church. The Presbyterians did keep some elements of the past, however: they maintained the hated and abusive tithe tax. Cromwell too was totally opposed to the Presbyterians who were soon more vehemently hated than the Church of England. This conflict, in addition to those concerning political governance, only added to the pervasive sense of anarchy.

England's economic house provided no stability in this age of religious and political strife. The first three decades of the seventeenth century witnessed what various historians consider the "seventeenth-century-crisis," a collapse of the international market structure in the Thirty Years' War, and the simultaneous bankruptcy of most western European governments. Additionally, England experienced poor harvests from 1646 to 1652, and as the price of corn soared, privation became common with even starvation reported in many rural parishes.[20] The fighting and destruction accompanying the civil wars from 1642 to 1646 further hurt a precarious supply of food and the two trade wars with Holland in the fifties further complicated matters.

The textile industry, England's most advanced and labor-saturated industry, failed in the forties, largely because of overproduction.[21] The resulting unemployment affected full-time urban workers as well as many semirural part-time farmers for whom the few pounds earned at the mills maintained the family on the land. This unemployment was further aggravated by the failure of the poor relief system which, during the best of times, was characterized as "harshness coupled with failure."[22] Incredibly, this system managed to deliver more of both during these years of religious idealism and constitutional reform. And to add to the burden, the revolutionary government created a new, and hated, excise tax to pay for a succession of failing governmental experiments while the old, and hated, tithe paid for a religious establishment viewed by many Englishmen with increasing hostility. There was also much social dissension because the poor believed the rich bought confiscated lands at low rates while they lost their land or raised barely enough to survive and pay their taxes.

Politically, economically and religiously, England was a mess. Traditional and legitimate sources of political authority had been destroyed while institutional spiritual authority had lost credibility. When Cromwell crushed the bulwark of Parliamentary conservatism and then destroyed the Leveller radicals of the left and the king on the right, he remained with little that might help him build a successful government. Religious dissension and economic instability further complicated Cromwell's efforts. Peculiar experiments in governance followed one another in rapid succession as Cromwell became increasingly frantic to create some form of government. Unable to achieve any measure of stability but unwilling to assume the title of king offered him, Cromwell eventually became Lord Protector and provided military rule through a series of major-generals. Cromwell died in 1658. He had been king in all essentials but name. Finally, in 1660, Charles II returned to England and took up matters where his father, executed for treason, had left them.

One change of major historical importance occurring during this two-decade flirtation with upheaval was the special role played by the lower classes. Since the Peasant Rebellions of the fourteenth century, when local noble institutions were unable to keep the peace, centralized government based its claim to superior authority in large part upon its ability to keep the poor in check. Strong executive rule by Tudors and Stuarts did in fact accomplish this, but, in opposing King Charles, Parliament was forced to call upon the peasant and commoner to rally to the side of "Parliamentary liberty" against royal abuse of authority. Hence, it is not surprising that the New Model Army was so vehement in demanding a role for the lower classes in the restructured England or that radical army officers in the Putney and Whitehall debates demanded a new political franchise and what they conceived as the return to Englishmen of those rights that had been theirs before the advent of the "Norman Yoke" in 1066.

11

BLASPHEMY, IMMORALITY, AND ANARCHY

The suppression of the Levellers in the army and Cromwell's increasing authoritarianism put an end to much radical activity and to many hopes and dreams. But renewed lower class conformity in the area of religion, equally desirable from a conservative Puritan or Anglican perspective, could not be easily accomplished. First, there was no single religious consensus. The Anglican episcopal clergy and their agencies of censorship and ecclesiastical courts and institutions were gone. The Presbyterians could not fill the void because the Puritan tyranny replacing the Anglican tyranny was even more hated and went far to destroy the very notion of a uniform religious social policy. Censorship was gone and, until 1660, there would be no new repressive legislation to replace the older ecclesiastical agencies of control. If there would be no widening of the political franchise and no redistribution of goods, another ideal of the common left, there would be no religious repression either.

The result was a curious state of affairs where social and religious radicals could not come to power, but the government and other agencies of authority could not repress publication of radical literature and suppress the freedom of religious speech. Radicals published thousands of treatises expressing opinions which would never have reached an audience a decade or so earlier. One Presbyterian observer called the situation "gangrenous" and bitterly lamented the *de facto* policy of religious toleration which the government was unable to circumscribe. Indeed, religion became the vehicle through which repressed class and political hopes were expressed. Hence, when we read of the proliferation of sects and small gathered churches led by ignorant, or informally trained, "mechanic" preachers teaching a radical social ethic which emphasized the Apostolic common ownership of goods, we understand that such phenomena represented both religious innovation as well as repressed lower class hopes for economic reform. Similarly, when we read of Quaker refusals to remove caps and hats in the presence of their social betters by those who were meek, mild and otherwise good subjects of legitimate authority, we witness the fierce social tension separating the social classes. Sectarianism proliferated because of political anarchy, economic depression, no single religious consensus, no credibility to any of the more orthodox religious institutions, and strong class divisions.

Cromwell aided the process of sectarian growth because he too distrusted religious establishments. Moreover, he may have understood that it was one thing for angry commoners to identify with a democratic and working man's vision of Jesus and quite another to redistribute actual property and share political power. Indeed, one might even forestall the latter by permitting the former. Hence, either with the approval of government or despite it, a multiplicity of religious sects inherited the social hopes, frustrations, dreams and yearnings of those whose only recourse was religious expression.

Perhaps the largest and certainly the most entertaining of the several different radical sectarian families would include those loosely described as Familists or Spiritualists. We would find in this group the religious descendants of Henry Niclaes' Family of Love which spread from the continent to England during the second half of the sixteenth century. More distant ancestors would include medieval mystics, especially those of the fourteenth century. Often, Familists did not constitute an organized sect, gathered or otherwise, though some within this category became ardent organizers and created firm sectarian institutions. By the middle of the seventeenth century this religious orientation was both numerically and theologically significant and would include, in order of radicalism, Seekers, Quakers, Muggletonians and Ranters.

Though these different sects employed somewhat different language to express their antinomianism, in part because their spiritual concepts and terms were also made to support political and social ideas as well, several ideas were generally held in common by all within the spiritualist household. All spiritualists emphasized the importance of the "inner light" within the soul as the meeting place between man and God, and hence recognized the spirit of God within themselves. The implications could be far-reaching and such ideas might include extreme varieties of antinomian individuality and libertinism, the allegorical interpretation of Scripture predicated upon the saint's communion with God, and apostolic common ownership of wealth by the saint. Antinomianism was a rejection of priestly authority and the haughty intellectual authority of the universities. The allegorical interpretation of Scripture was a rejection of the Protestant shibboleth of Scriptural literalism and all traditions of interpretation which did not deliver desired radical social formulae. Common ownership of property along New Testament lines of thought was a rejection of private property and therefore a rejection of all forms of contemporary social organization. Some seventeenth-century spiritualists were more extreme yet and rejected prayer as well as heaven and hell and the resurrection. Needless to say, if prayer were useless and if there were neither heaven nor hell, a final judgment nor a resurrection, there was no need to live as if these did exist. And Ranters, as we shall see, rejected everything altogether.

To one extent or another, the sects within this category opposed existing religious institutions, were suspicious of government, and believed private property was a source of moral difficulty and class antagonism. But on social issues as well as on religious grounds, these sects differed from one another in terms of sheer radicalism. Where Seekers were open to diverse individual expressions and stirrings of the spirit and sought truth where it might be found (hence their name), Ludwig Muggleton was primarily concerned with harnessing the free spirit within himself to create a single church bearing his name and existing as an extension of his personality. Hence, Muggletonians and Seekers possessed many of the same ideas but differed in temperament and political attitude. The Quakers, like the Seekers and Ranters, eschewed all formal religious expression in favor of the workings of the individual inner spirit. Seekers celebrated this individuality by staying out of churches, while the Quakers stayed out of formal churches, but created their own "meeting houses" where they sat around making sure nothing organized happened. Ranters drank and hooted. Both the Quakers and the Muggletonians had Seeker and Ranter origins but both were institutionally-oriented and therefore hated each other's efforts and maintained an active literary conflict. While intellectually very close, each, except the Ranters, committed, in the eyes of the other, the serious sin of possessing a separate organization. Hence, while Muggletonians, Quakers and Ranters all opposed the institutions repressing them, only the Ranters refrained from creating new institutions which, invariably, were used by each sect to repress deviant voices within their own community.

The Ranters were the most radical of all. Along with ideas from ancient and medieval mystical dualism and the legacy of the Brethren of the Free Spirit, Ranters incorporated elements taken from sixteenth-century Libertinism, Familist spiritualism and from the anticlerical popular culture of the day. Ranters used taverns as churches, drank, smoked, cursed and lived sexually promiscuous lives. Most believed sin absurd and, in the words of one such jolly fellow, "the devil was an old lady stuffed with parsley." They rejected heaven and hell and considered the resurrection nothing more than a clever "bogeyman" to keep the poorer and less educated sort in line. Most thought King Charles a fool and Cromwell somewhat worse than that, and had little patience with any of the political ideologies of the age. All were violently opposed to government, some dreaming of blood, gore, and divine vengeance. All accepted the idea that private property was as rotten as government and organized religion, and most noted how defenders of the one were usually, not coincidentally, stalwart defenders of the other.

The typical Ranter envisioned himself as a modern day traveller about to embark on a most significant trip but forced to wait at the railway station until such time as the track is cleared of snow. The traveller does not know how long he will be forced to wait in the station but he is certain that little good can come of this wasted time. One might engage in philosophical enterprises to appreciate one's position, but since one must wait in any event, there is no harm done by filling one's time in a variety of other ways. One might read a serious novel or a frivolous magazine, play pin ball, enjoy a larger than usual lunch with an extra martini or two. There are always movies or even the company of some young lovely. Whatever one does, it is meaningful only for the moment, to kill time or to alleviate boredom but it is totally meaningless when compared to the coming embarkation. If only the snow would melt! In any event by tomorrow, or the day after at the very latest, this dead time and how it was filled will be forgotten. Eventually the snow will melt.

Some of the main differences separating one group of Ranters from another concerned how they thought best to fill their time while waiting for God to take them. The more speculative and philosophical types believed one should abstain from the world one was about to abandon and should wonder and ponder the meaning of it all. Revolutionary Ranters wished to create a huge conflagration in which all corrupt social institutions such as government, the church, and private property would be destroyed. Such actions would lead to the "kingdom of God within you" of the more philosophical types, but also "the kingdom of heaven on earth" for all people while the saints awaited God. Others, the Sexual Libertines, sympathized with the revolutionary Ranters but believed that as long as one was forced to live in the senses and could not avoid doing so whatever one did, one might as well enjoy the pleasures of the satanic material world while the opportunity presented itself. Indeed, the Libertines advanced the fantastic notion that sainthood—in fact all redemption—could come through evil and sin which was, perhaps, why some Ranters sang, whistled, and danced. Once one accepted this crass material life for what it was and anticipated the next glorious life of merger with God for what it was, a little whiskey, some tobacco and the fine company of the opposite sex made the wait a little more pleasant. Anyway, if one actually did sin, which one could not, one only developed a better understanding of this evil material world. Divine Ranters were so consumed with their own sainthood here on earth, as were their adoring followers, that they believed themselves not merely followers of Christ's path, but actual Christs within themselves.

While probably also having some Seeker antecedents, the Ranters contributed more than their due share to other groups. For a short time between 1647 and 1659, the Ranters were the chief sectarian expression of radical frustration with the outcome of the civil wars, Cromwell, and the suppression of the Levellers. John Reeves, the major Muggletonian prophet and Ludwig's cousin, had been a Ranter; and Lawrence Clarkson, "Captain of the Rant," also ended up a Muggletonian. Because they had originally been Ranters, some Quakers were almost as boisterous as Ranters and were called Proud Quakers. Some Ranters were called Shakers, seemingly because it seemed like a good idea at the time. Perhaps because the Ranters formed the core from which the other groups drew ideas and membership, once these others separated, they often turned against their Ranter source and perhaps for this reason, too, Ranters were the most visible radical group in public. Indeed, while Englishmen could find no common religious consensus to create positive religious policy, orthodox and sectarian alike could agree that the Ranters were beyond the limits of acceptability. So dangerous did Ranters seem to the outside world that they were subjected to special repressive legislation particularly written to limit their activity.

On June 14, 1650, the Rump appointed a committee "to consider of a way for suppression of the obscene, licentious and impious practices used by persons under the pretense of Liberty, Religious or otherwise."[23] The committee drew up a report on "several abominable practices of a sect called Ranters" and was then instructed by Parliament to create legislation "suppressing and punishing these abominable opinions and practices." After considerable debate on June 14, July 5, 12, 19 and August 9, Parliament adopted an act entitled "Punishment of Atheistical, Blasphemous and Execrable Opinions," or the Blasphemy Act.

The main provisions of the act are easily enumerated. Declaring one's self to be God or denying that God exists was condemned as were specific types of behavior. Anyone advocating drunkenness, adultery or swearing, or declaring that there is no difference between moral and immoral behavior was also to be condemned. Denial of heaven and hell, salvation, damnation or teaching there was no difference between them was also to be condemned. The Blasphemy Act did recognize the difference between professing the above in private conversation and preaching the same before an audience or publishing such opinions. Only the latter public behavior was punishable, however regrettable the former. Any individual found guilty of these charges was to be jailed for six months for the first offense. For the second offense, the individual was to be banished on pain of death should he return to England. The preamble to the act clearly explained that such punishment was necessary because Ranters maintained "monstrous opinions, even such as tend to the dissolution of human society." The stipulations of the bill were to apply to both male and female in England, excluding only "persons distempered in their brains."

Eventually, the Quakers swallowed up the Ranters and all the rest because they were able to combine the social radicalism and extreme antinomianism of the Ranters and the tight organizational sense of the Muggletonians with a conventional middle class sexual morality which might also prove acceptable to the rest of society. "Had not the Quakers come," one Quaker observed, "the Ranters had overrun the nation." How fortunate.

16

Philosophical Ranters

2. Richard Coppin

More than any other single author, Richard Coppin was the theologian-philosopher of the Ranter movement. He was an associate of both Abiezer Coppe, the leading Libertine, and Joseph Salmon, the leading Revolutionary Ranter, before whose congregation Coppin preached during the summer of 1655. Indeed, before there were Ranters there were Coppinists. The small circle that formed about Coppin appears to have been the first consciously radical dualist congregation that later fused with other tendencies to form the larger and more diverse Ranter movement.

Much is known about Coppin's life as a Ranter, for in his 1655 treatise, *Truth's Testimony*, he wrote about his several trials and legal encounters. Little is known about his youth and education and nothing at all about his life subsequent to 1659, the year in which his last treatise was published.

Like other sectarian dissenters, Coppin had a religious background which was an odd composite of contemporary England's religious landscape. He was born into the Church of England in Kent, but became an ardent Presbyterian at an early age. No more content with what he considered the intellectual prison of Calvinism than with the mindless ritual of Anglicanism, Coppin became an Independent for a short time and an Anabaptist thereafter. In retrospect, these many religions seemed to Coppin only varying approaches to the same theme which combined a formidable concept of sin with a simplistic notion of good works emphasizing a variety of iron-clad practices, rituals, and observances guaranteed to provide salvation. Each group was quick to condemn the others while proceeding merely to offer an alternate ritual life built upon the same basic theory. None of these religions proved satisfactory, and finally Coppin became a Ranter.

Coppin's greatest contribution to the Ranter cause lay in his very effective preaching, but for the historian writing from the distance of over three centuries it is obvious that his written works also provided an invaluable source of ideas for other thinkers and preachers in the movement. It was perhaps Coppin's very success in providing an intellectual framework for Ranter dualism which more conventional Christians might find appealing

17

that led him into conflict with both religious and civil authorities. Following the publication of his very influential *Divine Teachings* in 1649, Coppin experienced several bouts with legal authorities. On March 23, 1652, Coppin was found guilty of denying the existence of true heaven and true hell. He was again tried for the same offense on March 10 of the following year before Judge Green of the Oxford Assize but was eventually discharged and released. In 1655 Coppin again found himself in court after being entrapped in a public debate. He was committed to Maidstone prison on Christmas Eve of 1655 and was released six months later in June of the following year. More will be written about these trials later in this chapter.

Coppin's writings fall into several categories. His earliest work and single most influential publication was the *Divine Teachings* trilogy of 1649 with an introduction by Abiezer Coppe. This work was so successful it was reprinted in 1653 with a different introduction and prefatory letters. In 1652 Coppin published a companion piece to it entitled *Man's Righteousness Examined*, which elucidated several themes inadequately treated in the earlier work. Later religious treatises include *A Man-Child Born* of 1654, the *Threefold State of a Christian* of 1656, which no longer exists, and *Crux Christi* of 1657.

Coppin wrote three polemical works including *A Blow at the Serpent*, and *The Twenty Five Articles*, both of 1656, and *Michael Opposing the Dragon* of 1659. Coppin's political views, as radical as his religious opinions, were presented in his *Saul Smitten for Not Smiting Amalek* of 1653, in which he argued against both king and parliament. His legal ordeals and his spiritual biography were presented in *Truth's Testimony* of 1655. Together, these works constitute the single most nearly complete corpus of Ranter writings in existence. Because Coppin's views underwent a process of inner conceptual development, his works will be treated thematically, in groups of religious, political and polemical treatises.

Religious Writings

The *Divine Teachings* trilogy was first published in 1649 and again in 1653 in slightly different form with new introductions and prefaces. These three treatises constitute the best systematic presentation of Ranter beliefs and might be considered a Ranter primer. Each of the three parts served a different function and was addressed to three different sorts of readers at different stages in their religious development. The first part, "The Glorious Mystery of Divine Teachings Between God, Christ, and the Saints," was addressed to the general reader curious about the beliefs of spiritual dualism. The second section, "Anti-Christ in Man Opposing Emmanuel, or God In Us," was directed to the reader committed to dualistic Christianity. The third section is both the most complex and most satisfying. "The Advancement of All Things in Christ and of Christ in All Things, with a discovery of good and evil inhabiting man," is a philosophical, religious and conceptual expression of hard core Ranter thought and was written for those readers progressing satisfactorily through the first two parts and desiring a stronger dualistic interpretation of Christianity. In short, the first section was devoted to the general orthodox Christian. The second was for the general believer and the third for the perfecting of the saint.

While the trilogy as a whole was popular, the third section was the most appreciated and was published separately under the title *The Exaltation of All Things in Christ* in 1649 and was probably the basis for his lost work of 1656, *The Threefold State of a Christian*. Although the trilogy was carefully constructed to bring the novice to complete Rantism, to avoid repetition and ease systematic considerations, we will treat the trilogy thematically rather than sequentially.

A. The Deplorable State of Nature

Like other dualists, Coppin believed the conflict between spirit and matter characterized all existence. Earlier dualists such as the Gnostics and Bogomils, among others, maintained that the source of this conflict lay in Lucifer's rebellion against God and the former's expropriation of the physical world of matter for his own domain of control. Coppin, too, accepted the idea that a cosmic war between God and Satan provided the foundation of all subsequent developments in heaven and on earth. He wrote, "We may read thus of Michael and the Dragon in Rev.12,7-10. There was a war in heaven. Michael and his angels faught against the Dragon and the Dragon faught with his angels and prevailed not . . . and the Dragon was cast out."(29)

Cast out of heaven, Satan had but one alternative. According to Coppin, "The Serpent was cast out of heaven to the earth and had nothing but the earth given him to feed upon, which is the habitation of sin." (89) Henceforth all reality and existence reflected the Manichaean polarity of God and Satan, heaven and earth, with humanity torn between these two warring principles. Since that time, "The Devil is the head of all things below God" (98) and consequently, hell and the earth were one and the same. "That which we call this world," Coppin explained, "is the Kingdom of Satan in which he reigns . . . we read that he is the God of this world, that is, the

Prince of Darkness, the Devil." (103) All creation was in fact evil for "creation is all from below and nothing from above, therefore is earthly, sensual and Devilish." (98–99)

Of all things created in matter, only man continued to reflect some divine element along with his more formal devilish physical nature. According to Coppin, "When God first made us we were without sin, beautiful, comely, pure, and holy . . . for we were made after the image of God." (80) The idea of man was close to God but the translation of the idea of man into matter was not celestial and ethereal and as a result, "The state in which we were *made* was a state far below the state in which God himself lives." (80) The corrupting influence of Devilish matter was soon evident and "we did not long continue in that image or state of moral holiness . . . we were soon overcome and so fell . . . to a state of sin and corruption where we were defiled and became filthy and polluted creatures." (80)

Rather than placing blame for the fall on human shoulders, Coppin believed that human corruption was a result of its material composition and not the result of mankind's willfully choosing evil. When writing about the earthly matter used to create mankind, Coppin noted, "This is the seat of sin where sin doth act and show itself; sin hath no other place and no other habitation but the earth."(90) Consequently, "that which troubles the creature arises from the darkness in the creature . . . and where darkness is, there will follow works of darkness."(100)

If Coppin's teachings of the fall and original sin echoed traditional dualistic teachings, so too did his understanding of the trees of wisdom and eternal life found in Eden. According to Scripture the trees forbidden to Adam and Eve were not for human use and one must therefore wonder why they were placed in Eden which allegedly was a home for human beings. For Coppin, the Garden of Eden was not God's habitation but the earthly domain of the Devil. The tree of wisdom possessed the carnal knowledge of this world and consequently was "a tree of unrighteousness that hath spread itself over the whole creation."(73) In turn, the snake who beguiled these first human beings was "the serpent [who] was cast out of heaven to the earth and had nothing but the earth given him to feed upon, which is the habitation of sin . . ."(89) The fruit consumed by the human beings, Coppin noted, "is the forbidden fruit which Adam and we all have and do still feed upon to satisfy our own lusts and desires, even to have a knowledge of things out of God."(73)

When man had eaten of the tree of wisdom, the balance within his composition was altered. The divinity mankind possessed was swallowed up in a fleshly carnality expressed in a material perception of the world. In every

20

person, this inclination was "to satisfy our own perverse wills in forming an image of ourselves contrary to the image of God. And thus, wicked man is never satisfied till he sees something in himself more than God made."(70) The "something in himself more than God made" was Coppin's explanation for the human spirit. This spirit or what we might call self-consciousness, might well have remained divine and truly spiritual had the connection between God and man not been severed. Because of the events in Eden, however, human self-consciousness was self-righteousness and became a physical and carnal spirit far more engrossed in pleasing the body than in pleasing the more elusive soul. Coppin explained that "the natural spirit of a man, which naturally belongs to the body, falls with the body."(49) It is this evil human spirit which mankind continually mistakes for its soul and the facility which gave birth to mankind's various religions, most recently Christianity. Through the perceptions of this carnal spirit, "the creature hath brought upon itself an image not like the image of God but the image of the Devil," Coppin taught, "an image which abides and remains a lie, in ignorance and darkness, in falsehood and error, as in the Devil."(70) Consequently, while man mistook the spirit for the soul, the spirit was in alliance with all the forces of evil within the world. Despite a show of religiosity, humanity was merely another vehicle through which the Devil might act and Coppin taught that "sin doth but make use of the person to act and show itself."(88) The result was that despite rituals and religion man "now became unhappy."(70)

The ancient Gnostics believed and all dualists ever since have believed that organized religion was the cult of the Devil and could never prove satisfying to the needs of the soul. From this perspective, organized religion traditionally emphasized the importance of ritual and other carnal busy work practices to divert mankind from inquiring into the needs of the soul. And yet, in its unhappiness and insecurity, humanity clings to these mindless rituals and becomes even more unhappy. The descending spiral of moral and spiritual dissatisfaction was not easily broken since the human spirit believed these religions true and thought that the Devil was God. For the Gnostics, no people had been more duped than the Hebrews and Coppin, too, explained that "while people lived under the law or before Christ, they had no life or peace but what seemed to be upon every performance of duty done and fulfilled by them . . . which not being done, could have no peace with him in the creature's apprehension."(92) Mankind was forever on a treadmill of observances, always blaming itself for its own lack of observance when the problem was elsewhere. Indeed, in view of the human predilection for ritual-oriented religions, all of mankind's efforts on its own behalf were frustrating and self-defeating. Such was humanity's deplorable condition in the state of nature, the state of the Devil and the state of man.

The depressing view of the human condition taught by Coppin was accepted in varying degrees by all Ranters. Ranter teachings concerning the Bible only compounded the sense of human isolation and inability to cope with the power of the Devil. Some people rejected Scripture altogether as a mere history of human devotion/depravity. Others, like Coppin, believed Scripture was in some sense true, but also contained much that was literally false or required thorough reinterpretation to redeem the kernal of truth from the carnal lie. "We and the Scripture," Coppin wrote, "are the grave in which the glorious God lies dead and buried."(10) In every age Scripture had been entrusted to the priests of devilish organized religion who maintained a properly carnal interpretation to please Satan. In his own time, Scripture was interpreted by university trained ministers, which universities, Coppin observed, were "the two well springs of this land, Oxford and Cambridge, which have been looked upon and much applauded by men as a well yielding clear and pure water . . . yet in the use of it hath proved muddy and full of corruption, boiling up in the stomachs of those who received it . . . and hath deceived both themselves and others."(22–23) As in previous ages, every word and sentiment of these accepted interpreters was venerated, "and this is the blindness of people these days, they worship and acknowledge a god . . . as they can beget to themselves with their own fancies."(9) All such learning was useless.

Rather than teaching that humanity could know little from the world but should look inside itself, all religions taught that the truth of Scripture was an open book, literally true, and all the while praised human reason and wisdom as the tool to understand that open book. Coppin warned, "He will destroy the wisdom of the wise and bring to nothing the understanding of the prudent."(2) There was a road back to God, but it did not pass through the universities.

B. Divine Knowledge

When writing about God, Coppin found himself in the same quandary experienced by other dualists and mystics in all ages. All existence seemed testimony to some form of divine activity and yet within himself God was removed from the world and impossible to understand. The medieval *docta ignorantia* attempted to overcome this limitation by first defining physical reality and then presenting God as above or distinct from that definition.

RICHARD COPPIN

Coppin's dilemma was more complicated, however, for as a strident dualist he rejected any goodness at all in physical creation. God was not simply above or different from the world, but necessarily opposed to creation and consequently even more difficult to understand. Hence, God "is not known by anything but himself for God himself must make himself known."(A4) Every true statement about God must be the product of a specific act of divine self-disclosure. Nothing in or of the world can indicate anything about God, and pragmatic human wisdom is of no value. Coppin wrote that "man, by all his wisdom and learning that ever he shall or hath attained to as human, is not able to give any truth and knowledge of God." (A4) Fortunately, Coppin had received a divine communication and could write truthfully about God "because," he wrote, "this truth, was given to me of God and then declared by me from him."(preface)

Despite his divine inspiration, Coppin warned that God "can not be declared or received in full but in part."(A2) He explained that "because God, who is a spirit, must be looked upon by the spirit" it followed that "therefore without the spirit it is impossible to see or discern any of the things of God."(24) Coppin may have had the spirit to teach, but he could not vouchsafe the reader's spirit to receive.

Even with the spirit, divine truth is not easily perceived and at no time has any person or age been able to comprehend what God is. Moses spoke to a burning bush, which was certainly miraculous although it did not indicate more to him about God than any other bush might have indicated. Similarly, the prophets were aware of a divine presence but could not explain what it was. Despite these disclaimers, Coppin believed that "those who lived in former ages had some theory of God manifested to them, though darkly and under a cloud and not so clearly as in these later ages."(9) Those living in Jesus' lifetime may also have had the Paraclete but even the apostles had little understanding of what is was. "The apostles," Coppin wrote, "then as well as now, held it but in part, though we have it fuller than they then, yet still but in part for that which is hid today may be revealed tomorrow . . ."(A2) Indeed, Coppin believed he was living in especially miraculous times when humanity would behold "the glorious breakings forth of truth [that] was hid from them and other ages before us."(4–5)

His awareness of the complexity of God's concept led Coppin to be contemptuous of contemporary religious leaders and ministers who were certain they possessed all religious truth. He condemned university trained ministers for "all the wisdom of men and learning of men will appear to be mere foolishness, madness, confusion . . ."(2) when God finally did reveal himself. Even Scripture, a subject we will return to in detail, gave man no true information about God. Coppin warned that "to know the *truth* of Scripture, which is the mind of God, is to know God himself which can not be taught by any natural man but by God himself."(13) Much as the world of creation was only a poor copy of God's original intentions and human behavior a poor expression of the divine soul within man, so, too, the Bible was a human document based upon human weaknesses and therefore it could not express the true divine inspiration contained within it. "To know the original of truth is to know God himself," Coppin wrote, "for the original is the truth of all things and God is this original and this truth."(1)

Lest the reader despair that all channels of knowledge were faulty and of little value, Coppin added that God grants knowledge of himself only to those whom he chooses, and then you "shall come to be made one with the Spirit for that is the knowledge of the truth, to be made one with it and being made one with truth thou art one with God . . . then thou wilt come to know all truth and not till then."(preface,A2)

C. The Process of Redemption

Despite the terrible distance separating man from God and human ignorance of God's existence, "as soon as the creature was fallen, God was ready to help him up, and as soon as he was thus filthy, God was ready to make him clean."(81) In the third section of his trilogy, Coppin explained the process through which the soul might be redeemed from its carnal confines. We are told "there is a three-fold kingdom in a three-fold state . . . two of which every Christian is to pass through before he can come to the third and last kingdom where he is to stay . . . which we call the kingdom of the Father." (103)

We have already encountered the first kingdom, for "the first stage a Christian is to pass through is the state of nature." (103) In this state man is, at best, confused and at the very worst, self-contentedly evil and beastly, using wisdom and learning to justify his every action and belief as the essence of God's desire. In either event, the Christian might pass from this condition to the second state only when God appeared to the believer's soul. Coppin warned, "We can not see God till he sees us and saith unto us, *Behold me.*"(41) In another place Coppin wrote "He turns us before we can turn and changes us before we can be changed." (39) Citing the verse, 'I will send the Spirit and he shall teach you all things'—an example of the type of Scripture of which he approved—Coppin added, "The true understanding . . . is only the work of God."(7)

RICHARD COPPIN

The second stage through which the Christian must pass is filled with pain and suffering, a condition no person would voluntarily accept unless he truly sought God. Objectively, "the second stage and kingdom a Christian comes into and is to pass through is that of the mediator, and this is the kingdom of Jesus Christ in the flesh which a Christian is brought into as soon as he is converted into the faith."(104) In the second part of his trilogy Coppin discussed the meaning of the kingdom of Jesus Christ in the flesh.

Coppin's Christology was a combination of two seemingly contradictory positions. On the one hand, none can enter the second phase without first being called by God. On the other hand, every Christian must willingly and voluntarily accept a life of total suffering as soon as he is called by God. In fact, these two strains come together through a very specific interpretation and understanding of Christ's nature and purpose. For Coppin, the great miracle of Jesus Christ was his ability to overcome the material world while being totally human. He was adopted by God and then crucified by God "that so he might destroy the works of the creature or the works of the Devil in the creature."(61) Life and death were both part of the same process of liberating the soul, and in Jesus' case "it was needful that Jesus Christ should die, that by him all things of God which at first came forth from God might again return to God."(55) And yet, Coppin rejected the notion of vicarious atonement, that Jesus' death expiated for the sins of others. Christ's humanity was a vital point because "the Son himself went as a pattern for all his saints to follow."(36) Choosing to follow Christ, however, was not merely an act of will. "We can not go after God nor follow Jesus Christ till God comes to us and turns us and saith unto us, *Follow me*."(41) And when called, and when one chooses to emulate Christ, the believer "shall drink the same cup, break the same bread, be baptized with the same baptism, tread the same steps, go the same way and together with him receive the same glory."(36)

Following Christ's example consisted of practicing deeds and not of assenting to beliefs and dogmas. "The way to glory," Coppin explained, "is by suffering, and Christ went this way or else he could not enjoy his kingdom."(31) Consequently, "we," like him, "are to pass through many persecutions and tribulations for the truth's sake, both inwardly and outwardly." (32) Speaking in Christ's name, Coppin wrote, "The way which I have gone, you shall go. The death which I have suffered, you shall suffer"(34) and again, "You must be tempted with the Serpent, buffeted with Satan, and persecuted with Herod."(34)

Emulating Christ's life did not entail simple suffering either, for there would always be those who might grit their teeth and indulge their vanity.

Indeed the carnal beast's ability to justify his every self-serving action and deed was pernicious and vain and hence the Christian must suffer but only after first becoming terrified of suffering. Consequently, the second stage of Jesus in the flesh was marked by conflict and tension between the two warring principles and components within man, with each event and moment in the believer's life testimony to this conflict. This was the same conflict which tore at the very innards of the universe itself.

Coppin explained that "in every person there is a believer and an unbeliever, one which is loved and one which is hated, 'Jacob have I loved and Esau have I hated' though they tumbled in one belly."(52) The desire to follow Christ, difficult in itself, is mixed with the desires of the flesh, and "he sees a mixture of things, something of God and something of man, something of nature and something of the spirit"(104) and as a result, "the soul is sometimes at peace and sometimes in trouble."(104) Even worse, there is no resolution to this condition. The tension "shall be heightened to its full state of light and darkness, pleasure and pain."(58)

The conflict between God and Satan within the believer and the latter's inability to resolve this conflict one way or the other leads him to a very unhappy state and condition. At this time, "as soon as we have sinned, we are ashamed to look God in the face."(94) The guilt produced by sin is difficult to bear, but Coppin noted, "God can not be said to punish us for our sins, but we do punish ourselves by sinning."(94) Each sin pushes us farther from God, and the soul "may well be said to be in hell for he that is in darkness is in hell . . . and therefore man need have no greater hell than not to see the sight of God shining within him."(100) But when the believer avoids the lure of the senses and abstains from carnal sin, "he can have no greater heaven than to be forever beholding of and dwelling in the light and glory of God's majesty."(100)

The second phase was necessarily painful because it entailed the difficult separation of the natural and the spiritual within the personality, "a separation made between *all* things that are good and *all* things that are evil."(75) The battle would rage "till one have overcome the other"(51) and hopefully would result in "the good overcoming the evil, the evil cast out."(75) Over and over again Coppin stressed that the conflict was between "two opposites, that is, the law of the spirit and the law of the flesh, which are said to be warring one against the other, as in Galatians 5:17, till they have one overcome the other."(27)

Coppin used a variety of images to explain the process of separation. God was envisioned as a goldsmith who "hath made a piece of gold [and] doth by permittance or sufferance let this gold fall into the dirt where it is defiled and then out of love to his gold take it up again and make it clean. He is not angry with his gold but with the defilement and seeks to take off that, but will not wrong his gold. Even so it is with us."(81) A page later he continued, God "takes away our corruptions but the goodness he preserves and keeps."(83) Coppin also used Biblical images. The liberation of the soul is likened to "when he brought the children of Israel out of Egypt or out of great bondage."(56) All these examples share one feature which Coppin emphasized over and again. "We can not come out of ourselves till God saith, *Behold me,* and when he speaks in us and to us, and then we are ready to answer."(62) But our answer is our pain.

Coppin devoted considerable space to describing the "double cup of suffering" of inward and outward pain to be endured by all who would seek to follow Christ and arrive at sainthood. The outward suffering was easily understood by Ranters. "At first, an outward persecution or suffering which we meet withal from men in time of our possessing the gospel, as Christ himself and his apostles did when they walked the earth declaring the gospel."(32) Merely declaring oneself a Ranter and suffering public opprobrium may have met this requirement. Coppin likened Cromwell to Herod, the former being called "that anti-Christ, that man of sin which exalts and sets up himself."(32) Like Herod of old, Cromwell will search for Ranters, and "will seek to oppose him and afflict him very sore."(32)

The second form of suffering is inward but no less severe. It is necessary, Coppin wrote, "to crucify the old man in us with all his corrupt deeds and self imaginations."(32–33) Speaking in Christ's name, Coppin explained, "as if he should say, the way that leads to my kingdom is a crucifying way, even from the beginning to the end . . . from my birth it is a way sprinkled with blood and burning with fire."(34) Once these two requirements are met, the individual would enter sainthood which was "the enjoyment of the new life, the end of the flesh crucified."(35)

Coppin considered sainthood the "plain seeing of the Father and this is the kingdom of Jesus Christ in the spirit which exceeds the kingdom of Jesus Christ in the flesh."(105) In this last phase all doubt is gone as the individual goes "from darkness to light, from night to day, from evening to morning, from winter to summer, from sorrow of heart to gladness, from earth to heaven and from this world to that which is to come."(39) Spiritually naked before God, the saint is an unencumbered free soul floating above life's demands and "we become dead to all things else and then we do live unto God, when we so live to and in him as to become dead to all else but him which we can not be till the God of life arises and manifests himself to us, to work all for us, in us, upon us and to be all to us, with us, about us, that so we may be nothing but what we are in him."(15) Fleshliness and carnality all gone, "we reflect again back unto him, as the sun shining upon the waters answers itself, so the Lord shining in us answers himself."(40) Elsewhere Coppin wrote, "Here is the union of the saints knit up in that one spirit, God, and Christ. For as Christ doth the work of the Father, so the saints the work of Christ, and all three the works one of another."(11–12)

The saint is beyond the need for human fraternity. "The spiritual man which is said to know all things and judge all things, can be no less than God,"(8) Coppin wrote, adding later, "We need not receive any witness from men to expect help, light or assistance from any created thing."(20) Because the saint is the very embodiment of truth, he has no need for religious practices for "the dead in the flesh are spiritually free and need observe nothing."(38) Included in this category are "holy worship, ordinances, prayers, duties, preachings, teachings, hearing, reading and the like."(19) Even more, because the saint is above material concerns, he "can not sin because it [i.e., the soul] is born of God for it came forth from God and is as divine as God. The New Man is divine spirit and therefore can not commit sin."(87) Surely no less a status could be granted to a being who was "the palace of God in which he dwells."(19)

There is one last phase in the life of every saint and believer alike. With physical death, the body decays and "to the earth it must return again, where it is dissolved and appears no more."(50) In turn, the soul is "reduced again to its original and divine image as at first . . . [and] will be as God."(105)

There should be no difference between the death of the saint and that of a sinner for in both cases the body decays while the soul returns to its source. In all cases, death brought about the complete division of body and soul but also the separation of the spirit and the soul. In the case of sinners, however, the soul returned to God but, unlike the saint's personality which remained intact, the sinner's spirit was destroyed: "the good for everlasting salvation and the evil for everlasting damnation" where "all things opposed to goodness [are] condemned to death, punished with everlasting destruction from the presence of the Lord. . . ."(58)

In this earliest treatise, Coppin wrote with the certainty of the saint. Coppin was convinced that he was a special divine messenger to an age strikingly similar to the time of Christ. Coppin saw himself as a poor man who "sits disputing with all the self righteous as he did in the Temple of old when he disputed with the doctors, posing them and asking them questions."(3) In the civil war, "God now comes forth from the great and learned of the world and exalts himself in the poor and ignorant . . . not only the poor as touching the world but poor and ignorant in the things of God."(3) What else could the civil war be but the same divine battle which led to the destruction of the Temple, "the like things we see in the world, with kings and with councils, even the greatest of men's wisdom, for what is it that hath dashed them to pieces and broke the bands of all human government but the Lord Jesus Christ disputing with them to bring in his own divine and everlasting government?"(4)

It is doubtful whether Coppin or other Ranters considered themselves to be actual God though the continual affirmation of their own divinity caused great friction with devotees of other sects and churches who, no doubt, considered themselves saintly expressions of God's true wisdom. Such self-congratulatory assessments seem to be quite the norm in the seventeenth century and contributed to the internecine warfare characterizing sectarian relations. From his own divine station Coppin bridled that he had been condemned by others on such secondary issues "as outward forms and outward observances, ceremonies and the like, for not going to church, as some call it, or for not having fellowship with men in their worldly worship." (A3 of preface) There could be but one reason he was criticized, "by reason of the enmity or man of sin who reigns in them . . . who makes all the breaches and offenses in and amongst men."(preface p.1) Coppin could have but one response, regarding "the truth concerning the things of God," Coppin wrote, "I shall therefore press it the more earnest in writing, and shall not refrain my pen."(preface p.1)

Coppin's remaining religious writings were intended to supplement and improve upon the basic teachings found in the *Divine Teachings* trilogy. Each examined additional concepts important to understanding Christianity from a dualist perspective. Coppin's second religious treatise, *Man's Righteousness Examined*, of 1652, studied the expression and manifestation of evil in the world. More than any other single issue, dualism is predicated upon a strong sense of evil and it is not surprising that Coppin should have devoted his first specialized treatise to this subject.

Coppin's conception of the devil was typical of the dualistic thought we have encountered. He noted that "The Devil was at first good and an angel of Light, but through covetousness he became evil and angel of Darkness, and so was cast out of heaven into hell, as out of light into darkness."(6) We have already observed in the *Divine Teachings* that the Devil was sent to the earth which he soon controlled for his own purposes. Humanity was material in orientation "and so like natural brute beasts, knowing only the things of nature, deceive their own souls and can not but speak evil."(17) As a result, humanity's many religions were dominated by the Devil, whom man considered God, and "the knowledge of evil from which they can not free or discharge themselves nor others, and so beguile both themselves and others."(17) Christian religious leaders may condemn others but are no different for "they have fellowship only with the Devil, the prince of this world or natural state . . . and so walk according to the course of this world and the prince of the power of air, worshipping a God after the flesh."(21) For this reason, the world's innocent but ignorant populations "are already in hell and damned."(19) The results of this unfortunate condition are "terror of conscience, ignorance of mind, rashness of spirit, discontent, envy, wrath, malice and so forth, which they burn in and are tormented with; this is the reward of sinners."(19) Despite unhappiness in this condition, they "can not cease from sin in that they can not cease from the knowledge of sin."(19)

Christians were evil people tortured with evil thoughts predicated upon their evil and carnal natures which in turn are predicated upon the Devil. The very essence of traditional Christianity was nothing more than the religious pursuit of evil and the devil to produce "a dead faith or no faith at all, or if it be a faith it is but the faith of devils who believe and tremble or believe they are damned."(16) All devilish religions meet human uncertainty with a treadmill of rituals, observances, ordinances, and practices, none of which can help man in the least but without which, the human being believes, there is no salvation. This, for Coppin, "is the damnable heresy and doctrine of devils, to deny that there is full end of sin for all men, past, present and to come."(10)

Though he divided the world into saints and sinners, Coppin saw some measure of variability in the devil's brood. Devils were a varied lot and Coppin found it possible to define several different categories of evil people. In general, all evil people were dogs and "by dogs is meant carnal men, such whose nature is doggish . . . as to be always barking, biting, snapping and snarling . . . and thus in men dwells the nature of dogs while they remain in that state of nature, and not only dogs, but also sorcerers, whore-mongers, murderers and idolators."(4) Sorcerers were those devils who taught "the art of man's wisdom, human learning"(4) or, in short, university men. Murderers were magistrates who "murder, kill, and slay every appearance of Christ in his people by persecuting some, imprisoning some, and killing others."(5) Ministers of other religions were whore-mongers, who "go a whoring after strange flesh (as after strange Gods), ways and worships which men set up as gods which in turn are no gods at all but creature inventions or men's inventions."(4) Their followers, the ordinary commons merely following their parish ministers were idolators who "idolize, set up and maintain any man, form, things, way, worship, and opinion contrary to Christ and the truth."(5) All such devils were like a dog which "turns again to his vomit, sin, and corruption . . . to the wallowing in the mire."(32)

Opposed to all these doggish devils are the saints. The saint was one who believed in "Jesus Christ, whose kingdom consists not in forms or outward worships and who is now throwing down all forms, religious worships and opinions whatsoever."(26) Additionally, the saint is one who "despises government and speaks evil of dignities."(21) This theme was developed in Coppin's political treatises.

Coppin's religious views became more radical during the next two years and his treatise *A Man-Child Born* of 1654 reflected a new polarization in his already dualistic views. Despite certain overall similarities to the views he expressed in the *Divine Teachings*, Coppin's more sharply defined views of evil led to his employing new images to express a new radicalism.

The major purpose of this treatise was to elucidate upon the incarnation of Christ from an allegorical perspective. As we recall, the *Divine Teachings* emphasized Christ's mortal suffering and the need for others to follow in his path. From this earlier vantage point, the incarnation, or the dressing of the Word in flesh, was an unnecessary concept. Indeed, it would have been difficult for Coppin to have explained how the material and spiritual might have existed in one being, how mortal human beings could have followed in the path of a divine Jesus and how human beings might shed their flesh and become divine by following the path of one who shed his divinity to become mortal.

Yet, despite his radical orientation, there are several reasons Coppin evidently felt the need to come to terms with this traditional Christian concept. His radical adoptionist Christology was condemned at both his earlier and later trials and Coppin may have realized that a systematic theologian must account for traditional concepts and opinions however useless these may have been to him. Second, it is possible that Coppin's many listeners and readers felt the need for an explanation of the incarnation and impressed upon him the need to explicate this concept from his own vantage point. Whatever his motivation, *A Man-Child Born* was written to reinterpret this cardinal orthodox teaching along dualistic lines. In the process, Coppin considerably strengthened his religious system and demonstrated how potent allegory might be. Also, Coppin found yet newer images through which his dualism might be expressed, and best of all, all the new images were compatible with his earlier ideas.

Coppin noted that "God in Christ declares himself to be ever clothed with flesh,"(4) which may have sounded vaguely orthodox but may also have meant that the divine soul was always clothed in flesh, a condition that applied both to Christ and to every other human being. Thus, when writing about Christ, the pattern for all humanity, Coppin cited Scripture, "*his name shall be called Emanuel,* which being interpreted is, God with us, that is, God declared, revealed and made manifest in our flesh"(6) which was a clear reference to all humanity. Thus, if the incarnation referred to the clothing of souls in flesh, every human being and not merely Jesus was incarnated. Conceivably, the resurrection, the soul's shedding of the flesh, was also true of every person and not only Jesus.

Applying terms and concepts usually reserved for Christ to all mankind could have radical implications. Rather than conceiving of the incarnation through the communication of idioms, as the very special clothing of the word in flesh to create a being both fully divine and fully human, Coppin taught that *every* human birth entailed an incarnation of the divine soul in a fleshy casing. Moreover, this was no great cause for joy, but the terrible damage done by the incarnation could be undone by the resurrection which entailed shedding the flesh. Not only had Coppin succeeded in neutralizing a cardinal Christian concept, but he had mocked its importance as something requiring not veneration but repair.

Coppin next turned his attention to the concept of the virgin birth. Dualists traditionally disparaged this view. Here again, Coppin ostensibly accepted the orthodox concept only to show his contempt for it. Again in near orthodox wording, Coppin stated, "Mary is the flesh or human nature"(29) as statement which might have one meaning for traditional Christians but another for dualists, especially when Coppin also argued, "It is written that a woman shall compass a man . . . for what is the woman but man's nature, weakness and flesh?"(7) Thus, the incarnation, which was also the fall of the soul, finds its systematic origins in femininity, the agency which created the evil-tainted matter and not coincidentally, the agency which led man to sin in the Garden of Eden. Coppin expressed this point by explaining that "God first creates us and forms us in our mother's womb and brings us forth from thence into particular bodies and appearances."(1)

From the earliest Gnostics, dualists of all ages have made use of the male-female dichotomy to vent their hatred of matter. Ranters such as Foster carried this to an extreme as did Salmon, and Thomas Tany went so far as to deny women a soul. Coppin was not so extreme and was willing, after making his argument, to retreat a bit and explain that all people, both male and female, are the material bearers of the soul. "This is a hard saying,"

Coppin wrote, "who can bear it, and also a paradox to the world that *we should all* be the mother of Jesus Christ."(10)

The "man-child" referred to in the title was in fact the status of every believer who possessed a divine soul and yet was also a mother of flesh. "This man-child, or Lord Jesus Christ," Coppin explained, is "thus born in you and given to you."(14) The mission of every true believer was to enable this man-child, the soul, to be free of the mother nature of flesh. Thus, "when he comes to show himself to you, [he] will strip you of it [i.e., flesh] and leave you destitute, naked, and childless to anything but the Lord."(13) This process, the resurrection, was also "the New Jerusalem . . . the state of the spirits of just men made perfect which is God descending in glory to us, to take us up to himself."(9) This in turn meant, "the change of man's nature into the nature of God, that makes it the same with God and so it is written, we are made partakers of the divine nature."(4)

From a systematic perspective, everything fits together quite nicely, for Coppin was able to explain his dualistic views through the use of orthodox terminology and concepts which usually carried orthodox intent but which now also carried heretical meaning. If nothing else it made prosecution of Ranters more difficult but no doubt helped spread the Ranter message as well.

Several new ideas which would be developed in other treatises were introduced by Coppin in *Man-Child Born*. His social radicalism was expressed when he wrote, "And this is the counsel that I give, saith the Lord, to deny thyself and follow me, to sell all that thou hast and give to the poor; a hard saying, who can bear it?"(19) Similarly, Coppin was able to demonstrate the allegorical method of interpreting Scripture which would be used very effectively in his political treatises. Rather than accepting the literal wording of Scripture, Coppin wrote, "Those enemies thus overcome by the Lord in us are the army of the Assyrians mentioned in Scripture that are said to come into our land . . . Now by Assyrians is meant devil, sin, sorrows, fears, doubts and unbelief, so by the land is meant the flesh or body corrupted into which those Assyrians come and there abide for a time to war against the peace of the soul."(23) In this more martial and more Manichaean vein, Coppin also referred to God as the Prince of Peace and the Devil as the Prince of War, when he wrote, "The Prince of War with all his oppressive army, to wit, sin, sorrows, fears, doubts and unbelief, shall be cast out and the Prince of Peace with all his army, to wit, love, joy, peace, rest and salvation shall come in."(23)

One additional new image used by Coppin was God as a "thief in the night." All of Coppin's works explained that one must wait for God to appear to the soul before the believer is capable of responding to God. Various Ranter authors used different images to make this same point and in this treatise Coppin wrote that God "will come as a thief in the night, stealing upon you unawares to you, and being once come you will own it and embrace it as the day of your salvation."(27) At that point the believer can "truly say that unto me a child is born"(14) but until then, "they can not yet see themselves to be saved and so have not this knowledge of their being the wife of God and mother of Jesus."(11) It is likely that Coppin borrowed this image from Abiezer Coppe whose writings were in wide circulation. He used this image with far more dramatic impact than did Coppin. For Coppe the Libertine, a "thief in the night" could actually be a real thief in the night.

Coppin's last two religious works were truly innovative. *Crux Christi* of 1657 and the equally unusual *Michael Opposing the Dragon* of 1659 completed Coppin's theological literary product with a curious history of sainthood and suffering for Christ. There were new departures in these treatises, and Coppin's elucidations are pointed, novel and innovative in tying together several loose threads from earlier volumes. These last writings are vintage Rantism, for more than any other author Coppin was prolific and able to follow up on previous thought and advance his dualism into a complete intellectual system.

Crux Christi and *Michael Opposing the Dragon* present the reader with interesting discussions of several themes usually neglected by radical theologians. In these writings, Coppin attempted to place his views within a larger conceptual and social framework. True sainthood was not a matter of proper belief but proper lifestyle; hence Coppin was concerned that believers would not adequately appreciate the need to institute Christ's cross within their daily lives. Earlier dualists such as the Bogomils and the Cathari were able to depend upon church life to translate the meaning of their beliefs into everyday life. Coppin did not enjoy the luxury of ecclesiastical support; hence he was forced to accomplish on paper what earlier dualists did through institutions.

Coppin did not attempt to create a moral code or list of practices dualists might adhere to. After all, he was not about to recreate the forms, rituals, ordinances and the like that he detested in other churches. Rather, he would provide a personal orientation through which each individual Ranter might view personal social relationships as well as his relationship with political power.

The world was not a friendly place. The Ranter could anticipate "sin and the devil and all iniquity, which is a flood out of the devil's mouth, rushing out upon you to devour you."(1-2*Crux.*) Against all the forces of Satan—and these included the ministers of Kent—the individual had but one recourse: "to follow him and take up his cross daily and carry it with you after him, suffering it to be placed on you, as the Lord's standard lifted up against the enemy."(1-2)

Taking up Christ's cross meant not merely suffering for one's beliefs but also suffering because one was alive in matter. To save one's soul, one must alienate oneself from all of life and withdraw. "In taking up this cross and following Christ," Coppin explained, "you forsake father, mother, husband and wife, children and brethren, house and lands, and all for Christ."(5) This was not simply a reiteration of Christ's own warning to those that would follow him, for Coppin explains in shockingly obvious dualistic terms why all of the above must be forsaken. If matter and fleshly carnality were evil and perverted, one's own parents were certainly the immediate authors of such perversion in the life of every individual believer and therefore, must be forsaken. "Your father whom you are to forsake," and who sired you, "is the devil that begets sin and wickedness in you and made all your knowledge and love amongst men to be devilish."(5) Even more to the point, "Your mother is the whore of Babylon and lust of the flesh, the mother of whoredoms and abominations of the earth in which sin is conceived and brought forth and of whom you at first were begotten by the devil."(5)

Worse than one's antecedent relationships, over which one had no control, were romantic entanglements involving members of the opposite sex. Coppin warned his reader, "You have been and still are by them matched and betrothed, united and coupled, marrying and giving in marriage with the daughters of men, your own inventions and imaginations which are as harlots and which as whores you make your spouses."(6) The evil nature of women was apparent to all if one but chose to see it. Women, "appearing fair and beautiful to you, you are in love with them and do go a whoring after them."(6) The result was that each generation compounded the evil horror of the previous one and "have begotten and brought forth strange children, children of whoredoms and of fornications, after the image of your father the devil and of the whore your mother."(6)

If one chose to follow Christ, like him you must "forsake all and follow him whether so ever he shall lead" and foremost, "all such marriages are to be broken, lost, and forsaken."(7) Only *after* such relationships are ended will "he lead his dearest saints that know him and are nearest in union with him for the trial of their faith."(10–11)

Coppin visualized human beings in a paradoxical situation. Many worry about the condition of their religious lives and the state of their souls and all the while honor their perverted progenitors, those who have dirtied and fouled the human nest in the previous generation. While worrying about their union with God in the future, mortals dirty their present existence and enter into the social relationship of marriage to justify the generation of foul offspring as God's blessing. The choice was simple: "Would you now die that you might live? Then this is the way to see yourselves and all things of yourself crucified in Christ."(8) Over and over again Coppin felt it necessary to remind his reader that following Christ was not a matter of words. "My Brethren" he wrote, "think it not strange concerning your fiery trials, persecutions and tribulations and suffering, as if some strange thing happened to you, for they are the companions with Christ on the cross."(10) Indeed, Jesus may have been fortunate that his life was taken from him by others. In the absence of such kind persecutors, "the way to this life is to die daily till you be dead to all things but God, for as you die the death of one life (which you must die and can not live) so you live another life which is for everlasting and can never die."(3)

Coppin's regimen was strident yet he believed this lifestyle expressed God's true desire for mankind throughout history. To demonstrate this point Coppin included in *Crux Christi* a thumbnail sketch of suffering in Biblical history. He cited the example of Abel who was persecuted by his materialistic brother Cain (16) and the Hebrews who were forced to labor with clay and mortar in their servitude in Egypt. This suffering was not the result of bad luck but of God's requirement that his saints suffer and thereby purify themselves. Thus "God *hardened Pharoah's heart that he should not let Israel go,* but should afflict them so long."(17) Even this was not sufficient, however, "and after he let them go, he hardened the hearts of the Egyptians to persist in persecution against them and to follow them through the Red Sea."(17) After that, Israel was harassed by Amalek as they wandered in the wilderness for forty years.

There was also the story of Joseph who was hated by this brothers and sold into slavery. Once in Egypt he was sold yet again, this time to a powerful nobleman and his lot became better but only so that it could become much worse. His master's spouse attempted to seduce him and when righteous Joseph failed to respond to her charms, she accused him of making sexual overtures and he was thrown into prison. Even worse, when God gave him the tool with which to free himself from prison, it consisted of an ability to read the Pharoah's dreams, all of which had Egypt and the royal family coming to a bad end.(13–14)

The story of Job provided a poignant example of suffering. Surely human logic and religious wisdom must confirm that Job, a righteous man, should prosper in his faith and in his dealings with his neighbors and society. Not so, claimed Coppin, for it was God himself who permitted Job to suffer as he did, for "neither could the devil touch Job in his person nor estate to afflict and punish him without God had bidden him and gave him commission, which God saw would be good for Job and therefore Job in all his afflictions accuseth none, neither devil nor witches, nor any other in the loss of anything."(19)

Even God's spokesmen were forced to suffer indignities. Citing the examples of Isaiah and Ezekial, Coppin noted, "And so did the Lord do by Isaiah when he made him to walk naked and barefoot three years for a sign. He made Ezekial to bake men's dung and eat it for a sign . . . yet all such are counted as mad men by those that knew not the Lord, though they did it by his command."(19) There were also the cases of Jonah, Jeremiah, Daniel and even Shadrack, Meshack and Abednego, "who at the wrath of King Nebuchadnezzar for their faithfulness . . . were cast into the midst of the hot and fiery furnace."(34)

In light of these earlier saints of God, Jesus' life on earth could have but one meaning. "He was a man himself in the flesh, [and] suffered such reproaches, whippings, scourgings and reviling of men, and yet, for the glory that was set before him he endured the cross . . . and as Christ was made perfect through sufferings, so shall we all that will be made perfect as he is perfect."(45, incorrectly 37) Hence, "think it not strange concerning your fiery trials, persecutions and tribulations and sufferings as if some strange thing happened to you, for they are the companions with Christ on the cross."(10) Rather than hating those who offer whippings and humiliation, "blessed are you when men shall hate you and persecute you and shall say all manner of evil sayings against you . . . and shall separate you from their company and shall reproach you and cast out your name as evil."(42) When such tribulations afflict you, "rejoice in that day and leap for joy."(42) Repression was not evil for "before any deliverance can be of any to any, there must first be a bondage."(17) Even after initial deliverance and God's call, he "gives them a thorn in the flesh, sends Satan to buffet them and the Serpent to bite them."(52, incorrectly printed as 44)

Coppin must have taken comfort that his legal ordeals provided him with more than adequate opportunity to suffer. He observed, "All my sufferings for the truth to this day bear me witness, that bands and afflictions, persecutions and trials through which a soul enters into the kingdom of God, are very good and in which much of God hath been manifested to me."(11) Coppin might have been as good a Christian with less strife in his life but the justification of suffering has been a common theme among persecuted radicals of most ages. If indeed Coppin was able to see his own trials as the equivalent of those suffered by "Adam, and the first fathers, the prophets, Christ and his apostles"(52) he had good reason to rejoice.

Political Writings

Coppin's political ideas found expression in two treatises, *Saul Smitten for Not Smiting Amalek* of 1653 and *Michael Opposing the Dragon* of 1659. Through a skillful use of allegory, Coppin was able to turn scriptural history into an explanation of contemporary England's woes and problems. In order to appreciate the strong relationship between his political views and his religious ideas, we will present the more general *Michael Opposing the Dragon* first and *Saul Smitten* last. First, however, we might consider why Coppin's earlier religious treatises give little indication of any personal political interest at all.

Several factors may help explain why there were few indications of the social radicalism in his earlier treatises and why this changed by 1653. The civil war and the execution of King Charles led many to anticipate serious change but by 1653 it was increasingly clear that neither Parliament nor Cromwell would initiate any of the reforms radicals anticipated. Additionally, Coppin's experience in the courts of law left him very bitter. Despite a more liberal religious atmosphere during the interregnum, Ranters could not avoid the strictures of the Blasphemy Act, and Coppin as well as many others suffered continual harassment. Last, the years 1652 to 1655 were the zenith of Ranter growth and influence. Consequently, Coppin's new radicalism may represent the Ranter self-confidence so evident in the writings of other Ranters in this period as well as disgust with the outcome of Cromwell's revolution.

In his last work, *Michael Opposing the Dragon*, of 1659, Coppin continued his efforts to expand his dualistic teachings into a larger intellectual framework, this time a political one. Early in the treatise Coppin argued that Scripture "is spiritually to be understood and not literally"(13) and that "even in the History of Kings and Acts of the Apostles may be an allegory."(11) Coppin would prove that biblical personalities are either "blessed or cursed, saved or damned, in heaven or hell"(21–22) and that such spiritual status held political meaning as well.

From the earliest times, humanity confronted a paradox. "Adam was created of the dust of the ground and that was the first and eldest part of man in the creation"(84) Coppin explained. Consequently, the carnal and fleshly perception of life was usually victorious in its conflict with the soul with the result of this eternal conflict becoming evident just one generation later. "Adam had two sons sprung up from him, Cain and Abel, a man earthly and a man spiritual (signifying flesh and spirit in us) and the Earthly rose up against the Heavenly and slew him."(84) Within a few generations the descendants of Sarah and Hagar, the sons of freedom in the spirit and the sons of bondage of the spirit were in contention but "now both signifying two nations, houses or families."(87)

Later we read of Jacob and Esau, "and we read that by Esau is signified the greatness and honor of the world which is the human, fleshly part, for Dukes, Kings, and Nobles came from him and he is called the father of the Edomites which were the enemies of God's people and despised them."(83) Subsequently, "these two seeds, flesh and spirit, the earthly and heavenly parts, do both grow together in one man till the regeneration and resurrection, then Christ appears to make a separation."(86)

The earthly influence was twofold and we have already had opportunity to view the spiritual dimension of this dichotomy of spirit and flesh. The Esau-principle of seeking power and position had a corroding effect upon the governance of the whole of humanity. Carnal monarchy always represented "the hands of the devil, to maintain his kingdom of worldly honor and pride, cruelty and oppression."(141–142) Hence, despite God's initial love of the Hebrews, they too soon became polluted with the spirit of Esau. Samuel warned against monarchy but the Hebrews wanted a king and we read that "Saul was the first king given them, of whom it was said he should make slaves of them and continue wickedness among them, as hath been continued to this day."(144) Subsequent human history entailed more of the same with church and state aiding each other in repressing the commoner. Eventually, "the Magistrates and Ministers of late times do uphold one another to maintain the kingdoms of the world against the Lord's kingdom, to serve not the Lord nor his people but to serve themselves of his people."(141)

Those who oppose either church or state are called sinners, blasphemers, and heretics when in reality it is they who are the saints. "But pray," Coppin asked, "what were the elect but sinners? Else they could not be saved nor said to be justified."(125) Those who blindly choose to follow the priests will find no solace, for "the best works a man can do will not carry him from hell to heaven, though it may help him towards hell when he doth it to be saved by it."(22)

This entire world of hellish government and devilish religion will come to a bad end. There was no hope for true reform and Coppin wrote, "All shall die, cast into the wine press of the wrath of God or Lake of Fire to be burned."(25) Only those willing to "tread the wine press of the wrath of God alone"(23) in this world had hope of salvation. So arduous was that path that even Jesus, who was chosen by God, declared, "My God, My God, why hast thou forsaken me?" and so great was his pain and "so great was the wrath of God upon him . . . [Jesus inquired] if it were possible that the cup might pass from him and he not drink it."(23) Christ's apostles fared no better and suffered "afflictions of diverse sorts, some were tortured . . . others had trials of cruel mockings and scourgings, bonds and imprisonments, they were stoned . . . were slain with the sword."(27) Hence, those who oppose the policy of fleshliness must do so politically as well as religiously.

Coppin's political views are easy to understand from the vantage point of his interpretation of Scriptural history. *Saul Smitten for Not Smiting Amalek* was an attempt to demonstrate how religious ideas and political ideas must be understood as parallel and interrelated. It is an interesting play upon the Old Testament story where God commands Saul to destroy every man, woman and child of the Amalek tribe and all of their property as well.

The Amalekites, a tribal people not significantly different from the Hebrews, plagued the latter during their forty years of wandering in the wilderness when Moses took them from Egypt. The two tribes may have been competitors at first but several centuries later, during Saul's reign, the relative positions of the two tribes had changed. The Hebrews were now organized into a tribal confederation with a new, if untested, monarchy while Amalek remained a band of wandering nomads. According to Scripture, God commanded Saul to obliterate this ancient enemy, but this order came in the midst of a power struggle between Saul and Samuel. The religious authorities of the day, most notably Samuel, had been opposed to monarchy. Samuel had warned the Hebrews that a monarchy would enslave them, tax them to death, and draft their sons. Hence it is possible that Saul wished to destroy Amalek to bolster popular support behind his new government.

Scripture recounts how Saul in fact destroyed Amalek but, quite against God's commands, retained some of their property for his own benefit. As a result, Saul suffered continuing erosion of religious support as well as the loss of this divine charisma which was the basis of his right to rule.

Through an imaginative use of allegory, and building upon the ideas that would later appear in *Michael Opposing the Dragon*, Coppin reinterpreted this story of Saul's perfidy into a political parable for his own times. He explained that Israel's release from Egypt was not only redemption from physical servitude but also liberation from spiritual bondage expressed "through forms, ordinances, outward observances"(2) borrowed from Egyptian religion. In turn, the "promised land" was a safe national refuge, but in a spiritual sense, "their rest, their heaven, their happiness."(2) In bringing his people from spiritual death to spiritual life, God told the Hebrews to "quietly pass along, through and by and over all the ways, laws, forms and religions of men and not suffer you to stay or rest in anything or abide in any house or form till you are come to that which is your rest."(2)

Unfortunately, Israel was plagued by the arch evil Amalek, a true threat to Israel's spiritual purity. We are to understand that Amalek's influence was essentially similar to that ascribed to Esau and Hagar's progeny, Cain. Thus, at long last Saul was told "to slay all, both men and women, infant and suckling, the great whore and her children, which have been the oppressors of the people."(13) Clearly, for Coppin, Amalek represented every evil from which Israel had been liberated by God. But Saul had already been influenced by Esau-inspired desire for power and wealth, and failed to respond to God's call when he retained some of Amalek's material wealth. This wealth, interpreted allegorically, represented Amalekite corruption and hence, Israel's first king was spiritually corrupt.

As a result of Saul's betrayal of God, the monarchy he founded was tainted and built upon a corrupt semi-Amalek foundation which in turn "brought forth many laws, acts and statutes, set up many particular interests on men's inventions."(9) These in turn created the whole panoply of tyranny "which may be known by the names of priests, lawyers, sheriffs, bailiffs, oppressive tithe mongers, committee men, excise men, common council men, and all sorts of clerks, courts and offices and whatsoever particulars else may appear to have been set up by men that have in any way been oppressive and in opposition to the true peace and freedom of the people's rights and privileges . . . ."(9)

Even worse than organized religion and government, the corrupting Amalekite foundation produced private property. Coppin wrote that after the foundation of an oppressive power structure from above, "next [came] the stores belonging to this house or family, to wit, sheep, camels and asses, and this may be said to be the people's privileges, lives, and liberties and estates, with all the wealth, honor, and riches of the land which men by their power, they have taken into their hands to make themselves fat and rich and which they carried captive by them from the right owners of it."(9)

Considering the foundation, the future was predictable. Thereafter David centralized worship in Jerusalem, and Solomon built a temple supported by taxes so heavy that ten tribes rebelled against Judah at his death and formed the separate kingdom of Israel. King replaced king with each increasing his power and encouraging the property rights of those that supported him. Each explained his exalted position with the religious justifications that organized religion supplied and traded for much royal financial support. In the space of a few centuries, Esau's principles, Egypt's bondage and Amalek's evil corruption were fully expressed in the house of Israel. "And now," Coppin explained, "are men still persecuted and have been to this day by both Pope, papists, bishops, prelates and presbyterians and [are] now like to be by the Independents and Anabaptists, all like those oppressive Amalekites still acting against the appearance of the Lord Jesus in his people."(6) Far from being a dead story buried in the pages of Scripture, "consider what and where he [i.e., Amalek] is," Coppin advised. "Some all along in all ages have still appeared to war against Israel in the way, as they have come up from Egypt."(5)

Turning his attention to contemporary England, Coppin used the images of Amalek and Israel to analyze the events of his own day. "Amalek," Coppin explained, "may be said to be a whole household or family with all that belongs to it and may relate to kings' houses and houses of former Parliaments . . ."(8) Like earlier kings of Israel and Judah, the previous governments of King Charles "tyranized over my people by their unlawful dealing, exacting upon them their persons, goods, labors and purses . . ."(12) Parliament was no better and replaced royal abuse with "their unjust laws and statutes in their unlawful offices, courts and councils, making preys of them, serving themselves by it."(12) Both king and Parliament, like their more ancient brothers in evil, make laws to protect themselves, so "if any that are oppressed by them complain of their oppression, they [Parliament] will plead the authority of Parliament for what they do . . . and say they have as law for what they do and a power that maintains them in it."(12–13)

Much as Saul was commanded to destroy Amalek, "so the like command might have come from the Lord to our general [i.e., Cromwell?] to smite the late Parliament and to slay them of their oppressive power, law and actions, rules and private interests and to spare none . . . and to return all the rest, to wit, the people's interest, rights, privileges, which the late Parliament with others before them had taken away."(9) To fulfill God's desire, Coppin would have Cromwell complete Saul's commission, where "ought all to be slain or taken out of the way and not any to be spared or left remaining as before, to rule in any power or sit in the place of justice." (13) Pride's Purge may have been a good beginning, but like the earlier Saul who did not

RICHARD COPPIN

slay Amalek and then expressed its corruption, Cromwell failed to reform the government and return the people's privilege.

Coppin sought reform in three areas of English life. Politically, Coppin could see little need for central government and demanded a system where "everyone shall have his freedom in things that are not hurtful to the peace, liberty, and freedom one of another."(25) In the area of property distribution, "all men shall have an equal proportion of satisfaction and where he that hath least shall know no want and he that hath shall have nothing over."(23) In matters of religion, "let all men act their freedom in point of worship towards God, which way they please."(27)

In presenting his demands upon contemporary English society, Coppin sought to demonstrate that Jesus fit the pattern of envisioned social reform. Jesus was a religious libertarian. Coppin noted that "Jesus Christ suffered all men in their several ways and opinions and forced no man to any way, form, or opinion of things by any outward rule or enforcement."(29) A page later Coppin wrote, "Jesus Christ is he that must recover again . . . and restore into our hands again all our freedom, liberties, and estates, both temporal and spiritual."(30) Jesus, then, was also a social revolutionary. Rather than writing of saints, *Saul Smitten* refers to "the Lord's Free Men"(30) whose purpose is to "restore to every man his own house, wealth, land, riches and honors, freedom and liberty which the Lord hath given to them, to wit, *the whole earth and all things therein.*"(28) This condition of general social sainthood which Coppin sought, "is the Kingdom of the Father which we all wait for, expect and pray for when we say 'Thy Kingdom Come'."(31)

The social radicalism expressed in *Saul Smitten* was predicated upon the successful application of dualism and an allegorical interpretation of Scripture to contemporary social issues. The result was an intellectual and conceptual consistency between the two areas of religious and social concerns. The destruction of Amalek was identified with the destruction of the carnal fleshliness from which Jesus came to show the path to freedom. The Pharisees of old who killed Christ found their origin in Amalek but were only an older version of the priests of the Church of England and/or their Presbyterian adversaries. Land owners were a sinful people both religiously and politically and they too found their origin in Amalek, who slew Jesus, who . . . .

The freedom of the soul from material fleshliness was its liberation from religious strictures but also the liberation of God's Free Men from the Amalekite land owners who killed Christ and represent the Devil. Kings are latter day Sauls, and Parliament is a latter day Esau. Jesus represented spiritual freedom, political freedom, religious freedom, and Amalek was the origin of everything opposed to Jesus. And in his day, Cromwell was Esau, and Coppin represented Jesus.

Legal and Polemical Treatises.

It is fitting that we conclude our treatment of Richard Coppin with his three legal and polemical treatises of 1655–1656 for these demonstrate how he was forced to tread the wine press of the wrath of God. *A Blow at the Serpent* and *The Twenty Five Articles* relate Coppin's experiences in 1655 at the hands of the religious and civil authorities of the city of Kent where he was first invited to participate in a public debate with orthodox ministers and then prosecuted for the views he expressed in those debates. *Truth's Testimony* tells of an early encounter with the legal system from 1651 to 1653 when Coppin was tried for heresy according to the terms of the Blasphemy Act. The treatises are neither harangues to the faithful nor castigations of the evil but clear and concise descriptions of his travails. Unlike other Ranters whose bold and dramatic lives made them controversial and liable to prosecution, Coppin disturbed none and his persecution is a case study in the religious intolerance of the age.

According to *Truth's Testimony*, Coppin noted that his troubles began in 1651 when he was invited to preach in Emload in Worcester. To the chagrin of the local religious authorities, he was very successful and each week attracted more and more people to his sermons. Finally, "the priests and elders decided to get a warrant from some JP and charge me with blasphemy"(28) and such local dignitaries and JPs as Eason of Basford, Collier of Bleachy, and Ralph Nevil said "They would knock me on the head or tread me under foot."(28)

On March 23, 1651, the three named gentlemen presented Coppin with a Bill of Indictment. He was ordered to appear before Lord Chief Baron Wilde, judge of General Assize in Worcester, and present testimony before a grand jury.(31) The Bill of Indictment listed seven charges, alleging that Coppin had preached the following: that all men would be saved, that those hearing him were in heaven, that God was as much in them as in Christ, that the day of judgment began 1600 years ago with no future day of judgment, and that there was neither heaven nor hell but what was in man.(31)

It is likely that Coppin did preach these themes for all can be found in his writing. His answers, as he recorded them, were simple and direct. Coppin admitted that those "who preach up sin unpardoned and held forth damnation . . . ought not to be heard or believed."(33–4) Concerning the second point, Coppin noted "It is most certain that God gave to every man his soul, therefore will he take every man's soul to himself again."(35) Hence, there was no damnation, all would be saved, and God was in fact in all people with souls. As to whether people were in heaven when hearing Coppin preach, the preacher answered "every man therefore may be said to be in heaven and glory in him, yea, in the same glory that Christ himself is in, though not yet revealed to them."(36) A similarly vague answer was given to the next question, whether God was in each man as he was in Christ. God, Coppin stated, "was the same in all men as he was in that one called Christ . . . though he be not yet fully manifested to and in all men as he was to and in him."(37)

Did judgment day begin 1600 years ago? Coppin answered that "the work of judgment was then begun with some, coming on to others, and is not ended to this day with all, neither will be . . ."(39) On all these issues Coppin gave vague answers which presented Ranter truth but should have given little offense to orthodox jurors. The most important points were the last two, however, concerning the existence of heaven and hell for these alone were covered by the provisions of the Blasphemy Act. In his inexperience, Coppin attempted to present candid and honest answers, though he soon learned from this mistake. He argued that according to Scripture, "the kingdom of heaven is within you" and he concluded, "I know no other heaven (as to me) in which man's salvation from sin, death, hell and the world . . . and they that will have another, let them declare what and where it is."(40) Concerning hell, "I yet know no other hell as to me than what I have found in my own conscience."(40)

Coppin stated that he was satisfied with his answers and also with the judge who gave him every opportunity to present his defense. He noted, "The hearing was fair [but] my accusors were troubled and added new charges" which included Coppin's alleged rejection of the Law of Moses and the Sabbath day, that he spoke in derision of heaven and that he denied the physical resurrection of the body, "and said there was no other but what was in flowers and grass."(42) The transcript continues, indicating Coppin's answers which generally agreed with the charges against himself. Again Coppin was satisfied with his answers and was therefore shocked to learn that the jury found him guilty on the two charges concerning heaven and hell.

Coppin explained that the judge, too, was surprised by the jury's findings and attempted to intervene on his behalf. Judge Wilde explained to the jury that none of the issues were covered by the law except the charges regarding heaven and hell. Even here Coppin fell outside the law's provisions, according to Wilde, because "Coppin did not deny them altogether." Moreover, the judge went on, "the witnesses claimed it was denied in private conversation and that was not covered by the Blasphemy Act."(43) Despite the judge's statement and explanation, the jury would not be moved and "the judge ordered me held until the next assize."(43)

In Coppin's mind the case was clear cut. Despite his innocence according to the letter of the law, "the reason why those men persecute me thus is for the malice they have against me for exercising these gifts that God hath given me for his glory . . . which gifts they know not."(44) It is possible that local ministers were in fact jealous of Coppin's oratorical skills, but he had himself to blame for his answers concerning heaven and hell.

It is likely that Coppin posted bail for he does not mention incarceration. Six months later, however, he was in court again, this time appearing before Judge Nicholas where a new list of charges was submitted by Nevil and Collier arguing for the prosecution.(48–49) The three charges read in court alleged that Coppin had preached that Christ suffered and died for his own sins, that there was neither heaven nor hell but what was in man and that "everlasting life" ended with the grave.(49) Since the prosecution could produce no witnesses, they asked Judge Nicholas to transfer Coppin to authorities in Oxford for the next assize and Nicholas agreed.(49) Coppin paid bail and was released.

Requesting a change of venue was a very skillful maneuver. Had the prosecution used only the charges of denial of heaven and hell and produced no witnesses and no evidence, Coppin would have walked out of court a free man for witnesses could testify only that in private conversation Coppin denied an afterlife. By adding new charges and requesting a continuance to a different location where Coppin was well known and where he preached regularly, prosecutors had a better chance of sending Coppin to jail. Nicholas, for his part, evidently did not care one way or the other and was probably happy to be rid of the case.

At some point during the following six months Coppin learned to plan his answers with greater care. His earlier statements were largely responsible for his present situation and he faced a far greater possibility of prosecution in Oxford, where he was known, than in Emload, where he was not. Thus, one year after the initial opening of the case against himself, on March 10, 1652, Coppin appeared before Judge Green of the Oxford Assize. When asked how he testified regarding the existence of heaven and hell, Coppin stated, "There is a heaven and a hell acknowledged, though not such a one as some men would have but such a one as in man which is according to Scripture."(52) He also noted that this opinion had been offered in private conversation and not in a sermon.

Coppin's optimism about the trial increased when two prosecution witnesses impugned their own integrity in court. One witness, Minister Beckingham of Emston in Oxfordshire, admitted being jealous of Coppin's popularity as a preacher, "finding the people to be more taken with my doctrine (which was the doctrine of free grace) than with his (which was not.)"(53) The second prosecution witness also hurt his testimony against Coppin when he ended his statement about the content of a Coppin sermon and "confessed to some others and said it was the best sermon that ever he heard in his life until his master, the said minister of the parish, had tutored him and made him change his opinion."(53)

Other factors also seemed to strengthen Coppin's position. Large petitions from the populace of Oxford and Emston were submitted by the defense, attesting "they heard not anything delivered by him but what was truth according to the Scriptures and our experience in which we were satisfied and should be glad . . . to hear the like again."(55) One petition went further, noting about Coppin's character, "as to his life and conversation, it hath been civil, honest, and representative towards all men," adding, "to all which particulars we have here subscribed our names and shall be ready to take out oaths."(56)

Though the other issues were not covered by the Blasphemy Act and hence were less important, Coppin was careful not to antagonize the jury with any answer they might find offensive. When asked if Christ died for his own sins or for the sins of all mankind, Coppin replied that "Christ suffered for the sins of his own body, whose body we are . . ."(58) Coppin's answer implied that Christ died for the sins of mankind, the orthodox understanding of vicarious atonement, when in fact he believed the very contrary.

Once again Coppin informed the reader that he found the judge fair and the proceeding according to the law. He noted that after all testimony had been entered and instructions given the jury, Judge Green "after he had heard my answers and understanding it, knowing it also not to come within the compass of any late act of Parliament, and with all perceiving the malice of my enemies . . . acquitted them [i.e., the jury] with the truth of the business that so justice and equity might take place."(64) Judge Green warned the jury that whatever their opinions of the issues involved, "we are to take his [i.e., Coppin's] sense and meaning upon the words and not another's, the words being his own."(64) Green also explained to the jury "There is nothing mentioned in the Act against it [i.e., Coppin's views] therefore we are not to meddle with it and you are not to bring him in guilty for anything he is here indicted, it being not within the compass of the act."(64)

Despite Green's instructions, the jury found Coppin guilty. Regarding their finding they explained to the court that "they could do not less [because] they were so followed by the priests from place to place and importuned to it that they could be at no quiet for them unless they did it."(65) The jury also informed Green of the "accusors and others that followed them forth, contradicting the words of the judge, saying they were not to take notice of what the judge hath said, neither of my answer but the Bill [of Indictment.]"(65) Judge Green, understandably angered, "perceiving their ignorance, showed them how it came not within the compass of the act and therefore ought not to be found."(65)

Because of the irregularities expressed by the jury, Judge Green declared a mistrial and "perceiving the malice of the accusors and the ignorance of the jury . . . [but] willing to do justice, took my bail for my appearance at the next Assize."(66) A judge issuing a directed verdict today, as Green did, might take the case away from the jury and dismiss the charges against Coppin. In seventeenth-century England, however, juries possessed greater independence and could indeed defy the judge's directed verdict. Consequently, the best Green could do for the defendant was to vacate the jury's findings and order a new trial. Coppin evidently believed this was the proper course for he called this action by Green "willingness to do justice" and it would appear the prosecution also believed Coppin had won his day in court. Coppin described how "my accusors began to fall mad, crying out again for my imprisonment, banishment, or silencing."(66) The prosecution attempted to force Coppin to sign a list of orthodox beliefs but he declined and so matters stood for the next six months.

In a modern American court of law, the judge declares a mistrial when it is clear that the prosecution's evidence is weak and that public sympathy for the defendant is very great. Under these circumstances, the state will often drop its case rather than attempt additional prosecution, thereby exonerating the defendant. Essentially the same thing occurred six months later when Coppin appeared before Judge Hutton at the next Oxford Assize. The prosecution did not appear to press charges and Coppin was released. This was hardly the end of Coppin's legal difficulties, however.

In March of 1653, two years after appearing before Emload's JPs, a year after his trial in Judge Green's court and six months after his acquittal in Judge Hutton's court, Coppin once again found himself in court and charged with maintaining radical religious views. It seems that Coppin

RICHARD COPPIN

had been invited to preach before a local congregation in Stow in Gloucester on the afternoon of Sunday, March 19, of that year. Arriving in Stow earlier that day, Coppin found that a certain Mr. Elmes of Winchcombe was currently presenting a guest sermon. Mr. Elmes was an orthodox Calvinist and when, according to custom, opportunity presented itself at the end of the sermon, Coppin made objection to certain points raised by the speaker. (78–79) The ensuing exchange of views was civil and cordial, but two local JPs, John Crofts and Richard Ayelworth, were so upset by the content of Coppin's questions that constables were ordered to arrest Coppin and bring him to the home of a local minister for interrogation.

After he arrived at the minister's house, the doors were bolted shut and the JPs and minister posed a series of questions to Coppin regarding God's relationship to the devil, heaven and hell, universal salvation, predestination, and the trinity. Coppin insisted he was civil and polite and presented very conventional answers, especially where the stipulations of the Blasphemy Act were concerned.(80) His captors were not content, however, and told Coppin "that I had formerly spoke things that were blasphemy [and] unless I would come to church in the afternoon and hear their minister without objecting to anything against him, they would still keep me as a prisoner."(81) Realizing the illegal nature of his abduction, Coppin cited article 36 on page 43 of the government document, *Commonwealth's Government*, signed by Cromwell. According to that document, "none should be compelled by penalty or otherwise to the public profession held forth and that all laws contrary to Christian liberty were to be null and void."(82)

Coppin does not tell us how he obtained his release, but he did not attend the orthodox minister's lecture and conducted his own sermon according to the terms of his invitation. It is possible that Coppin's abduction had been a contrived attempt to frighten him from speaking, for after thirty minutes of preaching before a very large audience, all hell broke loose. Justices Crofts and Ayelworth plus the local minister rode mounted horses into the assembly of people listening to Coppin and the horses were attacked by several bull mastiffs owned by members of the audience with a general free-for-all resulting.(82–83) Eventually constables arrived with a warrant for Coppin's arrest.

Now if it is strange that mounted horsemen would attack an assembled crowd, it is also peculiar that members of that audience would have with them their bull mastiffs. Consequently, it is possible that far more was occurring than Coppin indicated in his treatise. The lecture may have been more of an organized confrontation than a simple Sunday afternoon sermon. It is possible that Coppin accepted the invitation to force a confrontation or that once he accepted the invitation to preach and his coming was publicized, local orthodox authorities hoped to intimidate him, first by abducting him and then by breaking up the assembly.

The next day Coppin appeared before the two JPs and some local ministers. When he demanded to know the charges against him, Crofts "answered that my accusors were not yet known, neither the accusations. Neither was I to know until I came to trial."(84) Further complicating what appeared a rather arbitrary use of the law, letters were sent to local ministers of surrounding counties, including Worcester and Oxford, inviting them to come to present evidence against Coppin.(84)

Coppin does not indicate how he spent the next four months but on July 22, 1654, he appeared before Judge Green once again. The following charges were made against Coppin by Crofts: that Coppin assembled profane people and disturbed the peace; that he disturbed their local ministers; that he asserted that believers need not pray for the pardon of sin and that there was neither heaven nor hell. Coppin was also charged with rejecting the authority of the local JPs and called upon the local populace to demand their liberties and "not to suffer the justices to entrench upon it." Also, Coppin was called a continual troublemaker.

Once the charges were read, "the court told them that they could proceed no further by these informations but if they had anything to accuse me withal, they were to proceed by way of indictment."(87) The JPs were unable to produce any witnesses, however, and "I was freed to the shame of my enemies."(88)

One issue of interest that arose in the course of this last trial concerned the introduction of Coppin's written works as evidence against the author. Before Coppin was released, Crofts requested of Judge Green a continuance of several days to examine Coppin's books. This was a fairly standard procedure especially when there was little evidence of other wrongdoing. Coppin noted that "they presented to the court several books with my name to them and the court demanded if I would own them. To which I answered that I had written such books with such titles but whether those particular books they produced were the same I wrote, I knew not unless I heard them all read."(86) Eventually authorship was established and the prosecution attempted to enter into evidence parts of these works expressing Coppin's blasphemy. Coppin noted how "out of which books my accusors had picked here and there some part of some particular sentences which they preferred to the judge to examine me upon."(88)

Had Coppin's works been entered into evidence and had Crofts actually prepared his case, Coppin would have been hard pressed, for his works did in fact affirm the prosecution's charges against him. The JPs, however, had not prepared their selections with care and "the judge, after he read it, told them that they had given him that which was nonsense in taking part of a sentence and not the whole for in so doing (saith he) you may wrong the sense of any man's words . . . but you are to take the words before and after them and then one might explain the other."(88)

Richard Coppin was very fortunate that in both series of trials the Assize court judges were reasonable men. Justice Green in particular seems to have believed Coppin was not the dangerous radical the JPs continually made him out to be. Neither judge believed a court of law was the best place to determine religious truth. Had the charges against Coppin included sedition, immoral behavior, or even serious religious irregularity, Green might have seen merit to applying the Blasphemy Act. Indeed, several years later Coppin again found himself in court facing charges of blasphemy. In a long series of trials he was found guilty and was sentenced to six month's incarceration. To a large extent the difference between the earlier trials conducted by Justice Green and those which led to Coppin's incarceration had less to do with the nature of the evidence against the defendant than the judge's attitude towards Coppin.

From Coppin's point of view, all these conflicts were not a question of legality or illegality but of religious truth. Coppin was convinced that his legal victories were positive proof that God loved him and hated orthodox ministers. In his introductory letter to the reader Coppin wrote, "So that the truth of those transactions that have passed between me and my adversaries may appear, it is published as a narrative of what the Lord in these dividing times hath done and will do for the increase of the manifestation of truth amongst men." Like Jesus and the apostles or Daniel in the lion's den, those preaching truth must suffer at the hands of the powerful, "and so in all ages since, whatever of God hath by God revealed to men contrary to the law of the times, hath been by that law unlawful to utter and so by men counted as blasphemy . . . was it not so with Christ and with Paul and the rest of the apostles? Hath it not been so since? Is it not so now?"(18) Perhaps God's truth was involved and perhaps God watches over his true saints. Whatever it was, Richard Coppin was a very lucky man, but not for long. Just two years later Coppin was lured into a public debate and said more than he should have. *A Blow at the Serpent* and *The Twenty Five Articles* speak of his own foolishness but also of the duplicity of those who opposed him.

The debates were held in Rochester Cathedral during the month of December 1655. At four different meetings, Coppin debated with the leading orthodox ministers of Kent including Walter Rosewell, William Sanbroke, and Daniel French. Others, too, as we shall see, entered the debate against Coppin. The large audience included townspeople, soldiers and officers as well as such notables as the mayor of Rochester and other city dignitaries and Major General Kelsey, the regional Marshal.

Though Coppin's account may have been self-serving, his presentation of orthodoxy was honest and congruent with the treatises of most orthodox Ranter antagonists. Coppin's claims that he bested his opponents ring true for several reasons. There is much internal evidence to demonstrate why Coppin did well, and no less an individual than Major General Kelsey, to his chagrin, wrote as much in his private correspondence. In general, Coppin gauged his arguments toward his audience of laymen and soldiers where Rosewell and other orthodox leaders spoke to the officers and city officials. One continually senses Rosewell's frustration in his inability to get a firm grip on Coppin who turned every issue under discussion to his own advantage. Preaching in forests, town squares, in barns and behind closed doors may not have earned Richard Coppin a very good living but he did learn how to hold his audience and force his opponent into making regrettable statements.

The first session was held on Monday, December 3 with Rosewell taking the initiative by stating that Coppin was "a blasphemer of Christ, a perverter of Scripture and a venter of damnable errors."(2) Two main subjects were discussed that evening. First, Rosewell maintained that Coppin taught that Jesus Christ was of an ordinary sinful nature and was, consequently, no better than other mortals and unable to guarantee salvation for others. The second issue was the doctrine of universal salvation.

Rosewell argued that Christ possessed more than a mere mortal nature and in atoning for others, took on himself not man's sins but their punishments. Coppin simply responded by citing Scripture. He noted Isaiah 53:12, "He was numbered with the transgressors" and *Isaiah* 53:5, "He bears our sin" as well as 2 *Corinthians* 5:21 to the same effect. Rather than accepting Rosewell's basic charge regarding his unorthodox Christological teachings, a premise that was true, Coppin's citation of Scripture left Rosewell in the difficult position of being able to respond only, "You pervert Scripture," which was not the issue at hand. In great frustration Rosewell cried out, "Mr. Mayor and the rest, you may see with what a brazen face this blasphemer stands to maintain his damnable errors."(5) It was probably not lost on the audience that Coppin's defense had been Isaiah.

The second point discussed was Coppin's alleged doctrine of universal salvation, or in Rosewell's words, the "belief that all men shall be saved."(7)

RICHARD COPPIN

Rosewell presented a good description of the why and wherefore of divine election and predestination but Coppin again frustrated Rosewell's intentions when he refused to attack anything asserted. Rather, Coppin simply noted that even if some were predestined to hell and others to heaven, God was able and could redeem souls from hell if he so chose. To substantiate his position, Coppin cited *Amos* 9:2, "Though they dig down into hell, thence shall my hand take them," and then concluded "The Lord will have men to come in his way and not their own, they shall come to heaven but through hell."(8) In speaking of hell Coppin may have been merely affirming Ranter truth which identified life in the flesh with hell, but Rosewell was placed in the unfortunate position of having to argue that God could not redeem souls from hell, and hence was not omnipotent, or that God could redeem souls from hell and thereby discredit his own views of divine election and predestination. Here as elsewhere, Coppin remained true to his beliefs while refusing to argue the charge made against him. And if Amos might have dissented from Coppin's use of his views, Rosewell was not in a position to counter Coppin unless he was willing to open the discussion into an entirely new area of Scripture study.

Subsequent discussion that evening makes clear that Coppin was both articulate and shrewd. Unwilling and unable to deny Rosewell's charges, Coppin instead argued on his own ground and forced Rosewell again and again to defend his own orthodox views in light of Coppin's unorthodox reading of Scripture.

The second session was held on Sunday, December 9. Mr. French, another local orthodox minister, took Rosewell's place as Coppin's chief opponent. Mr. French observed, "You obscure the Scripture and turn it which way you list, into an allegory, as a nose of wax."(21) Rather than ducking the issue of allegory, Coppin embraced it and again defeated his opponent. Agreeing that "the Scriptures are an allegory and a great mystery," Coppin went on to argue that "there is a spiritual meaning to be understood in it all along."(21) Coppin might have explained why a dualist would choose this method, but instead he cited Paul's letter to the *Galatians* 4:23−24, concerning Abraham's children by his two wives Sarah and Hagar. "Speaking of the son of the Bondwoman and the son of the Freewoman, which things sayeth Paul is an allegory for these are the two great covenants, the one from Mount Sinai which gendereth to bondage and under which all men are bondsmen. The other," Coppin continued, "is from Mount Zion or heavenly Jerusalem, which is above, is free . . . and this also is an allegory and a great mystery."(21)

Coppin's use of Paul might have annoyed the apostle but one could hardly argue that Paul was wrong in embracing allegory or that the method was incorrect. Coppin must have stunned his opposition, for Captain Harrison, commander of locally quartered troops jumped up and interjected, "You pervert the Scriptures and are a blasphemer, and I will prove it so . . . first, I'll dispute with you and do it by the law of God, and then I'll take another course."(21) The atmosphere of the session grew so tense because of this clear threat to Coppin that another officer, Lieutenant Scott, tried to make clear that "there is nobody here that intends any hurt against you, to entrap you."(22) Unable to restrain himself, however, Harrison felt obliged to offer, "We came here on purpose to hear you and now we have heard blasphemy enough and *that* you shall know 'ere long."(24) Reasonably, this ended the second session.

Why Coppin continued to debate is a mystery. It must have been clear to him that these debates were only a pretext to draw him out and use his statements against him in court. This may explain why Coppin chose his approach to these debates and said as little as possible regarding issues punishable by the Blasphemy Act. In any event, the third session was held on December 11.

Rosewell again led the attack in this debate and attempted to raise the issues discussed in the first session. Both Coppin and the audience grew restless to the point where the moderator, Captain Smith, said to Rosewell, "Sir, I conceive that Mr. Coppin has given you satisfaction to this proposition in the last dispute. Therefore, if you have anything else Mr. Rosewell, you may please go on."(25) Rosewell must have been flustered and was unable to make any additional coherent points and the audience, largely favoring Coppin, began to laugh at Rosewell. This mocking laughter became so disruptive that Captain Smith warned the audience, "If any do laugh, it will be taken notice of."(28) Coppin diffused the situation when he added, "Friends, seeing sometimes you can not choose but laugh, henceforth laugh inwards and make no noise."(28)

Resuming the debate, Rosewell introduced the cardinal Christian tenet of the resurrection of the body, which, he claimed correctly, Coppin denied. Refusing to argue on Rosewell's terms, Coppin asserted, "Friends and Brethren: I do own a resurrection according to the Scriptures and such a resurrection you must all partake of before you can see the Kingdom of God."(33) This was a true if not a complete statement of Coppin's belief. But before Rosewell could question him concerning conventional ideas about the resurrection and his own more spiritual version that applied only to the spirit, Coppin added that in "1 Corinthians 15, there is a resurrection spoken of [by] the apostle which is the resurrection of the first Adam to the state of the second Adam. But there were some then as well as now that think the apostle had meant carnally, the rising of the same body of flesh and bones. Now take notice that I do not deny anything to Christ all this while but do advance him and also our own resurrection in him, as the Scripture sayeth, 'We are raised up together with him, to sit in heavenly places in Jesus Christ' and this is the mystery of the resurrection."(33–34) Once again, Coppin's carefully worded answer proved difficult to refute and nowhere did he agree with Rosewell nor abjure his own beliefs. He indicated that some interpreted Paul along physical lines but that he preferred a more spiritual explanation while nowhere categorically denying the actual physical resurrection.

Coppin must have felt quite comfortable with his answer and the audience's reaction for he elucidated upon this more spiritual interpretation. "This resurrection is to be within you," Coppin continued, "and you are to know it while you live in this body for it is your own rising from faith to faith, from glory to glory . . . that is, changed from one state of the first Adam to the state of the second Adam and so he tells us 'It was sown in Adam, it was raised in Christ.' It was sown a natural body and it was raised a spiritual body . . . that as you have born the image of the earthly so you shall bear the image of the heavenly, for there is a body natural and a body spiritual."(34–35) This wording was meaningful from a Ranter perspective yet also possessed orthodox meaning too. Hence, Coppin concluded, "Now take notice that I do not deny any resurrection at all, this which by any man may be proved, but I do declare to you the mystery of the spiritual resurrection."(35)

Rosewell was not deceived by Coppin's words, for he indicated, "Of all religions this is the most damnable, to say there is no resurrection of the body."(39) If that was not the logical conclusion of Coppin's words, certainly it was true of Coppin's belief. For his part, Coppin cautioned Rosewell, "I do not deny anything which any man can prove to be true from Scriptures."(39)

It must have been obvious to Rosewell that Coppin would say nothing to incriminate himself, and so he chose a different tactic to draw Coppin out and this too backfired. Taking up Coppin's challenge to prove a physical resurrection from Scripture, Rosewell asserted, "I prove a physical resurrection of our bodies from the example of Christ's resurrection of the body."(39) Thereafter the debate revolved about *Rosewell's* attempt to justify what *he* believed, with Coppin sniping at every one of Rosewell's scriptural allusions. The issue was thrown into confusion and Rosewell was discredited.

Coppin's care in answering Rosewell was not misplaced. Whatever fears he might have entertained in accepting the offer to debate, surely Harrison's threats of subsequent legal difficulty and more must have been disquieting. Hence, from Coppin's perspective, it was necessary to defeat Rosewell but without employing any language that might prove damaging in court. For his part, Rosewell might have chosen better issues to discuss in continuing their debate. When Rosewell raised the issue of the trinity, which was not covered by the Blasphemy Act, Coppin was careful to word his response so that civil authorities would not be antagonized. Complicating matters was the simple fact that Coppin rejected the trinity, as he must if he taught a truly mortal Jesus. Additionally, Coppin's soteriology rejected vicarious atonement.

Carefully wording his response, Coppin started by using a familiar debating mechanism. "I do not deny the three persons according to the Scriptures," Coppin stated, perhaps out of an awareness that Scripture nowhere mentioned the concept or term trinity. "First, there is a God, the Father, that did create all things and in whom all things live, and yet unknown to man. And that man might know him, that is true, he did appear as a son amongst men to manifest himself to men and so he is said to be Immanuel, God within us, which is also Christ within us . . . third, there is a Holy Spirit and this is the complete manifestation of the fullness of all things brought home to man's understanding wherein God, Christ, and man appear, all but one, in one God."(41)

Coppin's answer, which did not mention what kind of son Christ was and that the trinity was not a device used by God merely for human knowledge of his divine nature, elicited from Rosewell, "You have confounded the three persons."(42) In turn, Coppin retorted, "No, I have unified them together in their proper places."(42) When Rosewell attempted to pick at Coppin's statement, Captain Smith, perhaps expressing audience sentiment, exclaimed, "Mr. Rosewell, it is the plain Scripture. I conceive Mr. Coppin hath given the people satisfaction in those things."(42)

The last topic discussed that evening, universal salvation, once again demonstrated how Coppin had developed audience rapport. In the first debate Coppin had been able to control discussion of this subject by citing scriptural statements which forced Rosewell to concede that God could take all souls out of hell if he so chose and was not subject to human concepts of predestination. In this session, Coppin went on the offensive and challenged Rosewell, "Whereas you say this doctrine of salvation to all men gives men liberty to sin," Coppin asserted, "I say you, no . . . to the contrary of what you say, I declare that by your preaching of wrath, hell and damnation of poor souls that are weak in the faith, it doth cast them down from the knowledge of the love of God through which they should see themselves saved."(51) When Rosewell cited *Matthew* 22.14, 'Many are called but few are chosen' a member of the audience shouted out "We are well satisfied, may God keep us from this damnable doctrine."(51) The debate ended and Walter Rosewell must have felt distressed.

The last session of the debate was held the evening of December 13 with Mr. William Sanbroke taking the lead against Coppin. Few new issues were raised with discussion devoted to previous statements about universal salvation, damnation and Christ's nature. One new point was Coppin's rejection of conventional baptism, arguing, "That which I declare concerning baptism is that they have no ground for the Lord Jesus Christ by precept of example, to baptize with water."(76) When allegorical method was condemned, Coppin responded with a long statement demonstrating the richness of this method. Taking the phrase "Jacob have I loved and Esau have I hated," a standard Ranter touch-phrase which Rosewell and Sanbroke had cited in support of predestination, Coppin argued, "Though they tumbled both in one belly, *Jacob* is good, even the spirit; *Esau* is the evil, even the flesh, and everyone hath this Jacob and Esau within them for a time. But *Esau* which is the flesh, shall be burned by *Jacob* which is the spirit. The flesh shall be destroyed but the spirit saved and so saith the Lord, 'The house of Jacob shall be a fire and the house of Esau shall be stubble and they shall kindle in them and devour them and there shall be nothing left of the house of Esau (*Isaiah* 4.4.).' "(77) Once again, the orthodox ministers were at a loss for they could not explain why their specific interpretation of these words was more accurate than Coppin's since the text itself spoke neither of predestination nor of the dualism of spirit and matter.

Coppin's account of these debates would have the reader understand that he vanquished his many opponents and won the hearts of the audience. In fact, the most immediate response to these debates came on December 24 when Major General Kelsey and the three Justices of the Peace, John Parker, Charles Bowles, and Richard Watson, together with Captain Harrison and several local ministers, met at the Crown Inn in Rochester to take witnesses' depositions to charge Richard Coppin with preaching blasphemy. Their motivation may be apparent from Major General Kelsey's letter to Cromwell in which he attempted to explain why, after the debates, he forbade Coppin from preaching and finally arrested him. In this letter Kelsey expressed shock and horror when he discovered how popular Coppin had become with townspeople and soldiers. "I am afraid that they [Kelsey's own soldiers] may have drunk in so much of these tenets that I fear they may do hurt by laying there [in Rochester] because the townsmen, being tainted, will be ready to strengthen them in their opinions."[24]

Coppin was arrested and charged with blasphemy on December 24. The twenty-five charges made against him by the ministers of Kent are contained in the short treatise by that name appended to *Michael Opposing the Dragon*. In themselves neither the charges nor Coppin's responses break new ground. Indeed, the wording of both sides was often a paraphrase of the earlier public discussions. Considering Harrison's threats, one must wonder why such issues as Coppin's rejection of heaven and hell were not raised in debate or in the charges. If Coppin's trial was not the result of a conspiracy, it may have been the result of Rosewell's having lost the debate, and presumably, having lost face in the community as well.

Coppin could not be found guilty of blasphemy since none of the twenty-five charges were covered under the terms of the Blasphemy Act. In the meantime, however, he sat in jail for six months waiting for the next assize and his eventual release. *Crux Christi* and *Michael Opposing the Dragon*, both of which emphasized suffering and the need to withdraw from the world, were written while Coppin sat in jail.

Richard Coppin was not necessarily a typical Ranter. He was far more prolific, intelligent and systematic than most Ranter authors. Moreover, that his moral and personal life were beyond reproach was hardly true of others. His views, however, were standard Ranter fare. Dualism, allegory, the denial of sin and rejection of the physical resurrection, heaven and hell, and all ritual, were commonly held Ranter views. These were often combined with yet other ideas to create various composites of Ranter thought. Other Ranters, especially those who were insane, were also far more entertaining than Richard Coppin who was sincere, but terribly sour and dour. However much other Ranters differed from Coppin in moral, psychological or intellectual senses, we will find similar views and methods of argument because no one more than Richard Coppin laid the intellectual foundation from which all other Ranter tendencies might draw.

3.   Jacob Bauthumley

Jacob Bauthumley was born in Leicester in 1613 and served as an apprentice to his father William Bauthumley, a shoemaker.[25] The Bauthumley household was decidedly radical and in 1619, William Bauthumley was excommunicated by the Church of England as was Jacob in 1634. Both had been found guilty of preaching unacceptable doctrine to groups of parishioners meeting in the Bauthumley home.

The civil war found Jacob Bauthumley a strong supporter of Parliament against the monarchy. He continued to serve in the army after the war and in 1650 we find him serving as quartermaster of Colonel Cox's regiment. In November 1650, Bauthumley published the small treatise *The Light and Dark Sides of God*, and as a result, on March 11 of that year was cashiered from the army.[26] One pamphleteer noted that "he was bored through the tongue and had his book burned, his sword broken over his coxcomb and so his arrears were paid him."[27]

While in jail in 1655, Fox met Bauthumley and reported the latter among the Ranters who sang, whistled and danced, and otherwise upset him.[28] By 1660 Bauthumley appears to have returned to Leicester where he was employed as a librarian. Other than the few personal glimpses of his religious experiences he volunteered in his treatise, nothing else is known about Jacob Bauthumley.

However much Bauthumley shared with Coppin as a philosophical Ranter, there were important differences between them. Coppin sought to create an entire dualistic intellectual framework within the contours of traditional Christianity and hence engaged in constant struggle with the conceptual baggage he acquired during his travels to Ranter truth. Bauthumley's vision and confidence in his mystical message is never in doubt and his writing is typical of those who write from an altered state of awareness while they gaze upon the magnificence and brilliance of the ineffable God. Coppin's dualism was a continually developing organism, constantly discovering new conceptual avenues of expression and new areas of conflict with historical Christianity. Bauthumley's single little treatise is a self-contained quietist expression leaving little else to add. Coppin's writings circle and circle a dualistic center with each treatise adding some new component with which to fight conventional Christianity, but Bauthumley wrote from inside the truth he attempted to impart to others. In a word,

BLASPHEMY, IMMORALITY, AND ANARCHY

Coppin was an intellectual and preacher hoping to explain his dualism to others, and Bauthumley was a mystic expressing the certainty and confidence of one who has little need for others.

The title of his treatise indicates the dualistic nature of Bauthumley's thought and the work itself provides a fine example of the manner in which Ranters combined ideas from dualist, Free Spirit, and medieval mystical sources. The light and dark sides of God are the spiritual and carnal appreciations of the universe. The light side includes God, his angels and the human soul. The dark side consists of the world of matter, the devil, and man's corporeal body. Man shares qualities of both realms and is thus caught between them. The purpose of this treatise was to enable man to move from the dark side to the light side of God.

Using words reminiscent of late medieval mystics, the very opening verse of the treatise posed the central problem facing material man in his search for the ethereal God. "Oh God, what shall I say thou art when thou canst be named? What shall I speak of thee when in speaking of thee I speak nothing but contradictions?"(1) Even terms specifically applying to God are useless, for "I say thou art infinite but what that is I can not tell because I am finite."(3) The *docta ignorantia*, too, proves insufficient for "I can say of thee thou art only, and there is none besides thee, but what thou art I can not tell."(3)

Opposed to God was the material world of the devil. The devil too was difficult to define, but Bauthumley was more successful here. "The Devil," we are told, "is darkness and in him there is no light at all . . . the Devil is falsehood, his ways lead to darkness and end in death and destruction."(29) Unlike God, the devil is less of a cosmic force in a Manichaean sense than the spirit of actual mundane matter itself. Consequently, "men fear a devil without them and so fancy him to be terrible in their apprehensions, never considering that he is in them."(29) Despite the divine soul within man, the human body was unalterably corrupt. The resurrection of the body was absurd, for human bodies, like those of cows or flowers, are matter pure and simple. "The flesh of man and of all other creatures," Bauthumley explained, "differs not in anything in the nature of them, indeed, . . . none of them are capable of any more glory than one another, all being of the same mold and coming to the same end . . . returning to the dust from whence it came."(57)

From an objective material understanding of mankind, God and man must be alienated from each other. Bauthumley wrote that "it is apparent that God speaks spiritually . . . and man can not hear God speak."(83) This condition did not result from any physical deficiency within man, and

Bauthumley pointed out that "we are as perfect as we shall ever be."(21) Yet, the soul is not alienated from God. Bauthumley could therefore conclude that "the soul, being of him, it must needs be pure and holy, not admitting any mixture of the flesh . . ."(59) Bauthumley labored to explain how the soul, somehow within the flesh was still not of the flesh. "Though it was fused into the body, yet I am sure it was not of the body nor could the flesh be capable of such a thing as we call union with the spirit, so the soul is in the body but really distinct and so it is in flesh but not flesh, and so it is God manifest in flesh."(50)

Because the soul is God, *it* understands God, but man understands neither God nor his own soul and is hardly aware of the existence of either. Consequently, man truly reflects the dualism characteristic of all existence. Finite man cannot understand infinite God and finite man cannot appreciate his infinite soul. As a result, "If I say I see thee, it is nothing but the seeing of thyself for there is nothing in me capable of seeing thee but thyself. If I say I know thee, that is no other thing but the knowledge of thyself for I am rather known to thee than know thee."(2) Bauthumley explains the same is true of other terms of familiarity such as loving God, seeking God, or praising God for in all cases there is nothing about man capable of such comprehension. The soul may understand God, but the soul is alienated from man much as God is alienated from matter.

The soul is purely rented equipment for which man has neither self-apparent need, nor an instruction manual. "Thou dost not speak to man," Bauthumley explained, "because there is nothing in man capable of thy speaking or hearing but thyself."(3) Hence, alleged divine-human communication is a charade, a game in which both participants sit in different rooms, facing different directions and attempt to speak with each other in mutually incomprehensible languages. From the human perspective, one cannot truly be sure there is anyone in the next room.

Bauthumley did not elaborate upon the nature of creation nor explain how these two levels of existence came into being. Neither did he present any of the standard dualistic concepts concerning the rebellion of Satan and his subsequent control of the universe. In one location he does note "before he [God] lived in himself, so there could be no sin, there being nothing but God."(59) Elsewhere he wrote, "When I read of Michael and his angels and the Dragon and his angels fighting against one another, I see nothing there but the fleshly and dark apprehensions of God against the pure and spiritual, and as Michael overcame the Devil, so too the more spiritual and pure dispensation of God shall overcome the dark and carnal."(27) It would appear that Bauthumley's dualism was not cosmic or mythic but the distinction between God's purity, which cannot transcend material reality, and the material reality of the world which cannot reflect, express or even conceive God's ethereal spirituality.

Despite the soul, humanity is limited by a finite nature and therefore must sin. On a theoretical level, "sin is properly the dark side of God which is a mere privation of light"(33) or, "sin is a coming short or a deprivation of the glory of God."(32) In other places the identification of sin and matter is more explicit. "Inasmuch as this flesh is a veil or covering wherein the soul or divine nature (call it what you will) the glory and beauty, the purity and excellence, there is being darkened and obscured; there is the sin."(51) And elsewhere Bauthumley again explained that if matter is not itself sinful, sin can exist only because of sin. Sin, like matter, is a "veil or covering over the face and glory of God that hinders the showing of it in the spirit. For the sun doth shine as clearly when the clouds interpose betwixt us as it does when it is a clear day, only it doth not appear to us."(34) Simply stated, the world is material, flesh is sin, man is flesh, and God is none of these. Under these circumstances, self-serving behavior and the inability to sustain faith in anything beyond itself are easily understood human qualities.

Bauthumley's appraisal of human alienation from God and proclivity to sin should have proved very distressing but just the opposite seems true. It was true that most human beings sinned while a few maintained a moral existence, and that "some live in the light side of God and some in the dark side, but in respect of God, light and darkness are all one to him for there is nothing contrary to God but only our apprehension."(10) Indeed, "God is no more provoked by sin to wrath than he is allured to blessing by any holiness of a people or person."(33) Even more extreme yet, "sin itself doth as well fall in compliance with the glory of God as well as that which we call grace and goodness."(33) Sin may result from human alienation from God, but God was not concerned with what deeds might be anticipated from life in matter.

The extent of Bauthumley's amoralism and indifference to conventional morality must have shocked his contemporaries. He wrote, "Neither the evil act nor the good act are [sic] evil or good as they are mere acts and men can do no more evil than they can do good."(37) Consequently, "Men may drink, swear, and be profane and live as they list," Bauthumley explained; "the sin lies not in these outward acts for a man can do the selfsame acts and yet not sin." (37) Bauthumley wrote that he did "not mean to countenance any unseemly act or evil in anyone" but on the same page he also noted that "they did not more that crucified him than they that embraced him."(39)

Man acts as he does because he is clump of clay and clay is not subject to

moral or religious standards. God is neither pleased not displeased by human actions for both good and evil are functions of God's removal from
matter and the material construction of the universe. Bauthumley's logical
conclusion was that "people are as near and ready to be helped and saved of
God when they sin as when they do good . ."(34) Indeed, it is only luck
"that one man acts not as vilely as another."(38)

Had Bauthumley's treatise continued no further, he would have constructed a firm conceptual foundation for justifying libertinism. In fact,
Bauthumley did believe that true evil existed and that man must attempt to
liberate himself from this force, but that its expression was not reflected in
the petty little sins people commit and then hide from their neighbors.
True evil consisted of a specific self-centered attitude which glorified man's
central importance in the universe. From the very beginning in the Garden
of Eden, man was unable and unwilling to perceive or appreciate the soul
within himself and consequently believed himself to be the center of the
universe and the standard of total truth. Thus, from the very beginning
human beings disregarded divine attempts to communicate or twisted such
messages to justify human glorification. Adam's sin, for instance, was his
choice to "live in himself . . . to procure a self happiness . . . which was
his own holiness, righteousness."(42)

The self-centered materialistic approach to life did not yield sweet fruit.
Frustration, confusion, and continued human alienation from God characterized human religion with the result that "all is cursed to him and so
man is in hell," Bauthumley wrote, "so that our ceasing to live in God and
living in the self, the being is in hell."(42–43) All ancient religions relied
upon magical formulas expressed in ornate rituals practiced by a class of
priests using human fear to maintain themselves as a powerful financial
elite. Of all the ancient religions, none was more corrupt than Christianity.

Christianity: Religion of the Dark Side of God

With great regret did Bauthumley note that the fundamental basis of
Christianity was the concept of reward and punishment, the same concept
used to train a dog. "They imagine God is angry and he is pleased, he
threatens and he promises and he punishes."(10) As a result, the Christian
concept of heaven, among many others, was perverted. God is envisioned to
be a powerful nobleman; "They fancy a high place for him above the stars, I
know not where" when in reality, "God is the high and lofty one that in-
habits eternity and not any circumscribed place."(18) Even worse, some
have attempted to locate and describe heaven and hell on a map of the earth.

"How many have puzzled and beat their brains out, as if it were a local place," lamented Bauthumley, "and therefore some, because they would make it [i.e., hell] contrary to heaven, and as they fancy that the highest place so they will be sure to make hell the lowest [place] and therefore being as carnal in one as in the other, make it to be the lowest part of the earth."(44)

The attempt to fix the locations of heaven and hell was only a trace less absurd to Bauthumley than the human attempt to outline the contours of God himself. The doctrine of the trinity demonstrated ignorance and arrogance for "there is nothing in Scripture or reason to countenance such a gross and carnal conceit of God."(11) Trinitarianism was another form of human idolatry for its adherents "fancy some corporeal shape in him, though they call it spiritual."(6) The same carnal conceit which would have a human Jesus understood as a divine being also presents other absurdities.

Surpassing foolish Christian concepts of heaven and hell and the trinity were that religion's concepts of angels, and Bauthumley noted, "I see the world as much mistaken in them as in the former."(24) People believed angels "are created spiritual substances distinct from God and waiting upon God as serving men about their lord to see what his pleasure is."(25) Placing angels in a menial position was a carnal appreciation of God's desires, as if he wanted or needed servants, but a very self-serving one as well. Christians hoped such angels would serve them at their own physical resurrection, when "they dream of a heaven wherein they shall sit at the right hand of God, another at the left, and hope to have much outward felicity and glory when they have their glorified bodies, as they imagine."(21–22) Once again the truth was contrary to carnal expectations: "for however much men speak that the corporeal body shall be made spiritual, to me it is ridiculous because the Scripture saith that which is born of the flesh is flesh and can remain in no other capacity."(57) But then, what else should a clump of clay desire?

The carnal understanding of God as a nobleman served by ministering angels demanded a religion of rites, rituals, and ordinances. Such practices have little meaning in themselves for Bauthumley other than inducing a sharp sense of guilt in the believer should a small detail go unobserved. Arguing much like Paul and Luther, Bauthumley wished to eliminate all such "historical" rituals the only purpose of which was intimidation. "He that is under the law or in any formal way or outward duty, and is so possessed with a spirit of bondage that he must do so and so or else he must be damned, and if in the doing of such and such he shall be saved, this man is in hell and hell in him and needs no other devil to torment him but his own self and carnal apprehensions of God."(44)

Christianity taught foolishness and proceeded to justify these views through a carnal understanding of Scripture to match its other carnal views. Like other Ranters, Bauthumley maintained that God did not write Scripture but that it was written by men, for men, in "the outward speaking and hearing of men"(73) and consequently, "it reaches no further but to an historical and fleshly knowledge of God."(81) Despite the fact that the Bible "is clothed in fleshly terms and expressions and speaks in the languages of men"(74) orthodox Christianity venerates the text as if it were divine. Scholars make a fetish of words and terms and "having attained a little skill in several languages of several countries and received ordination (as they call it) they think themselves so invested with powers above their brethren."(79) Having learned languages and terms and words, scholars "will believe nothing but what they think Scripture speaks in the letter, though indeed they err, not knowing it or the power of God."(59)

Bauthumley did not believe the Bible was the best source for religious inspiration and people "need not run so often to a great Bible to relieve themselves in straights and doubts as men generally do, never reflecting upon their spirits to see what God speaks there."(75) For his own part, "I must not build my faith upon it or any saying of it"(72) and "I do not care whether ever I look upon one again or no."(75) Yet Bauthumley also understood that many received solace from Scripture and could write "I do not speak to condemn the practice, neither is the fault in the Bible but in men's carnal conceits of it, and seeing men make an idol of it."(75) Perhaps out of compassion for the weak in the spirit, Bauthumley could add, "I am willing to give way to their weakness because I have been childish myself."(58)

In fact, Bauthumley's attitude toward Scripture, like that of other Ranters, tended toward opportunism. Where Scripture supported his views, he cited liberally from those places while criticizing other locations as carnal conceit. In other places Bauthumley "retrieved" the spiritual intention of the Bible by allegorizing the text as we have already observed concerning his interpretation of the battle of Michael and the Dragon. Organized religion, literal Scripture, the religion of times and rituals—these were the hallmarks of a perverted Christianity expressing the dark side of God.

Christianity: *The Path to the Light Side of God.*

The most direct path to God was through the soul for "God speaks spiritually in man, not in any audible voice or form of words."(80) In itself, the soul was dormant and unknown to man until God spoke to the soul and brought it to life. Bauthumley explained that before the soul's awakening by God, the believer "is reserved in chains of darkness till the judgment of the great day of God's appearing in the spirit, till then he is in hell, until God judge and burn up that flesh and carnal knowing of him and reduce him to his first being."(43)

Bauthumley referred to the divine message to the soul as an angel, noting, "I look upon every glorious manifestation of the power and wisdom of God to be an angel"(25) and cited the example of Lot in Sodom. "Lot received two angels which is spiritually true for there was something more than ordinary of God's mind discovered to him."(26) When they come, these messages are simple, direct, and very compelling. Bauthumley shared his own experience with the reader about his reception of God's angel. "And this is what I found till God appeared spiritually and showed me that he was all glory and happiness himself and that flesh was nothing and should enjoy nothing and then I could not but cease from my former fleshly actings which caused nothing but fear and trouble. [I] saw God or rather, God made out himself in me, joy, peace, and brought me into the glorious liberty of the sons of God."(47)

The process leading from the dark side to the light side of God does not involve great activity, learning, specific rituals or benedictions, or the proper social connections. It involves nothing more than responding to God's angel and therefore becoming emotionally and psychologically closed to the demands of the body and the world and thereby permitting the enlivened soul control of the personality. Bauthumley described the effect of an angel upon the soul in the following manner: "When there is nothing of the self being appearing, in a word, when to the world he appears to act nothing, do nothing in an outward and formal way, so that men think there is no spiritual life in him"(63) and "when he wholly resigns up all his grace, abilities, knowledge of God unto God, and knows not what he doth or is or should know, ceasing from his own reaching forth unto God, living and being to any self enjoyment or expectation of any future felicity, life, or comfort out of God."(64)

The self-contained spiritual state described by Bauthumley is essentially similar to zen or nirvana and represents the traditional Christian mystic's quietist union with God. In words reminiscent of so many authors Bauthumley wrote, "I can willingly resolve all my comforts, joy, and peace unto God who is the infinite ocean, and rather desire to be comprehended of it than comprehend it."(71) The opening verse of Bauthumley's treatise asked who God was. It is clear that he never discovered the answer and ceased to care or believe the question had merit.

Mankind was weak and unimaginative and consequently God provided humanity with a role model whose very life was a guide to the transition from fleshliness and carnality to spirituality. Like other Ranters, Bauthumley believed Jesus was fully mortal, writing, "The Son of Man, being of the first Adam after the flesh, must as well be subdued and perish with the fleshly forms and administrations that did accompany him."(61) Elsewhere on the same page Bauthumley wrote, "It is not the earthly man that is raised but the spiritual and so Christ after the flesh was but an earthly man and so must be destroyed and subdued."(61) In Christ's case, as in the case of every other human being, "there is no spiritual exaltation of God but when the creature ceases from being."(41)

Most Ranters taught that a final resting within God could come only with death but that even in this life some measure of unity with God was possible. In this vein Bauthumley wrote, " 'The Kingdom of God is within you,' and I see heaven to be there where God displays his own glory and excellence. For heaven is nothing but God at large or God making out himself in spirit and glory."(14) The status of sainthood carried with it some measure of God's presence within the live being, and Bauthumley wrote, "I am fully satisfied in my own spirit with those words of Christ where he saith, 'I am the resurrection and the life' and see it fully made out in me."(55)

Such phrases as "the kingdom of heaven is within you" or "I am the resurrection and the life" were used by all Ranters to apply to the state of the soul within this life once the individual attained sainthood. Eventually, however, as in Jesus' case, the human being must give up the outer being for "till the fleshly and outer form or formal being suffers, the divine can not reign and therefore in the midst of death there is life and God doth but die in weakness and rise in power."(66) Far from a cause for sorrow, "There is sweet truth in the Scripture where is said that the day of man's death is better than the day that a man is born."(64) For the saintly, death was a vindication of their earthly search for God. For the wicked, death brought a first realization of who God was and how fortunate that the earthly life of error was ended. Bauthumley, however, refused to accept any concept of an afterlife or the physical resurrection of the body after death. The body was corrupt and hence, "As the man dieth, so dieth the beast. As dieth the wise man, so dieth the fool; one end to them all."(57)

Rejection of the physical resurrection of the body, like the rejection of heaven and hell, was a controversial position. The Blasphemy Act demanded adherence to such orthodox ideas which represented the hopes of great numbers of Christians for a better life than the one they presently enjoyed. Perhaps because he was aware of treading controversial soil, Bauthumley attempted to present his views in the best orthodox guise possible. In the opening epistle to the reader, Bauthumley noted that "we neither deny there is a God, heaven, hell, resurrection or Scripture, as the world is made to believe we do."(A3b) Yet, we have already observed that Bauthumley in fact did reject most of the views he claimed to accept. He might say "Concerning a hell hereafter, what it should be or what should be tormented in it, I do not as yet apprehend"(52) which might indicate neutrality on the issue. And yet just a few pages away he might argue against a true hell by writing "If there be any that think it is not hell enough to be inwardly and spiritually tormented, let them but consult with those that have been under spiritual dissertions, as are called, and have cried out as if their bones had been broken and would have chosen death rather than life and thought they could have endured many burnings to have been rid of such a condition. And I think they will tell them there is no other, or need be, no other hell."(48)

Bauthumley's concept of heaven was also unorthodox. He wrote, "It is plain to me that the spiritual presence of Christ or God in the spirit is the Kingdom of Heaven."(20) In another location he noted that "Scripture speaks of no other heaven but what is spiritual and not consisting of any corporeal or bodily felicity, as men conceive."(17)

The illumination experienced by the resurrected soul leaves the Christian in a unique position. Conceivably, most orthodox Christians would maintain that once the soul was in heaven, religious rituals would be unnecessary. Bauthumley also maintained that the soul in heaven had no need for any religious practices. We repeatedly read that those who live in the heaven within themselves "should enjoy such a life as that they should not worship in any outward external way or form and should not need to be taught by any man or means of any outward administrations or ordinances."(22) Similarly, civil and moral law had no meaning for the resurrected. For those living in God, "there need be no laws of men to compel or restrain them."(76) At the very least, one could certainly sing, whistle, and dance.

While his prose is often abstract and the mystical message he taught not easily comprehended by the ordinary layman, it is not hard to understand why Bauthumley's religion would prove attractive to those reading his treatise. Indeed, Bauthumley may have spoken more directly to his times than is at first apparent. Considering the religious unrest in England, the lack of certainty many experienced regarding the rituals of the Church of England and the anger felt by many toward compulsory tithes, Bauthumley's account of his personal life as an orthodox Christian may have sounded familiar. "The truth is . . . so long as I was in bondage to days, times, and set times, that I must pray so often and do so much, frequent such ordinances, so long was I in trouble and sorrow . . . and so I was continually suffering the torment of hell, and tossed up and down, being condemned of myself."(46) Bauthumley could also speak to those who journeyed from church to church in search of teachings and practices that would bear scrutiny. "I can not but take notice," he wrote, "of the babel and confusion that men are in and yet think themselves the only ambassadors of peace as if all knowledge and spiritual learning were confined to them."(58)

Whether the individual consciously desired to be the sole judge of religious truth or even believed himself able to determine which of England's competing religions was true, no one more than Bauthumley could speak to their needs. Like them he understood that despite their best efforts at religious goodness, some group or another would condemn them and their efforts as satanic and evil. Hence, Bauthumley could write, "I do not do anything or abstain from anything because the outward letter commands it or forbids it but by reason of that commanding power which is God in me . . . and it is that by which I live and by which I act."(76) And those who were timid might have been reassured by Bauthumley's reminder that "the soul or substance which is God, lives to all eternity."(9)

Bauthumley neither chastised his reader for being weak and referring to Scripture nor demanded anything of him. He offered no tortured interpretations of Scripture which only the very clever or well educated might understand and did not parade any special credentials indicating his monopoly of religious wisdom. "I shall receive sweet content in my own spirit," he wrote, "however my person and parts be mean to the world's eye and so may cast an odium upon the things that I hold forth."(A2b) One did not have to be influenced by his views to admire the self-confidence of Bauthumley's religious peace. He could write, "I reflect upon my own spirit and trace the goings of God there and then I can find God rising from one degree of glory to another . . . and so I see how he hath led me from one dispensation to another and from one ordinance to another till at last he appears so spiritually that he overpowers all flesh and forms which I admired in my carnal condition."(55) Indeed, few sincere followers of any church could testify that "it is one thing to believe the Scripture because such and such write it, as most men do, and it is another to believe it because God said so *in me.*"(73)

Bauthumley's appeal, like that of Luther before him, was in freeing the individual from the tyranny of a religiosity imposed by others. Much as Paul liberated the spirit from ordinances of the Pharisees and Luther freed Christian belief from the strictures of a human Catholic priestly class, Bauthumley appealed to the individual's inner sense of religiosity to oppose the structured religious life developed by the Episcopal church hierarchy. Surpassing both Paul and Luther, however, Bauthumley noted, "I do not go to the letter of Scripture to know the mind of God, but having the mind of God within, I am able to [see] it witnessed and made out in the letter."(72)

Bauthumley's views paralleled those advanced several centuries earlier by the Brethren of the Free Spirit. He, too, wrote of the same in-life deification for which they were known and expressed the same ideas of heaven and hell as internal psychological states of mind. Like them, Bauthumley rejected Christ's vicarious atonement for mankind and instead presented Christ as a human role model for man to emulate. Also like the Brethren, Bauthumley allegorized Scripture or dispensed with it entirely much as he dispensed with conventional morality. Some Free Spirits were libertine and Bauthumley's views would indicate that he had no argument with those wishing to pursue such a life.

Bauthumley's views also remind us of Coppin's nearly identical positions on the same issues. Indeed, other than tone, the emphasis on suffering and strong asceticism of Coppin, and the obviously more powerful individualism of Bauthumley, both philosophical Ranters seem variations on the same theme. Yet, some historians have pointed to what they believe was Bauthumley's "pantheism" which must certainly distinguish his teachings from those of Coppin. If indeed Bauthumley was a pantheist, he would have been quite a queer duck. Surely it must be obvious to the reader that Bauthumley did not identify God with matter, as a pantheist must, but divorced the two entirely, as a dualist must. The citation often used to support the notion that Bauthumley was a pantheist appears early in the treatise where the author wrote, "I see that God is in all creatures, man and beast, fish and fowl, and every green thing from the highest cedar to the ivy on the wall."(4) Yet on the very same page Bauthumley explains that God is not the substance of these things but "the life and being of them all" which is a neoplatonic code phrase for God's being the source of all ideal forms but certainly not the substance of things. On the contrary, we have observed over and over and over again how Bauthumley disparaged the flesh, considered it sinful and at best transitory. Moreover, to identify an author as a pantheist because he presents God as "the spirit of life" is to determine that all religions and all religious thinkers, with the sole exception of dualists, are pantheists. Even more, that identification determines that Scripture itself is pantheistic for it too tells how God created man in his own image and proceeded to breathe the spirit of life into Adam's nostrils.

More than Coppin but much like other Ranters, Bauthumley was a strong individualist who neither cared for what most people thought nor cared that other people existed. In the epistle to the reader he warned, "I know the most unto whose hands it [i.e., the treatise] may come can not read it . . . and I shall wish no man to embrace it or condemn me, so I shall neither thank them that do the one or condemn them that do the other." (A2–A3) Perhaps this explains why Jacob Bauthumley never wrote another treatise.

4. J. F.

Though J.F.'s treatise, *John The Divine's Divinity*, was published in 1649, it was written before then. Abiezer Coppe's introduction was dated January 1649; hence, the original manuscript which caught Coppe's eye was of an earlier date but is no longer in existence. It is not surprising that Coppe would have been intrigued by this little work, for in a vague sense its ideas and expression were similar to his own and yet also different in being more philosophical than libertine. Coppe, the eloquent spokesman for the Sexual Libertine wing wrote, "something hereof sparkles through these papers and I only let thee *know* there's *some sweetness* in them, and that I durst not turn my back upon them." Regarding the identity of the author of the book he conceded, "I know not whose they are or who writ them." Hence, J. F. must rank as an early exponent of Rantism, though the work is conceptually undeveloped compared with early works by Coppin, Salmon and Clarkson.

The author called God "pure," "immutable," "original, i.e.—all others flow from it" and is finally given the name "I AM" a term appearing in many subsequent Ranter writings.(3) J. F. then awkwardly attempted to explain how mundane physical reality might flow or emanate from a transmundane God. In turn, the dichotomy of matter and spirit in the universe is also evident in the individual human being. On the one hand every human being possesses a soul which "hath God for its being, from him it's given and breathed (with the life) into the creature."(51) Opposed to the divine soul is the fleshly casing in which the soul is forced to reside, about which J. F. wrote, "It seeketh to destroy the remnant of *the seed of God in me*," but, the author added, "My flesh can not have its will in this."(24) Thus, every human being reflects the same basic tension evident in the universe.

Jesus Christ was adopted by God to provide a model to teach mankind to subdue the flesh and liberate the soul. J. F. wrote, "The fleshly death [of Christ] is but a *type*, further, it is a sign."(29) Christ's crucifixion together with the subsequent resurrection from the flesh was the pathway to be followed by all his followers so that the soul might be liberated from the body. Before one may follow Christ's path, however, God must first appear to the soul and enliven it. J. F. warned that "the workings of God in us and with souls are diverse; his grace and love commeth [*sic*] to some as a *thief*, when they are asleep."(45–46) In its illuminated state the soul is capable of discerning the spiritual aspect of the dichotomy characterizing the universe, "that divine love is heaven, to behold God . . . [while] this *tophet*, this hell, is dreadful apprehensions of God . . . base hard thoughts of God."(50) This condition of divine illumination when "my mind is raised from all things beneath to things above"(31) leads to the status of sainthood, described as "a *shadow* of Christ's rising in my soul out of the first sepulchre of my lusts, parts, righteousness, in which he lay buried."(30) This "in-life" resurrection was called by J. F. the "NEW CREATION, THE NEW HEAVEN AND NEW EARTH; THE KINGDOM OF GOD IN US."(10) Sainthood, however, could liberate the soul from the body but not completely redeem the soul from the material world. This final redemption came only with death, when "after the spirit hath been awhile in the body, it returneth with the life (with which it came) immediately into God again."(52) With the final return of the soul to God, "the natural shall be made spiritual, the mortal immortal."(31)

To a greater extent than was true to most Christians, the Ranter saw in death a final and complete resting place when the soul returns to God from the hell of his life. There is no other concept of an afterlife complicated by reward and punishment, or conventional ideas of heaven, hell, or purgatory. "Why are thou then cast down O my soul" J. F. could write, "thou must ascend as Christ is who also descended to that state of thine; as I am in hell with him and he there with me, so we shall be in heaven together, as we suffer together."(33–34)

J. F. expressed many bench-mark Ranter views. Ceremony and ritual such as "preaching, baptism, supper, church fellowship," were but external celebrations, "and many of God's [saints] so enjoying them have no need (as to themselves) of these outward signs."(14) Similarly, Scripture was qualified in terms to be found in every Ranter treatise. "The *history* is not the gold, it's the mine, it is not the jewel, it is only the cabinet."(16) On the same page J. F. added, "neither can the letter *teach* or *reveal* the mind of God, but the spirit only . . . thus *God* in his *working* in us is our *Scripture* and *rule of life*."(16–17)

Despite his stated ambivalence to Scripture, J. F., like other Ranters, cited those passages of the Bible that supported the views he espoused while he denigrated the *history* when it expressed views contrary to his own. Scripture could be interpreted away from the carnal and dead letter of the history and J. F. presented an example of the allegorical method necessary when interpreting the Bible. Referring to the scripture's description of Herod's efforts to seek out the Jesus child whom he feared, J. F. did not interpret this story to refer to an actual person named Herod or even to all governmental authority. Rather, J. F. wrote, "This *Herod* is my reigning sin, who, hearing of Christ coming to reign in my soul (which they for a long season ruled) opposed it all they can. Send out their wise men, (humane arts, learning) to betray (to declare) the ways and things of Christ foolishness and childishness. Sin by this would murder the child Jesus in me."(24)

This short treatise presented only hints of developing Ranter thought, yet the basic components were all in place. J. F. taught, if often in embryonic form, a thorough spiritualism predicated upon dualism, allegorical interpretation of Scripture to support this dualism, a Christology emphasizing Jesus' humanity and the rejection of vicarious atonement in favor of a soteriological system demanding that every person act to save his own soul, and the rejection of ritual as the expression of a meaningful religious experience. If J. F. did not condone the immoral behavior favored by the Libertines, he did write that "sin is a non-entity"(47) and, further, interpreted heaven and hell as psychological states of the soul. In all these many issues, J. F. was on firm Ranter ground.

J. F.'s treatise reflected one additional virtue of importance. Despite the author's silence on most themes important to the Libertine Ranters, Abiezer Coppe, a leading spokesman for that tendency, felt comfortable enough with the treatise's content to add his own name to the work when even its author would present only his initials. This is significant for it may indicate that divisions between Ranters (and there were many) were of less importance to seventeenth-century Ranters than the outline of this book would indicate. Despite significant differences, it would appear that Ranters recognized one another and the common core of views that each expressed.

Sexual Libertines

5. Abiezer Coppe

At first glance it is difficult to imagine two more different orientations than Philosophical Ranterism and Sexual Libertinism. Indeed, it is difficult to imagine two more different sorts of personalities than the sane, sober and ascetic Richard Coppin and the ecstatic, spectacular, bizarre and probably insane Abiezer Coppe. Yet, both intellectual tendencies represented recognized wings of a movement wide enough to include both, much as Protestantism included high Episcopalians and Presbyterian Puritans. Indeed, Richard Coppin's first and most important work was introduced by Abiezer Coppe.

The literary styles of the two schools differed much as did their authors. Where the former wrote in a detached and systematic manner, admonishing the readers to avoid the lures of the flesh and find God within their own spirits, Libertines envisioned themselves as latter day Christs and expressed themselves in the ecstatic language of the prophets of doom. Philosophical Ranters attempted a concise statement of faith, but Libertines were disorganized and expressed their views in haphazard fashion, depending upon shock effect as often as logic to make their arguments. Both were dualists but where the former hoped to avoid the world and retreat from sensuality, the Libertines preached an embracing of the world and sensuality as the surest path to God through concepts generally known as the redemption through evil. Hence, whatever differences in literary and personal style separated the Libertines from their more austere brethren, they did not differ so much in their appraisal of the world as in their prescriptions of how to deal with it and overcome it.

More is known about Abiezer Coppe's life than is usual with Ranters, perhaps because he came from a dignified family of some local standing. He was born in Warwick in 1619 and, after attending a local grammar school, was enrolled in All Souls College of Oxford University in 1636. Shortly thereafter, Coppe became a postmaster at Merton. Coppe acquired a reputation for immoral living and at the outbreak of the civil war left the university without having taken a degree. Like other Ranters, Coppe followed a spiritual odyssey which took him from the Church of England through Presbyterianism, Baptism, and finally to Rantism.

Early in his career as an itinerant preacher and leader of an extremely radical following, Coppe earned a reputation as a powerful preacher. His writings, too, reflect great rhetorical flourish and it is likely they were more effective when recited than when read silently. Adding to Coppe's fame as a preacher was his manner of preaching in the nude, which contributed to his imprisonment. Coppe was considered unstable, at least by his critics, and there is ample evidence even within his own writings of a most unusual temperament and frame of mind. When he was facing charges of blasphemy before Parliament, his books were condemned and burned, but Coppe taunted his prosecutors by shelling peanuts and throwing the husks at his opponents and officers of the court.

Coppe enjoyed good relations with other Ranters. His association with Coppin has been indicated and we have also observed that he introduced J. F.'s treatise to the London Ranter community. He knew Lawrence Clarkson, a competitor within the London community, and was taken in by Dr. John Pordage during a particularly bad time in his life. He knew Thomas Tany and others as well.

Coppe's writings are few but exceptional. His first treatise, *Some Sweet Sips of Spiritual Wine* [hereafter SW], written in 1649, set out many basic ideas and reflected his general orientation to life. In 1650 Coppe published his most notorious work, for which he was condemned in Parliament, *The Fiery Flying Roll, Parts 1 and 2*. This treatise is one of the clearest expositions of Rantism and one of the most poetic as well. Indeed, it was so outrageous that it left him imprisoned and he retracted it entirely a year later in 1651 in his *Remonstrance*, written primarily to win his release from prison. When the last treatise did not accomplish the desired end, he wrote *Coppe's Return to the Ways of Truth* which was the formal apology Parliament sought from him and a total abjuration of his views.

After his release from prison, Coppe led a very retiring life in Surrey where he practiced medicine under the name Dr. Higham. He died in 1672. During his last years as a respectable country doctor Coppe did not advance the Ranter cause. He did preach an occasional antinomian sermon but learned to express his views in far more acceptable fashion and to preach with his clothes on.

The table of contents of SW described the purpose of the treatise as "a call to arise out of the flesh into the spirit, out of form into power, out of type into truth, out of signs into the thing signified."(A3b) The dichotomy of the false and the true pervades all of Coppe's writings. We are told, for instance, that human beings, too, fall into one of two categories. Coppe explained that "Abraham had two sons, the one by a bondmaid . . . the other by a free woman," (18) and a page away he explained "Isaac is the heir, the son of the free woman, not Ishmael, the son of the bondwoman, for he is cast out."(17) In turn, this dichotomy is expressed in yet another context, "The son of that free woman is free indeed," Coppe explained, "the son of the free woman is a Libertine." (18) These same dichotomies are expressed in yet other ways. Coppe tells the reader, "Some are at home and within, some abroad and without. They that are at home are such as know their union with God and live upon and in and not upon anything below or beside him."(6) Those who are outside, live "at a distance from God (in their own apprehensions) and are strangers to a powerful and glorious manifestation of their union with God."(6) One method to determine whether one was at home or without, inside or outside, concerned the degree of one's alienation from organized religion. Coppe explained that "these [that] are without, abroad, not at home, would fill their bellies with *husks*, the outsides of the grain."(6) Those living within know "that their being [is] one in God and God one in them; that Christ and they are not twain but *one*."(6)

Those "without" can make no sense of the SW, Coppe writes, for "that which is here (mostly) spoken is inside and mystery. And as far as anyone hath the mystery of God opened to him, *in him*, can plainly read every word of the same here. The rest is sealed up from the rest."(5) However, Coppe promised, "If I speak in an unknown tongue, I pray that I may interpret when I may."(5) Thus, in phrases that are very effective when recited aloud, Coppe often digresses from his own discussion to ask, "Dear Hearts, where are you, can you tell? Ho! Where are you? Ho! Are you within? What, nobody at home? Where are you? Are you asleep? For shame, rise, it's break of day, the day breaks, the shadows file away, the dawning of the day woos you to arise and let him into your heart."(10) And yet elsewhere, in simpler language, "Here is the voice of one crying, Arise."(2)

Like other Ranters, Coppe taught that each human being must wait for God to appear within the soul. Using a Scriptural allusion, he wrote, "If the grain of a mustard seed be buried in the earth, wait for it because it will surely spring up into a tree."(5) Hence, this treatise was a "vision for an appropriate season . . . wait for it, it will surely come."(5) Anticipating God's action was futile for "if thou shouldst arise . . . before the spring of life enter thee, thou shouldst run before the Lord and outrun thyself."(3) In a word, "this cautional hint: Arise, but rise not till the Lord awakens thee."(3)

BLASPHEMY, IMMORALITY, AND ANARCHY

Thus far Coppe's ideas remained fairly close to those of Bauthumley or Coppin. Dualism, allegorical use of Scripture, the necessary passivity of the soul, and the division of humanity into saints and outsiders were common ideas among Ranters. Other similarities will be noted, but Coppe differed in terms of who he believed he was. Bauthumley claimed to be no one in particular, and Coppin was a preacher of a divinely inspired truth imparted to him by God. Coppe, however, held a more exalted view of himself. In terms reminiscent of Moses' encounter with God before the burning bush where God tells Moses 'I am that which I am,' Coppe wrote about himself, "I am what I am, and what I am [is] in *I AM*, so I am in the spirit."(7) Coppe would elucidate upon this identity in his later works.

Having established that there are those within and without and that Coppe is *I AM*, Coppe turned his attention to the message of this written sermon. Addressing those who wished to be free, he wrote, "O! Open your doors, hearts, open, I, the King of Glory come in. Open dear hearts! Dear Hearts, I should be loath to be arraigned for burglary."(12) Welcoming the new initiates within their ranks, Coppe explained how God converts the individual mustard seed into a saint. Essentially, the novice must undergo a trial referred to by Coppe as the "Day of the Lord" and elsewhere as "the anointing." This was a form of spiritual rape. "O day of the Lord," Coppe intoned, "come as a thief in the night, suddenly and unexpectedly and the night too, that they may not help themselves. O come . . . come quickly, as a thief in the night . . . come quickly, the long dark nights, come in the night."(14) Once this thief is taken within, the believer will find "the winter is past, the rain is over, the flowers appear on the earth, the time of the singing birds come [*sic*]." (15) In another location Coppe described the emotions of the newly sainted that "then you will sing one of the songs of zion, a Hebrew song, and say *Eli Avi atah*, thou art my father, my God . . . for you are no more twain but one." (35) These same marriage images are used elsewhere. Coppe asked, "What is man? Man is the woman, thou art the man . . . our maker is our husband, we are no more twain but one." (54) Later, these same typical Ranter ideas will receive strong sexual imagery.

Like other Ranters, Coppe believed spiritual union with God obviated any need for human religious institutions. Those experiencing "the anointing which you received of him abideth *in you* and you need not *that any man teach you.*"(26) Similarly, "They shall know no pastor, teacher, elder, or presbyter but the Lord, that spirit."(21) Human wisdom will be as nothing and "you will fall upon your books . . . and bring your books together and burn them before all men."(34) The anointed saints "live according to God in the spirit, cannot be offended at anything and in them there is no occasion of stumbling."(A3b) Simply stated, the saint cannot sin.

The life of the saint was not an easy one. At the same time that "the Lord will take you up into himself and say 'Live in me, Dwell in me, Walk with me' "(34) others will hate you. If you try to explain your feelings, "men shall say you are not only a lunatic but quite besides yourself . . . and your father and mother are troubled at you, grieve for you and at length forsake you."(34) Even worse, many will persecute you. Coppe recounted how "they caught one (true saint) and treated him shamefully, sent him away empty and shamefully handled him. At another they cast stones and wounded him in the head. Another they beat, smote with the tongue and devised evil devices against him saying, 'Report ye and we will report it' and another they killed and so would they all if they could."(17) Raising his voice, at least literarily, Coppe shouted, "Touch not the apple of his eye, his saints" and "if any man will hurt them, fire proceedeth out of their mouths and devoureth their enemies and if any will hurt them, he . . . shall be miserable (at least mystically) destroyed."(19) Turning to the saints, Coppe admonished, "Sodom must be destroyed and Lot must be saved . . . divorce them from their fleshly fellowships."(37)

Coppe believed that Sodom was being destroyed right before his eyes in England. Taking note of the civil war and the resulting political and religious confusion, he wrote "Many pastors have destroyed my vineyard, Jere. 12. Thus my father's vineyard goes to wrack while it is let out to husbandmen."(17) This allusion to Cromwell and Parliament reflected typical Ranter sentiment. "It is but a little while and behold," Coppin warned, "the Lord of the vineyard cometh and will miserably destroy (and that very suddenly) the husbandmen."(17) In the coming days of conflict, the saints would be protected by God. When the ancient Hebrews were led through the wilderness of Sinai as they left Egyptian bondage "he protected them, led and lighted his people by a pillar of fire and a cloud."(29) These were not the same sources of light known to others, Coppe noted, "It was not the sun and the moon which the Egyptians were acquainted with."(29)

The second half of the treatise was an exchange of letters between Coppe and Mrs. T.P., one of his devotees. While it would seem to be a separate or an unrelated section of the treatise, this was not the case. Through this exchange we get a very clear and intimate picture of Coppe's view of himself, the nature of the thief in the night, and why family members, especially husbands, might "grieve for you and at length forsake you."

Mrs. T.P., described by Coppe as "another converted," was a perfect example of the sort of disciple Coppe sought. Her letter includes many kind words expressing deep feelings for Coppe and a dream with definite sexual meaning. His reply returns her feelings of love and expresses the essence of Libertine thought through sexual-social imagery.

Mrs. T.P. began her letter as follows: "Dear Brother—My True Love in the Spirit of One-ness . . . It hath pleased the Father of late so sweetly to manifest his love to my soul that I can not but return it to you, who are the image of my Father. I should rejoice, if the Father pleases also, to see you and have some spiritual communion with you that I might impart those soul ravishing consolations . . ."(39–40) Mrs. T.P. then noted, "Of late the Father teaches me by visions of the night" in which "I have been at the holy land and have tasted the good fruit."(40) Mrs. T.P. was troubled by a recent dream, however, and turned to Coppe to interpret it for her. In this curious dream, "I was at a place where I saw all kinds of beasts of the field, wild and tame together . . . and all kinds of fishes in a pleasant river where the water was exceedingly clear."(41) While roaming in this lush place, "we had so free a correspondence together [i.e., with the animals] as I oft-times would take the wildest of them and put it to my bosom." So pleasurable was this that Mrs. T.P. writes that after she put all the different animals to her bosom, and "at last I took one of the wildest, as a tiger or such like, and brought it to my bosom and away from all the rest, and put a collar about him for mine own . . . but not withstanding all my care, it ran away."(41–42)

Perceiving the sexual imagery of this dream hardly requires extensive psychological training. The physical communion Mrs. T.P. experienced came from putting all the different animals to her bosom. All the different animals (i.e., men) were pleasant enough but she wished to reserve one very wild animal for her own use. The beast, however, would not be confined by her collar (i.e., wedding ring? leash?) and it ran away, leaving Mrs. T.P. feeling rejected and low.

Mrs. T.P. had several ideas about the meaning of the dream and, not surprisingly, they were social-sexual. The "holy land" was the internal heaven we have read about in previous sections, and the lush river location was living in the Garden of Eden where there was neither right nor wrong. Indeed, "it was shown to me that my having so free a commerce with all sorts of appearances [i.e., animals at her breast] was my spiritual liberty and certainly did I know it; it would be a very glorious liberty."(42) Mrs. T.P., no slouch pop-psychologist herself, also understood her relationship with the tiger. "Now concerning my taking one of them from all the rest (as distinct) and setting a collar about it, this was my weakness and here comes in all our bondage and death by appropriating of things to ourselves and for ourselves."(42)

The essence of sin, it would appear, lay not in indulging her desires with as many as she wished but in attempting to possess one of them for her exclusive use. It is possible that Mrs. T.P. was writing about property, but marriage and sexual exclusivity were as contractual as property. In any event, we will see that Coppe was as opposed to property as he was to sexual exclusivity. In either case, Mrs. T.P. laments her weakness, observing, "Could I have been content to have enjoyed this little, this one thing in the liberty of the spirit, I have never been brought to that tedious care in keeping nor that exceeding grief in losing."(42–43) Essentially, Mrs. T.P. seems to be drawing the moral that one should own only what one is willing to lose, or enjoy freely of all that is available as the essence of liberty.

Mrs. T.P.'s concluding remarks lead the reader to wonder if Coppe were not that wild tiger she had taken to her breast and attempted to own and perhaps was now afraid she lost through possessiveness. She requests of Coppe, "Wait therefore upon God for a further understanding in this thing and when you have it, I make no question but I shall partake of it."(43) Demonstrating her own proper subservience to his desire, she concluded, "I know you have the *anointing* which showeth you all things, to which anointing I now commit you and rest."(43)

Coppe's response was in keeping with the tone set by his correspondent. "Dear Sister in the Best Fellowship; mine entire love," Coppe began. "I know you are a vessel in the Lord's house, filled with a heavenly liquor and I see your love . . . I love the vessel well and I see your love, the Father's love, in the sweet returns of your (I mean) his sweets to me."(45) The next several pages present Coppe's enthusiastic approval of his lover, "filled with a heavenly liquor." Finally Coppe wrote, "How sweet thou art,—O Word, O God—to my taste. Yea, sweeter than honey and the honey comb, my God, sweet God, awake Lute, awake Harp, awake Deborah, awake, it is a song, a song, a song of love, one of the songs of Zion."(48) It is difficult to envision Bishop Laud, George Fox or Sidrach Simpson answering fan mail with the words, "Here in the spirit! O Spirit of Burning! Consuming Fire! O God, our joy."(48)

Turning his attention to her dream, Coppe accepted Mrs. T.P.'s interpretation and added a few images of his own. The lush garden was the condition of her spiritual liberty which she correctly enjoyed, and the river represented her baptism into God's freedom. The river is also, Coppe advised, "the fountain of life, the living God, [it] is clear pure. It is good to be here, to drink deep draughts . . . to wade up to the ankles . . . we should be up to the knees . . . to the loins."(58)

Coppe sympathized with her sorry experience with the tiger. "It seems you have took some of the wildest appearances, forms and figures to your bosom. So have I, but most of them are gone, vanished in a moment."(59) Coppe indicated that such was the way of the world, for "they are all wild and will run away (when the day breaks, the shadows fly away). They will all turn wild and run away and we shall be besides ourselves."(59) Agreeing that her sin lay in attempted possession of a free being, from which he too suffered, he wrote, "Let us not therefore any longer single out any appearances and appropriate it to ourselves, no . . . all is yours if you will not set a collar upon the neck."(60) Soothing her feelings, Coppe noted "Here, thou hast wine and milk and honey, without money, without price,"(52) and a page later he concluded, "Here all tears are wiped away from thine eyes . . . for thou art in the holy land, the holy land, and the Lord thy God in the midst of thee, who rejoiceth over thee . . . Sing O daughter, the Lord sings in thee. Shout, O daughter, the shout of the king is in thee. Take a timbrel O Miriam, the Lord danceth in thee."(53) Despite Coppe's imagery, most of the ideas he expressed can be found in both Bauthumley and Coppin, though there is little evidence that either of the latter received such fan mail.

SW was a minor work compared to Coppe's more famous treatises, *The Fiery Flying Roll, Part 1* and the *Fiery Flying Roule, Part 2*. Coppe's rhetoric reached a high point in these works and they are wonderful to recite aloud. It was this flamboyant style which first earned Coppe the reputation of a madman, though his last works indicate an even more flamboyant style plus true insanity.

The Fiery Flying Roll was subtitled "a word from the Lord to all the Great Ones" and presented a strident and vehement attack upon the rich and powerful of the civil war years. Like other messianic writers, Coppe felt the need to clarify his credentials and possession of a divine inspiration before presenting his special message. The preface, therefore, was devoted to explaining how he came to write this treatise.

Coppe informs the reader that he had been passing through a particularly bad time of his life several years earlier when, "first, all my strength, my forces were utterly routed, my house I dwelt in fired, my father and mother forsook me, and I was utterly plagued, consumed, damned, rammed and sunk into nothing."(A2, no printed page number) When he had sunk to his lowest, Coppe claims to have met God. "I heard with my outer ear (to my apprehension) a most terrible thunderbolt and after that a second . . . which was exceeding terrible, I saw a great body of light like the light of the sun and red as fire . . ."(A2, no printed page number) Though very much frightened, "with joy unspeakable in the spirit, I clapped my hands and cried out, 'Amen Hallelujah, hallellujah, amen . . . [and] with a loud voice I inwardly cried out 'Lord, what wilt thou do with me?' My most excellent majesty and eternal glory (in me) answered and said, 'Fear not, I will take thee up into mine everlasting Kingdom. But thou shalt first drink a bitter cup, a bitter cup."(A2—A3)

Despite divine assurances of eventual salvation, Coppe lay "trembling, sweating, and smoking for a space of half an hour" and then "was thrown into the belly of hell . . . among all the devils in hell, even in their most hideous hew."(A2—A3) Yet, with all the terrible torments of hell and devils, that is, the internal psychological strains of insecurity within his personality, there was "a little spark of transcendent transplendant unspeakable glory which survived and sustained itself."(A3) Coppe then experienced a wonderful vision in which "a mighty angel is proclaiming (with a loud voice) that sin and transgression is [sic] finished and ended and everlasting righteousness brought in."(A1)

During the next four days and nights Coppe experienced many more visions. He was ordered, in Jonah-like fashion, to seek the redemption of his fellow human beings, to "go up to London, to London that Great City. Write, write, write. And behold, I write and lo a hand was sent to me, a roll of a book was therein . . ."(A4) It was this very same divine message which Coppe would make known to the rich and powerful. It was not a happy message, however, and it "filled my bowels with it where it was as bitter as wormwood and lay boiling and burning in my stomach till I brought it forth in this form. And now I sent it flying to thee . . ."

The general theme of this first *Fiery Flying Roll* was far removed from the lush Eden-like atmosphere enjoyed by Mrs. T.P. There were no harps, no timbrels and no songs, but Coppe was equally ecstatic. *"Blood, blood, where, where? Upon the hypocritical holy heart* . . . vengeance, vengeance, vengeance, plagues, plagues, upon the inhabitants of the earth. Fire, fire, fire, sword, sword, upon all that bow not down to eternal majesty, universal love; I'll recover, recover, my wool, my flax, my money. Declare, declare, fear thou not . . ."(A4) The body of the treatise is no more ambivalent about Coppe's, or God's, intentions. The civil war was nothing but God's revenge upon evil England which included Parliament. "Thus saith the Lord, I inform you that I overturn, overturn, overturn. And as bishops, Charles, and the Lords have had their turn, overturn, so your turn shall be next."(1) The civil war rich grow more and more fat, but all will be taken from them and "it is not for nothing that I the Lord with a strong wind cut off (as with a sickel) [*sic*] the fullest, fairest ears of corn this harvest. . . . It is not for nothing that such various strange kinds of worms, grubs, and caterpillars (my strong host saith the Lord of Hosts) have been sent into some grain. Neither is it in vain that I the Lord sent rot among so many sheep last year."(16) The world was coming full term and all that is presently will be no more, for "never was there such a time since the world stood as now is."(9) The day of judgment was coming, "and the sea, the earth, yea, all things are now giving up their dead. All things that ever were, are, or shall be visible are the graves wherein the king of glory (the eternal, invisible almightiness hath lain, as it were) dead and buried."(A1)

The remainder of the treatise was an enumeration of the many things God was about to destroy. Foremost among the institutions God hated was the religious establishment, "the ministers, fat parsons, vicars, lecturers, etc. who . . . have been the chief instruments of all these horrid abominations, hellish, cruel, devilish persecutions in this nation which cry out for vengeance."(3) The crimes of the clergy were twofold. In a religious vein, the clergy "call good evil and evil good. Light darkness and darkness light, truth blasphemy and blasphemy truth."(8) Both bishops and now presbyters seek out dissenters whom they "set branding with the letter B . . . to judge what is sin, what not, what evil and what not, what blasphemy and what not."(7)

Equally grievous were the crimes of the clergy. They converted a spiritual message to love God into a money-making enterprise for their own support through "that plaguey, unsupportable, hellish burden and oppression of the tythes."(5) It was this perversion of religion which permitted the church of the poor apostles to become the church of the fat benefices. In the process, all of Christianity had been turned on its head. Where Jesus clearly stated the rich would not go to heaven, the clergy "tellest him he may break bread with all such believers who believe their horses and their cows are their own."(20) Those preaching Jesus' own poverty are "branded with the letter *B*, banished or imprisoned."(20)

The clergy was guilty of providing the spiritual justification for the accumulation of wealth, but Coppe's greatest criticism was of the wealthy themselves. Coppe asked, "How long shall I hear the sighs and groans and see the tears of poor widows . . . and all sorts of people crying out, oppression, oppression, tyranny, tyranny?"(10) Rather than collecting rents the rich should "cover the naked . . . a cripple, a rogue, a beggar."(7) Rather than raising prices, Coppe asked the rich to "kiss beggars, prison-

84

ers, warm them, feed them, clothe them, money them, relieve them, take them into your houses, don't serve them as dogs, without doors. Own them, they are your flesh, your own brethren, your own sisters."(6) Using the very words of the Brethren of the Free Spirit, Coppe wrote, "mine ears are filled brim full with cries of poor prisoners, Newgate, Ludgate cries (*of late*) are seldom out of mine ears. Those doleful cries, *Bread, Bread, Bread, for the Lord's sake* . . ."(7) Coppe warned the rich, "Repent, repent, repent, bow down, bow or howl, resign or be damned."(6)

Like other Ranters, Coppe sympathized with the Levellers and expressed sentiments no doubt quite common in the army. In pointedly plain and direct language for Coppe, he wrote, "You can little endure the word *Levelling* as could the late slain or dead Charles."(12) And turning to Parliament he noted, "You mostly hate those called Levellers who (for aught you know) acted as they did out of sincerity, simplicity, and fidelity of hearts."(11) Referring to the Leveller mutinies in the army in 1649 crushed by Cromwell at Burford and his subsequent execution of three Leveller ringleaders, Coppe declared, "Then were they most barbarously unnaturally, hellishly murdered and they died martyrs for God and their country."(11) The more flamboyant Coppe added, "You have killed the just, you have killed, you have killed, you have killed the just."(11) Expressing God's own compassion for the suffering poor, Coppe lamented, "O London, London, . . . my compassions within me are kindled toward thee . . . to proclaim the day of the Lord throughout thy streets."(13)

Despite his warning, Coppe did not expect "the abominable, false hearted, self seeking, self enriching, kingdom depopulating and devastating"(10) rich to permit change. To such he noted, "I, the eternal God, the Lord of Hosts, who am that mighty Leveller, am coming . . . to level the hills with the valleys, and to lay the mountains low."(2) Coppe warned, "High Mountains! Lofty Cedars! It's high time for you to enter into the Rocks."(2)

The tone and mood of this treatise are far different from those of the SW, and yet Coppe expressed the same hatred of possession, ownership, and property in both treatises. The wealthy place collars about the world's wealth and have stolen God's bounty for all humankind for themselves. Scriptural admonitions against the accumulation of wealth went unheeded by a religious establishment collecting the tithe. Government brings change only in how it will repress the sincere of heart like the Levellers. In actuality, the two works present the same ideas, but in a different format expressed with different images. Tigers and saintly poor, collars, leashes and private property are the themes of both works. There is one very big difference, however. Coppe didn't write to Mrs. T.P. the same way he addressed England's governing-owning class. Perhaps they did not write him fan mail.

The second *Fiery Flying Roule* was both conceptually superior to the two earlier works, and more radical as well. Several new ideas were presented along with a radical concept of ideal human-divine relations, and a graphic picture of what God will do to destroy the world. Ever mindful of the importance of good introductions, Coppe opened this treatise with a refresher concerning his credentials. He reminded the reader that "the word of the Lord came expressly to me saying, write, write, write,"(1) and then warned his audience, "Read it through and laugh not at it; if thou dost, I'll laugh at thee and laugh at thy destruction."(1) A far more militant Coppe added to Parliament, "I charge thee burn it not, tear it not for if thou dost, I'll tear thee to pieces."(1)

A more aggressive and strident tone is evident throughout the treatise. In the first *First Flying Roll* Coppe made clear that he himself was no "sword Leveller" and that "this hand (which now writes) never drew sword or shed one drop of any man's blood . . . and sword levelling or digger levelling is neither of them his principles."(2) The second treatise presents a far bolder and more radical image. "Thou hast many bags of money and behold now I come as a thief in the night with my sword drawn in my hand and like a thief as I am I say, 'Deliver your purse, deliver sirrah, deliver or I'll cut your throat.' "(2) Similarly, Coppe's social message was expressed now in sharpened language. Speaking for God, Coppe wrote, "Thou hast robbed me (saith the Lord) of my corn, my wool, my flax, etc. Thou hast robbed me of my tithes for the tithes are mine. And the beasts on a thousand hills, yea, all the bags of money, hayriches, horses, yea, all that thou callest thine own are mine."(1) And here again, "I am now come to recover my corn, my wool, and my flax, to discover thy lewdness."(1)

Considering the sin committed, the penance required was obvious. Turning to Scripture, Coppe taught, "For our parts we hear the apostle preach, will also have all things in common; neither will we call anything that we have our own."(19) Translated into Coppese, "Give, give, give, give up, give up your houses, goods, gold, lands, give up, account nothing your own, have ALL THINGS common."(3-4)

Coppe's earlier criticism of the religious establishment was amplified in this work. Coppe noted that Christ presented two sorts of messages to his disciples. The first was purely religious and spiritual to be understood metaphorically in the spirit. The second was a clear and literal social message regarding property relations in the carnal and material world. Organized religion, however, turned everything upside down and now the purely spiritual message was understood literally while the social message was understood metaphorically. The result was the creation of many literal religious rituals and lists of dogmas of the sort practiced in the Temple during Jesus' lifetime. The social message which warned against hoarding property, however, was not accepted literally, but spiritually, to explain it away as referring to some other kingdom. "O fool!" Coppin exclaimed, "Who hath bewitched thee, art thou so foolish to begin in the spirit and wilt thou now be made perfect in the flesh?"(17) adding, "Wilt thou not cease to pervert the right ways of the Lord?"(18) Concerning spiritual matters, Coppin advised, "Keep thee to the spirit, go not back to the letter, keep thee to the mystery . . ."(17)

The world was upside down with current property, social, and religious conventions reflecting this confusion. Previously Coppe advised the rich to surrender voluntarily before the day of God. Earlier in this treatise Coppe redefined the "thief in the night" from a spiritual overwhelming to a regular thief in the night. The intellectual justification for this change was provided by Coppe in the concept of redemption through evil.

Though never widespread, this concept has had adherents in many religions. The Cainites and Ophites, among others in the ancient world, believed the Old Testament was written by Satan and consequently, one did God's work by doing the opposite of what Scripture required. Hence, one must be redeemed through 'evil.' During the Middle Ages Adamite sects followed the path of Adam and welcomed sin, believing that sexual libertinism, even debauchery, advanced the soul along the path to salvation. For these devotees, the believer must saturate the soul with evil and defile the body, created in his image, with foul practices.

Curiously, dualists in particular have been drawn to this form of redemption. It is reasonable that extreme dualists would see Satan as the God who created the world of matter and would therefore reverse Old Testament restrictions/liberties. Additionally, this reversal represented an attempt, albeit a weird one, to come to terms with a world which was so hated. One can see that philosophical dualism emphasized the needs of the soul and advised an ascetic life to avoid overt pollution by matter. But the world must be overcome or transcended, and where Coppin demonstrated the suffering path to punish the body, and Bauthumley disparaged and finally ignored the body as simply a dumb beast, Coppe would teach the believer to embrace the perverted and disgusting as the only way to turn the world back right-side up. One comes to terms with evil matter and is liberated from it by becoming it.

BLASPHEMY, IMMORALITY, AND ANARCHY

Those acts which are low and base and disgusting are the very deeds that will bring about the downfall of what is presently considered good, proper, and righteous. He noted that "God hath chosen BASE things and things that are despised, to confound the things (that) are."(10) As an example, Ezekial "seems to be higher than the rest by the shoulders upward and was more seraphical than his predecessors, yet he is the son of *buzi* (Ezek. 1) which being interpreted is, the son of contempt. It pleases me (right well) that I am his brother, a son of *buzi*."(7) Similarly, Hosea was commanded to marry a whore.

To demonstrate his own continuity with the prophets, Coppe noted that he too did strange things such as "hugging, embracing, kissing a poor deformed wretch in London who had no nose on his face . . . but only two little holes in the place where the nose used to stand." (9) Yet other strange forms of behavior which Coppe could boast of included "falling down flat on the ground before rogues, beggars, cripples, halt, maimed and blind etc. kissing the feet of many, rising up again and giving them money."(10) Some of these activities were Christlike for he too embraced the palsied and gave succor to the socially unacceptable. Then again, Coppe's list also included a few other things not usually associated with Jesus such as, "skipping, leaping, dancing like one of the fools; vile base fellows, shamelessly, basely uncovered, too, before the handmaids."(10) In short, "BASE things so called, have been confounded into eternal majesty."(13) Perhaps this was why Ranters sang, whistled and danced.

Coppe's general rule of thumb was that anything base or in poor taste was good and redeeming while things that "are" represent the Devil and must be overturned. Coppe's list was extensive. "Family duties are no BASE things . . ."(10) and should be discouraged. Similarly, "grace before meat and after meat are no *base* things, these are things that ARE."(11) Coppe repeatedly admonished the reader, "Give over thy base nasty thinking formal grace before meat and after . . . give over thy stinking family duties and thy gospel ordinances, as thou callest them."(12)

In turn there were many positive BASE actions one might act upon to enable the BASE to overcome the things that ARE. Other than skipping and playing the fool, Coppe noted, "Lust is numbered amongst transgressors, a BASE thing"(13) and hence "I chose base things when I sat down and ate and drank around on the ground with gypsies and clipped and hugged and kissed them, putting my hand in their bosoms, loving the gypsies dearly. O BASE!"(11) As an afterthought Coppe added that some readers "could have better borne this if I had done it to ladies, so I can for a need, if it be my will . . . without sin." (11) Indeed, not merely ladies rather than gypsies, but married ladies too and Coppe explained that he could "love my neighbor's wife . . . without sin"(11) and "I have concubines without number, which I can not be without."(14) Coppe admitted, however, that he had a particular fondness for gypsies for "at that time when I was hugging the gypsies, I abandoned thoughts of Ladies, their beauty can not bewitch mine eyes or snare my lips or entangle my hands in their bosoms."(11) Coppe relished the anticipated reaction of some readers, and "the least spark of modesty would be as red as crimson or scarlet to hear this." (11) More shocking yet was this prophet of God's statement that such that are shocked, because they represent the things that ARE, will experience even more unsettling shock when God "will make thine own child . . . lie with a whore before thine eyes." (12)

Sexual liberty did not exhaust the totality of human potential for goodness, and there were yet other forms of behavior which encouraged holiness. Coppe noted for instance, "It's meat and drink to an angel (who knows none evil and no sin) to swear a full mouthed oath (Rev. 10:6). It's a joy to Nehemiah to come in like a madman and pluck folks' hair off their heads and curse like a devil."(12) Through such actions "my plaguey holiness hath been confounded" and these deeds "have been made fiery chariots to mount me swiftly into the bosom of him whom my soul loves . . ."(13) Or again, "Through BASE things (as upon the wings of the wind) have I been carried into the arms of my love which is invisible glory, eternal majesty, purity itself . . . which transcendent unspeakable beauty is my crown and joy, my life and love."(14) It is perhaps characteristic of the libertine attitude that Coppe's description of the joys of unity with God should receive strong sexual imagery. Coppe looked to a day "when I have been hugged, hugged, hugged, embraced and kissed with the kisses of his mouth whose loves are better than wine, and have been utterly overcome therewith, beyond expression, beyond admiration."(13)

However different Coppe's expression and imagery, his ideas were essentially similar to those of Bauthumley and Coppin. All three thinkers rejected religious rituals and church organization, political frameworks and private property. Moreover, all three thinkers believed it possible to transcend the physical world. Where Bauthumley wished the world would go away and would ignore it until it did, and Coppin would torment the body to strengthen the soul against the world, Coppe would overturn the world and make it into what it was not. He would replace all of yesterday's creations, both social and civil, with their opposites, and thereby return man to the innocence of a pure soul in Eden. SW described the Eden Coppe would seek, where mankind existed with neither personal nor social restraint. Sin was limitation and exclusion, and merger with God would come by abandoning the forms, formulas, and conventions of life. If Philosophical Ranters were more erudite and intellectually consistent in describing their mystical merger with God, they could draw upon a long tradition of spiritual mysticism and dualism. The difference between Coppe and Coppin was primarily one of imagery. Sexual ethic was personal choice.

All denied the reality of heaven and hell, sin and social convention in favor of a greater reality into which they sought to merge themselves. Bauthumley and Coppin described the soul's relationship with God as the relationship of the individual rays of light to the sun or water returning to its source in the sea. Coppe wrote of the simplicity of Eden where man would "become a little child and let mother *Eternity*, almightiness, who is universal love and whose service is perfect freedom, dress thee and undress thee."(12) Despite the difference in imagery all would agree with Coppe that for man "to see no more evil, he must first lose all his righteousness, every bit of his holiness and every crumb of his religion."(12) Bauthumley and Coppin wrote of God speaking to the poor and unlettered of the world much as Christ spoke to the poor and unlettered of his time. Coppe too reasoned that the world must "be plagued and confounded (by base things) into nothing. *By Base things which God and I have chosen.*"(12)

Abiezer Coppe was an anarchist who would destroy the world's institutions to permit a better, more original plan to reemerge and take its place. Programs, alternative systems of organization and platforms were not serious considerations, for the present was an infection to be destroyed but not reformed. Consequently, Coppe proved very unsettling to contemporaries and his works were condemned by Parliament and ordered to be burned on May 10 and August 9, 1650. Later that year Coppe found himself in court facing half a dozen charges of blasphemy, sedition and immorality. It was to answer these charges that Coppe wrote his *Remonstrance* in 1651 in which he attempted to argue that he did not maintain the views charged against him, which, in any event, were correct. This was Coppe's first attempt to retreat from the positions expressed in his writings. The *Remonstrance* is the only account of Coppe's legal difficulties we possess and, unfortunately, he wrote very little about the nature of the process itself.

Even when facing prosecution, Coppe had difficulty taking his situation seriously. Writing of himself he noted, "Some said he is good man, others said nay, but he is mad and hath a devil. He is a wine bibber, a glutton and a drunkard, a friend of publicans and harlots." (1) He congratulated Parliament's desire "to suppress profanity and wickedness, superstition and formality" (2) none of which, he explained, applied to him. Indeed, Coppe claimed not to be writing on his own behalf, "but for the sakes of others (since) my pure innocence supports me and lifts up my head above all these things."(1)

Coppe rejected all the charges against himself. He denied that he "ignorantly and blasphemously affirm myself or any other creature to be God."(4) He protested the accusation that his writings and lifestyle advanced "uncleanness, profane swearing, drunkenness, filthiness . . . lying, stealing, cozening and defrauding others."(4) Coppe solemnly swore that "murder, adultery, incest, fornication, uncleanness, sodomy, are things sinful, shameful, wicked, impious, and abominable in any person."(4) Additionally, Coppe affirmed "that there is a heaven and a hell, salvation and damnation"(5) denial of which, Coppe knew, was punishable under the terms of the Blasphemy Act.

Having explained that he was completely orthodox and civil, Coppe went on to expound on some of the views he did maintain which might have caused some confusion and difficulty. Regarding "liberty, I own none but the glorious liberty of the sons of God . . . and I do from my heart detest and protest against all sinful liberty that is destructive to soul or body."(5) Concerning his views of property, "I own none but that apostolic saint-like community spoken of in the Scriptures" and "I am for dealing bread to the hungry, for clothing the naked, for the breaking of every yoke and for the letting of the oppressed go free."(5) Believing there was nothing wrong with these views, Coppe asked, "Whose ox have I taken? Or whose ass have I taken? Or to whom have I done any wrong? Whom have I dealt unjustly with? Where is even a drop of blood that I have shed? Whom have I defrauded of a shoe latcht or a thread?"(3)

Coppe thought he understood why so innocent an individual as he would be forced to defend himself. It was his vehemence against "idolatry, superstition and idolatrous formality . . . that the coals were first kindled against me,"(2) he explained. Comparing himself to Christ, Coppe observed, "I have been by all men (except those that knew me) cried up (as my *forerunner* before me was by all sorts even the most religious and righteous, except a handful that knew him) for the worst of sinners, the vilest of persons; for a *Blasphemer*, a *Devil*."(2) With less than Christ-like humility Coppe warned his prosecutors, "Hell and damnation to all that *touch the apple of his eye*, that oppose the *Lord's Anointed*, and *that do his prophets any harm*."(5)

This treatise failed to win his release from prison, and he remained incarcerated for much of 1651. Despite Coppe's denial of his published views, the judges may have had little respect for an admitted drunkard, glutton and associate of whores. Later in 1651 Coppe again attempted to gain his release from prison by writing *Coppe's Return to the Ways of Truth*, his last treatise.

Coppe must have found prison life extremely difficult, for this treatise gives evidence of severe psychological debilitation and deterioration. Coppe's prose was poetic and picturesque and his imagery was colorful as always, but there is also an uncomfortable tone of desperation that is difficult to miss. It is possible that the treatise gained his release on humanitarian grounds of compassion.

Coppe apologized for disturbing Parliament but explained that he found prison life extremely unpleasant especially now that his wife was ill and was being attended by a physician.(2) Rather than simply recanting his views and condemning his earlier life, he attempted to explain to his censors why he had acted and lived so poorly. He compared himself to a confused Israel wandering in the wilderness where "God took me by the hand and hath transacted and done over the same things (in a spiritual sense) pitching and removing my tents from place to place, setting and seating me in various forms. In all which I have lived and acted zealously and conscientiously, never stirring a foot till I clearly apprehended this voice (all along) 'Arise, get thee hence, remove thy tent to such a place.' "(3) One wonders whether it was wise for Coppe to ascribe his behavior to God since he acted in so bizarre a fashion, as he would describe, and because he would in the end recant of all his divinely inspired activity. In any event, he continued in this vein. "At length the terrible notable day of the Lord stole upon me unawares, like a thief in the night . . . my bowels trembled, my lips quivered, rottenness entered into my bones. Why? Before him came the pestilence and burning coals at his feet. And the cup of the Lord's hand was put into mine hand. And it was filled brimful of intoxicating wine and I drank it off, even the dregs thereof."(4) The result was not the closeness to God Coppe desperately sought but "being made drunk," he explained, "I so strongly spake and acted I knew not what. To the amazement of some, to the perplexity of others and to the great grief of others. For I was (really, in very deed) besides myself, and till that cup passed from me, I knew not what I spake or did."(4)

The sudden initiation, the sense of being overwhelmed, the period of the bitter cup and the resulting period of tribulation were experiences common to all Ranters. According to Coppe, the results of this heady wine were particularly difficult. "I was driven from MEN. From MEN. That pure spark of reason (was for a season) taken from me. From men, from RATIONALITY, from PURE humanity. And thus I was driven from MEN.

And I have been with the beasts of the field. I have been with the BEASTS. I have fed with BEASTS. I have eaten GRASS with OXEN. Have been conversant with BEASTS and have been company for BEASTS. And sure I am my hairs were grown like EAGLES' feathers and my nails like Bird's CLAWS."(5) During this period of beastliness many of his ideas spread far and wide, and Coppe agreed, "There are many spurious brats (current errors) lately born . . . some of them (indeed) look somewhat like my children . . . whether they are mine or no . . . I will turn them out of doors and starve them to death . . . I will be so holily cruel as to dispatch them."(6–7)

Fortunately, the bitter cup eventually passed from him and Coppe could now report "mine UNDERSTANDING is returned to me."(5) He indicated, "I have been (a long while) clothed with filthy garments and have been in the channel. Everyone that hath passed by me have cast dirt upon me . . . but now (in these days) I shake off the dirt, rags, and all."(6)

Hoping to convince his captors that he was now able to live a normal life, Coppe described how his life would be if released. This description is rather tragic for it is clear that the bitter cup had not yet passed him by. "I will deal with my WIFE as a man of knowledge," Coppe wrote, "I will love my little CHILDREN. I will love all my BRETHREN, though of different statures, ages and complexions. My strong brethren and my weak also I will not offend. My sickly ones I will pity and visit and be serviceable to them. And my babe brethren I will dandle on my knee and do the best I can to quiet them when they cry and are crabbed. And my brethren that are at age I will dine and sup. With them I will talk and confer. With them I will eat, drink, and be merry in the Lord."(6)

After this long prefatory section Coppe addressed the various charges made against him in court. His answers reflect a shift in Coppe's thinking away from Libertinism to views more akin to those espoused by Coppin. There is still, of course, a healthy dose of Theatre Coppiana, or perhaps it was just his madness.

The first charge against him was that he maintained there was no sin. Earlier Coppe had argued that BASE things were needed to overturn things that ARE, but now he wrote, "Everyman on earth here below sinneth, is a sinner, a sinner all over, brimful of sin. And of sinners, I am the chief."(2) A few pages later we are treated to one of Coppe's soliloquies on the subject of sin. "O Sin! Sin! Sin!" he declared, "There is Sin, Murder, Theft, Adultery, Drunkenness, Swearing, Cursing, Uncleanness, Covetousness, Pride, Cruelty, Oppression, Hypocrisy, Hatred, Envy, Malice, Evil surmising in Sin. Nothing but Villainy, Sin, and Transgression in me, the Chief of Sinners.

In man, in every man. There is none righteous, no, not one. None that doth good, no, not one. All are sinners. The very little thieves and great thieves, drunkards, adulterers and adulteresses. Murderers, little murderers and great murderers. All are sinners, sinners all."(4)

Coppe was also charged with teaching there was no God. He denied maintaining that position and explained that God was "a spirit having his being in himself . . . the fountain of life and light."(6) The third charge, curiously, was that Coppe also believed "that man, or the mere creature, is very God." Rejecting this altogether, Coppe noted, "Neither do I know any one on the face of the earth that affirmeth that the mere creature is very God."(9) Using good Ranter terms, Coppe added, "The mere creature is finite but God is infinite. Ergo, the mere creature is not very God."(9)

There were other differences between man and God enumerated by Coppe. God can do whatever he pleases. Only God, Coppe explained, could demand circumcision on pain of death and just as firmly abolish the practice altogether. Only God can forbid murder, punish Cain, and then demand that Abraham kill his son. God can forbid adultery but command Hosea to marry a whore. In a word, the mere creature cannot possibly be God, because "He doth what he pleases [whereas] the creature is limited in weakness."(8)

The next charge, "that God is in man or in the creature only and nowhere else"(9) was also covered by the Blasphemy Act. He wrote, "I know that he is (Hic et Ubique) here and there and everywhere. He is in the heights, in the depths, above and below." (10) Recalling the Psalmist, Coppe noted, "If I ascend up to heaven thou art there. If I make my bed in hell, behold thou art there."

The last charges concerned some of the more colorful aspects of Coppe's Ranter lifestyle. He now argued, as he had in the *Remonstrance*, that cursing, swearing, adultery and fornication were prohibited by Scripture and therefore sinful.(12–13) Similarly, the community of women and property was eschewed as destructive to society, but he continued to affirm the need for "dealing bread to the hungry, for clothing the naked, for the breaking of every yoke, for the letting of the oppressed go free."(14)

The last few pages of the treatise presented an exchange of letters with Rev. John Dury, a member of the committee charged with dealing with Coppe. Dury's letter was friendly in tone and advised Coppe to write a treatise of recantation addressed to Parliament and concerning the following issues: sin, the Law of God, the human soul and its relationship to God, the resurrection, and last judgment. Additionally Dury advised Coppe to show real regret and remorse about his earlier life. (16–18) The letter was dated June 23, 1651, and it is likely Coppe received it after he had written *Coppe's Return* because he subsequently addressed the various points raised in Dury's letter.

In general, Coppe summarized relevant points made earlier and attacked moral sin even more vehemently than in his soliloquy. Even the desire and thought of sin were declared sins.(20) The Law of God, an idea that would have previously sent Coppe into a fit of hysterical laughter, was now taken quite seriously. It was "a rule to all men, of their lives in thoughts, words and deeds . . . whereunto all men must appeal and submit."(24) In simple direct statements he affirmed the resurrection of the body and the final day of judgment (25, 26) and noted that he did not express these views in order to win release from prison but out of sincere belief and that he had no "desire to seek after my liberty to this end, that I might return again and wallow in the mire."(18) He sought release from prison, he explained, "that I might be in a better way, place or posture and capacity to glorify God than I possibly can in here. For how can I sing the songs of my God in a strange land?" (18–19) Coppin continued to assert, in Ranter-like fashion, "We are partakers of the divine nature"(25) but Coppe's orthodox critics were evidently content with Coppe's more spiritual orientation.

Coppe left prison and did not resume his Ranter lifestyle. Whether his views actually changed is not clear. On December 23, 1651, Coppe, fully clothed, preached a recantation sermon at Burford in Oxfordshire and later practiced medicine in Barnes parish in Surrey under the alias Dr Higham until his death in 1672.

When Coppe abdicated his position as the leading spokesman for Sexual Libertine Rantism, Lawrence Clarkson was ready to fill that position himself. Like Coppe, Clarkson was charismatic, intelligent, and literate and in a short time he was known as the "Captain of the Rant." In that position, Clarkson led Sexual Libertine Rantism to a new level of radicalism far surpassing that of Coppe at his most extreme.

6. Lawrence Clarkson

Lawrence Clarkson, or Claxton as he also called himself, combined a flamboyant lifestyle with a sharp intellect and a charismatic preaching ability and soon emerged as the outstanding leader of the Libertine wing of Rantism. Much as Coppin was the complete Ranter intellectual, Clarkson, as "Captain of the Rant," was the complete Ranter activist and must rank as one of the most outstanding personalities of the civil war years.

Clarkson's many writings fall into two distinct categories. His early writings include *A Pilgrimage of Saints by Church Cast Out* (1646); *Truth Released from Prison to Its Former Liberty* (1647); *A General Charge or Impeachment of High Treason* (1647) and *A Single Eye All Light, No Darkness* (1650). These works reflect his growing radicalism and Ranter phase. Though the first of these is no longer extant, enough is known about the circumstances of its creation to follow the unified thread tying all these very radical works together.

Clarkson's later writings are less radical and of less interest to our purposes as they express his post-Ranter religious beliefs as a Muggletonian. Of these later writings we will review *The Lost Sheep Found* (1660), Clarkson's spiritual autobiography, in which he described his Ranter life. Later in this volume we will have the opportunity to study *The Right Devil Discovered*, written in 1659, a far different sort of work from that which might have been anticipated from Lawrence Clarkson. Other works written during this period include *The Quakers' Downfall* (1659), a Muggletonian attack upon the Society of Friends with no Ranter content at all, and *A Paradisical Dialogue Between Reason and Faith* (1660), a rather tedious piece that might have been written by almost anyone from the Antinomian left. His last treatise, *A Wonder of Wonders* (1660), like his first, is no longer in existence.

Unlike his heavy-handed later works, Clarkson's early writings are all important. Each one expresses an additional element or component that would coalesce into his mature Rantism. Each was written at a specific point in his life when new insights and concepts might be grafted onto an increasingly sophisticated bank of ideas. Together, these works provide a clear picture of the development of a truly radical mind.

Before analyzing Clarkson's writings, we might first read what he wrote about his early life and how he became a Ranter. Though his spiritual

LAWRENCE CLARKSON

biography, *The Lost Sheep Found,* was written in 1660 when Clarkson was no longer a Ranter, this work is still of enormous value. This interesting and often humorous treatise sheds light on the Ranting life and indicates much about the general religious turmoil and confusion marking the interregnum years.

Clarkson begins his story when he was a youth. At the age of fifteen he discovered he was unhappy with his upbringing in the Church of England. Seeking a faith with more vehemence, Clarkson became a Puritan and for a short time experienced the extreme religious fervor of the newly converted adolescent. Pursuing piety, however, proved difficult. In order to attend the Puritan church, he wrote, "Several times I have gone 10 miles, more or less, fasting all the day . . . and though I have been weary and hungry, yet I came home rejoycing."(4) Clarkson offered no explanations for his intense religiosity but noted that he had "many times privately prayed with rough hard cinders under my bare knees . . . with tears running down my cheeks."(6) He had become a Presbyterian because the Presbyterians seemed more committed to an austere and hard life than the Church of England. In time Clarkson grew disillusioned because "as the Presbyterians got power so their pride and cruelty increased against such as was contrary to them."(8) Ever in search of a spiritual home, Clarkson spent the next few years travelling through the maze of England's sectarian thicket. In this spiritual odyssey, Clarkson became an Independent, later an Antinomian, and finally a Baptist, a Seeker, a Ranter and eventually a Muggletonian.(8–10)

Clarkson did not explain how his actual views changed during these years or why he turned to inner light theology, but wrote that it was during his stay with the Antinomians that he discovered "I had a small gift of preaching and so by degrees increased [it] into a method."(10) Several congregations in Norwich, Yarmouth, Pulom, and Russel paid Clarkson to preach sermons and finally he was offered a permanent position in Pulham Market in Norfolk where "for a time I was settled for 20 shillings a week and very gallantly provided for, so that I thought I was in heaven."(11) After serving in this first position for six months, Clarkson experienced his first bout of religious controversy and notoriety. His doctrine of free grace, the doctrine that God granted grace to all people freely and without merit or requirement, proved so seductive to members of other churches that Clarkson acquired the name "'sheep-stealer'" and was not well liked by other local ministers.(11) At one point Clarkson was arrested for disturbing the peace but was soon released.

Clarkson soon fell under the influence of John Tyler, the Baptist leader, and on November 6, 1644, he came to realize "that the baptism of the apostles was as much in force now as in their days and that the command did as really belong to me as to them."(12) Evidently Clarkson was not an insignificant catch in the game of sectarian musical chairs for he was invited to live in the house of the well-to-do Baptist leader Robert Marchant where he was accepted as a family member. Clarkson returned the confidence of his host family by "amusing all four daughters," as he put it, and finally by marrying Frances Marchant.(12) Both spiritually and materially, this was a good period in Clarkson's life "so that really I thought if ever I was in a true happy condition, then I was . . . I was satisfied we were the only Church of Christ in this world."(12)

Eden proved ephemeral, however, and Clarkson soon found himself in trouble with the local authorities. Two constables, several soldiers, and an officer from Parliament came to arrest Clarkson and he was charged with irregular religious activity. He was detained and questioned at Bury St. Edmunds Prison where Captain Blayes of Woodbridge served as chairman of an investigating committee. Clarkson was questioned regarding his baptizing activities in general but more specifically the court complained, "We are informed you dip both men and women naked,"(15) and more serious yet, "We are informed you dipped six sisters one night naked . . . nay further, it is reported that which of them you liked best, you lay with her in the water."(15) In this first of many challenges to Clarkson's sexual integrity, he was sentenced to sit in jail for an unspecified period of time. Clarkson wrote that prison was tedious but he was in good spirits, met with many visiting friends, and preached to large audiences from his cell window. One visitor, the famous Seeker William Erbury, was able to show Clarkson the folly of his ways and, in any event, Clarkson believed this was an auspicious time to change his views. A full renunciation of his Baptist opinions and practices might win his release, and anyway, Clarkson said he was no longer sure of Baptist truth. He now believed, "I could not read there was ever any that had power by imposition of hands, to give the Holy Ghost and work miracles . . . I concluded that Baptism to either young or old was ceased."(19) His erstwhile Baptist brothers in Christ were shocked by his evident guilt of the charges and his change of views, "and seeing the vanity of the Baptists, I renounced them and had my freedom."(19)

Becoming a Seeker "who worshipped God only by prayer and preaching"(19) was agreeable to Clarkson's spirit and it was during this phase of his peregrinations that he wrote his first book, *The Pilgrimage of Saints, by Church Cast out, in Christ Found, Seeking Truth*, (1646). This treatise is no longer extant but one can imagine that in it Clarkson described his heroic battle of conscience in being expelled by the Baptists and his having found truth in the Seekers. In any event, Clarkson reports that the volume was well received and won him the respect and admiration of many who stopped him on the street to talk with him.(21)

During his tenure as a Seeker, Clarkson made an important discovery about himself: he was filled with lust. Clarkson wrote that despite his popularity and fame as a man of God, and "notwithstanding I had great knowledge in the things of God, yet I found that my heart was not right to what I pretended, but full of lust . . . [and] I was subject to that sin . . . that I concluded there was none could live without sin in this world."(20)

Clarkson made a meager living as an itinerant Seeker preacher but he was free to live as wished. "I set my cane upright upon the ground and which way it fell, that way would I go,"(21) he wrote. He also enjoyed a very fine social life with the ladies. In Canterbury there "was a maid of pretty knowledge who with my doctrine was affected and I affected to lie with her . . . and satisfied my lust, afterwards the maid was highly in love with me." There was also deceit involved, for "not knowing I had a wife she was in hopes to marry me . . . and would travel with me."(22) Clarkson promised the maid he would return quickly but avoided the city thereafter. In those instances when Clarkson did return to a town he had preached in earlier he "found none of the people so zealous as formerly."(22)

Finally, Clarkson was offered a permanent position in Sandridge in Herefordshire where he was well received "so that I was in heaven again."(23) Less than a year later, having been dismissed for "not being a university man," Clarkson was on the road once again. Never suspecting that his individual sexual ethic may have troubled his congregations, Clarkson lamented, "I was very often turned out of employment."(23) Not understanding why this should have been so, Clarkson was upset for once again Eden proved ephemeral.

Clarkson's continual rejection by various communities proved depressing and he noted "I think there was not any poor soul so tossed in judgment and for a poor livelihood as then I was." Preaching pick-up sermons in Herefordshire, Bedford and Buckinghamshire, Clarkson reported, "by my subtlety of reason got monies more or less."(24)

Intellectually and spiritually depressed, Clarkson no longer found comfort with the Seekers, indeed, "I concluded all was a cheat, yea, preaching itself."(23) Frustrated, angry, depressed and isolated, Clarkson wrote his treatise, *A General Charge or Impeachment*, (1647), one of the most sophisticated pieces of political writing of the age, for the sum of £12. Generally left-Leveller in tone, this treatise was an indictment of England's political, social, and religious institutions and a condemnation of those who call for reform but then justify tyranny when their own interests are satisfied.

Eventually Clarkson received the call from a small congregation in Lincolnshire parish, but found life there unbearably boring. He was saved from the tedium of small town life and uncertainty of the itinerant life by a Captain Cambridge who appointed Clarkson teacher and preacher to his company. Though he called this appointment "the mercy of God to me, my distress being great,"(24) he abandoned his charges at the first opportunity when they travelled to London.

It was in London that Clarkson made first contact with a group called "My One Flesh" as Coppe's London Ranters were known. An unidentified friend introduced Clarkson to the radical publisher Giles Calvert who in turn took him to hear the radical preacher Mary Lake. As Calvert grew confident that Clarkson was not a police informer, he was introduced into the circle led by Abiezer Coppe, the best known London Ranter. Clarkson reports that once again he was taken up with what he heard. "Now observe," he noted, "at this time my judgment was this, that there was no man that could be freed from sin till he had acted that so called sin as no sin. This a certain time had been burning within me yet durst [sic] not reveal it to any in that I thought none was able to receive it."(25) Thus, finding a new circle of friends, Clarkson became a Ranter. Before a large audience he affirmed "there was no sin but as man esteemed it sin, and therefore none can be freed from sin till in purity it be acted as no sin . . . for to be pure all things, yea, all acts were pure."(25)

Demonstrating the oratorical skills that had carried him through life, Clarkson addressed other Ranter assemblies, "making the Scripture a writing of wax, *I pleaded the words of Paul, That I know I am persuaded by the Lord Jesus Christ that there was nothing unclean but as men esteemed it,* unfolding that was intended all acts as well as meats and drinks and therefore till you lie with all women as one woman and not judge it sin, you can do nothing but sin . . . so that I understood no man could attain perfection but this way." (25) Using Scripture in a new more general manner, sort of like wax, Clarkson often preached from Solomon's *Song of Songs*, "supposing that I might take the same liberty as he did."(26)

There is little reason to doubt Clarkson when he reports that he was soon a very effective Ranter preacher and that many came to hear him preach. As we will observe when we analyze his writings, Clarkson had a first-rate mind and was able to express himself with clarity and force. His sermons were evidently unusually effective with the ladies and at one meeting a "Sarah Kuelin, being then present, did invite me to make trial of what I had

LAWRENCE CLARKSON

expressed . . . she invited me to Mr. Wat's [residence] in Road Lane where was one or two more like her felt [*sic*] and as I take it, lay with her that night."(26) The spiritual communion with Sarah Kuelin and friends was so satisfying that Clarkson took up permanent residence in Road Lane to practice his religious calling. He was evidently quite successful and he noted, "I had clients many that I was not able to answer all desires, yet none knew our actions but ourselves."(26)

Up to this time Abiezer Coppe had been the most important Ranter leader in London, a position Clarkson coveted, and he is vehement in his disapproval of Coppe's licentious life. While closing one eye to his own lifestyle, Clarkson complained, "Now Coppe was himself with a company ranting and swearing, which I was seldom addicted to, only proving by Scripture the truth of what I acted."(26) To challenge Coppe, "I was moved to write to the world what my principle was, [and] so brought to public view a book called *The Single Eye [All light, no Darkness]*".(26) Like his earlier efforts, this volume, published in 1650, was successful and Clarkson found even greater acceptance and popularity, "being, as they said, Captain of the Rant, I had most of the principal women come to my lodging for knowledge."(26)

Clarkson was successful in providing a rival to Coppe as a preacher and intellectual but his popularity with the women, especially married women it seems, soon brought him to the attention of the authorities. Though he "was careful with whom I had to do, this lustful principle increased so much that the Lord Mayor with his officers came at midnight to take me."(26) There were other reasons why leaving London as quickly as possible seemed wise. His volume, *A Single Eye*, was causing something of a scandal and even his service to women had become tedious and "at last it became a trade so common that all the froth and scum broke forth . . . that I broke up my quarters and went to the country to my wife where I had by the way disciples plenty."(26) Clarkson evidently saw no contradiction between his promiscuous social life and his fidelity to his spouse for over and again he informs the reader, "I was made still careful [*sic*] for moneys for my wife, only my body was given to other women."(26) And so, if only to permit the London atmosphere to become a little less charged, Clarkson returned to house, home and hearth. And wife.

We might pause for a moment to examine a few of Clarkson's teachings. His notion of redemption through evil, somewhat different than Coppe's, had adherents among ancient and medieval dualists. The strange logic was as follows. In order to store the soul, God had been forced to create Adam's body from mundane matter. According to dualists, this was not a happy arrangement, for the soul and body were alien and yet could not be separated within this lifetime. Consequently, out of confusion, Adam and Eve sinned at the first opportunity. True spirituality was impossible for as long as the soul was forced to reside within the body. Praying could not make the corrupt material body go away, and fasting could not strengthen the already divine soul. Thus, the individual was in the paradoxical position of knowing within the soul that all was evil and yet feeling within the body that all was sexually desirable. Those who would avoid the world through ascetic practice leave the soul in the unfortunate position of never being tested by carnal temptation. In any event, asceticism was an avoidance of the problem, but not a solution to the problem. The denial of the flesh and senses led not to salvation, as some insisted, but to a very frustrated soul unable to cope with the fleshly albatross permanently poisoning its spiritual existence. Some argued that much as the soul was alienated from the body, the soul was also strengthened by its contact with sin. Hence, the more one would sin, the more pure the soul would be. Indeed, the only way to overcome sin within this world was to sin and thereby strengthen the soul. Since everything done *for* the body was sinful but all done to strengthen the soul was necessarily pure, all things done in purity were pure and only an action conceived as sin was sin.

This concept of redemption through evil was more clearly articulated and developed in Clarkson's writings, but even in this brief spiritual biography he attempted to justify his thinking. Like all dualists Clarkson maintained that "the spirit of man while in the body was distinct from God."(28) Hence, human beings were constitutionally alienated from goodness and incapable of morality. As an example, "If the creature had brought into this world no propriety as *mine and thine* there had been no such title as theft, cheat, or lie."(26) Arguing, like Paul, that the existence of the law or prohibition created the crime, Clarkson reasoned, "I apprehended there was no such thing as theft, cheat, or a lie but as men made it so." (27) God could not lie, cheat or fornicate and hence sin was peculiar to fallen, mundane, material mankind. Indeed, all prohibitions against such behavior were human and hence the product of an evil humanity, or as Clarkson wrote, "nothing was evil but as man judged it so." (26) Their disregard was essentially righteous and Clarkson thanked God, who owned no property, for "what great and glorious things the Lord had done in bringing us out of bondage to the perfect liberty of the sons of God."(27) True liberty of the soul did not result from some futile battle against the flesh but when the believer became indifferent to the mores, laws, and conventions of human society which foolishly condemned sin.

102

LAWRENCE CLARKSON

Clarkson also felt justified in participating in the joys of the flesh for other reasons. Like all dualists Clarkson claimed, "When death came it [i.e., the soul] returned to God and so became one with God, yea, God itself." (28) Using typical Ranter imagery Clarkson explained, "even as a stream from the ocean was distinct while it was a stream, but when returned to the ocean was therein swallowed and became one with the ocean."(28) Sin was ephemeral and a function of this corrupted world. It meant less than nothing to the divine soul and to those living within the soul.

Eventually Clarkson grew tired of life with his wife. Since the authorities no longer sought him out, he returned to his Ranter associates. "Mary Midleton of Chelsford and Mrs. Star was [sic] deeply in love with me, so having parted with Mrs. Midleton, Mrs. Star and I went up and down the countries as man and wife spending our time in feasting and drinking."(28) Returning to London, Clarkson officiated over a full Ranter community. "Taverns I called the house of God, and the Drawers [of wine] Messengers; and sack, Divinity; reading in Solomon's writings it must be so in that it made glad the heart of God."(28) Such meetings had a profound religious effect upon participants and "improved their liberty, as where Doctor Pagit's maid stripped herself naked and skipped among them."(28) Being a modest sort, Clarkson would not describe the nature of their communal commitment, but he did note, "Being in a cook's shop, there was no hunger."(28)

Clarkson's fame spread among his supporters and opponents. Parliament issued a warrant for his arrest and set a £100 bounty for his capture. Eventually, a bounty hunter named Jones apprehended him and Clarkson was brought before Parliament to answer for his sexual conduct while in residence at Road Lane. When asked about his promiscuity, Clarkson responded, "I never lay with any but my own wife."(30) Another charge was, "As you were preaching you took a pipe of tobacco, and women came and saluted you and others above were committing adultery."(30) He was also questioned about his treatise *A Single Eye*, and his relationship with Abiezer Coppe and other Ranters as well. The result of the investigation was that his treatise was burned and he was to serve at hard labor and then suffer banishment from England on pain of death. In fact, the sentence was never put into effect and Clarkson was soon preaching in Cambridgeshire, "where still I continued my Ranting principle with a high hand."(32)

If his adversaries hoped that a brush with the law might quiet this free-living Antinomian, they were to be proven wrong and the next few years of Clarkson's life were more riotous than those resulting in his Parliamentary censure. In addition to the gospel of free grace and spiritual libertinism, "I attempted the art of astrology and physic which in a short time I gained

. . . improving my skill to the utmost that I had clients many, yet could not be therewith contented but aspired to the art of magic."(32) Clarkson was soon performing all sorts of miraculous deeds: "I improved my genius to fetch goods back that were stolen, yea, to raise spirits and fetch treasure out of the earth."(32) In performing these feats, "a woman of Sudbury assisted me pretending she could do by witch-craft whatever she pleased."(32)

Despite his own admission that he was involved in a confidence game Clarkson believed that he did have some sort of power. While he admitted "something was done but nothing to what I pretended," he also noted, "I have cured many desperate diseases" and in one instance he was able to cure a bewitched young lady with the result that "it puffed up my spirit and made many fools believe in me."(32) In any event, these activities were lucrative, and "monies I gained and was up and down looked upon as a dangerous man."(32)

Among the fools who came to believe in Clarkson's power was Clarkson himself. He reported that "several times [I] attempted to raise the devil that so I might see what he was, but all in vain so that I judged it was all a lie and that there was no devil at all, nor indeed no God but only nature."(32) In this disaffected mood, Clarkson came to reject many other ideas. The Bible was "no more than a history . . . for when I have pursued the Scriptures I have found so much contradiction."(32) The only belief Clarkson continued to maintain was the general core of Ranter thought, "that which was life in man went into that infinite . . . bulk and bigness, so called God, as a drop into the ocean, and the body rotted in the grave and forever so to remain."(33)

During the next few years Clarkson resumed his religious odyssey. He found Quaker views congenial for "their God, their Devil, their resurrection and mine was [sic] all one," he reported, "only they had a righteousness of the Law which I had not, which righteousness I then judged was to be destroyed."(33) Eventually, in 1657, Clarkson fell under the influence of John Reeves and spent his remaining years as a Muggletonian. His last writings come from this phase of his life.

It is difficult to assess Clarkson's account of his Ranter years. His candor is both refreshing and disarming but it is also possible that he exaggerated the misdeeds of this phase of his life, for *Lost Sheep Found* was written when Clarkson was a Muggletonian. Despite these misgivings, Clarkson's account must be accepted as an accurate portrayal of the lifestyle common at least to London Ranters of the Libertine orientation. Of course, not all Ranters were Libertines. Philosophical Ranters and Revolutionary Ranters, on the contrary, were usually ascetic, living austere lives of self-deprivation and self-denial. If not all Ranters lived so dramatic a life, certainly the community as a whole tolerated such behavior.

Clarkson's writings were as provocative and radical as his life was flamboyant. Indeed, few radicals of his age expressed so biting a cynicism and so sarcastic a rejection of normative social values.

Though his first work, *A Pilgrimage of Saints*, no longer exists, it is possible to piece together the circumstances of its creation from Clarkson's spiritual autobiography and other sources. It would appear that during his Baptist phase, Clarkson developed a fairly large following as a preacher but allegations of immoral conduct with female parishioners led to his incarceration as a serious troublemaker. In January of 1645, Clarkson was imprisoned at Bury St. Edmunds where he was detained for six months and finally released on July 15, 1645. His confinement ended, in part, because Clarkson was willing to renounce his practice of nude dipping. If we recall, Clarkson had been living in the household of Robert Marchant, a wealthy Baptist leader, and one might assume that Clarkson's Baptist colleagues had less than complete faith in his ministry once his moral life was disclosed. It is likely, therefore, that Clarkson's first treatise, *A Pilgrimage of Saints by Church Cast Out*, explained the circumstances of his ejection from both the Marchant household and the Baptist church. The full title indicated that he was no longer a Baptist but a Seeker, and it is likely that Clarkson put the best face possible on his ejection by explaining that it was he who first lost faith in the Baptists rather than the reverse. Shortly thereafter Clarkson was appointed minister to a Seeker community at Sandridge in Herefordshire.

Clarkson's second work, *Truth Released From Prison to Its Former Liberty*, of 1647, defended his reputation as a troublemaker and radical. It is a curious work, less conspicuous for significant ideas than for its attempt to justify the concept of social disruption in general. Thus, even before Clarkson developed his anarchistic ideas, he had already discovered the intellectual means to vindicate the rejection of authority.

The work is dedicated "to the mayor, aldermen, and inhabitants of Preston in Lancaster" and is subtitled "A True Discovery who are the Troublers of True Israel, the Disturbers of England's Peace." The general question posed in this treatise was how a community can determine whether or not an individual is a troublemaker and it is likely that those to whom the work was dedicated were in fact the very people who thought Clarkson a troublemaker. Clarkson noted, "You shall hear the outcry of the people saying, 'These men do exceedingly trouble our city, yea, for preaching the truth, you shall be the men that turn the kingdom upside down.' "(B3a–B3b) As a general rule of thumb, Clarkson provided "that he that is the troubled is the troubler, he that takes offence gives the offence and so the offender."(B8a)

Most people would maintain that he that is offended could not be the offender; that is, the victim of the crime can not be the perpetrator as well. Clarkson disagreed and presented several examples from his own experience to demonstrate his logic. He wrote of one community where a peaceful congregation of Baptists met regularly. Some townspeople were upset by the presence of sectarians in their midst and influenced the constable to look into these dissenters. The officer attended their meetings and found the Baptists a peaceable group offending no one while they went about their devotion. The orthodox citizenry, hearing the constable's report, became incensed and raised a ruckus and a tumult and the officer's professional services were truly required. This led the constable to declare that the Baptists were not the troublemakers but that the leaders of the orthodox community certainly were. (B7a–B8a) Hence, those who were the offended were in fact the offenders as well.

Clarkson cited a second example from within the Baptist community where there was sharp disagreement concerning proper procedure. Some dipped while others sprinkled with neither side content. Since both groups were tolerant, however, they accepted their differences and the general validity of their baptism.(B7a) Had either group been intolerant and caused trouble for the other, they would have been the true troublemakers. From these two examples Clarkson concluded, "Thus dear friends, the conclusion is clear, that the troublers are first troubled,"(B2b) and, "that the disobedient and troublers of Israel do first complain that they are troubled."(A8a)

Clarkson further attempted to bolster his argument through the use of Scriptural examples. Citing 1 Kings 18.17, "Art thou he that troubleth Israel?" Clarkson explained Elijah's relationship with King Ahab. He noted that Ahab called Elijah a troublemaker because "a truth prophesied or preached by poor Elijah, a poor saint, is esteemed a trouble to the nobility of Israel."(A7b) Speaking for himself and Elijah, Clarkson commented, "I (yea I) a poor despised *prophet* am not the trouble of Israel, but thou (yea, thou) *King Ahab* art he that troubleth Israel."(A6) Similarly, "Jeremiah, for prophesying a truth was counted a troubler of Israel, so even the disciples of Christ . . ."(B3a) In more recent times too, Clarkson was pleased to report, "God hath been pleased to call out the poorest and weakest of his saints, adorning them with gifts . . ."(A3a) Clarkson believed these Scriptural examples should convince the most antagonistic reader and he noted, "I hope by this time you are satisfied that my conclusions do not consist of untempered mortar as philosophy only or logic patched together with linsey-woolsey and such like stuff."(B2b)

One technique employed by Clarkson in all his treatises was to present his own views as well as those of his opponent, which he then went on to demolish. In this instance Clarkson presented several popularly held opinions used against him as a troublemaker. One common view was that the majority of the population was troubled by just a handful of wicked troublemakers. Clarkson's answer was that "notwithstanding the prophets of Baal be 450 in opposition to one poor Elijah . . . you shall find that the people of God, the family of love, are not many but few, yea, the fewest of all sects or churches whatsoever."(B5a) Others pointed out that the very best in the community including the powerful, the educated, the governors and others of quality know what is best for the population as a whole. Clarkson countered by asking, "What if he pleases to refute the greatness of the Elders, Scribes, and Pharisees and accept of beggars as Peter and John? What if it please God to reject the nobility of King Ahab and approbate the prophecy of poor Elijah, or poor tradesmen as taylors, weavers, etc? Should this displease you, that [this] is the pleasure of God?"(A3b) Rejecting the view that only the educated knew God's mind Clarkson reasoned, "I say to thee it matters not whether learned or unlearned, whether a tradesman or no. If God hath given thee a *talent,* you must *traffic* with it, as Christ hath . . ."(B4a)

Still another common argument was that the times were troubled while a great reformation was under way, and therefore not proper for dissent. Clarkson asked, "The question is when is the season if not to reprove a child when it offends . . . so it is clear there is no season."(B4a) As for the great reformation currently under way, "Truths should be silent that we understand a reformation . . . I do conceive too, provided that the reformation be *real,* not *verbal,* that under the pretense of Reformation in religion you do not root up religion."(B3a)

Clarkson was convinced that he could not possibly be a troublemaker any more than earlier prophets of God might have been. Like Elijah, Jeremiah, and Jesus, Clarkson believed himself one of God's chosen and obliged to respond as they did in the face of universal condemnation. "Notwithstanding your displeasure herein," Clarkson wrote, "I dare not, I can not but . . . declare unto you, (yea you) *my* countrymen, *my* townsmen, *my* neighbors, and *my* acquaintances . . . *I am engaged to present my light* before you, to traffic with my talent *amongst you* to the end that you may see and acknowledge God."(A3b) He came "to divulge truth in opposition to errors"(B4a) which is never well received. So too with Christ, "for whereas before they applauded him, now saith the text, they were offended by him."(A2b–A3a) Indeed, opposition to him was so great that Clarkson feared, "I may not have the occasion to weep over you as Christ had over Jerusalem saying, O Jerusalem, Jerusalem . . . so that I may not say, O Preston, Preston, thou hast been seduced by blind guides."(A4)

Clarkson saw evidence of corruption all around him. A thorough reformation was needed, but not of the presbyterian verbal sort. "I say, if your reformation be real it must be in truth. So that *truth* prophesied or preached can in no kind be said to hinder further reformation in that truth must be the *foundation*, truth must be the *instrumental* cause; yea, truth must be all in all in a *true reformation*."(B3b)

In his next two treatises, *A General Charge or Impeachment of High Treason* and *A Single Eye All Light, No Darkness*, Clarkson would elucidate upon the content of his commission. Both works were excellent expressions of the Ranter social and religious radicalism.

Radical political treatises demanding wholesale political change were common enough in this age of instability and turmoil, but Clarkson's political treatise *A General Charge* was unusual in at least two senses. First, it was a complete condemnation of English life, directing blows at the many powerful institutions of society. But Clarkson harbored no illusions that the ruling class would disappear simply to please Clarkson and his Ranting friends and he also condemned the common man as well for accepting allegedly "revolutionary" ideology which in fact maintained the power of the preexisting elite. To his credit, Clarkson proposed no simplistic formula reforms through which all of English political life might be made harmonious.

In his letter to the reader entitled "The Speech of Experienced Reason," Clarkson set down the fundamental democratic theories of political power which would serve as a conceptual base to the remainder of the treatise. This was Clarkson's only treatise in which he cited no Scriptural sources, though the influence of Ranter religious thought is evident from the outset. He wrote, "First, know that which giveth Being to a thing is greater than the thing being . . . as the sun above the beam, the fountain above the stream."(1) Hence, "that which giveth power is greater than to whom power is given."(1) Parliament and king might wrangle for supremacy, but with the ascendency of the former, Clarkson asked, "From or by whom had Parliament *their* power or being?"(1) Following his earlier thought he wrote, "From themselves it could not be in that they can not choose themselves . . . therefore from you (yea, you) the Communality of England had the Parliament their rise and origin, by you it was they were chosen and enabled to sit as a Parliament. So that by you they have their power to prosecute, not against you but for you, not to destroy you but preserve you . . . for to that end you have chosen and employed them."(1–2) If such an agency does not fulfill its task, it must be removed, "for from you they derived their authority, therefore unto you they must empty that authority that as without you they could have no power so that at your demand they must give up that power."(2) Theory, as Clarkson was aware, had its limitations, but provided a conceptual foundation.

The reality of power in England was far from ideal. Hypothetically, Parliament "are not your masters but your servants," (1) but in fact, "consider what oppression, what cruelty soever is acted by the Parliament . . . (to wit) Judges, Sheriffs, Committees, Justices of the Peace and Ministers whatsoever, so that what cruelty and tyranny these excercise on you, the Communality, is countenanced by that Parliament, by that power that you the Communality have given them."(2) Unlike others anticipating great change from the Parliament or the army, Clarkson damned both, writing, "The Parliament and the army neglect the great affairs of the Kingdom, through which delays they honor and enrich themselves to the ruin and slavery of the communality."(5)

Governmental ruin of the populace took many forms, the foremost of which was a heavy and repressive system of taxation. "You, the said communality of England," Clarkson wrote, "have suffered heavy and unjust taxations to be imposed on the Communality to the impoverishment and undoing of many of your brethren . . . for the destruction and slavery of the Communality."(5) The worst of these impositions was "that grand oppression of excise . . . when as they have not had so much as bread for themselves, their wives and their children."(6) While the poor paid and paid, "yet to those to whom they were to pay it have not only had a redundance of the best and choicest . . . [but] being the richest, they have paid nothing at all."(6)

Another tax, the tithe in support of the clergy, also fell heavily upon the poor. Clarkson condemned a society which "authorizes a sort of people (to wit) the clergy and impropriators to require a tenth part of your estates as though it were not yours but theirs."(8) Clarkson fumed in recounting how these men of God "demand your corn, your cattle, your cheese, your eggs and your poultry . . . to demand, as they say, their due, their maintenance by way of tithe, protesting it is theirs and not yours." (8) Though there was little difference between government and clergy in their ability to milk the domesticated common cow, Clarkson thought less of the latter for they alone spoke in God's name. Yet, "not one in a thousand, not withstanding their humane arts, are [sic] able to unfold the mystery of divine justice."(9)

The local parish priest, always present to collect his due but never available to perform his duties, does not escape Clarkson's cynicism. "Where is the priest," Clarkson asked, "what is his name, in what parish doth he dwell yet seeks to be your servant and not your Lord?"(9) Even worse than the local priest was the Justice of the Peace, and "experience may teach you none is so much against justice and peace as they . . . not one in a hundred observe what he saith, not one of a hundred of them since the first cause came before them."(7) Like the local clergyman, the Justice of the Peace should serve his constituency's interest, but, Clarkson noted, "They sold it for bribery to the Communality's slavery."(7)

Governing bodies maintained their power through extortion levelled against the poor and defenseless. When, through the press, one attempted "to make known to the community the illegal, confused, and destructive proceedings of Parliament, Army, and Clergy,"(7) Clarkson observed, "They do cause the press to be locked up with a silver key and entrusted the said key with none but such that were true and faithful to injustice."(7) Even that was not the worst of it, however, for the established classes "have prisoned many of the faithful subjects of Justice and Equity for no other cause than endeavoring to free the communality from the insufferable bondage that unjust men have imposed upon the communality . . . [they have been] kept in prison, to lie the space of many years, to utter ruin of themselves, their wives and their children."(8)

Clarkson accounted for the dreadful state of affairs in contemporary England in two ways. The first cause was simple and unvarnished class hatred. Office holders, army officers, and the clergy all represented those owning land, and, Clarkson asked, "Who are the oppressors but the nobility and gentry, and who are the oppressed, is it not the yeoman, the farmer, the tradesman and the laborer?"(11) Generation after generation of class division, Clarkson believed, led to an attitude where "it is naturally inbred in the major part of the nobility and gentry to oppress the persons of such that are not as rich and honorable as themselves, to judge the poor but fools and themselves wise."(11) There were simple reasons why the present served the interests of the rich. Clarkson explained that "your slavery is their liberty, your poverty is their prosperity," (11) and worst of all, "experience may teach you," Clarkson added, "injustice will continue, oppression will reign."(11).

Most radical authors have been content to castigate the evil wealthy and

110

defend the virtuous and righteous poor. Clarkson, however, was too so-phisticated and intelligent to follow in so thoughtless an assessment. It was understandable that the wealthy and powerful would wish to gain and keep their power. Hence, attacking their venality and hypocrisy was easy but also useless. Less clear were the reasons why the poor and despised tolerated such a system when they were so many and the rich so few. Hence Clarkson might condemn the policies of the rich and powerful but it was more important for him to explain why the wealthless and powerless did not use their force of numbers to bring about change.

Clarkson believed that the nobility, through the agencies of Parliament, the church and the army, were able to maintain themselves by convincing the common man that class tyranny was what the commoner wanted and what was in his best interest. Throughout the treatise Clarkson reminded the reader that "the Parliament and Army have done no more than you the communality have permitted them."(13) On the very first page of this work Clarkson wrote, "You, (yea, you) the Communality of England, are guilty of high treason against the law and statute of Justice-Equity,"(1) and again later, "When you oppose them, they oppress you in that you have armed them with your own armor so that if they destroy you, it is by your own weapon."(11) Commoners grumbled and complained about their ill treatment at Parliament's hands but, Clarkson observed, "You, the said communality of England, or the major part of you, have assisted the Parliament in the late unjust actions and held correspondence and intelligence with the Parliament against the law of Justice-Equity."(4)

In sophisticated fashion, Clarkson detailed how commoners aided and abetted their own undoing. He cited several examples of those beliefs and concepts fostered by the wealthy and powerful and accepted by the commoner who then acted to hobble themselves. The most common myth of those years was the argument in favor of an excise tax to support the army. The myth was that "the Parliament in their wisdom found the excise was the readiest way for raising the monies and yet not burdensome to the communality in that it is but small that was required, of wine, beer, cattle and such like things, which could not be prejudicial to any of the communality . . . and yet raise a great sum toward the maintenance of the soldiery then . . . in great need of their pay."(18) According to Clarkson this commonly held belief was so erroneous in so many ways that it was difficult for him to counter it in a single treatise. In fact, Clarkson argued, the excise was "the greatest benefit that ever they invented to beggar the communality and enrich themselves for that is the end for which they raised it, witness the soldiers' complaint of not having been paid so that it is clear they must have it themselves, by which the yeoman is turned a farmer, the farmer becomes poor and the poor turned beggars in so much that the whole kingdom is undone and is in extreme famine."(19) Clarkson conceded that some monies did go toward army salaries, but even then it was the common soldiers "who want necessaries for so hard employment while officers doth brave it out in scarlet, silk, and silver."(5)

Some argued that some form of taxation was needed and the excise could be borne by all alike, that "it was not the communality's doing in the least that any of the poorer sort should be taxed and the rich go free."(17) In reality, however, "men of the greatest estates have paid nothing at all while those that are not able to pay rents were compelled to pay the rich their taxations."(18) Clarkson even doubted that there was a genuine need for an army to begin with. Like most Ranters, Clarkson remained aloof from Parliament's war against the king, arguing instead, "Peace is their war, peace is their poverty, yea, peace is their ruin and by war they are enriched, by war they are honored and promoted to this and that office."(14) This alone was the cause of the civil war.

Organized religion, too, thrived on myth. The myth was that "we find it requisite, so for the body so for the soul, some wise men should be set apart for the prescribing a way for the ignorant to walk in, in that all men are not able to judge of the truth in the historical part of Scripture, not having understanding in the original, (to wit) Hebrew and Greek, without which none, as we conceive, is able to give a true definition of the way, discipline and government of Jesus Christ."(25) Here again Clarkson had grievances against this commonly vaunted myth. As a matter of principle, "It is unjust that such of the communality be forced to maintain . . . another man's faith."(27) On a more practical level there was reason to believe that such regimented religion, even if desirable, could not work. Clarkson asked what was special about "the clergy, as though they were more able than others to find out a way and discipline for the communality, which is as possible as a shoemaker to make a last to fit all men's feet."(25) Moreover, this clerical authority must be ever present in every hill and dale for it was necessary "to have ministers in every parish and that because the communality may not do what is right in their eyes."(26)

The reality of clerical authority was far different. Should every person find God on his own, there would be little need for an organized church or a clergy. Hence there would be no justification for the tithe, and we have already observed that "the clergy and impropriators require a tenth part of our estates, as though it were not ours but theirs."(26) Those opposing the tithe are punished "and thousands better than the parish priest have saluted the gallows."(27) More evil than the army, organized religion "compelled the communality not only in their bodies but consciences, to execute unjust designs one against another, viz. to worship that for God which to them was no God."(5)

No less grievous for the individual or for society was the myth used to muzzle the free publication of opinion. Once again, Clarkson provided the popular rationale why there could be no free press. "We hold the free press for all," the argument ran, "provided the use thereof be not improved to raise division in our kingdom . . . by which the peace of the kingdom is broken. So we think it requisite there should be men appointed to peruse the writings of all men's opinions whatsoever."(23)

Clarkson believed three errors characterized this commonplace. First, control of the press was not imposed to avoid divisions; surely Parliament's actions against the king accomplished this, but out of fear "that thereby their villainy might be discovered."(23) Second, those responsible for intellectual censorship were mediocre. Clarkson observed that "You have chosen a sort of men that have no more wit than a goose or religion than a horse to judge other men's writings, and they alone pass sentence what is orthodox what is not, who are religious and who not."(23) Third, censorship was merely another form of taxation, for "truly, their religion consisteth of little else than fee and bribery."(23) In short, censorship was a literary toll bridge used to tax commoners wishing to write and publish much as other taxes expropriated other areas of human enterprise.

Of the many groups benefitting from the general milking of the common cow, no single group angered Clarkson more than lawyers and judges. The popularly accepted myth justifying their importance to society was no less attractive than other myths but essentially no more meaningful. Presenting this social myth, Clarkson wrote about judges, "It is requisite to be for the decidings of differences among the communality, they being set apart for that work are experts in all points of law, yea, able to judge of matters of controversy . . . we cannot discern how they can enslave or beggar the communality, they having but what is requisite for their pains . . . [and] can not subsist without something from those of the communality."(19)

Once again Clarkson believed that the myth differed from the reality. The justice system was "a fair character of a shell without kernal, yet no other than a cloak for their knavery"(22) involving "Judges, Sheriffs, Attorneys, Solicitors, Sargeants and Promoters . . . to keep terms, Assizes and Sessions by which they enslave and beggar the communality pretending what they do is by the Law, though never so much against it."(19) Clarkson believed that in many instances differing parties might have

113

reached some amicable agreement but "instead of directing them a way of peace and agreements, they [i.e., lawyers] advise them to try it out by the Law and they will assure them damages one against the other, when therein they really intend nothing but to enrich themselves."(20) Lawyers are willing to argue even bad cases for "these said locusts, finding the said parties so grieved, well feathered with gold and silver, they declare that both their cases is [*sic*] good whereas reason may certify you one of them must be at fault, yet this they do to the end they may not put it up betwixt themselves till such time that they have sucked out the sweetness of the case into their own purses."(20) Clarkson was dismayed by such a system of justice, "as though it were impossible to have any piece of justice or equity executed without them" and stoutly defended a far simpler system where "all differences may be debated and ended among the communality themselves."(20)

The collective effect of these institutions upon the lives of English commoners was dreadful. The government taxed, the church taxed, the legal system confounded everything so that those who complained were sent to jail. Parliament passed laws to favor the rich but convinced the commoners the laws were for their own benefit. The commoners applauded their leaders' efforts which "maintain error to be truth and truth to be error, injustice to be justice."(6) In fact, this leadership consisted of "the corruptest of men . . . none were so unjust or malignant as themselves"(6) and should one see through the tissue of lies, they "tell you to your face that they are your magistrates, your ministers, you must obey."(9) Those remaining unconvinced confront a legal system "imprisoning many of the just and faithful subjects of Justice-Equity for no other cause than endeavoring the communality's freedom from insufferable bondage . . . [These] have been kept in prison year after year to the ruin of themselves, their wives and their children."(24)

There was one additional myth which was the most perverted of all those propagated by the wealthy and powerful. When all else failed, the individual possessed the right of petition and could address government when society's institutions seemed to falter. Clarkson noted, "Surely experience should teach you that petitions, though never so prevalent, are not of the virtue to move the hearts of those men . . . yea, how many petitions have you offered and yet where is your expectation answered?"(14) Clarkson added, "O that you could produce that man that will say, 'I had my petition granted, yea, I am the man that had justice done me.' "(14)

Clarkson was not naive and did not believe there would be reform. Historians have criticized Ranters for not proposing a program for change, as did the Levellers, often forgetting that those radicals who did so were usually executed for their efforts. Moreover, England was involved in precisely such a revolution in the name of constitutional liberty and involving programs which succeeded only in creating tyranny and finally the restoration of monarchy. Thus, when Clarkson asked, "What shall we do?" as did other radicals, he seems to have understood the nature of power. "To bear it we can not and to contradict it we dare not and that because we are their tenants, they are our lords, our patrons and impropriators. If we oppose them, they will oppose us, prison us and beggar us. So that the case is clear."(10) Clarkson's pessimism was no doubt very discouraging to many of his readers but surely the wisdom of his words was borne out. A decade later, with Parliament's cooperation, Charles II returned to England without that body requesting a single reform. And the common man once again thought his betters had acted for the best.

Clarkson's powerful religious treatise *A Single Eye All Light, No Darkness* was the flip side of the Ranter coin the political and social attitudes of which were so well expressed in *A General Charge*. Despite differences in theme, both works share the view that truth transcends the usual method of discovery employed by others. Consequently, Clarkson believed that most people were not only wrong but unaware of how to be correct, and he lamented, "The present state of the gentiles, they being then as it were prisoners and in a state of darkness."(1) In religion, as in political life, many people accepted so many slogans and rationalizations that "rare it is to find the creature that is awakened out of his deep sleep, that hath shaken off the covering."(A2a) And again, as in the case of Parliament's revolution which would promise liberty but grant tyranny instead, so, too, in the area of religion, "never was there more superstition, more darkness in the churches than now, therefore never more need to have the light of God expell those dark mists."(1)

Like his Gnostic predecessors, Clarkson believed that mankind experienced earlier periods of blindness where organized religion taught bondage to ritual rather than freedom in the spirit. In one such instance, at the time of the temple in Jerusalem, "in reference to their bondage, Christ, called the Son of God, was promised, to redeem them from the region of darkness, that notwithstanding they had worshipped that for God which was no God."(1) Clarkson was confident that he could lift the veil of darkness for his age and help others shake off their deep sleep. "I do not in the least tremble but rejoice," Clarkson wrote, "that I have this opportunity to declare it unto you, however it may be received by you."(8) In elucidating this truth, Clarkson noted that all conventional forms of authority were useless. "I find the unfoldings of God in this would seem to appear contrary to most that is quoted in the history,"(2) Clarkson observed, adding, "The censures of Scripture, churches and devils are no more than the cutting off a dog's neck."(A2b) Evidently, Clarkson did not care for dogs.

At first glance Clarkson's views appear deceptively simple and seem to bear similarities to Bauthumley's ideas. Explaining that "there is but one God whose name is Light," Clarkson taught that "where God said, 'Let there be light' it was no more than if he had said, 'Let there be God and there was God' for God is light."(3) Similarly, God made the sun and the moon in the heavens and "in the making of these he made nothing but himself."(3) All light, including the stars and even candles, possessed some measure of divinity for "their rise is from the sun, they were but one with the sun; nay, indeed, they were nothing but the sun but after they issued out of the sun, one this way, one that way . . ."(4) Through a process of divine illumination, this divine light became diffused in a variety of ways, created shapes and forms but all reflect divine illumination just as sunbeams when "reduced to their being, they are no longer called a beam but a sun."(4) Different forms and types might appear to be quite different but all are divine. "The light in the creature is not the same light of the sun," Clarkson explained, yet "one is as much divine as the other."(4) "Why may not the whole creation," Clarkson asked, "say with their brother Jacob, 'Surely God were in these and we knew it not?' " (4)

Were light the total expression of existence, God's character would dominate reality but there was also the world of matter which was not divine. "You shall find in Scripture a two-fold power, to wit, more powers than one . . . a power of darkness, a power of light, a power in the wicked, a power on the Godly."(5) The world of matter was as corrupt as the world of light was divine, but Clarkson nowhere explained if matter was in itself corrupting or whether, like Bauthumley, that matter shrouded God's illumination and was therefore corrupting. Within man, the physical body was the material shrouding the soul and hence, "the body hath several denominations as *earthly, dishonorable, weak, vile, etc.*"(13) Because man is both divine and corrupt, "his majesty, the being and operation of all things appeareth in and to the creature under a two-fold form or visage."(A2a) Were man spiritual and immaterial, he could see God's light, and were man merely material, he would not care. Because man is both material and celestial, corrupt and spiritual, he can not differentiate between these two opposite forms of existence which dominate his perceptions of reality and himself.

Within each human being, these two rival forces compete with each other. Like other Ranters, Clarkson could find apt Scriptural images to express these views: "So that consider; though two powers, yet they have but one womb, one birth, so both [are] twins, both brethren, as Esau and Jacob . . . Pharoah and Moses, Pilate and Christ . . . as two streams runneth contrary ways, yet they are but of one nature and that from one foundation."(6) When man pursued wealth or worldly grandeur, this was "the power in Esau in Pharoah, the power in Herod and Pilate by which they crucified Christ . . . this was the power of darkness of sin."(5)

Other dualists, like Coppin, might believe it possible to transcend the world of matter, but the essence of Clarkson's libertinism was the belief that life can not be transcended and that no act of will can wish matter away. Moreover, only human beings experienced existence in both spirit and in matter. Consequently, good and evil were terms that applied only to those who perceived the dichotomy within their being and this did not include God, "for light and darkness are both alike to God,"(2) Clarkson wrote. Pontius Pilate and Esau lived within the flesh and cared not at all for the spirit, while Jacob and Christ lived within the spirit and overcame the material world. Thus, perception of the world was fundamental and "it is called darkness but only to the creature's apprehension, to its appearance; so nothing but imagined darkness."(6) Elsewhere too Clarkson attempted to explain that evil was a perception of the universe: "It *appeareth* but a darkness in the creature's apprehension, so but an imagined darkness."(2) What then was imagined sin?

Clarkson's theory of sin was the most radical presented by any Ranter. Essentially, Clarkson dismissed sin as a fiction. "The very title sin," he informs the reader, "is only a name without substance."(9) Concerning the variety of behavior found objectionable by most religions, he wrote, "There is no act whatsoever that is impure in God or sinful with or before God . . ."(7-8) Acts of deceit and all forms of antisocial behavior were shrugged off as meaningless for all "those acts called swearing, drunkenness, adultery, theft, etc. these acts, simply as acts are not as they are called (and by thee imagined) Drunkenness, Adultery, and Theft, that is, in and from thy imagination . . . by which thou apprehendest and esteemeth them to be acts of sin."(9) Indeed, Clarkson courted the outrageous when he asserted that "these acts, simply as acts, were produced by the power of God, yea, perfected by the wisdom of God."(8) And a page later he reiterated that "by his power and wisdom thou executest this act and that act."(9)

Clarkson was not the only Ranter to diminish the significance of sin, but only he was willing to make God responsible for all human weakness. "What said I," he asked in mockery of orthodox objections, "a swearer, a drunkard, an adulterer, a thief, these had the power and wisdom of God to swear, drink, whore and steal? O Dangerous Tenant! O blasphemy of the highest nature! What? Make God the author of sin? So, a sinful God."(8) Even more offensive to conventional sensitivities, Clarkson, asked, "Was it not a sinful act to crucify Christ? That I know you will all conclude it was a wicked act, and yet this act was according to the will of God."(5) A page later Clarkson reiterated that "this power in Pilate was a dark sinful power, yet it comes from God: yea, it was the power of God."(6) If sin did not truly exist, it followed that "these acts, yea, nakedly as acts, are nothing distinct from the acts of prayers and praises . . . no more holiness, no more purity in the one than the other."(9) The difference between them was how they wished to perceive themselves and how they chose to act. Hence, "again and again it is recorded that to the pure, yea, all things are pure, but to the defiled, all things are defiled."(10) As a result, if one acted out of good intentions, one's deeds were so judged, "so that consider, what act so ever is done by thee in light and love is light and lovely, though it be that act called adultery."(10) Since intentions and not deeds determined true righteousness and goodness, "to that man that so esteemeth one act unclean, to him it is unclean (as saith the history) there is nothing unclean of itself but to him that esteemeth it unclean."(10)

Since intentions and conscience were the only bases for distinguishing good from evil, unfortunate persons with plagued consciences can find redemption and relief only through acting out sinful behavior with a better mental attitude. In short, redemption from evil deeds and evil thoughts can come only through the practice of those evil deeds. "Sin must not be thrown out," Clarkson warned, "but cast within, there being in the vat it is dyed of the same color of the liquor, as safron converts milk to its own color, so doth the fountain of light convert sin, hell, and devil into its own nature and light as itself."(12)

Clarkson's views were certainly controversial to non-Ranters and might be condemned by the provisions of the Blasphemy Act. Clarkson, however, expressed distaste for those who would judge him and find him lacking. He wrote, "No matter what Scripture, saints, or churches say, if that within thee do not condemn thee, thou shalt not be condemned for saith the history *Out of thine own mouth*, not another's, *will I judge thee*."(12) Other sects might teach a variety of rituals but Clarkson warned, "One man esteemeth one day above another, another esteemeth every day alike. What is to one pure to another is impure; herein appeareth but a bare estimation."(9) All such practices were idols or fetishes and Clarkson advised, "Say with the apostle, *we know that an idol is nothing*."(11)

Clarkson's religious views expressed a combination of moral anarchism, strong individualism and even an element of existentialism. Each individual comprised a total religious universe responsible to and for himself alone. No authorities or sources could be of benefit to anyone and even the judgments of friends and colleagues could be harmful. Clarkson warned, "Neither canst thou upon the bare report hear of say, 'Well, if it be as [this] man esteemeth it, then I will esteem it so too.' Alas friend, let me tell thee. Whatever thy tongue saith, yet thy imagination in thee declares sad things against thee in that [if] thou esteemeth them acts of sin, thy imagination will torment thee for this sin in that thou condemnest thyself, thou art tormented in that condemnation with endless misery. So that happy is the man that condemns not himself in those things he alloweth of."(11)

Every individual, whether he wished it so or not, was condemned to freedom because there was no higher authority. After reiterating that "there is nothing that I do that is unclean to me, no more than it is unclean of itself,"(11) Clarkson reminded the reader "that if thou judge not thyself, let thy life be what it will be, yea, act what thou canst . . . but if the reproach and slander of saints and churches do cause thee to question thyself, then thou art ready to say within what they report without, 'I am guilty of what they accuse me.' "(12) When one accepts the criticism of others and converts this condemnation into guilt, all is lost, "so that true is the saying, *O Adam, thy destruction is of thyself.*"(12)

Clarkson's other religious views were well within the tolerances of Ranter thought. Writing "where else is heaven but in our present peace" (opening poem) Clarkson rejected the resurrection as "a palpable tenet of darkness." If neither the soul nor the body could be dispensed with in this hellish material life, it made little sense to have both in some spiritual nonmaterial heaven. Indeed, "It is destructive for the fowl to live in the water or the fish in the firmament, so to raise the body to a local place called heaven would to thy body become a hell."(13) Hence, "Look not above the skies for God in heaven," Clarkson taught, "for here your treasure lies, even in these forms."(poem)

Clarkson's treatises were uncommonly seditious. Though he called for no revolution and presented no program for violent change, Clarkson's views demonstrated the poverty of political reform and the bankruptcy of common political mythology. Indeed, even the call for reform would lead only to new forms of tyranny justified with yet newer sorts of popular mythology. In the end, the common man would suffer as he always had suffered.

Clarkson's religious views may not have rivalled existing dogma, but they were an acid bath sure to corrode the social and intellectual fabric of any organized religious policy. That evil existed in the mind of evil people might explain why Puritans found evil in so many places and why Parliament acted so poorly. Both government and church were true troublemakers because they found trouble all over. Rituals, practices, fasts and feasts were all created to foster some feeling of guilt which might find amelioration only through the efforts of a tithing clergy. Monarchy might disappear and the Church of England might be disbanded, but taxes, the tithe, and arbitrary and repressive authority would remain.

The righteous individual seeking the path to goodness need look only within himself to determine whether his actions, carried out with good intentions, were good or evil. Those plagued by pangs of conscience were advised to internalize their sin, for redemption came not from avoiding evil but from confronting evil and personalizing it. Those given to actions condemned by others, whether it be drinking too much or loving one's neighbor too literally, were told to continue in their action in love. Those confused by the plethora of religious choices facing the Christian were told that no one knew anything about God and, in any event, God was not concerned with the little rituals performed by man. Drinking or praying, fornicating or praising, it was all one to a God who merely wished to spread his divine light through the world.

Clarkson was no empty prophet mouthing empty words. Surely his life as we know it was adequate testimony to his willingness to live what he preached and suffer jail for preaching these beliefs. His amoral writings, an ability to preach effectively and a charismatic personality all help explain why Clarkson was Captain of the Rant.

Parliament took Lawrence Clarkson very seriously. On September 27, 1650, the Committee for Suppressing Licentious and Impious Practices labelled *The Single Eye* an "impious and blasphemous book." Further, Parliament resolved, "That the said Lawrence Clarkson be forthwith sent to the House of Corrections, there to be kept at labor for one month and from that time to be banished out of this Commonwealth and the territories thereof, and not to return upon pain of death." Further, it was "resolved by the Parliament that the book called *The Single Eye* and all printed copies thereof, be forthwith seized and burned by the hand of the common hangman . . . that all and every person and persons whatsoever who have in their hands or custody any of the books entitled *The Single Eye*, or printed copies thereof, be, and are required and enjoined forthwith to deliver the same to the next Justice of the Peace . . . to be publicly burned."

Clarkson may have gone to jail for a month's labor but he was not banished. Indeed, his subsequent life, as retold in his *Lost Sheep Found*, described this period as the most tumultuous in Clarkson's career as he added astrology and magic to his repertoire of preaching aides.

After a respite of almost a decade Clarkson's writings again flooded the radical book market. By this time, however, his ideas had changed considerably and he emerged from his Ranter phase a very different person. Somehow Clarkson lost his sense of individuality, his intellectual clarity and strength of personality. He fell under the spell of John Reeves, a former Ranter turned prophet and disciplinarian, and joined his sect. When Reeves died shortly thereafter, Clarkson fought Reeves' cousin, Ludwig Muggleton, for control of this independent church. He was beaten in this battle for supremacy and the sect soon became known as the Muggletonians, in large part because the latter had been able to forge the sect around himself as a tight cult of personality. Clarkson was permitted to remain within the fold but only should he agree never to write again and concede that Ludwig Muggleton alone enjoyed the status of divine prophet. Agreeing to these humiliating conditions, Clarkson was quiet for several years but he did eventually take up his pen by the end of the fifties to write the boring and tedious works alluded to earlier in this section. We will next meet him again in a later section of this volume devoted to anti-Ranter writings.

7. Anonymous

Were Clarkson's and Coppe's writings the sole expressions of Libertine Ranter literature, it would be easy to conclude that this tendency consisted of madmen like Coppe and charlatans like Clarkson. Fortunately, the integrity of this special branch of Rantism can be vindicated by an author who was neither a madman nor a charlatan. Moreover, this sane and sincere author was very much aware that others thought Libertines mad and wrote his treatise to justify Libertinism from such charges. Unfortunately, we do not know this author's name, though the treatise makes clear that the combination of a sexually permissive morality and a very radical social platform was the province of more than the weird and insincere.

Anonymous' treatise *A Justification of the Mad Crew in Their Ways and Principles* of 1650, is conceptually well developed and surpasses the writings of Clarkson and Coppe in all but literary style and sheer amusement. What it lacks in literature is more than compensated for in the sheer radicalism of its content.

Anonymous' conversion experience would appear to be very similar to those described by other Ranters. He was born into an orthodox family and only much later in life experienced a personality-shattering divine illumination which dramatically changed his life. About his earlier life he wrote, "It pleased the Lord . . . to train me up in the childish things where I was pleased with his back-parts . . . and truly I must needs confess that I had great joy and satisfaction in this estate."(22) This condition of ignorant bliss did not continue indefinitely. "One day, the day of God's wrath and vengeance fell upon me and burnt up all my childish things," he explained, "and there was such an everlasting fire about my ears that I could keep nothing I had but was burned up both body and soul with all that I had, righteousness, holiness, preaching, teaching, prayers, wife, children and all that I had ."(22–23)

Stripped of all religious pretense and familial relationships, the author was spiritually denuded by God coming as a thief in the night. Rather than experiencing any pleasure from his spiritual awakening, the author explained that he felt only grief and depression for "by this fire I then (by God) began to be plagued with my holiness and my prayers became sin to me and all things a burdon."(23) In this crisis of identity and faith, and perhaps a midlife crisis as well, "my former joys became my sorrows and my pleasure torments, and I was a spectacle to myself and to all about me. I wondered where I was and I fell down dead."(23) Only later did the author come to understand why God had appeared so suddenly and why so violent a conversion experience was necessary. Speaking in Christ's name, as Libertines were wont to do, the author wrote that such violence was required "that I might thereby damn, ram, and plague you into myself who am Jesus the Son of God."(A3b)

After losing family, friends, and possessions, the author eventually came to his senses when "the power of God set me on my feet . . . and then I looked and could see nothing but purity."(23) Having been damned, rammed and plagued into Christ, the author felt a new spiritual peace where "I have been made to see a blessing in everything. The earth hath ceased to bring forth briars and thorns to me and the curse to me is taken away."(25) In this illuminated state God, or "that within me said, 'Call thou not anything common or unclean for I have made all things clean for thee.' "(23) The author recounts how in this state he could finally read Scripture and understand its central message. "Sayeth the history," he explained, "to the pure all things are pure"(8) and "I looked and could see nothing but purity."(23)

The author's new spiritual awareness had dramatic results within his daily life. "I had never sworn, been drunk or given to any outward prophaneness [sic] or looseness in all my life,"(23) he explained, but "I have sometimes since then been (as I have formerly called it) unclean and yet never more clean; uncivil and yet never more civil; I have been since then a great transgressor and yet never a less transgressor."(25) Anonymous' life had been turned upside down with a previous identity gone and a new one gained. "I have lost all things and I have found all things, my loss being my gain and my death my life. I am come to the spirits of just men made perfect, to Abraham's spirit, to Moses', to David's spirit, Daniel's, Paul's and John's spirit. I familiarly talk with them and they with me."(26) In this spiritual resurrection, "death is swallowed up in victory. O Death, where is thy sting? O Grave, where is thy Victory?"(13) the author queried.

In the language of those who know the truth, the anonymous author explained, "There is none good but one, this is God, and that whoever calls anything good, unless God, and so hugs it to himself as good, falls down to an idol and worships a lie, that which his own fingers have made."(A3b)

Worshipping the produce of one's hands would appear foolish and yet all society, Anonymous claimed, worshipped foolish material possessions as if they were divine. Writing in God's voice and using words reminiscent of Coppe, the author noted, "The Earth is mine and the beasts on a thousand hills are mine"(18) and directed to society's leaders, "You hypocrits, why do you call anything you own? Why do you say, 'So much I have, so much land, so many children, such a woman is *my* wife.'"(16–17)

The author explained that human possessiveness was a result of events in Eden. Initially, "Man, innocent, holy, upright man, tasting of the tree of Knowledge of good and evil, comes to divide and separate that which God had joined together and thereby became accursed, calling one holy, another unholy."(7) Human possessiveness, or what the author calls the spirit of division, was the root social evil. Humans venerated accumulated wealth, he explained, "I could tell all of you that money is your god, that all your care, industry, pains, is to get and keep this god money."(3) All distinctions between people were arbitrary social inventions created by a few for their own glorification at the expense of others. The author explained that the world had been created for the use of all equally. "The rich and the poor are both made by God," he explained, "the saint and the sinner, they have one being, one fountain, one source and rise."(9)

Elsewhere Anonymous condemned the organized ministry: "You righteous men are in hell and at a distance from heaven and can not by all your holiness, prayings, preachings, reach this heaven."(11) Asking in mocking tones, "Would you know God? To Jerusalem you must go."(A2) To reach heaven one needed no benedictions, no rituals, and no priesthood. One had merely to give away one's wealth and undo the spirit of division. "I say, come give me your money, your land, your wives, your children," the author preached, "call it our money, our wives, our children, our table, our meats, our drink."(18)

Those preaching common ownership of property are called madmen and Ranters "hold all things in common and truly enjoy all things in common."(16) Consequently, "they are named the Mad Crew, but so was Paul a mad man, one that turned the world upside down, so was Christ a devil, yea, the Prince of Devils."(1) The apostles, also a mad crew, "on whom the sprinklings of the spirit fell were (as saith the scripture, which you profess to own) made to see and act in this community, Acts 2:44–45 nay, they call nothing they possessed their own."(16) The author asked the reader, "Go and sell all thou hast and come and follow me who am numbered among the rogues, thieves, whore masters, and base persons of the world. Cast away your bags of money, your riches, your substance, your trades, your wives, your children. Be without a horse and without a home, to know not where in the morning to lay your heads at night."(3) Wherever such madmen have lived, "these wicked men, as you call them, are singing,

124

rejoicing, feasted with the everlasting of fat things."(11) Those who trust in God's bounty will not want, for "there is meat enough in our father's house . . . it is a full house, a rich house."(18)

The anonymous author devoted considerable space to describing the saintly lives of the Ranters. "Those who shall be accounted worthy of the world to come and the resurrection from the dead, viz., dead carnal cursed apprehensions and concernments, never marry, never join or disjoin, never love one and hate another . . . but they have the same pure perfect entire love to one as the other."(14) Consequently, "these creatures," the Ranters, "are married to all, every woman is their wife, not one woman apart from another, but all in one and one in all . . . lie with one another every night, the bed is large enough to hold them all."(15) Acting out of true saintliness, "They can not kiss one but they kiss all and love one but they love all and can not take one to bed with them and leave out another."(15) In this spirit of apostolic common ownership the author added, "Every woman is my wife, my joy and my delight."(18)

Other aspects of Ranter behavior such as swearing, whoring, and drinking also elicited universal condemnation. In fact, "the sons of God when they eat, eat God and when they drink, drink God, that they walk in God and tread upon God and are covered with God. They swear in God and abstain from swearing in God; that they live one with another in God and are not ashamed because God is in them. That they whore in God, that God is the whore and the whore master."(A3) Such activities might be considered sinful by some Christians, but there is no sin for Ranters: "This is taken away and they can sin no more."(12) All others worship their man-made gods through man-made rituals, but the Ranters "like little children they can play together, lay [sic] together, dance together, drink together, eat together, and yet think no evil, do no evil."(A3a) Consequently, all Ranter activity is the height of spirituality for "they serve God and he serves them . . . [they] serve him in hell, . . . in the taverns, in the ale houses, in a whore house and thus he is in these things served and yet spiritually."(6) Conducting himself in this fashion, the Ranter "contains him, hugs him, nay is really and truly God, even the living God."(A2b)

This anonymous libertine message was unusual for rarely was God adoringly called a whore and a whore master. It is perhaps for this reason that the author of this treatise declined to add his name to the treatise. And yet, most of the ideas this author presented were not really outrageous. Spiritual religion, common ownership of goods and a free sexual ethic are the hallmarks of radical sects and political groups in all ages.

BLASPHEMY, IMMORALITY, AND ANARCHY

Anonymous shared much with Abiezer Coppe. Both condemned private property, understood Eden as heaven, and original sin as possessiveness. Both wrote in praise of sexual liberty and the return of God's possessions "on a thousand hills" to poor people but most of all, both called themselves rogues and a friend of whores. London was large enough for more than one Libertine author but it is also possible that Anonymous was Abiezer Coppe.

Revolutionary Ranters

8. George Foster

Revolutionary Ranters combined Ranter religious ideas with an ardent desire to see England and the world destroyed. This destruction might be part of some apocalyptic scheme, as in George Foster's case, or part of a system of divine progressive revelation where such contemporary events as the civil war and execution of Charles I were positive steps in the process of divine destruction. Other Ranters too wrote of the coming great day of divine wrath but revolutionary Ranters differed in that this destruction was often the central theme of their message.

George Foster was a most outspoken revolutionary Ranter. His two treatises of 1650, *The Sounding of the Last Trumpet* and *The Pouring Forth of the Last Vial*, condemned contemporary property relations, government, and religion and gleefully looked forward to the coming destruction. Though the works were published within a few months of each other and present some of the same ideas, they differ in several respects. The first is chaotic, presenting most ideas in incomplete and sloppy fashion, while the second is better organized, more thoughtful, and more nearly complete. Both writings are important in understanding Foster's bizarre ideas and bizarre is the only term aptly describing them. Other than these two treatises, nothing is known about Foster himself or his relations with other Ranters.

The cover page of *The Sounding of the Last Trumpet* indicates the volume consists of "several visions declaring the universal overturning and rooting up of all Earthly powers in England . . . which shall come to pass in this year 1650." The several dozen visions in this volume commenced January 14, 1650, continued for well over two months and presented a vivid description of what Foster believed was about to occur.

Foster writes that he awoke in the middle of the night of January 14 to the sound of music and began to tremble and shake very violently. He began to laugh uncontrollably, indeed, "so heartily that I scarce ever laughed so heartily before."(5) Finally, a voice declared, "I am come to torment thee, to consume and burn thee up to nothing," which scared Foster and "I cried out that I was in hell."(6) Later visions were often so violent and were accompanied by convulsions so serious that Foster requested that his friends sit on him and tie him to his bed so that he would not be injured.(18, 40, 44ff)

The visions themselves took two forms. At times God would speak directly to Foster and impart some truth in direct conversation. More often, however, God would show Foster an image and ask him what he saw. Foster would describe the images in detail and God would them explain their meanings. The two formats were used interchangeably with little bearing on the content of the vision, though the latter format was often more graphic and dramatic.

Foster's love of vivid imagery is apparent in all his visions though the images often seem to have little relation to the content of the vision itself. Among the more common images he saw were angels that call other angels, angels with sickles, and angels with books. Natural images included dogs, pigs, horses of various colors and sizes, roaring waters, oceans, winds, trees, rivers, rainbows and mountains. Other images include iron rods, armies, women in dresses of various colors, men with swords, set tables, temples, cities and scores of people involved in a great many activities. Mystical images of a more conventional nature are also employed and include seven torches, seven trumpets, seven angels, seven chariots and a bush seven feet high.

Foster's message often seems independent of the many varied, colorful and dramatic images he employs. In one instance Foster saw the sun, moon and stars fall to earth and turn to blood with a company of swine and dogs appearing to lick up all the blood. God explains this vision in the following manner. "And by this heaven and the stars and the sun and the moon mentioned in Scripture turned into blood, is meant, all outward administrations as forms, governments and rulers and ways of worship which have been as lights that people have seen something of God in . . . and by the dogs and swine licking them up is nothing but a total extinction of them that they may be no more."(26) In another vision Foster saw a temple enveloped in billows of smoke. Upon asking the meaning of the vision, Foster was told that the temple is God's shrine and the billows of smoke "are all the ways of worship, forms and government which by wit of man are set up."(24) In yet a third vision Foster saw a throne, "and I asked, what is meant by this throne? and the Lord said, by this throne is meant my sons and daughters."(20) A page later Foster added that the throne was also a symbol for "all earthly powers, governments, forms and ways of worship, all outward administrations."(21) When Foster saw a great city he was told it is Rome, "that is, the laws, forms and customs."(22) Indeed, because "this city is forms, laws, governments and ways of worship which is in all nations and so is the spiritual Sodom and Egypt that crucified my son and hath from time to time murdered my saints."(22)

It must be clear to the reader that a great many things reminded Foster of laws, ordinances, forms and governments, ways of worship and administrations. This theme dominated much of Foster's thought and there is hardly a single page without some reference made to these institutions. God's prescription is the same in all instances. In the case of Rome, "I have sentenced this city to be burnt for I the Lord of Hosts do burn up and consume all forms and governments of men."(22) Or, more generally, "So this is the ultimate end of burning up all the forms and ways of worship and rules of men, that they may see that they have not had me to be their foundation . . . and see me to be their lives and their all in all."(28) God is hate filled, vengeful, angry and comes to punish devilish man and not to redeem the soul or the saint. As we shall see, this awesome sense of divine wrath and vengeance fuels Foster's visions.

In general, Foster's religious thought is consistently Ranter, though somewhat bloodier. God is defined as the universal idea behind all existence. "I, who am the life and fullness of all things," God tells Foster, "have been always the life of all creatures and the life of man and have been in man but not known to be there, but have been covered under the clods of proud flesh."(30) Within man, God is "the soul, which is the life of the body, which life is my own invisible being."(53) Like Coppin and Bauthumley, Foster too observed how God "had a long time been in me buried under the clods of proud flesh and I was ignorant of him . . . yet he did dwell in me and was the life of me."(1) Death will bring the final resting, for "their bodies are returned to earth from whence they came,"(53) while the soul "returns to its center." The resurrection is not the rebirth of the physical body, but in common with Ranter thought Foster maintained, "The resurrection in Scripture mentioned is not a resurrection of the body out of the earth, but a resurrection of the body from darkness to light, from wrath of me to the love and favor of me."(54-55)

The appearance of God in the soul has much the same meaning for Foster as for other Ranters. He wrote, "It is such a change in you that those things that you thought were unlawful before will now appear lawful . . . sin and transgression being finished with you and everlasting righteousness brought into you."(15) In yet other places Foster emphasized that God's "saints shall see that they shall no longer commit sin."(30) These saints understand the folly of organized religion for "they shall know how to worship me which will be without ordinances and forms, only waiting for me to teach them and no longer to wait upon the teaching of man."(37)

The individual saint thus liberated from his physical being and from all social restraints, obligations of the law, all ritual of any type becomes an angel, a term largely misunderstood. "My sons are angels and ministering spirits, they are angels," Foster wrote, "And the angels mentioned in Scripture are no other than my sons and daughters. And the two angels that came to Lot in Sodom were but two men but because I made them my messengers, they were called angels."(34–35) In all of these views Foster was well within the common Ranter consensus.

The bulk of Foster's first treatise concerns property relations, government, and social and religious institutions in order to explain how and why God must destroy everything. Early in the treatise Foster wrote, "O Earth, earth, earth, hear the word of the Lord and tremble thou earth at the presence of the mighty God of Jacob, for behold, he comes to take vengeance on his enemies."(A2a) Foster is not reticent about identifying the enemies of God and their fate. Over and again we read, "All power shall become as nothing and the mighty and great men, as kings and Lord, . . . shall run into the holes of the rocks and into the dens of the earth hide themselves for fear . . . and all the earth shall become dung before him."(A2a–b)

More than other Ranters, Foster was excited about the civil war and execution of the king but became depressed when Parliament did not destroy government and other institutions. Still, there were some promising signs at first. Foster described a vision in which a southern and a northern army met on a field of battle with the southern army winning a great victory. Afterwards, the southern army "marched away presently to London and searched a great house, pulling those that were in it out of it."(7) This apparent reference to Prides' Purge had Foster's blessing for he believed God was using the army as "my instruments to destroy all power and to bring to nothing those that are in power."(7)

Cromwell, too, appeared in Foster's visions and at first this great leader enjoyed God's support for what Foster understood as God's commission to the army. "And I saw the general and his officers sit as a Parliament in the room of the others and did promise that they would now restore freedom to the people. And I saw the general and his officers go into the halls where money was and threw it to the soldiers and the soldiers had so much that they gave it away to the poor and I heard the poor say one unto the other, these are joyful days . . . there may be universal love and freedom and want shall cease."(11)

130

Alas, Parliament soon took control of the army and oppressed the people in the manner of the previous government. Foster explained that "the Parliament hath pretended to change times, that is, to take off the oppression of people and laws."(38) Indeed, under the name of reform, Parliament actually increased governmental tyranny and "though King Charles did oppress the people with ship money which he should not have done and so he did show his cruelty and tyranny, yet the Parliament hath exercised as much cruelty upon the people as he did. For as Charles laid his little finger upon the people, the Parliament hath laid their loins and for matter of oppression of the people have been far more cruel than Charles ever was before."(37–38) Foster was thoroughly unimpressed by Parliament's activities for clearly they ignored God's mandate that they "shall wholly deny themselves from usurping a power over others, as to make laws for others to walk by."(7) Parliament was the most ungodly of England's revolutionary institutions and Foster repeatedly referred to it as the "beast" and the "anti-Christ" and noted that it "must be burned or destroyed."(39) Foster was convinced that this evil body would not long thwart God's plan and he predicted, "The Parliament shall be destroyed and brought to nothing before January next [i.e., 1651],"(43)

Like other Ranters, Foster expressed a burning hatred for organized religion. Calling priests and ministers "locusts that devour the fruits of the earth" and "spiritual merchants," Foster noted that religion "made merchandise of the souls of men and all this they have done pretending they did preach to bring them to heaven."(34) The religion of the churches is predicated upon the power "to make laws for them to worship God by, as they call it, and so poor creatures have been deluded by them to worship something but the priests know not what."(33) The purpose of these laws and ordinances "was more for their fat benefices than to bring souls to me, as they have made it appear to be."(34) Consequently, despite changes in government and religious structures, little else changed and "instead of being governed or having bishops, we must now have classes and presbyters."(38)

The propertied classes, landowners in particular, were also great enemies of God. In one vision God declared to Foster, "All is mine, saith the Lord of Hosts, all the beasts of the fields and all the riches of the world are mine and not thine. And though I have lent thee them, and thou having not made a right use of them, I take them from thee and give them to thy fellow creatures for their use as well as thine for when thou hadst these things as I have now taken from thee, thou madest them but instruments of cruelty to thy fellow creatures."(42) In the end, the mercenary of spirit will gain nothing for their efforts, "for it shall be that they that have strived for honor and greatness and have laid up bags of gold and silver for 5 or 12 or 20 or 30 or 40 years together, shall have no more than he that hath not laid up anything at all."(41) In one of Foster's visions, "I beheld a man in gay clothes and he had a bag in his hand and he put his other hand and took all the money that was in it and threw it about so long as any was in it. And thus shall all misers in time throw away their money that they have hoarded up."(45) It may have been naive for Foster to imagine the wealthy throwing their wealth away to the poor, but no other more realistic plan of property distribution has ever been actually instituted.

Foster believed that society would return to the pristine and equitable conditions of Eden once the many abuses of the existing order were eliminated. In one vision Foster saw God's sons and daughters dancing, with the explanation that "all things with them become new, former things passed away."(9) In many locations Foster indicated that God's purpose was "to restore the whole creation from bondage and slavery into glorious liberty."(15) When this came about, God would "restore the creation to the first estate, as Adam was set in, that as I made Adam lord over all creatures and all creatures were for the use of Adam (saith the Lord) so now shall all the creatures, men and women, have that privilege . . ."(16) It may have been naive to anticipate Eden, but then Cromwell was not naive and did not anticipate Eden; he created the first modern military dictatorship which led to the reestablishment of monarchy. At least Foster did not do that.

Foster hated the rich so much that he was willing to make a major alteration in Ranter thought to accommodate this hatred. It rankled Foster that the souls of the rich, like those of the poor, would join God at death. In one location Foster demanded of God, "What is to become of the wicked that have ceased if there be no hell nor no other life?"(53) If indeed the rich collected gold in this life and enjoyed God in the hereafter, they would have gotten the best of both worlds. Foster, however, found a way to maintain Ranter views of heaven and hell and the return of the soul to God, and still punish the rich.

Foster's problem was that there was little left to punish if the body decayed and the soul returned to God. Hence, Foster elucidated upon the spirit of man. Foster explained that "the spirit and the soul being two distinct [entities], the spirit of a man it is that is and shall be tormented."(53) Unlike the soul which is divine in origin, the "spirit, which is his conscience, that is, compounded of reason, wisdom, and knowledge, and so proceeds from man, and is called the spirit of a man, shall be tormented forever and that in a body though it be not in the same body."(53) Teaching a variant of the transmigration of souls—which applied only to the spirit and not the soul—Foster taught that when a person died the body rotted and the soul returned to God. The spirit, however, "as soon as it comes out of one man where I the God of Gods do not rule, it goes into another wicked man and there acts the same things which it did in the first."(53) Once in a new body, the spirit will be tormented by God with Foster gleefully noting, "I will be such a terror to the wicked that they shall be afraid of me and shall howl for sorrow and grief."(52)

There was one potential catch in the system. If evil continued to live in each succeeding generation and repeated itself with even greater force, each generation presented an increasing balance of the evil of the past with less and less possibility of reform as time went on. The fact that there was no possibility that society could improve and every probability that it would become increasingly corrupt may explain why the world must be destroyed. To accommodate these problems, Foster added another novel element. "There are some things in the likeness of hens or dogs or anything else that can speak . . . these are the spirit of wicked men whom I can make in any shape."(54) Surely no one would wish to return as a chicken or a dog, about whom Foster wrote, "Dogs are a most beastly creature and seem to be creature good for little . . . for all dogs are cruel and envious and are ready to destroy themselves by fighting with one another . . . always grumbling and snapping at one another."(21, *Pouring Forth*). Foster did not elaborate upon the personality of chickens, but there is little doubt that he thought much the same of them.

Foster's first religious treatise was fragmentary, often incoherent, and unsystematic. His criticism of government and other institutions was less thorough than Clarkson's for the latter explained what was wrong and also why people permitted the situation to remain unchanged. Foster's religious views were scattered all over the treatise with little bits here and there that can be pieced together only after one becomes familiar with the general outlines of Ranter thought and has read Foster over and over. Fortunately, Foster's second treatise was far better in all these deficient areas. Indeed, *The Pouring Forth of the Last Vial* is a good piece of revolutionary writing. Many of the ideas of the first work are presented in far more coherent and systematic fashion and many new interesting ideas not found in other Ranter writings are presented for the first time. Moreover, the structure of the visions and the use of imagery are clearer and more hard hitting than in the first work published just months earlier.

The second treatise consists of about a dozen visions, which, Foster tells the reader, came from God and were "so burning hot and powerful that I have not been able to resist as to keep them in secret . . . I was forced to write them, it being the good pleasure of my Father for to make choice of me, so poor and unable a despised instrument, to reveal and make known such things as shall surely come to pass." (1 Epist.#1) All the visions came to Foster "in a trance and lying dead for almost 22 hours."(1)

Having explained that he was speaking for God, Foster turned the reader's attention to the question of his sanity. As we have observed, many Ranters claimed to represent God and many were a little peculiar. Hence, Foster noted, "However you think of me, let not the notion of madness possess your spirits as for you to think that I am mad."(7) Perhaps because his first treatise was a little weird, Foster was particularly concerned that people would think "I have a devil."(8) Foster consoled himself with the thought that he was not the only person considered weird by his contemporaries. "If my Father's only chosen son met with such hard servants for to deal with him so cruelly and to tell him he had a devil, it is no wonder in this age of ours why I should . . . meet with any other but the same."(8) But where Christ came to deliver a message of salvation and demonstrate the path of redemption, "it is the good pleasure of my Father to make me so that I may give you warning of what he will do."(7) What God would do was easily stated: "It is the pleasure of the Father to turn the world upside down."(8) It is doubtful whether skeptical readers were much consoled by Foster's denials of insanity, but perhaps Foster felt better for the clarification.

The essence of Foster's social message was much the same as that of the earlier treatise. Turning the world upside down "concerned the Levelling of that which men for the present call their own and so hoard up riches and treasures here on earth for to make themselves great."(1) Foster's even greater hatred for the rich is also evident in this treatise. God says, "Because of your riches you have thought yourselves better than others and must have your fellow creatures in bondage to you, and they must serve you as to work for you and moyl [sic] and toil for you, standing cap in hand to you and must not displease you, no, by no means."(2) The rich were not content with owning the wealth of the land or even with controlling the lives of others, but "you through the hardness of your hearts have rather seen them starve for want of food than to give them a piece of bread."(2) All this will soon change for "I am come to take vengeance on such hypocrites as you"(2) with Foster adding, "I say he comes to plague you, torment you, and so to make you weary of your idols which you have made to yourselves."(3)

134

GEORGE FOSTER

Religious themes are also reminiscent of the earlier work. God is understood to be "in everything and that the whole world is but a garment to cover me from the visible sight of men."(31) Humanity is once again presented as consisting of flesh and soul (47) and "when any of my saints returns from the earth so that the body becomes dust again, then I draw up the soul and its spirit to their centers . . . their souls must return to me again, I being its fountain."(50) The remainder of the treatise presented new material.

Two areas where Foster improved upon his earlier effort were his description of events in Eden and how the day of wrath would come about. Both were important from a systematic viewpoint, for where the first explains why and how the world developed as it did, the second presents an explanation of divine judgment and justice and the logic of God's vengeance.

Foster explained that at first Adam "was holy, just, and upright, being a pure angel of mine."(48) Among his many other gifts "the Lord gave him reason, knowledge, and wisdom, which in themselves were very good."(48) With these facilities, Adam named all the animals and took dominion over Eden. The problem, in a word, was Eve, "being the weaker vessel and not able to contain herself in that condition as to know much and do little, but she did put herself forward in a way for to eat the apple . . . [knowing] well enough that if she did eat of the fruit she would have been as God."(48) In sinning, Adam and Eve wanted to "know more than they should have and so by presuming to go higher, even to be as God."(48) This traditional reading of Eden is colored with a dualistic interpretation of Lucifer's rebellion against God. The identification of Eve with weakness and finally evil was an idea also found in Coppin and one which would be amplified by Salmon, Tany and other Ranters able to turn Eve's accident into a dichotomy of good and evil predicated upon the social role of women as inferiors in English society.

When dealing with the serpent, Foster was on firm Ranter ground. He wrote, "This serpent was not a serpent, a creature that poisons . . . but this serpent was within Adam and Eve."(48) This more allegorical reading of the serpent was coupled with a more powerful interpretation of the fall. Where Christianity would place blame squarely upon the shoulders of Adam and Eve, Foster explained that it was God who placed Adam's and Eve's souls within flesh and therefore God who was responsible for the fall. Foster wrote, "It was the pleasure of I [sic], the creator, to set him in such a condition as I knew well enough he should fall."(48) Eve then may not have been the cause of evil, but merely its tool and agency of expression. The prevalence of ideas of this sort may explain why so many seemingly sane Englishmen believed in the existence of witches.

The results of these events were depressing. Despite divine responsibility, Adam was chased from Eden so that "he could not have free commerce or enjoyment of me as formerly he had as to talk with me . . ."(57) As a result, "he was naked, being stripped of my glory . . . [and] covered himself with fig leaves that he sews together [which] was nothing but his own right-eousness by which he would fain have hid his fault from me and so would have made Eve lain [*sic*] in all the fault."(57) And thus Adam is as evil as Eve for while she introduced evil, Adam partook of it but would make her the only source of evil.

The original divine gifts of reason, wisdom, and intelligence were re-tained by man, and used henceforth as additional fig leaves to rationalize, justify and self-justify and blame others whenever possible for his own shortcomings. "And so ever since men being driven out of the garden . . . have been inventing and sewing fig leaves together, that is, have been justifying themselves in their ways and so will not be ready to confess their faults but to lay it to another as Adam did his."(57)

Adam and Eve acted no better out of Eden than they had before. When they were cut off from God, humanity's worst quality emerged in "exalting itself against God and not becoming subject to God."(50) Foster wrote that "God, not appearing to the creature, [the creature] shall be in hell . . . and this hell will be every place where I do not appear in love to the crea-ture."(54) Rather than recognize the hell he had created, man created ever more fig leaves to cover his self-interest. The civilized society man created did not seek God's praise, but "who shall be the greatest and the richest, who shall have the most power, and who shall be the most applauded, and so have the most praise of men?"(16)

In his own times Foster could see terrible social inequities justified into righteousness by those with power. The mercenary greed of the rich was severely condemned. In one vision, Foster wrote, "I saw in a vision one give away all that he had and would not have anything as his own and I heard a voice say this man was come up to be His own son and was a true con-vert."(6) The rich, however, were evil and would not give up their wealth. "I hear all and everyone almost say, 'This is a hard saying, must we sell houses and land and give them away? What a condition we should bring ourselves into if we should do so.' "(5) To such sentiment Foster answered, "If you will not freely give up before I come in power, I will make you do it against your will when I come in power."(5) Even before he comes in power, God will torment the wealthy. "I will be such a terror to them that have abundance of riches," Foster intoned, "that I will make you weep to think you must part from them . . ."(4) With malice aforethought, God said "I am risen to destroy you and bring you to nothing"(4) and "to make you howl and weep."(2)

Foster possessed feelings no more kind for the clergy who "make religion to serve their own ends"(17) than for the rich, "especially those under the name Presbyterians and Independents who seem very white, that is, they had gilded outsides, as forms and ways of worship as observing the Sabbath and being zealous for their way of worship, even so zealous as to judge, censure, and condemn those that were not of their opinion. Yet notwithstanding all this, their hearts are full of hypocrisy."(17) Parishioners were no better, for the common man thoughtlessly accepted the priests' teachings, and "notwithstanding you go to church and hear sermons and have your children baptised, as you call it, and observe Sunday, that you have disobeyed my voice and have not walked humbly with me."(24) Foster believed that most people were content believing in empty religious rituals and avoided a true religion of the spirit. He described this condition of spiritual degeneration in a vision. "Behold and lo, I saw men and women running together and every one said, 'Save my God, save my God' as if men and women had each of them a god which must now be destroyed . . . and I said, 'Lord, what meaneth the people to call these their gods?' They call these their gods because they have set their hearts more upon these things than upon me and have with all eagerness run after these things."(8) Even the Golden Rule appears too difficult for most people. "You know that you must love all men and yet you hate all."(18) Foster asked, "How doest thou love thy neighbor as thyself when . . . freeing yourself from hard labor which thy poor neighbors are made, for your cruelty over them, to undergo?"(23) and noted how "many poor creatures starve for want of food and others have been driven to extreme poverty as to steal for something whereby to keep life in the body."(28)

The essence of good religion was not esoteric but consisted of following Christ's moral and ethical commandments. Christ's person was as important to Foster as it was to other Ranters who believed that Jesus' life should be emulated. Thus, it was not a small point to this class conscious author that "he did not come in pomp and glory but came of a carpenter's wife who descended from so low a lineage."(63) God's love of the poor was also evident in his selection of the apostles. "I have stirred up poor herdsmen and tradesmen before in the gospel in old times and in primitive times when I refused the priests, pharisees and leaders of the people in those days."(61) In modern times, too, God's message was only for the poor and the unlearned, a message "which I will hide from the learned ones of the world and will make choice of the unlearned."(60)

Foster did not believe many wealthy people would voluntarily surrender their riches or that those following false religions would seek the truth. Hence, God, the great Leveller, would turn the world upside down. The saints, alternately the poor and the righteous, are "good angels" and "the spirits of just men made perfect"(50) would be given "a sharp two-edged sword . . . and so execute vengeance on them."(10) The saints were told to "bind their kings and great men in fetters of iron and execute the doom that is written, even utter desolation upon all the high lofty ones, bring them to utter confusion, *that they may howl and weep* because they have made you even my chosen ones to be in slavery to them."(10) The shaking of the earth would have worldwide results, for "even the Pope of Rome shall lose his life in 1654 [and] the great head Turk shall lose his life in the year 1656."(65) Foster had evidently lost faith in his earlier prediction of 1650 as the year of God's wrath.

One assumes that the poor would be the greatest beneficiaries of this coming world revolution for only they were sainted and Christ-like. In fact, the greatest beneficiaries of this world shaking and first leaders in this coming time of troubles would be the Jews. In the few months separating the first and second treatise, Foster came to identify with the Jewish people. This is surprising since there were very few Jews in England, essentially a handful of Marranos, living as Portuguese Christians in London. Nevertheless, Foster came to believe that the Jewish people would herald the coming time of troubles and in the epistle to the reader Foster informs us that "the reason why I write my name to be Jacob Israel is because my name was changed from George in a vision, to Jacob Israel Foster, and so I subscribe."(10 of Epistle) At the end of the treatise Foster described how the patriarch Jacob, whose name God changed from Jacob to Israel, wrestled with an evil angel through the night. Believing this Bible story expressed his own conflict with evil and his change of name by God as well as the signifying of the coming time of conflict, Foster wrote of himself and the Jews, "I will give them a new name which none shall know but them that have it. My name changed from George Foster to Jacob Israel Foster."(68)

Two reasons help explain why Foster might have identified with Jews. First, if the world were to be turned upside down, no group of people so permanently resided at the bottom of the heap as the Jewish people who had been expelled from England in 1290, from France in 1315 and again in 1394, from Austria in 1421, from most German cities and states in the 1480s and 1490s, and from Spain in 1492. Then, in 1650, before the publication of this treatise, Polish Jewry, the repository of all those exiled communities, was massacred when Chmelnitski led a nationalist Ukrainian rebellion against both Poles and Russians. Unable to dislodge their true opponents, the rebels settled for massacring over 100,000 Jews. Thus, if the bottom were to rise to the top, none could rival the Jews as the lowest of the low.

A second reason for adopting the Jews may have reflected the general interest in the question of readmitting Jews to England at that time. A great policy debate within government was conducted during these years with many pamphlets written both for and against a more liberal policy regarding Jewish residence. Millenarian sectarians in particular favored the readmission of Jews. They believed that the world would end more quickly were Jews scattered over all the world but contemporary England possessed no Jewish community at all. A date of apocalyptic significance most often cited by millenarians was 1656, a date also popular in Jewish messianic and enthusiast circles for the coming of the Messiah.[29]

Foster believed that England would play a special role in subsequent Jewish history and "shall be the first that strive to go after my people who have a long time been cast off."(63) It was the divine commission of "Englishmen for to bring them word," about the coming revolution "even the Jews that are disperse about in Holland, Spain, Germany and Italy."(64)

When discussing the Jews, Foster made his messianic beliefs very explicit. He wrote, "O Zion who hath been made a laughing stock of all the nations, but now shall be made the praise of all the nations."(63) Following Jewish Zionist messianic thought, he added, "O ye Jews, whom I will gather out of all the countries wherein you have been dispersed, even they shall come to see that light that I will make known unto you when I have brought you out of captivity and bondage into the place of rest."(59) From bondage, the Jews would go "into their own country even into the land of Canaan . . . even to make the material city which the Jews formerly did inhabit."(61)

Together, Jews and saints would usher in the new world of God. Foster wrote, "All that hinder you or raise arms against you shall be drowned in my wrath . . ."(20) and together, the two groups "shall now rule all their enemies and all their enemies shall be but their footstool and they shall trample that wicked spirit which hath persecuted them to nothing."(33)

Foster was not a Judaizer and did not envision the glorious reemergence of Judaism as the religion of the future. Instead, his vision of God's tomorrow was characterized by freedom from economic and spiritual want.(7) In one vision Foster saw men and women singing and dancing and God informed Foster that "these men and women represent my sons and daughters and that which was in the cup which the men and women drank of was wine, which holds forth thus much; that it is the pleasure of the Lord of Hosts to give unto my sons and daughters for to drink wine, for as much as wine is set forth to be a nourisher of the nature of man and as thou sawest them that drink of the wine which I gave them were merry and did fall to singing and dancing."(15) The saints will be the envy of all peoples and "all nations shall long and desire for to come to thy light because my glory shall be upon thee."(59)

Not everyone would benefit from the coming new age. All those who were not Jews or saints would suffer a form of hell within this life. In his first treatise Foster envisioned the damned turning into disembodied souls eventually making their way into chickens and dogs and other beings. Here again Foster noted that "these devils are nothing but the spirits of wicked men deceased, which as soon as they go out of the body they are not at rest, neither can they rest or be at quiet but they are always seeking about in whom they can enter."(51) When a new host is found, "there he becomes a worse devil than he was before . . . and [when] that ceases, it goes into another, and these are witches, to plague and punish other wicked men and to bewitch the cattle of men."(51) This pattern would be broken when God came in his glory. God would "draw himself inward into himself and leave the rest of the world in darkness . . . when nothing but sorrow and pricks of conscience shall accompany these that go not up to Jerusalem."(54) Those that remain will have no souls and will consist of the rich, the wicked, and the witches who torment them.

George Foster was an atypical Ranter even when Ranters were each quite individual. He maintained all the benchmark Ranter ideas such as the rejection of heaven and hell, all ritual, and existing social structures. He affirmed a dualistic perception of the universe and a dualistic understanding of the soul within the body. Foster differed from other Ranters in his revolutionary apocalyptic thought. While others also despised the rich and wished them ill, Foster built much of his thought around the theme of punishing the rich both in this world and in some world to come. Foster's attitude toward Jews was also somewhat unusual though Joshua Garment and a few others also adopted a Jewish identity. The biggest difference of all lay in Foster's general disinterest in the meaning of sainthood, preferring to dwell upon punishing the devils. One senses that George Foster was a very bitter man.

9. Joseph Salmon

Joseph Salmon is another Ranter about whom very little is known. Since he was an associate of Coppe, Coppin, and John Pordage, it is likely that Salmon also knew Clarkson. Nothing is known about his early life and education, but Salmon served in the army until approximately 1650 when, like Bauthumley, he was discharged because of his irregular religious and social views.

Salmon's three treatises are all very individual. The first, *Anti-Christ in Man*, of 1647, was an extremely strident presentation of Ranter dualism. *A Rout, A Rout*, a political treatise written two years later, was Salmon's most important work. In this tract Salmon expressed revolutionary apocalyptic views very different than those of Foster. Salmon's last treatise, *Heights in Depths* of 1651, was written during a six-month prison term after he was dismissed from the army. In this very painful and personal work, Salmon attempted to abjure his extreme views, rephrase others in more acceptable fashion and present a short spiritual autobiography to explain how he finally arrived at a position close to philosophical Rantism. Though the second work is his most important, and his last the most personal and informative, it was Salmon's earliest treatise which best expressed the extremism of which both he and other Ranters were capable.

Anti-Christ in Man, authored by "a member of the army," is a rather distasteful expression of dualism. Salmon never discussed who God was, how creation came about, God's relationship with matter, or any other theme important to dualists. Yet few Ranter writings presented so clear a dichotomy of spirituality and material fleshliness and none did so with such poor taste. Matter, referred to in the title as the "anti-Christ," is the essence of evil. The treatise continually referred to fleshliness as "the Great Whore" with Salmon cryptically noting on the very first page, "Some there are that affirm this great whore to be the Pope, some the Presbyter, some the Episcopacy . . . they have seen her outside but not her inside, they know her in the history but not in the mystery."(1–2) Hardly wishing to diminish the perceived evil of these institutions, Salmon explained, "Know first then O man, that this great whore is in thee."(2)

According to the author, flesh and spirit have been warring principles within man since the creation of Adam. The soul, originally part of God and "clothed with such divine robes, was inconsistent to fleshly Adam."(4)

In this precarious balance, "now comes the serpent, which is . . . namely self and flesh."(4) As Scripture explained, spiritual man was defeated by carnal man with subsequent human history a dismal record of human sinfulness and materialism. Salmon wrote, "This whore, this Babylon, this Anti-Christ, is thy fleshly wisdom . . . the wisdom of the flesh [is] the carnal policy of the creature."(3) Matter is evil, man is matter, self is sin and the soul is lost.

Describing the great whore posed little difficulty for Salmon and throughout this treatise devoted to discovering the anti-Christ within humanity, Salmon used only feminine pronouns to refer to evil. Indeed, no Ranter was more extreme in using the male/female dichotomy to explain the distinction between good and evil. When discussing Eve, Salmon explained the nature of the feminine principle and its origin. "Out of the womb of fleshly wisdom proceeds all that actual transgression that is committed against the Lord. All outward appearances of sins are but the bastards of this whore, the children of this strange woman and the brats of this great adulteress."(7) Similarly, rather than condemning man's lustfulness, Salmon consistently asked, "O Man, seest thou not how the whore deceives thee?"(8) The identification of femininity with evil is the single point made in this treatise.

The whore's guile in seducing man was simple enough for Salmon to explain. "She will tell thee," Salmon observed, "thou art better than other Christians . . . thus she will make thee drink of her fornication by proposing her *golden cup* to thee"(16) or, "She will tell thee that she can supply all thy wants and relieve all thy necessities and therefore thou needest not to be beholden to God for anything."(19) Elsewhere Salmon wrote, "She will persuade thee that thou mayest take a little liberty to sin, that thou mayest exalt thyself a little . . ."(26) In all these instances, man is innocent but her evil is so powerful that innocent man is deceived. This theme will become more and more extreme.

Hatred of femininity is an idea deeply buried in all Christian dualism because it is the woman who made Adam sin in Eden, it is the woman who brings material life into this world, it is woman who is envisioned as the essence of weakness, and taken all together, it is the woman who is evil in herself and doubly evil because she is a seductress, a temptress and a whore. In all this, man is innocent. Christianity has traditionally attempted to soften this negative view with an equally unrealistic view of Mary. But Mary's very purity and immaculate conception stand as an indictment of every other lesser woman in this world. Dualists have used the male/female dichotomy as a likely image to polarized evil within the world, much as

God and Satan are divided in the ethereal world, and thus also circumscribe
evil into the woman. In effect, this leaves man sufficiently innocent to place
blame upon Eve as a seducer. In building his indictment, Salmon makes
use of every anti-female stereotype he can find. "It is a property of the
strumpet to pretend what she doth not intend to her lovers," Salmon advised, "She always pretends what she never intends . . . she will pretend a
glorious show but there is nothing but wickedness and harlotry intended."(13–14) For instance, evil will indicate that religion can be material
"and she is willing to let thee understand that Christ hath been flesh for
thee."(28) Even worse, "she propounds her own ways to the creatures
. . . to go feed upon the husks as namely, upon prayers, fasting or some
outward and carnal ordinances."(18) The poor innocent male Christian is
so confused that "a poor Christian many times can find no Christ in his
forms, no comfort in ordinances, no joys in duties and performances
. . ."(31)

If the great whore is evil in teaching the wrong path to God, how much
more evil she is when, deceitfully, she teaches the correct path to God! Salmon explained that "evil is very changeable in her appearance" and is
therefore difficult to root out. "It is a policy of a harlot to suit herself to the
humor and fancy of her lovers and that so thereby she may still retain and
keep them in her favor."(22–23) Under this more devious guise, evil will see
man's desire for goodness and "she will lead thee forth to the presence of
many good moral actions, as to extend alms, to feed the hungry, to clothe
the naked, to visit the sick, and to leave off thy old vices thou hast formerly
lived in."(23–24) In appearing to lead man toward goodness, she is doubly
evil for "she exacts herself above all that is called God, she sits as God in
God's temple, in a place where she hath no right to rule and govern."(11) In
short, femininity is sinful, domineering, deceitful and evil.

It was not God's purpose to leave innocent man in the clutches of the
whore, but one must wait for God to appear within the soul before redemption is possible. Salmon warned, "Thou canst never behold self aright till
God take thee up or carry thee away in the spirit."(35) We are informed
about those without illumination, "the highest discovery of Christ that they
have attained to is the fleshly forms and fleshly ordinances."(30) Those
illuminated by God, on the other hand, experience, "in a word, all the
inferior with the superior discerning of God that the creature hath had
formerly, shall be extinguished."(59) Yet, illumination brings difficulties,
too, because the temptations of the great whore are heightened and made
more intense. Coppin referred to this period of pain and suffering as "the
double cup of glory and suffering" and Coppe too spoke of a "bitter cup"

when he was with the BEASTS and ate GRASS. Salmon writes of "a period in the wilderness" where the innocent-*he* is finally released from the evil-*she*, and where "he loathes the scarlet color, the glorious attire of the whore"(39) and "he spies the vanity of all that was flesh below Christ"(37–38) and then "he now wonders that he should become drawn to commit folly by so filthy a harlot."(46) Through divine illumination, "he now sees the whore and her various pretenses and how she hath formerly deceived him in her several dresses, he sees her not only in her gaudy attire but in the height of her modesty, even in her religious garment."(41) The greatest realization of all comes when he realizes that her religion of self-righteousness is "but a *menstrous cloth and a filthy rag.*"(40) Certainly there can be no illumination greater than that.

Salmon's concepts of sainthood paralleled those of other Ranters. He used such terms as "New Jerusalem," "heaven" and "resurrection" to refer to the new status of sainthood which he described as "to swallow up the soul in himself, to drown, confound and bring to an end all creature glory in his own incomprehensible excellence."(60)

Salmon's first treatise was really poor quality stuff. The male/female dichotomy was effective with all who hated women, no doubt, but explained little about the anti-Christ within man. Unless one actually assumed that femininity was the root of all evil and masculinity was essentially innocent, and that one actually can distinguish between evil-female-fleshliness and innocent-male-fleshliness, which is somehow not material and carnal, the argument was stupid and a ruse. Rather than expressing the soul's difficulties in living in a carnal world of deceit, Salmon in fact parodied the relationship with women experienced by many army personnel in that age and all others. Salmon believed the whore exploited her innocent Christian but it was the less than total innocence of the Christian that in fact created the whore. Fortunately, Salmon's later treatises were more coherent and tackled real issues rather than fanciful allegories of them. We can understand why in later life Salmon may have wished to recant some of his earlier views; unfortunately, these were not those views.

Salmon's next work, *A Rout, A Rout*, of 1649, was a very different sort of treatise. Rather than discussing a religious theme, Salmon concentrated upon providing an intellectual justification for revolution and the continuing role of the army in bringing about radical change. This effort was more successful. Indeed, Salmon produced an interesting piece of revolutionary literature mixing religious dualism, Ranter themes and the fact of the English revolution.

Salmon's basic premise was that while God was unknown within himself, his presence within history can be observed as can his actions in the life of a society in crisis. He explained that "this power (which is God) comes forth and offers itself in a diversity of appearances and still (by a divine progress in the affairs of the earth) moves from one power to another, from one dispensation to another, from one party to another."(1)

The idea that God acted within history was certainly not novel. Isaiah refers to Cyrus as a Messiah for liberating the Hebrews, and Scripture recounted how Saul first gained and then lost his divine charisma as David then gained what Saul had lost. The New Covenant replaced the Old Covenant and antique Christian authors repeatedly wrote about divine dispensations and manifestations. Joachim taught about three different ages in God's manifestation, and historians are still writing about the effects of his ideas on subsequent thought. Reformation age spiritualists such as Michael Servetus and Sebastian Franck divided history into ages according to chronological schemes predicated upon God's activities. Millenarians hoped God would play a more active role in history, and the Fifth Monarchists believed he was about to do so. In all of this, Salmon had been preceded and superceded. It is true that none of the above used their views of God's activity in the past as a justification for present violence and bloody revolution. Yet Salmon's views are special for none of the above was a dualist.

It is quite one thing for a Christian thinker to find God's presence in a world he created and found 'good,' and quite another thing for a dualist to find God, who is remote and removed from this satanic world of the Great Whore and anti-Christ, active in the affairs of men. The dualist can always ascribe all the terrible things occurring in the world to the Devil who controls the world. If God is active in history, he must then take some measure of responsibility for the world controlled by Satan. We have encountered standard Ranter antihistorical biases in their rejection of Scripture as the "mere history" or the fleshly record of God which possessed no spiritual truth in itself. In his lamentable first treatise Salmon indicated that the ritualistic religion of the apostles was inferior to the spiritual religion of later times and in that same treatise he wrote, "He is not a Christian indeed that doth by the power of nature believe what is naturally and historically reported of Christ in the Scripture, but he that by the power of the spirit believes all this history to be verified in him[self] in the mystery."(27 *Anti-Christ*) Moreover, unlike Foster, Salmon was not apocalyptic. Foster, we recall, believed God would enter history in order to overturn it. For Salmon, however, God had always been in history; moreover, he did not foresee the end of times coming for religious reasons, but for political ones. For all these reasons Salmon's accomplishment in providing a structured portrayal of God's activity in the civil war is significant and if his earlier work was conceptually weak, his second treatise was a major improvement.

On the opening page of this treatise Salmon described how God has changed his pattern of expression over the ages. Salmon explained that other than appearing to Moses as a burning bush, the first religious guise chosen by God "was when God had faced the Jewish ceremonies (those carnal manifestations) with a great beauty and splendor of divine majesty."(1) God employed rituals of this time because mankind was so inured to devilish and material religious concept and worship that little spirituality was possible.

A second stage in God's changing pattern of divine self-expression came in the person of Jesus Christ who was "a more true pattern and exact resemblance of God, the divine power."(1) Salmon believed Jesus was an ordinary mortal who "gradually ascends out of the creature into a more complete image or likeness of himself."(2) To ascend from the mortal, however, Jesus needed to extinguish his life and "in the fullness of time he lays this [human] form aside . . . he must be crucified."(2) In this spiritual form, Christ expressed "all the brightness and luster of divine appearance,"(1) and provided mankind with a role model. In short, God moved from crass representation in rituals to clearer representation in the human form of Christ, and finally to transcendent spirituality in the crucified spirit within Christ. This is the same transition every person must emulate in his passage from the carnal and beastly to the suffering flesh of Christ to the spiritual resurrection within the soul.

The same progressively spiritual manifestation of God is found in God's "daily motion out of one dispensation spiritual into another in civil or outward dispensation."(2) Consequently, different forms of government, like different forms of religion, received God's sanction at different times. Salmon explained, "time was when God dwelt among us in the darkness of absolute and arbitrary monarchy [but now] comes forth to rend this vessel in pieces . . . and clothe himself in another."(2–3) Indeed, this was precisely the significance of England's civil war for it marked a turning point on God's pattern of civil expression. God used the Parliament to destroy monarchy but never intended that Parliament should itself be the basis for future governance. Salmon explained that "the very soul of monarchy sunk into Parliament and here it lost its name barely, but not its nature, its form but not its power, they making themselves as absolute and tyrannical as ever the king in his reign."(3)

God's most recent guise was already apparent to Salmon and "we see in a short time he lays aside that glorious show and idol and clothes himself with the army. And thus both monarchy and Parliament fell into the hands and upon the swords of the army. And thus the army are to be the executioners of that beast [i.e., monarchy] which they [i.e., Parliament] had formerly wounded."(3) "You have taken away from Charles his life," Salmon wrote, "and you are led forth in a way of vengeance upon your adversaries."(8) It was through the army that "the Lord besmears himself with blood and vengeance." (3–4)

The divine mission set for the army was to destroy all that lay in its path. "You sentence and shoot to death at your pleasure. It little moves you to trample upon the blood of your enemies; this is your victory, glory and triumph."(8) God's final purpose was not yet apparent and Salmon believed that the army had not yet reached its true role. Writing to the leadership of the army, Salmon intoned, "He turns your hearts, ways, and enterprises upside down before you."(8) Soon, Salmon warned, "The Lord, (ere long) will come forth in another appearance amongst you . . . he will let out a more pure glory upon you."(8) Elsewhere Salmon warned," And know this: That God will ere long leave you exceeding dark and dead in your enterprises."(5)

Salmon believed the revolution would continue when the regular soldiers overthrew their officers. Much as monarchy was destroyed by a Parliament which then ruled in the same tyrannical manner as its former adversary, the army would overturn Parliament and in turn the officers would be pushed aside by the common soldier. The dedicatory letters indicate Salmon's strong class orientation and his antiofficer bias. In the letter addressed to the 'Commanding Power in the Army' Salmon wrote, "My speech is intended especially (as I said before) to my fellow soldiers, those of inferior rank and quality."(A2a) It was to these common soldiers that he wrote, "You strike through king, gentry, and nobility, they all fall before you. You have a commission from the Lord to scourge England's oppressors; do it in the name of God, do it (I say) fully, hotly, sharply . . ."(A2b)

Salmon's hopes lay especially with a group he identified as radical "saints" in the army even more than with the general common soldier. In an introductory letter dedicated "To the Fellowship of Saints Scattered in the Army," Salmon wrote, "You are a scattered seed amongst tares and it is your name that upholds the fame of the whole. Your are that little leaven hid in the meal whose reputation seasons the whole lump" and further, "the day is coming and now is when I will gather up my jewels in the army." Early in the treatise Salmon described how "the Lord besmears himself with blood and vengeance"(3–4) and "Friends! Look about you for the Lord is now coming forth to rip up your bowels . . . yea, to let loose the imprisoned light of himself in you."(4) This was a cause for joy. "Oh, it will be a glorious day," Salmon observed, "wait for it."(13)

Like other Ranters, Salmon saw the coming day of troubles as signalling the end of the world. The purpose of the present crisis was obvious: "The Lord will kindle a burning . . . God himself shall be the burning, the holy one shall be the flame and all fleshly regality . . . shall be burned up and consumed."(3) The army saint would help bring about this universal conflagration, but preaching violence against superiors would not necessarily sit well with many of his readers. Salmon conceded, "I know . . . the form, method, and language invites not the curious and nice spirit in any man,"(13) but a page later he explained why he was willing to take such a radical position: "I was once wise as well as you, but I am now a fool, I care not who knows it. I once also enjoyed myself but I am now carried out of my wits, a fool, a madman beside myself. If you think me any other, you are mistaken. And it is for your sakes that I am so."(14)

Like other Ranters, Salmon believed that the true saint must be prepared to suffer for Christ's truth. Writing that "suffering is our crown, death our life,"(6) Salmon also warned "You know not yet what it is to be dead to your own interests."(5) At the end of the treatise he wrote, "I know many of you are almost spent under your burden. You are lost in a wilderness of confusion."(11) And a page later he added, "You fear the world and they are afraid of you. You are at a distance involved in a bloody contest, an earthly, lustful and carnal warfare."(12). Salmon reminded the reader of the central teaching that must motivate them in the coming struggle, that "God to us is light in darkness, glory in shame, beauty in deformity, liberty in bondage; we possess nothing yet enjoy all things."(6) Perhaps indicating his own spiritual state Salmon noted, "I am now dead with the Lord. I am at rest from my labor. Oh happy death! O blessed loss! How far better it is, O Lord, to be dissolved and gathered up into thy rest than to live the life of worldly and carnal labor."(5)

This treatise led to Salmon's dismissal from the army and subsequent prosecution for blasphemy. How these events transpired and whether this treatise had any positive effect upon his soldier colleagues is unknown. Salmon's last treatise, as we shall see, gives us some information, though not nearly so much as might be desired.

By 1651 Joseph Salmon was a very changed person. His last treatise, *Heights in Depths*, gives no indication of his earlier revolutionary views in which the army played so prominent a role. He no longer writes about God's role in history and instead wonders whether history has any meaning at all. This last work is pervaded by a mood of depression, despair, and the futility of existence. Like Clarkson and Coppe, Salmon ended his literary career as a more reserved philosophical Ranter, and *Heights in Depths* is an eloquent plea for the religious quietism characterizing Bauthumley's and Coppin's writings. We can only surmise that contributing to this depressed mood was Salmon's dismissal from the army, the failure of the army to express the revolutionary role he had envisioned for it, prosecution for blasphemy, and perhaps, a midlife crisis as well.

Heights in Depths was written to serve several different ends. It was partly a recantation of earlier views made necessary by his prosecution for blasphemy but also a rephrasing of his views into a more acceptable whole. Salmon listed the charges made against him and attempted to answer each point while maintaining the overall integrity of his Rantism. He also presented a short spiritual autobiography not unlike those composed by Clarkson and Coppe, to clarify for both himself and others how he arrived at his present position.

The title page indicates that Salmon's purpose was "a sincere abdication of certain tenets, either formerly vented by him or now charged upon him." While not indicating how he came to be charged with blasphemy, Salmon wrote, "My manner of walking being adjudged by those in power to be contrary to the peace and civil order of the commonwealth, I was just apprehended as an offender."(A3b) The initial action against him was military for he writes of a Major Beak, "a man much honored in my thoughts, though once a professed enemy to me,"(A5b) and a Colonel Purefoy, who "presented my discharge to the Major and aldermen then present"(A6b) on condition "that I would with all convenient speed declare myself in print against all those things which I was then charged with and still am by many."(A7a) This treatise was evidently written to satisfy this agreement. Previous to this, "I suffered above half a year's imprisonment under the notion of a blasphemer, which . . . becomes very irksome and tedious to my outward man."(A4) Had he not abjured his faith, Salmon might have feared continual punishment on the part of the local civic authorities present at his discharge.

Salmon explained that he sat in jail with "my door fast bolted on the other [side], I had time enough afforded me to ponder my state and condition."(A4) When he was in this condition "armed thoughts all at once beleaguered my soul as if they had agreed with one consent to devour me."(A4b) Despite depression and loneliness, Salmon wrote that he never lost his faith for "I knew the Lord had a special end to accomplish through all these declinings, [I] got by degrees more ground upon spirit and I forthwith addressed myself to those who had been the causes of my present confinement."(A5)

The body of the treatise itself begins with Salmon's spiritual autobiography to explain how he came to be apprehended by authorities and how his views changed over the years. He noted that as a young man "I found in myself a secret longing to soar in a more celestial orb . . . towards this more heavenly center [of God]."(9) Through a series of visions, Salmon explained how he came to "some quickenings of a divine principle within me . . . and shook off my night dresses and appeared to myself like the sun dawning out of its refulgent splendor from behind the dark canopies of the earth."(9)

As a result of this wisdom, Salmon left home and the Church of England for Presbyterianism and "became a zealous hearer." (10) He was still spiritually unsatisfied, however, and Salmon soon became an Independent because Independents were very controversial. "I understood they were a people decried by the vulgarity, which made me imagine that there was something of God amongst them."(11) In search of greater spirituality, Salmon became an Anabaptist "in the hottest time of persecution I was made one eminent, both in holding forth this way to the world and also in suffering for the same."(12)

Despite Salmon's willingness to suffer for Anabaptist truth, God appeared to Salmon saying, "Arise and depart for this is not your rest."(12) Like other Ranters, Salmon was ambivalent about God's call to him. In a word, he did not understand what God wanted of him. He described his condition as "weeping with Mary at the sepulchre; fain I would have found Christ where I left him, but alas he was risen."(13) Searching Scripture was of little value for "I found nothing in form but a few signals of mortality; as for Jesus, he was risen and departed."(13) After three days of extreme depression God again appeared to Salmon who felt himself "wrapped up in the embrace of such pure love and peace as that I knew not oft times whether I were in or out of this fading [human] form."(14) It was in the state that "I saw heaven opened upon me and the new Jerusalem . . . greeted my soul."(14) Like most mystics, Salmon often felt at a loss to describe his feelings. He wrote that "I can give you no perfect account of that glory which then covered me; the lisps and slips of my tongue will but render that imperfect"(16) yet he was able to observe a wonderful feeling "full of liberty," of coming "into the abyss of eternity," that "all my former enjoyments being nothing in appearance to that glory which now rested on my spirit"(14) and finally, "I walked with the Lord and was not."(16)

JOSEPH SALMON

Salmon's discussion of the heavenly bliss enfolding him at God's call was typical of the feelings experienced by most Ranters. Also similar was the period of confusion that followed this bliss when the fleshly principle reemerged with renewed vigor. This period of "the bitter cup" comes about when "angry flesh being struck at the heart . . . begins to swell and contracting all the evil humors of the body of death in one lump."(18) The resulting conflict between spirituality and fleshliness was difficult. Salmon wrote, "I was now sent into a strange land and made to eat unclean things in Assyria, walked in unknown paths and became a mad man, a fool amongst men."(18) He also wrote of his "tumbling in my own vomit, I became a derision to all and even loathed by those by whom I had been loved."(18) Salmon "was led into paths that I had not known and turned from a king to become a beast" and consequently, "I knew not whether I walked or what I did."(A3a)

Salmon must have lived a very carefree life during those years when he "tumbled in his own vomit." He remembered "the deep drunken bewitching besotting draughts of the wine of astonishment that hath been forced upon me."(19) The result was, "I lay as a spectacle of scorn and contempt to every eye, yea, my mother's children were angry with me."(19) Rather than elaborating upon his sinful behavior Salmon summarized all these years by noting, "I have seen and heard things unlawful to be uttered amongst men, but I shall at present spare myself the labor and prevent the world's inconsiderate censure."(17) During this phase he knew many who "reel, stagger, stumble, and fall with the desperate intoxicating draughts of wrath, madness, tumble up again and down in their own filthiness and bestiality."(20) In his own defense, Salmon wrote that orthodox Christians were no better for if they bothered to look, "they should soon discover as bad or worse in themselves as they hate and despise in others."(19) For his misdeeds, Salmon was apprehended, "judged, censured, stripped, persecuted, imprisoned by others."(20) He asked his censors, "What if God should uncloak you and strip you of your lovely garbs or pretended holiness and should let that appear which is hidden under this pleasing vesture?"(22) Urging moderation from those who would censure him, Salmon warned that "you little think and less know how soon the cup of fury may be put into your hands."(22)

Salmon believed that his experiences with the bitter cup were in fact part of God's plan for mankind to enable it to overcome a material composition. "It was given that I might drink, I drank that I might stumble, I stumbled that I might fall, I fell and through my fall was made happy."(25) Coming

151

to redemption through a process of failure may seem a mystery and "this I know is a riddle to many which none but the true Nazarite can expound."(25)

The final stage of Salmon's spiritual odyssey came after the cup of fury and bitterness passed leaving him in a quietism not far removed from Bathumley's philosophical Rantism. After "all the waves and billows of the Almighty have gone over me," Salmon wrote, "I am now at rest in the silent deeps of eternity, sunk into the abyss of silence and (having shot this perilous gulf) am safely into the bosom of love, the land of rest."(26) Like Bauthumley, Salmon felt himself far removed from the affairs of the world, and like Bauthumley, he did not much care. "I sometimes hear from the world which I have now forsaken," Salmon observed, "of the same clamor, strife and contention which abounded in it when I left it. I give it the hearing and that's all."(26) He added a page later, "My great desire . . . is to see and say nothing."(28) Rather than attempting to overthrow existing authority, Salmon wrote, "I am made willing to give my cheek to the smiter, to sit alone (keeping silence) and put my mouth in the dust."(32-33)

Like Coppe and others making a formal recantation, nowhere in Salmon's brief account of his spiritual development was there anything approaching an actual abjuring of his views. Nowhere was there any indication of why and how Major Beak and Colonel Purefoy, greatly lauded in the preface, were anything but opponents. Perhaps when Salmon praised them he was indicating his willingness to submit to an authority he could not defeat, but he may also have experienced a change of heart concerning the futility of human action in the corrupt world. Less like a revolutionary and more like the Jesus he would emulate, Salmon wrote, "I am able both to do and suffer all things . . . and resolved I am to gain conquest over the world by prostrating myself, a subject to their weakness . . . I must submit to them that I may reign over them."(33)

The next section of the *Heights in Depths* lists the charges made against himself and his replies to these. Salmon wrote that his trouble began with the publication of a treatise entitled *Divinity Anatomized*, a work no longer in existence. If we assume this work was as extreme as his other writings, especially *Anti-Christ in Man*, it is possible that Salmon had much to regret. Salmon claimed there was little truly wrong with this treatise or its views. "Somewhat I have formerly vented in certain pages, which the weak stomachs of many can hardly digest. And truly I could heartily wish that some expressions had been better pondered and not untimely exposed to a public view. Though I also believe that if they were well chewed (and not so suddenly swallowed without relishing the nature of them) they would be better digested than they are."(33–34) Indeed, Salmon continued this strange recantation of his former views by arguing that had there been something inherently wrong with these views, "that which men call truth today they proclaim error tomorrow, and that which now is adjudged and condemned as error, anon is embraced and extolled as truth."(35)

His critics, Salmon complained in this strange recantation, were small-minded, and "whatsoever stands out of their sphere or bears no proximity to their commonly received maxims must presently be deemed as blasphemy and sentenced to the infernal lake as most odious and abominable."(34–35) Rather than list all the charges made against himself, Salmon wrote, "I have here thought meet to cite a small parcel of the most crying errors of the time."(35–36)

The issues raised by Salmon were typical of the charges generally made against Ranters. These included "that there is no God, no devil, no hell; as one that denies the Scripture and the blessed trinity of the Godhead; that saith there is no sin or otherwise, that God is the author of sin."(37) Most of these accusations were condemned by provisions of the Blasphemy Act: consequently, Salmon treated each point separately and used orthodox language when possible.

Concerning God and atheism Salmon wrote, "What madman or fool will then deny a divine and eternal being?"(39) He defined God along traditional Ranter lines as "that pure and perfect being in whom we all are, move, and live; that secret blood, breath, and life that silently courseth through the hidden veins and closed arteries of the whole creation"(38) and "a pure light whose glorious nature can not be touched with the least tincture of darkness."(50) Less orthodox were Ranter views of the devil and Salmon must have been aware of the need for caution for he began on a very tentative note. "The devil is understood variously amongst men, either grossly or corpulently by some or more subtly and mystically by other."(40) Calling the devil "a recepticle of darkness" and "mystery of iniquity,"(41) Salmon never did provide an explanation that was orthodox.

Salmon's definitions of heaven and hell were no more orthodox. The former was described as "the center of the soul's bliss," the "Christian's rest," the "divine sabbath" and "to live with and in God,"(42) all of which follow good Ranter logic. Hell, too, was described along lines we have already seen elsewhere as "the appointed portion of the sinner," or "tophet of scorching displeasure" and "a dying life or rather a living death." (42–43) None of these descriptions recanted Ranter positions.

No less serious than the previous was the charge that Salmon did not accept Scripture as the written word of God. Salmon wrote, "I do not remember that in anything which I have written or declared, I have given the captious world the least ground to render me guilty of denying the Scriptures."(44–45) Yet, his definition was typically Ranter when he called the Bible "a history or a map of truth wherein (if our learned translators have not deceived us) is contained a true discovery of the dealings of God with his people in former times and ages of the world."(45) In short, the Bible was a history.

The last points concerned the nature of sin and were important because of the reputation Ranters acquired as libertines. Trying to belittle the charge that he rejected sin, Salmon pointed to a common inconsistency in Ranter prosecutions. "Some say I hold no sin and with the same mouth will be apt to conclude that I make God the author of sin. Here must needs be a gross mistake on the one hand or other certainly."(47) Nevertheless, whatever his real views had been, Salmon tells us, "I here recede them."(47) Salmon then proceeded to describe sin in terms that are pure Ranter but could carry orthodox intent if not inspected too vigorously. He wrote, "Man as man, growing from the root of the first Adam (the Earthly fallen principle) is nothing else but a massive heap of sin."(48) Hence, "Men, the best of men, things, the most excellent of things, they are all vanity and a lie, worse than vanity, vexation of the spirit."(50) A page later he added that "all that you see below besides God it is a lie, froth, emptiness, wind, and corruption"(51) which is the distinction between God as pure spirit and creation as pure matter.

Salmon addressed the trinity last. Historically, rejection of the unified godhead has been a touchstone indicator of religious radicalism. Ranters were particularly vulnerable to charges of heterodox trinitarianism for they maintained that God was remote, Jesus was totally human, and the spirit was in the believer's soul. Although rejection of the trinity was not condemned by the Blasphemy Act, Salmon did not wish to alienate his censors and thus noted, "I may lawfully and must necessarily maintain three."(53) Yet, his definitions did more to confuse than enlighten the reader. Indicating that "without controversy, great is the mystery"(52) he also wrote, "God is one, simple, single, uncompounded glory,"(52) and also that "the Father is not the Son, the Son is not the spirit as multiplied into form and distance."(53) If all this sounded confusing, Salmon concluded, "I love the unity as it orderly discovers itself in the trinity. I prize the trinity as it bears correspondence with the unity. Let the skillful Oedipus unfold this."(54)

It is likely that the army was less interested in the content of Salmon's recantation than in its mere existence coupled with a six-month prison sentence. The army won its point because the treatise is filled with indications that prison broke Salmon's spirit. We have already noted his disinterest in the world's events and his belief that his mission was to suffer and "put his mouth to the dust." If he had once believed contemporary events possessed great significance, he now asked, "What means this great noise and stir . . . the bitter contention that intermixes itself with men's ways and worships? The perpetual clashings of one form against another?"(5) Rather than having any meaning, "The world travels perpetually and everyone is swollen full big with particularity of interest."(4)

There is great weariness of spirit in this man who would dash government to the ground. "I am almost weary of speaking,"(A7B) Salmon tells us, "it is but vanity for me to write, vanity for you to read. Words are but wind; you read you know not what and perhaps I write I know not what."(7) Like Bauthumley, Salmon just did not care any longer. "I have lived to see an end to all perfections; that which I now long for is to see perfection itself perfected."(8)

With the publication of *Heights in Depths* Salmon disappeared from radical religious life. Tired of the contention he once sought, frightened by the authorities he once challenged and perhaps humiliated by the very institution in which he had placed so much hope, Salmon wrote, "All that man can do to acquire satisfaction does but multiply his sorrows upon his head and augment cares upon his spirit."(6) His prayer was simple. "O my soul," he wrote, "enter thou into thy chamber, shut thy doors about thee, hide thyself in silence."(A8b) Salmon did just that and was never heard from again.

Divine Ranters

10. John and Mary Robins: Joshua Garment

In addition to sexual libertines, strict dualists, quietists and apocalypticians, there were Ranters whose message was their identification as God. Other Ranters claimed special status as prophets and servants but Divine Ranters insisted they were God himself, or Jesus and Mary themselves. Consequently, the abstention from ritual, indeed the very end of religion, had arrived because these people thought themselves the essence of the second coming. Unlike the Scriptural account which presents Mary as Jesus' mother, the divine Ranters followed the pattern of Simon Magus and Helen where Jesus and Mary were husband and wife. In this section we will encounter two such expressions of divine Rantism in the case of John and Mary Robins, and in the far more infamous, and amusing, story of William Franklin and Mary Gadbury.

John Robins' legal difficulties were described in a small treatise entitled *The Declaration of John Robins* of 1651, written by GH who described himself as an "ear witness." GH attended the several trials involving Robins' followers and interviewed many of them while they sat in Clarkenwell Prison. Though he never indicated his specific interest in these hearings or his own religious orientation, GH was an honest reporter and does not seem to have misrepresented court statements.

According to GH, Robins taught that he was the son of God and his followers appeared convinced of this. In one interview held on Saturday, May 24, 1651, with Mr. John King, GH asked if "the report was true, that they acknowledge John Robins to be their God and (his wife) Mary Robins the Virgin Mary, and the child conceived by her (for indeed she is very big) to be Christ."(3) John King answered, "Yes, all this I verily believe for this man whom you call John Robins is God, he is both King, Priest, and Prophet, he is that Malchizedek formerly spoken of and is now come to redeem the world to its former condition as it was before the fall of the first Adam."(3)

GH was able to raise other issues in his interview with John Robins. He asked, "How have you the power to cast down and raise up unless it be by some satanical art and abominable witchcraft?" and Robins answered, "All

156

arts come from the Devil but mine proceeds from the inspiration of the Holy Ghost." When asked by GH, "Why do your followers term you a third Adam?" John Robins explained, "So I am for these reasons. The first Adam was made a living soul, the second a quickening spirit . . . the first, the servant of Death appointed, the second the Son of Life thereunto foreordained. And I am the third Adam and must gain that which the first lost."

Robins and his followers appear to have used various terms of divinity interchangeably but all applied to Robins and perhaps indicated his, and their, belief that all human history and divine expression were summed up in him. Yet, once in court Robins was willing to make a fairly standard orthodox statement of faith. When asked by a judge, "I pray Sir, what belief are you on?" Robins prudently replied, "I believe in one God the Father (said he) the maker of heaven and earth and I believe in the communion of the saints and the resurrection of the dead."(5) The last page of the short account presented Robins' signed abjuration of all claims to divinity. It is possible that this statement was intended to keep himself from going to jail. He swore, "Whereas I John Robins do at this very instant lie under the censure of the people to be the God of the Shakers and their only Lord in whom they put their trust. I do here declare . . . that I am free from assuming any such power or title to myself . . . only to have received the inspiration of the Holy Ghost and have had great things revealed to me and am now sent to call the Jews to conversion, which will be accomplished this present year, 1651."

GH's account, which assumed Shakers were Ranters, as did the court itself, presents very little information about their beliefs. Fortunately, additional information is available from a short nameless treatise published by the *Justices of the Peace of Westminister* on July 22, 1651. It seems that a month after Robins went to court, another group of his followers were tried for blasphemy at the Assize session in Westminister. The defendants listed in this account include Thomas Tydford, Elizabeth Sorrell the Elder and Elizabeth Sorrell the Younger, Margaret Dunlape, Anne Burley, Frances Bedwell and Thomas Kearby. The group appeared before the JP Lawrence Whitaker and at that time Thomas Tydford testified that Robins "is the God the Father of our Lord and Savior Jesus Christ, and saith that the wife of the said Robins, alias Roberts, shall bring forth a man child that shall be the savior of all that be saved in this world. He affirmeth further that Cain who slew his brother Abel, is the third person of the trinity and that those that deny it deny their own salvation. He saith further that the said John Robins, alias Roberts, hath power to raise the dead."(3) Tydford and the others put their mark on the confession to indicate their acceptance of its

157

contents with Francis Bedwell adding that she had in fact witnessed Robins "striking a woman dead and raising her again."(4) The account continued, noting that "they were all committed to prison without bail and mainprize until the next general session."(4)

It is not clear how long the group remained in jail but on June 20, with the exception of Thomas Kearby, all submitted petitions abjuring their former beliefs. The court accepted their petition and "upon this they were ordered to send for good bail to appear at the next sessions and to be of good behavior in the meantime, and so putting in bail and paying their fees, were dismissed."(7)

It appears that both groups of Robins' followers held similar views with Tydford's addition that Cain was a member of the trinity. The Bogomils too subscribed to this view and other early dualists maintained that both Jesus and Satan were sons of God. Unfortunately, neither Tydford nor the others were educated folk, indeed none could read or write. Consequently, none could elucidate their views.

It is probable that none of them, with the exception of Kearby, returned to court. There are no records indicating a subsequent hearing and it is probable the court was satisfied with the general abjuration of faith that they had submitted. The court asked them to be good people and it is doubtful that the justices believed them very harmful. Similarly, a different court had accepted Robins' recantation as well.

Thomas Kearby continued to maintain his faith and he alone returned to court where he was tried before justices Thomas Latham and John Hooker. After reiterating his views about Robins' divinity, Kearby was found guilty of blasphemy and the court demanded that he "be removed from hence to the Gatehouse prison from whence he was brought and shall be immediately removed from thence to the house of correction for the said city and Liberty, there to remain for the space of six months without bail or mainprize, according to the direction of the said late [Blasphemy] Act and the keeper of the said house of correction is hereby strictly required to set the said Thomas Kearby to hard labor and to give him corporal punishment as occasion requireth."(8–9)

It is likely that Kearby's punishment resulted more from his unwillingness to recant his views than from originally maintaining them. Not only were the others released and warned to stay out of trouble, but the court's treatment of Kearby's statement of faith also indicates that they did not take his views very seriously. When Kearby asserted that Robins could raise the dead, the court noted in droll fashion, "If he have power to raise the dead, there is work enough not far off to try his skill. Here are good store of

JOHN AND MARY ROBINS: JOSHUA GARMENT

churches and churchyards about the city and upon which he may make experiment."(12) Elsewhere the same humor is evident. One justice observed, "I have heard also the said disciple [i.e., Kearby] give out that Robins either hath or shall have the power to divide the sea as Moses, and pass over dry land. The Thames is near, he may do well to try experiments there first."(14)

On the basis of these two short treatises it is difficult to know how to evaluate Robins. His followers, gentle if ignorant folk, may have been charmed by a charismatic personality and some sleight of hand faith healing. If we recall, Clarkson too found such endeavors very rewarding and it is reasonable that Robins, like Clarkson, was a charlatan.

It would be a mistake to dismiss Robins too readily for he seemed to have attracted at least some serious and educated followers as well as simple and perhaps gullible devotees. One such disciple was the articulate Joshua Garment, the author of the treatise *The Hebrews' Deliverance At Hand*, published on August 23, 1651, just a few months after Robins abjured his divinity. This treatise was more than an affirmation of Robins' divinity for Garment claimed to be a prophet in his own right and may have written this treatise to propel himself into a now vacant position of leadership.

Garment's views are strikingly similar to those we have already encountered. His definition of God as "one God eternal, not defined nor confined, not clothed with mortal flesh and bone as we are"(7–8) was pure Coppin and Bauthumley. Similarly, Garment's dualist credentials were established when he noted that God "is not the creation nor any part of creation, whose being is in itself only"(8) and hence in a "state being kept closed from men."(6)

Garment's social thought is very reminiscent of Foster's and other apocalyptic strains. Like them Garment warned that "he that shall come and rule with a rod of iron all nations, breaking them to pieces like a potter's vessel and the nations shall not avoid his government for in righteousness he will judge and make war . . . yet the kings of the earth must rage and murmur, fighting against the peaceable multitude."(5) And again like so many Ranters, Garment noted the role the poor and uneducated would play in God's revolution. "In the day of his power," Garment wrote, "he will come and none shall hinder. O then! Who shall stand? Not the wise, not the prudent, not them that would be lords over men's consciences . . ."(5)

No less than other revolutionary Ranters, Garment enthusiastically endorsed God's violent plans for evil civil and religious authorities. "Haste, haste, haste thou man of sin, thy time is running short. God will plague thee for thy judging truth to be blasphemy," he wrote, "but thou shalt come to thine end and none shall help thee."(7) Religious authorities, too, would be judged and found lacking. "The bloody prelates, you must all bow down. Your tything laws must have no room . . . it is like thy fathers, the bishops, thy end like theirs. Think not thou proud new prelate that judgement will not seize on thee as on them."(7) Garment wrote that originally there had been hope for change when "I had hopes God would reform thee but now I know he will destroy thee and that suddenly, even before next March 1652."(7)

One great difference between Garment and other Revolutionary Ranters lay in his deep personal belief in the divine office of John Robins. Garment explained, "In the year 1650 I saw the man called John Robins riding up on the wings of the wind in great glory. Then the word of the Lord came unto me saying, *this* is thy Lord, Israel's King, Judge and Law giver, thou must proclaim his day . . . so that he may enter in."(4) With language identical to that used by Tydford and other Robins disciples, Garment continued, "This is the Melchizedek that Abraham met in the way, even the Abraham that was the first created who is restored, set and sent by God his creator with the name of God his creator, God Almighty, written on him."(4)

Though Robins' mission was to overturn all the world's institutions and redeem mankind, his special task was to deliver the Jews. About this more specific commission Garment observed, "I tell you in the name of God that John Robins is the man ordained by the creator of heaven and earth to lead the Hebrews, dividing the sea in the power of God his creator."(5) Like Moses, Robins would part the seas and "twenty days before next Michaelmas day the sea shall be divided and many Jews that are here in England shall go through on dry foot towards Judea and the Lord said, I will gather all Jews in the world in one place and with signs and wonders in great power bring them through all countries."(5)

It is unfortunate that nothing additional is known about either John Robins or Joshua Garment. The former wrote no treatises at all and the *Hebrews' Deliverance* would seem to be Garment's only work. Yet, the phenomenon of a husband and wife team declaring themselves Jesus and Mary presented itself again in even more dramatic fashion in the persons of William Franklin and Mary Gadbury.

11. William Franklin and Mary Gadbury

We are fortunate in knowing about Franklin and Gadbury. The only record of their activities is the treatise *Pseudo-Christus* (1651) by Humphrey Ellis, a local Southampton minister who attended their trial, interviewed the defendants and their followers and knew many of the townspeople who believed in them. We are also fortunate that Ellis was a fair and objective man who did not polemicize but simply permitted the court records to tell the incredible story. Ellis was confident that his readers would draw the correct—that is, orthodox—conclusions. He was more than a good observer, however, and through conversations with townspeople and neighbors Ellis scrupulously traced the defendants' individual histories. He was as curious about these two people as he assumed his readers might be and like them, he too wished to know how such a strange story could have come about.

At the time of his trial in 1650 William Franklin was forty years old, was married and had three children. He originally came from Overton in Southampton but more recently resided in Stepney Parish and made his living as an apprentice rope maker in London.(6) All who had known him in Overton thought well of him. Neighbors considered him "a civil man, diligent in his calling, honest in his dealings, careful to provide for his family."(6) Similarly, local religious authorities also thought well of Franklin, calling him "very zealous in the duties of religion and very constant in the practice and observance of the ordinances of the gospel."(6)

This praise was universal until 1646, some four years earlier, when Franklin became seriously ill. His physician, Dr. Charles Stamford, claimed that Franklin had been distracted since that time and often suffered from "fits." Though he recovered, he was changed and began to proclaim "that he was God, that he was Christ."(7) He soon denied the truth of Scripture and Church ordinances, spoke in tongues and made prophecies. In short, William Franklin was acting after a strange fashion. Either he became insane during his illness or he had become a Ranter, but in either event his congregation expelled him from their fellowship.

Mary Gadbury was an equally interesting person. About thirty years old at the time of the trial, she had been deserted by her husband seven years earlier when he ran off to Holland with a domestic servant. Since that time Mary had lived in Watling Street in London where she sold lace, pins, and other small wares for a meager living. Her neighbors thought well of her, considering her "to have been of honest conversation and to have lived in good repute and religiously amongst them."(8)

According to her confession, Mary met Franklin through a neighbor and she explained that each had a peculiar effect upon the other. He spoke in tongues and had visions and she too would experience visions each time she met Franklin. In one instance she suffered terrible shaking and trembling fits and then a voice sounded to her, declaring, "It is the Lord, it is the Lord."(10) At other times she saw bright lights and heard trumpets and on one occasion she experienced a very severe convulsion and afterwards proceeded to tell Franklin many intimate details of his earlier life. She continued to have visions, he continued to speak in tongues, and they continued to see each other as often as possible.

Franklin became aware of the spiritual significance of their extraordinary relationship very quickly. He explained to Mary that all of his past and even his current domestic situation consisting of wife and children no longer applied to him but to the old William Franklin born of the flesh. Franklin also explained to Mary that God had sent her to him and set her apart for his use.(11)

Soon after this conversation the two began experiencing the same visions. In one vision she was told to sell all her goods and give the money to the poor and then depart for the land of Ham which she understood to be the county of Hampshire.(14) Since he had experienced the exact same vision they determined this was the divine commission they had expected. Then she had an additional vision in which she was told, "I have made an end to sin and transgression for me and my people."(15) Finally, "he [Franklin] was proclaimed by her to be the Christ, so she declared herself and was acknowledged by their seduced followers to be the Spouse of Christ . . . to apply to herself the Scripture of the *Lamb's marriage being come and his bride to have made herself ready.* . . . Thus is Franklin now in the room of Christ to her . . . and she putting herself in the room of the Church, Christ's mystical body, to be the *Spouse of Christ, the Bride, the Lamb's Wife.*"(16) In short, Franklin and Gadbury were about to reenact the lives of Simon Magus and Helen in the land of Ham, where the divine Mary was not Christ's mother but his spouse and lover, and, as we shall see, a great deal more, too.

In November of 1649 Franklin and Gadbury took lodging at the Inn of the Star in Andover.(17) She appears to have been the brains of the operation, and according to her confession they devised an interesting strategy to make converts to their cause. While Franklin returned to London for two

162

weeks to borrow money, Gadbury would stay in Andover and "tell abroad that she had seen Christ in the person of a man, not declaring him to be the person at present whom she did thereby intend, that so by the time he should return it would somewhat appear how their design would take and what might be the effect of it."(17)

Accounts of Mary's strange visions soon took hold in this market town and many people sought her out at the inn where she stayed, hoping to obtain help for their problems. Mary was enchanting and alluring and during the two-week trial period she developed a very large following. She would enter a trance and prophesy for her visitors that Christ would appear within two weeks. The Christ she described fit the form of William Franklin. She told them how each of them would be "reborn in Mary" and how the labor pains with which she suffered throughout this period were for all those about to be so reborn. From his own personal investigations Ellis recounted how individuals would come to her and "then she would pretend her travail to be for such a one, who, being at length wholly wrought upon and seduced by her, it must be ascribed to her travails an effect of them, that must be the person for whom she was in travail and such a person the spiritual birth now brought forth by her."(21–22)

The narrative continues, describing the conversions of Edward Spradbury, Mrs. Woodward, and later, Mr. Woodward, a local minister. In each case Mary's visions and prophecies were geared to each individual personality and in every instance the convert became an ardent enthusiast for Franklin as Christ. Gadbury created so large a congregation of *his* supporters that when Franklin returned from London he and Mary were forced to leave the Inn of the Star where they caused continual disruptions. Those with the spirit never want, however, and the divine duo were invited by the Woodwards to live in their large house and use it as their special quarters.(25) This move provided excellent opportunities and Ellis could report that "multitudes of persons now resort to Mrs. Woodwards, to see, hear, and speak with them."(31)

Franklin was so successful as Christ that it soon became impossible for the divine duo to meet the needs of the community in person. Ellis does not know whether credit should be given to Gadbury or Franklin, but they created a full church structure and appointed the "very active persons to be the Preachers, spreaders and publishers of it abroad to the people."(31) One John Noyce was made John the Baptist. Henry Dixon was appointed one of the destroying angels mentioned in the book of *Revelation,* and Edward Spradbury was to be a witness mentioned in *Revelation* and also a healing angel. William Holmes was also appointed a destroying angel. Despite the

163

use of such silly titles, these second tier ministers were effective missionaries with Ellis reporting, not happily, "This infection dispersed abroad by such active publishers of it, began to spread exceedingly that too many now began to be taken with it." (33)

In Ellis' opinion, the majority of Franklin's followers consisted of "credulous persons, wavering and uncertain in matters of religion, having itching ears after some new things, were soon drawn away and seduced by them."(31) He described Franklin as possessing a charismatic personality with Mary Gadbury able to deliver powerful sermons in a slow, austere and eerie voice. Through the efforts of their special angel helpers, the new church grew so rapidly throughout the region that ministers from other denominations became increasingly upset. Ellis wrote how "such notice and great offence is a justly taken threat by diverse godly and well affected ministers and others." These in turn decided "to stop the further spreading of this so great an evil"(33) and it was at this point the local JPs were brought into the picture.

The Justices of the Peace of Southampton issued arrest warrants during the January quarter session of 1650 for William Franklin and Mary Gadbury and Mr. and Mrs. Woodward, Henry Dixon, Edward Spradbury and Goody Waterman. Noyce and Holmes could not be located.(34) This assorted crew appeared before the Justices Thomas Bettesworth and Richard Cobbe and from the very outset of the hearing the trial was a veritable circus with the court in an uproar every time one of the defendants rose to speak. Witnesses for the prosecution testified that Franklin had indeed presented himself as God with one Fortunatus of Woodhay swearing that he had heard Franklin affirm he was "Christ, the Son of the living God, the Messiah that sits at the right hand of God . . . that his spirit was abroad gathering souls and that he now came in the fullness of time to save the very Elect." Others testified that Franklin called himself by the oft-used Ranter name for God, 'I AM' and "the very King of Heaven."(36) Franklin's disciples were also condemned for teaching that Franklin was the risen Christ, indeed God himself. The examination of the defendants indicated that all conceded that they had indeed preached as charged and continued to maintain these opinions. Margaret Woodward declared to the court that Franklin "is her Lord and her King, and that she is saved by his death and passion."(39) Others testified that they had been spiritually reborn through the efforts of Mary Gadbury, "the Queen of Heaven."(39) It was also established that Franklin and Gadbury "did call themselves man and wife and that they lay together in one bed in his [i.e., Woodward's] house." (39)

Franklin's testimony confirmed the statements made by prosecution

164

witnesses. After presenting his personal background and history he noted "that it was revealed to him a vision that she [i.e., Mary] should be set aside for his use. He claimed to be the Son of God."(41) Mary Gadbury did not wish to testify but denied having had sexual intercourse with Franklin and affirmed that it had been revealed to her in a vision that Franklin was Christ.(41)

If JPs were often incompetent, this trial indicated how shrewd some others might be when most of those charged with crimes are known to them. Rather than throwing the whole lot into jail, for indeed all were guilty under the terms of the Blasphemy Act, the justices thought it best to influence Franklin into making a recantation. If indeed the two had as many followers as orthodox observers believed, finding them guilty as charged would have been easy but would also create martyrs and do little about their followers who would continue to keep faith in them. Meeting with him in private chambers, the JPs threatened and evidently sufficiently scared Franklin so that he entered the court and made a full recantation that he was neither Jesus Christ nor God after all. (42–43) His followers were shocked and dismayed and began jumping and shouting with Mary crying out, "Hast thou done this? Is this by thy hand?" Edward Spradbury shouted, "Thou villain, how hast thou deceived us by thy lies?" Franklin's sole response was to turn to his followers, shrug and declare, "You see what the times are."

The outcome of the trial was as follows. Dixon, Spradbury and the Woodwards were bound over to the next Assize for trial according to the terms of the Blasphemy Act. Mary Gadbury and William Franklin were sent to Bridewell and the common jail, respectively, having been found guilty of adultery and bigamy. Later, at Franklin's request, Mary was transferred to the common jail so that they might be together. (44–45) Ellis did not explain why the JPs would have honored Franklin's request.

The entire issue of Franklin and Gadbury might have ended here but such was not the case. According to Ellis, many people came to see Franklin and Gadbury in jail and their fame continued to spread through the region. Ellis reports letters coming to the prison and protesting their imprisonment and declaring Franklin and Gadbury miracle workers and "how they never miss to make trumpets sound in the very bellies of their converts and great ships appear to the view of all people near them."(46) Perhaps shaking his head in amazement, Ellis concluded about these converts, "Let them discourse with whom they will, priests or else, they are all converted, leave all and follow them."(46) Rather than inhibiting the growth of the sect, imprisoning the spiritual set seemed to have the opposite effect with

Ellis admitting that since going to jail, "for the most part it is thought they have converted to them five or six hundred."(47)

Despite the recantation, Ellis found Franklin less than contrite when interviewing him in prison. According to Ellis, Franklin "rather labored to put it off, to deny it, to make it to be the mistakes of others . . . [and] no particular acknowledgement of anything could be got from him."(47) Mary Gadbury seemed more confused. At times she continued to affirm the truth of her visions and the content of her spiritual message but at other times "she would say she was deceived, even undone by him and lay all blame upon him."(48)

The next court of Assize session met in March with Franklin and company heard on the seventh and eighth of the month by Lord Chief Justice Rolls. Both Franklin and Gadbury issued recantations with the latter denying ever having had sexual intercourse with Franklin. The outcome was that all the women were sentenced to stay in Bridewell until the next assize. Mary Gadbury, however, petitioned for her freedom and was released on April 22, 1650, and returned to London. William Franklin, the Woodwards, Spradbury and Dixon were sentenced to the common jail, there to remain till they put in good security for their good behavior. To the best of anyone's knowledge, this ended the short careers of Franklin and Gadbury.

It is obvious that both of our divine couples were a different sort of Ranter from those encountered in previous chapters. First, the element of chicanery, so obvious in both these last cases, removed them from Salmon, Coppe, Coppin and Foster whose religious beliefs were quite sincere. Even Clarkson assumed the role of a charlatan and confidence man only after becoming confused and disillusioned with both himself and Rantism. Chicanery, however, does little to explain why so many people could be convinced of Franklin's divinity. Many, no doubt, as Ellis believed, were very gullible and willing to believe any new thing. And yet, we noted earlier that Garment was no fool but a legitimate Ranter and willing to accept Robins as God. If it proves impossible to explain how so humble a foursome as those treated here might attract ardent followers, we might do well to think of Jim Jones, Daddy Grace, Elijah Mohammed and many others in our own time. Should the reader find these would-be Elmer Gantrys curious and mischievous, several later figures will surely seem even more mischievous and definitely more curious.

12. Thomas Tany

Thomas Tany was perhaps the most provocative and radical of all Ranters and he was certainly the most insane. He combined neo-Gnostic dualism with an extreme intellectual anarchism and an absolute faith in his divinity. Nothing is known about his origins or his education and one contemporary called him a "mad transylvanian" though there is evidence to support only half this assertion.[30] When employed, Tany earned a meager living as an itinerant goldsmith but he also lived with John Pordage and other Ranters during particularly bad times. He was an associate of Captain Robert Norwood, who may also have supported him, and who wrote an introduction for one of Tany's works.

Tany was a very prolific author and during the period 1649–1655, the only period of his life about which anything is known, he wrote some sensational treatises. Like other Ranters, Tany spent his six months in jail for denying the existence of heaven and hell and seemed to have had his share of devotees and followers. Yet, few have read his treatises and even those devoting a paragraph to this unhappy radical may, in fact, never have read his works and therefore may never have described his views.

Tany's obvious madness is one problem confronting the curious scholar. Other Ranters were certainly peculiar. Salmon and Foster were neurotic; Coppe, psychotic. The young Clarkson may have been a sociopath. Tany, however, exceeded these Ranter peers for he was incoherently mad. From the first page of his first treatise to the very last page of his last treatise, one cannot escape the feeling that this author of so many curious views and creator of an entire intellectual system was an absolute madman. Such an evaluation need not prejudice the reader, however. Tany's works may appear an incoherent and incomprehensible jumble but once his insanity is separated from the core of Gnostic views he espoused, a clear pattern emerges that is far more radical than anything we have thus far encountered.

Tany's writings fall into two general categories: single sheets and long works. The single sheets, *I Proclaim . . . the Return of the Jews* (1650), *Hear O' Earth* (1654) and *Thau Ram Tonjah* (1654) were expressly written to elucidate Tany's divine calling and identity. His longer works, some of which are very long indeed, bear titles that are bizarre even in an age of strange titles. In 1651 Tany published two treatises, the *Theauraujohn His*

BLASPHEMY, IMMORALITY, AND ANARCHY

Theous-Ori Apokoliptical (hereafter *Apok.*) and the *Theauraujohn His Aurora in Tranlogorum in Salem Gloria* (hereafter *Aurora*). These two interesting writings were followed in the next year by Tany's *Theauraujohn High Priest to the Jews* (hereafter *High Priest*). In 1653 Tany published two additional treatises. His *Theauraujohn Tani, His Second Part,* (hereafter *Tany2*) was the second part of the earlier *Theous-Ori Apokoliptical* of 1651, and Tany's last treatise, *Theauraujohn, His Epitah,* (hereafter *Epitah*) was his last long work. The only work Tany wrote bearing a title both understandable and reasonable was his political treatise of 1651, *Nation's Right in Magna Charta.*

In writing about Tany, we will digress from our usual method. Thus far each author's individual treatise was analyzed separately so that the reader might appreciate the full range and development of that author's views. This method proves impossible when one is writing about Tany. Many of the same ideas are presented in these treatises with each work presenting only a vaguely different context for the idea in question, almost as if Tany had forgotten discussing the idea earlier. Additionally, some ideas are introduced in the earliest works but are developed only in the latest. Even worse, Tany often contradicted himself and while some of his works are very coherent, others are off all four walls at the same time. Last, Tany's peculiar theory of languages and grammar was presented in the last works though their comprehension helps understand the earlier works as well. In short, presenting Tany's writings in serial form would involve incredible repetition and would actually hinder comprehension. Rather, Tany's overall system will be analyzed with differences between earlier and later works noted and explained. Or, to put this all in Tany's own words, "I shall open unto you as the unfoldings are opened unto me . . . the world is round, the gospel is round, the soul of man is round . . . for know, the more near the spheres you come, the more spiritual you must be."(*Tany2.* 88–89) Such statements may appear confusing, but Tany continued, "This is a strange metaphorical expression, but tis a true assertion." Let us then, without further ado, enter the circle of strange metaphorical expressions but true assertions.

There is usually little need to introduce an author to the reader before proceeding to that author's works, other than through the author's background or education, means of livelihood and other pertinent data. This is not the case when dealing with Thomas Tany, however, if only because the author possessed several different identities. Indeed, all three of his single sheet publications were written to establish some new identity, and the

168

introductions of most of his treatises also present vital information about how the author conceived of himself at that point. If one takes all his publications into account, several different personalities emerge, some the product of Tany's insanity but others the product of the Gnostic dualism he espoused.

Identity #1. Prophet to the World

Like other Ranters, Tany envisioned himself as a divine messenger commissioned to impart divine truth to the remainder of mankind. In his *Theous-Ori Apokoliptical* Tany explained the nature of his role. "But know Beloved," Tany wrote, "I am sent to unlock the locked depths of man's darkness and unveil truth," and a few pages later he added, "I shall, brethren, discover to you through God's mystery that that is hid to Sons of Man."(45, 59)

Tany's message was a wisdom or gnosis the essence of which must be kept secret. He explained that "the apostles themselves were ignorant of this mystery . . . [or] else they would have declared it in some one place or other."(22) Indeed, he could not be sure who would read his treatise and therefore cautioned, "I beseech you, mind, for this discovery is not revealed to the Sons of Man."(22) Tany explained that he did not fall upon this great truth by accident, for "After fourteen weeks in humiliation, in fasting and prayer frequently, the power fell upon me in my shop and smote me dumb and then blind and then dead in the beholding of hundreds of people. Then I was corded and bound in my bed and then I received instruction."(A2b) Foster, too, we noted earlier, was tied to his bed and like Coppe, Tany claimed he was unaware or unconscious of the workings of the spirit. "I was forced to write, I neither understood nor knew what I wrote and when it was wrote."(*Epitah.* p. 1)

Throughout his many treatises Tany claimed to be the explicator of a divine truth which was variably manifested to him. On the most obvious level, he was prepared to discern the differences between illusion and truth, an important role for any dualist preacher. "Now if our eyes were fully open we might see the full state," he explained, "for the whole mystery lies in the sun and the moon."(*Apok.* p. 17) Together, these two images "fully represent all things and contain under their hieroglyphics whatever is and is not."(*Apok.* p. 38) While both images appeared to be equally real and equally valid, they expressed the dual illusions of physical and spiritual reality. "The sun is the true light and the moon is a false light . . . for she received [light] from the sun and shows it to us as if it were her own light and that is false deceit."(*Apok.* p. 17) Use of the feminine to describe deceit was not accidental, as we shall see, but fortunately for the reader, Tany could lead toward a wisdom which might enable him to avoid error.

The content of Tany's message was variable. Like other Ranters, he espoused a mild Joachite apocalyptic millenarianism. Accepting a trifold partition of time Tany explained that "the Jews' ceremonies were beauteous for a time and then vanished, the apostolic beauteous for a time, which time is ended . . . now comes the Evangelical living."(*Tany2*, p. 57) Also like other Ranters Tany came to preach to an England seemingly unwilling to accept God's new plan for mankind and noted, "Therefore tremble O' England and woe unto thee O' France, thy judgment is appointed and the time hastens." Like Salmon, Foster and others Tany believed days of trouble would come. "Beloved," he consoled, "days of mourning and sorrow are at hand for the earth is ripe, ready to be reaped . . . and storm is coming."(*Tany2*, p. 91) To this point, Tany's identity paralleled those of other Ranters who also claimed divine insight and a social message for the world. The mysterious quality of Tany's message was similar in expression to that of earlier Gnostics who also claimed the secret gnosis. Tany did not stop at this point.

Identity #2. Theauraujohn: Prophet to the Jews.

Even before Tany assumed a world-redeeming commission, he claimed the special role of redeemer of the Jews. Like so many other Ranters, Thomas Tany found the Jews irresistible and his first publication, *I Proclaim from the Lord of Hosts, the Return of the Jews*, of 1650, marked Tany's debut as a radical pamphleteer. In this single-sheet, Thomas Tany introduced himself to a waiting world as follows: "Hear ye O Jews my Brethren. I am a Jew from the Tribe of Reuben but unknown to me till the Lord spake unto me by VOICE . . . and he changed my name from Thomas to Theauraujohn, since November 23, 1649." Tany signed all subsequent treatises with this name, among others, and the theme of the return of the Jews to Zion would also recur. A new Israel, Tany informs us, "shall be the glory of all the Earth and the Fear of the Nations."

Thomas Tany was neither Jewish nor of the Tribe of Reuben, but he was not the only Ranter to identify with Jews. Foster, Garment and others also linked their vision of the saint's future with that of the Jewish people. This identification was also affirmed in Tany's first serious treatise, the *Theauraujohn His Aurora in Tranlogorum in Salem Gloria* of 1651. The opening letter of that work explained, "I am Reuben, the Lord's first born and the first of the first trine [i.e., tribe]" and he signed the letter "Theaurau-john Tannijour, Allah Al, High Priest, Sabbah Scribajail." The treatise itself refers to Tany as "my servant, I have chosen thee,"(50) but on the last page of the work Tany referred to himself as "I, Theauraujohn, the Jew of the Tribe of Judah of the seed of David according to the flesh and spirit, wrote this book . . . for I am sent forth for the gathering of the Jews, my Brethren, home [which] you say you pray for."(58) Though Tany claimed to be of both the tribe of Judah and Reuben, it is doubtful that too many readers held him to this inconsistency. Any Englishman wishing to iden-tify with a persecuted Jewish people was probably peculiar from the outset and as such could claim a lineage from as many tribes as he liked.

Tany's identity underwent modification in his *Theous-Ori Apokolipti-cal*. Here Tany claimed "I, Theauraujohn saw what John [the apostle] saw," adding a page later who he truly was when he explained, "I am the alpha and omega, the end and the beginning . . . My brother John was a beginning flowing forth in that Makkademical expression, I come to put an end to that Makkademical expression."(36) Makkademical or no, 1651 saw other elucidations on Tany's identity. In his political treatise, *Nation's Right in Magna Charta*, he wrote on the opening page "written by me, Theauraujohn Tannijjour High Priest Scribajail, Earl of Essex or other-wise Essex Tenet of Norms or Normandi, Lord Paulet of sens in France . . . of the royal desentive from Aaron of the Lord's High Priest, desen-tive from the right Henry VII which was of the race of Jews of the Tartarian line."(1)

Tany's *Theauroujohn High Priest to the Jews* of 1652 combined a little of the old with some new. On the one hand he wrote, "My brethren, God has sent me forth (the High Priest and Recorder of the thirteen tribes of the Jews) for their return from captivity." He also noted, however, "My descent is in the Tribe of Reuben, of the House of Austria, as England, France, and Spain shall witness."(1) The year 1654 also saw new elucidations. The single-sheet *Hear O Earth* indicated that Tany's name had been changed to Thau Ram Tonjah, Leader of the People, with the single sheet *Thau Ram Tonjah* claiming, "I demand the crown of FRANCE as lineally descended from Charles of Castille who was son in law to Charles the Great. Next I demand the crown both of REME and ROME, from my ancient parent Pope Nicholas of the House of Austria who married the Flamina of Flan-dria in whose RIGHT lies included the title unto NAPLES, SICILY, and JERUSALEM, *the inheritance of all my Brethren, the Jews.*"

As we can see, Tany had one overriding identity and several more minor claims. Had the redemption of the Jews been his only divine commission,

Tany would have proved far less controversial. Rather than censoring him and locking him up in jail for six months, Parliament might have wished him well and sent a delegation to see him off to the holy land from the port of his choice. His claims to several European thrones were not taken seriously because other radicals made the same claims and, in any event, these thrones were occupied at the time. Tany, however, was the alpha to omega from the Makkedemical expression. No other Ranter claimed so divine an identity.

Identity #3. Madman for God

Tany was very much annoyed when readers and others thought him mad. To settle the issue once and for all he wrote, "And from this day know I am not mad as they have accounted me, but it is the blindness in them that counts it madness in me."(*Apok.* p. 33) Tany had little difficulty explaining why he was condemned. "I am but one and the whole world is against me," he complained and others thought him mad because "I must untie their tied ceremony and destroy their foundation."(*Apok.* p. 21).

The essence of the condemnation, Tany believed, was misunderstanding of his divine commission and role. He conceded that it was "the gospel in me that you count blasphemy, hath made me act so strangely."(*Apok.* p. A2a) And a page later he continued, "Now if you condemn me for blasphemy . . . I can say then that my blasphemy is holiness and you are found blasphemers with your high cry of holiness."(*Apok.* A2b) Even admirers thought Tany insane. In one introductory letter to the *Apokoliptical* written by a certain Dr. Johns, that gentleman refers to Tany as "the accounted madman of the times, who can speak somewhat experimentally"(*Apok.* p. 1) and even Tany's more coherent writings are often plagued by lapses into incoherence. In his perfectly clear and well-organized political treatise *Nation's Right in Magna Charta*, Tany halted his discussion of English political development to make the following statement:

> I have put three small queries in this little manuscript that by them I may know it to be my own. 1.) What is the creative part of the Cabbalestrial incline in the terrestrial orbs of the Theabarick. That word is Calde. 2.) What is the incline of the Philiades in her coertive part in the New Trine in the hemisphere of sol; that word now seems strange but to let you know there is a new birth in the Planitoriam scheme or scine. 3.) What is the inclusive PERTINEAT at the conclave of the Mediterranean assome?(6)

Fortunately for the reader, Tany did not attempt to answer these weighty queries. It can be very frustrating to read a complicated argument and have Tany provide a final proof in the following words: "Take this from me that am a man unlearned in any art or tongue. *Arki, vea, arni, ophiat, al sabi, arni, ary, alpha, am, O Threarpha, alba army anat.*" (*Epitah*, p. 8) Perhaps no less might be expected from the rightful ruler of REME and ROME. Tany was very intelligent and also very insane. Sometimes these qualities came together and made for strange reading and sometimes Tany was clear and coherent, and very, very radical. One must, in all cases, be very patient.

Scripture and God's Truth

Tany's views of Scripture were essentially neo-Gnostic. Like other Ranters, he espoused a spiritual reading of the text and disparaged the literal value of the words. But like Marcion and the Cathari, Tany also taught that much of Scripture was erroneous and the work of the Devil. Hence, at the same time that he could state that "it is true that I do deny the Scriptures as you hold them forth"(*Tany2*, p. 49) Tany could also assert, "I deny not the Scriptures but the lie that is added to or set for Scripture."(*Apok.* p. 28) Other Ranters thought that error crept into Scripture through ignorance or through improper translation, but Tany accounted for these errors through the active influence of the Devil upon humanity wishing to turn Christians to evil. This erroneous part of the Bible "is only a lie made by men to fetch about (their) designs."(*Apok.* p. 64) As a result, Christianity itself too was a lie. "A lie you have learned and a lie you have conceived and a lie you have declared," Tany wrote, "the root a lie, the branchings forth they are the same."(*Tany2*, p. 9) To the Church of England Tany declared, "You Priests in England, you have been founded from the anti-Christ and not from the true Christ, you have been and are a lie."(*Tany2*, p. 5) Since the Scriptural root was a lie, and the ecclesiastical branchings forth no better, it did not surprise Tany that normal Christians were also evil. "The reason you act so wickedly, you Christians," Tany explained, "is because you have gotten the dead apostles' dead expressions contained in their writings, which you count the gospel."(*Tany2*, p. 11)

Tany never clarified which sections of the Bible were acceptable and which tainted though such distinctions were important to him. "I am come not to asperse the true Scriptures," he explained, "but to take one man's inventions that is indeed inserted for the true Scriptures for all is not Scriptures that is written in the Bible and the New Testament."(*Tany2*, p. 1) There was an easy method to determine which parts of Scripture were true.

Since the soul and true Scripture were both divine, the former instinctively responded to the latter. Tany observed that "the true Scriptures, tis the divine life of God in the soul and it is written by and with the *Digitus Dei*, the Spiritual finger or finger spirit of God."(*Tany2*, p. 67).

The test of Scriptural truth lay within the believer himself and where Protestantism would have its followers read the Bible, Tany widened this spiritual franchise with "everyman being a gospel unto himself."(*Tany2*, p. 55)

Calling the true Bible "the mystery of mysteries" and "none but the Evangelical eye can view it."(*Tany2*, p. 80) Tany was at pains to express how the words and their meaning, like the soul and the body, might in fact be very different. "Let me tell you," Tany confided, "there is not one word that came from Christ and his apostles but all were mystery." (*Tany2*, p. 85) Those venerating the literal word are mistaken for "the written letters are not holy but the intendant spirit it is holy and [the] holy can not stand on paper and ink but in the souls of men."(*Tany2*, p. 48, incorrectly numbered 41)

Tany presented several examples of the proper interpretation of the dead literal words of Scripture. In the story of Daniel's resistance to the pagan king, Tany asked, "What is meant by the kingdom or Prince of Persia that opposeth Daniel? Was it a temporal prince? No." Rather, he explained, "It was that spirit of darkness that opposeth Daniel."(*Tany2*, p. 30) No princes, no lions, indeed, nothing outside of Daniel's own internal fears. Another example of misleading Scriptural wording concerned the virgin birth. Virginity referred not to Christ's mother, but "the virgin is the womb of our souls . . . in which is inherent the deity."(*Apok*. p. 8) Later we will have additional opportunities to see how Tany spiritualized the wording of Scripture away from the apparent literal meaning of the words.

Thus far, Tany's spiritualized reading of the text would seem standard Ranter fare. But even the proper allegorical and spiritual methods might not elicit from the text the true depth of God's meaning. Unlike his Ranter colleagues but very much like earlier Gnostics, Tany, too, believed in verbal codes and verbal formulae through which truth might be expressed. Hence, allegory might conceivably be aided by numerology or other letter codes. Gnostics believed that the archons ruling the universe were fooled by Christ into letting him pass through from the heavens to the earth. Through his use of similar secret language codes the believer, too, might pass from this mundane to the transmundane world. Indeed, such codes often constituted the essence of the Gnostics' special "gnosis" and the basis upon which all divine-human communication must occur. Hence, Tany, like his spiritual ancestors and intellectual forebears, had a theory of languages to explain not merely the allegory but the mystery as well.

Tany's Theory of Language

Thomas Tany's theory of languages is one of several great hurdles the reader must overcome because it is central to his use of Scripture as well as his insanity and to the way the two were interwoven. In his *Theauraujohn His Aurora* . . . Tany explained that he wrote this treatise "to let you and all people know that there is now a restoring the people to a pure language . . . [and] to unseal that sealed book and evangelical light that lies wrapped in the womb of the so called Law and Gospel."(54) This admirable project of deciphering the language of the gnosis must be applauded by all serious minded students of the truth. Yet, from the earliest pages of this important work through the remainder of Tany's corpus of writings, there was something very peculiar about all of Tany's biblical citations. Like other students of Scripture, Tany made extensive use of Greek, Latin and Hebrew and several other languages as well. The problem, one soon realizes, is that despite his confident use of them, in fact Thomas Tany knew none of these languages at all. At least one eminent historian has been fooled by Tany's gibberish but Tany himself tells us, "As the Lord lives, I neither can or ever could read any Hebrew or Greek or any tongue but English. Neither do I know any Hebrew but my own characters and then . . . I could write them down but knew not the meaning of any one of them."(*Apok*.6) Indeed, Tany acknowledged having difficulties with English, too, and a great deal more when he admitted "I am not well Englished for many words I understand not; neither have I memory." (*Apok*.62) Like Moses, Tany possessed a speech impediment, writing, "I am not learned in what I declare and neither yet could I ever speak unto people nor dispute, but read unto the people what I wrote."(*High Priest*, 3.)

To make a very long and bizarre story much shorter and simpler, almost every one of Tany's hundreds of citations drawn from Scripture allegedly in the original languages was gibberish and made no sense at all, at least from the vantage point of Hebrew, Latin, Greek, and Arabic. The English citations, often paraphrases, were usually close to a standard English rendering of the text, but one might wonder why an author would cite foreign sources and then voluntarily disown any knowledge of those languages. Much more interesting is why those scholars who have written about Tany and who claim to have read his works, did not recognize these languages for what they were.

BLASPHEMY, IMMORALITY, AND ANARCHY

To explain how an ignorant person came to know all these languages, Tany shared with the reader that "I had no learning but in seven days when I was apart I received my divine learning by inspiration so that my light is over all languages and truth in which I can read."(*Aurora*, p. 2) A few pages later Tany added, "God taught me and now I am able to translate the bible itself, which is truth, then insert that truth into any language under heaven."(*Aurora*, p. 11) Tany explained that others, too, claimed the ability to divine the spirit but "much more unto me is this *grace given* that I should *unseal* the hidden *depth of depths* in all *mysteries* and *languages*."(*Aurora*, p. 27) Lest his more educated readers click their tongues in despair Tany reminded them, "Did not the *apostles* at being *called* speak with *new tongues*?" (*Aurora*, p. 27)

The best place to begin Tany's theory of languages is with the letters of the alphabet and his rules of grammar. In the opening epistle to the reader of the *Aurora*, Tany wrote, "I except against five letters in the English alphabet, as W, X, Y, Q, F and OF, is not proper in any state substantial, but the four [6?] are false according to any true state for a true state can not be wrote with a false letter. I write VV for W; for X, K; for Y, I; for Q, G; for F, PH. Now C is weak but tis a true impede."(*Aurora*, A2). Later in that same treatise Tany explained why it was necessary for him to use these different letters. "F is imperfect and to be laid by when I write the Divine mysteries."(40) Similarly, "Q is another of the duplexes to be cast out when I come to my main work, that is, the translation of the hidden truth that lies vilified in the lie that is the Greek tongue."(22) Equally upsetting for Tany was the preposition OF, about which he sagely observed, "O' this English OF doth all the mischief in the whole tongue."(21) The very worst linguistic offense, however, was the use of dipthongs: "Now here comes the birth of generations of deceit in their forged dipthongs as ae, ei, oa, au, el, vieu, etc., of this sort is to be found 2 in 1, 1 in 3, 5 in 1, and from this invention comes the new logic."(34)

The "new logic" that Tany found so upsetting was what others called translation according to standard rules of grammar and vocabulary. Tany rejected all such rigid and formal methods in favor of his more subjective but fluid approach. The benefits of his system were varied. He noted for instance, "I can read a negative derivacy from an affirmative state out of the same radaxes by the collateral conjunct and adjunct."(36) In simpler English Tany essentially believed he could change the affirmative or negative content of the passage according to how he appraised the context of the words involved. Even more beneficial, his method permitted him to transcend individual languages. "The major includes the minor as part Hebrew, part Latin. The major tis properly wrote in, but I am forced to cite many simblims [sic] or words for the radical examplication of the sentence for one language can carry the truth in its full species radically."(1–2) And since the subject of "simblims" has been raised, one should note that "an hieroglyphic is an emblem of somewhat more than is expressed in that semblence, that semblence cited is to allude to somewhat more significant."(40) How wonderful.

All of these rules, which must have made sense to Tany since he made them up, helped in the proper rendition of Scripture. Through their scrupulous application, divine truth might be expressed in all languages and translated from one language to another. "Now when I cite any Latin, Hebrew, Greek, or Arabic or Syriac, or Transilvanian or Muscovian or Orcadialis Orientalis, in any one of these with any word I can *influence the whole sentence*, I can impede the whole *sentence or any word in the sentence* stating it betwixt two *radical words* in any *method I can lessen* or weaken the *tie* of any *bar* in that *word* or *letter* or *semblence* I please, and you can not do this, you can not write true."(16) Tany was certain that few scholars could make these claims and from the distance of three centuries it would appear that he was correct.

Even the most fluid system of translation cannot disregard the peculiarities of the individual languages involved. Consequently, Tany had much to offer about the several languages of which he was ignorant. Greek was very important because it was the language of the gospels. Few scholars, Tany believed, truly understood how complicated Greek translation was. Tany wrote, "Mind, there is *Grekus Ariaback*, there is *Grekus Muscovitus*, there is *Grekus Orientalis* sub luna in 54 degrees Saturn transcendent . . . [and] the four Greek tongues of East Arminia."(*Tani2*, p. 74)

The four Greek tongues of East Arminia find their origin in Hebrew and Tany wrote, "*Alah Almanah alvah asanah ob si heroclock absalah mons in Somann in arararum sola mana aclelab abdonarulabo sonator alma roi delit meco.* This is wrote in the Tartarian tongue in the East Arminia from the Hebrew radaxes, the third descent in that language from the creation."(*Aurora*, p. 19) Other languages too found their origin in Hebrew, Tany explained, "for I know that the Arabic and Chaldee and Syriac and the Muscovy in their original center are, as it were, in the edge or verge of the Hebrew. Now you will say that the majority of them languages is Hebrew; it is granted, but write you in any one of them languages, it is not Hebrew."(*Tany2*, p. 66) All this in turn, is important for translating these many languages into English for "now in English hath the Chaldee tongue been the proper tongue . . . now you think it strange but tis true." (*Tany2*, p. 75)

There can be no doubt that of all the languages Tany did not know, his favorite by far was Hebrew, the language of the Old Testament. Hebrew was also the language of the Devil, however, for the Old Testament far more than the gospels possessed the fleshly hallmarks of satanic evil. Consequently Tany felt obliged to explain, "Now know I write Hebrew in the virgin state, as Moses wrote it, and the same spirit [is] in me dictating forth what itself pleases to insert."(*Aurora*, p. 5) Describing his method as "cabbalestrial," (*Aurora*, p. 81) Tany gave examples of his profound Hebrew usage when treating the non-existent Hebrew word *gabest*. "The Hebrew word doth denominate thus much, *a root, a strength, irresistible, a form, a tower, a cave, a circle*." (*Tany2*, p. 68) But when considering the same term elswhere he explained that even more might be elicited from this term. "I can make it stand for dark or light, heaven or hell, or sea or land or angel or sun or devil."(*Tany2*, p. 82) Tany was tremendously pleased with his linguistic accomplishments and congratulated himself for skills so rare in the scholarly community. He wrote of himself, "Now you will say, 'The man is *learned*, I say, in knowledge' . . . [and] now you admire."(*Aurora*38.). Elsewhere he wrote, "Brethren, you differ and are astounded when I speak two or three words of Latin, then Hebrew, then both."(*Tany2*, p. 82)

Could Tany, in his madness, have believed he could use these languages? Could Tany, in his cynicism, have believed his own creations from Scripture were neither more nor less valid than the equally inspired creations of those who knew the languages but who forced their interpretations in any event? Could Tany, in his silliness, have believed that there was essentially no difference between ignorance and wisdom if the method of reasoning seemed convincing?

Divine Ignorance and Satanic Truth

The scholar devoting many years to language study must condemn Tany outright and yet the issue of Tany's language usage is more complicated than we might at first realize. We have encountered many Ranters claiming some ability, perhaps like that of Paul, to write or interpret the Scriptures. Essentially, Tany went one step further and actually wrote his own Bible citations. Whenever he wished to argue a point or cite Scripture for support, Tany simply made one up and presented it to the reader, allegedly in the original language, to add further credibility. To an extent Tany was forced into this extreme creativity, for the dualism he espoused, as we shall see, was quite extreme. Moreover, centuries of medieval exegetical tradition had successfully elicited from Scripture a variety of meanings through the careful manipulation of the text according to the four-fold method of interpretation where any given word might mean anything from its literal meaning to its virtual opposite.[31] Jerusalem might be a city in Israel or it might represent human perfection, heavenly wisdom, or the future kingdom of God depending upon whether the noun was translated literally, allegorically, anagogically, tropologically, or typologically. The method employed by Coppin, Foster and Salmon relied very heavily upon allegory to strip the text of its literal meaning and was fully consistent with the limits of medieval method.

Even the "literal" method of interpretation vaunted by Protestants during and after the Reformation proved quite flexible.[32] Protestantism objected to the medieval four-fold method as far too flexible and preferred a more literal method that still succeeded in delivering desired meaning from the text. Lefevre D'Étaples, long considered an important source for Protestant method, condemned the spiritualizing of the text away from its plain literal truth and then used Cabbalistic numerological method to determine the literal meaning. This fine author knew medieval exegesis, but, unfortunately, knew very little Hebrew. Perhaps this accounts for his use of numerology.[33]

Martin Luther translated the Bible into German and influenced the development of modern German culture. Unfortunately, Luther, too, knew very little Hebrew and even boasted that he could dispense with grammar in favor of the truths imparted by the holy spirit. Despite these limitations, Luther and his defenders made great claims for the accuracy of his literal translation of Scripture from a language of which he was largely ignorant.[34] Indeed, Martin Bucer, the great Strasbourg reformer and fine student of Hebrew, refused to call himself a translator, preferring instead the term "paraphrast" which he believed better summarized his efforts.

Despite widespread disavowal of medieval linguistic flexibility, the sixteenth and seventeenth centuries produced no consensus regarding method and interpretation of Scripture. Tany's ignorance of Scriptural languages may have been outrageous, yet most Ranter critics were no more educated in Greek or Hebrew than he, and if they did not actually create Scriptural allusions to support their views, they were able to take enough phrases out of context to justify their ideas. Most Ranters, we have seen, were fully able to find adequate Scriptural citation for their views much as those who rejected Ranters found adequate phrases with which to oppose the Ranter's

Scriptural phrases. Indeed, in all the religious, political and social conflicts of the century, all sides found the Bible a true source of quotations for almost any view one wished to advance. Those educated in Scripture could play that instrument like a harp and we have noted the contempt Ranter mechanic preachers had for these Oxbridge products. Similarly, Tany noted that "the love of learning is that beauteous whore that bewitches the natural ingenious spirit in man unto death for her lovely sight is but death." (*Tany2*, p. 82) Such sentiments were common Ranter fare but few advanced compensating concepts as radical as those taught by Tany. In a word, all learning was evil, of human invention and of little value in studying God. "Learning is a *lie*," Tany declared, "it is the name of a thing, it is not the thing but the sound of a substance and it is nothing in itself."(*Tany2*, p. 31) Anticipating the censure of the scholarly world and those who accepted scholarly method, Tany attempted to explain his complicated position. In one of his lucid moments he wrote, "Scholars, you think I speak false Latin because I follow not the learned lying rule," and then added the lynchpin of his logic, "Know, a rule can not be true that is learned."(*Aurora*, p. 2). That which is learned is human, fleshly, evil and far removed from God. Divine truth was obvious within the soul, but human learning was not obvious, required close reasoning and many years of education. On the theory that one cannot hide the sun under a rock, that which is true must be obvious and consequently, that which must be taught, must be false. Hence, as we have seen, Tany condemned learning as a lie and that which must be learned as false.

The logical result of Tany's thought was that the ignorant are truthful while the learned are error prone and actually evil. Tany taught, for instance, "I say it is the learned . . . that pervert Scripture," and logically, "the unlearned can not pervert the Scriptures . . . [because] the unlearned are free from [the] destruction of or by the perverting of the Scripture." (*Tany2*, p. 31)

There can be no question that Tany was very well qualified to speak for the unlettered and ignorant. Indeed, he emphasized how little he knew about anything at all. "When I *write*, I have no knowledge," Tany wrote, affirming what many readers probably thought, "neither *behind* nor *before* but the word that comes . . . it is *itself* expressing *itself*."(*Tany2*, p. 30) Like Coppe and many others, Tany explained that he was not the true author of his views, for "I was forced to write, I neither understood nor knew what I wrote and when it was wrote."(*Tany2*, p. 1) Hardly defensive about his continuing ignorance, Tany prayed to God, "In Thy strength, O my God, deliver me from my own wisdom for it is of the Devil."(*High*

180

THOMAS TANY

Priest, p. 3) He also believed he was in good company. Tany reminded his readers that perhaps "you have forgotten the apostles, being unlearned, that they overcame the great rabbis,"(*High Priest* p. 7) and in the same spirit of divine ignorance Tany also did the same, writing, "I do challenge the universities of Oxford and Cambridge, also the assembly of dissembling, deceived and deceiving clergy."(*High Priest*, p. 2)

Tany did not believe himself to be perpetrating a hoax by creating his own Scriptural allusions and translations. Exact Latin or Hebrew was less essential than capturing the true spirit of the text, and no less an authority than Martin Luther would have agreed. Moreover, Ranters believed in the spirit for it was this agency which enlivened the dormant soul within the dead body for all Ranter systems. It was but a short jump to conclude that the same spirit might certify Scriptural truth. "Know that *the spirit composeth all tongues into one truth.*" Tany informed the reader, "but not as you compose."(*Tany2*, p. 8) Luther, the Anglicans and Oxbridge did not truly trust the spirit for they would not trust human learning if they did. Tany, however, could be sure of two great truths. He was certain he was ignorant and he was certain the spirit was not and that was all there was to know. If asked how he could be certain he was ignorant, Tany would give an answer with a familiar ring. "I return a strange answer that hath not been returned in multitudes of ages, and that is this: I know they are both true because I know neither of them false by reason that I have no knowledge."(*Apok* p. 63) Other scholars would scratch around in libraries consulting lexicons, grammars, concordances, word lists and the like and might still never understand the text while Tany need only question his soul whose integrity was certified and guaranteed by his ignorance. To such scholars Tany could only sigh, "Say what you can for mind, saying is nothing and knowing is all things."(*Tany2*, p. 84) When confronted with his obviously superior intellectual system, Tany believed others must give way in the end. Tany concluded, "Your wisdom in your learned method is lost, for that end I have come forth, to confound your lying learning . . . and I shall put an end to it and save your brains."(*Tany2*, p. 82) Was Tany grinning when he wrote, "Now you brethren, you great ones, be not angry if a *mad* man tell you the truth."(*Tany2*, p. 33) If he was not grinning, it was because he was mad.

It should be obvious to the reader why Thomas Tany was the consummate Ranter, though we have not as yet approached the actual substance of the views he espoused. He created an entire intellectual system with its own languages, phrases, concepts, grammars through which he would express truths coming from the spirit in cooperation with his ignorance. Tany was

181

not merely a radical but an intellectual anarchist unwilling to accept the most basic presuppositions of normative intellectual life: a commonly agreed upon set of sources expressed in commonly accepted languages. Rather than using conventional methods and sources but drawing radical conclusions, Tany created a bizarre system which guaranteed total freedom to his imagination, his uncultivated and ignorant soul, and his madness.

Tany's method at once hinders and helps the reader of his works. Because the reader must struggle through some of the most incredibly bizarre citations allegedly drawn from other languages, the reader is hindered and must have patience. Citation after citation of gibberish can test one's endurance, however, and one may fall into Tany's trap and actually begin reading these quotations for content. But the reader is helped as well as hindered. There is never any doubt about the content of Tany's views because every citation rendered in English from Grekus Orcadialis or anything else was sure to support the very essence of Tany's views for why else would he have created it in the first place? Consequently, if one can accept Tany's Scriptural citations as a tool through which he expressed his opinions, albeit a bogus tool, one can read Tany with ease. Indeed, it may be easier to read Tany than other authors for one never need be concerned with the textual accuracy of his citations or the degree of agreement between his views and his sources. Just follow the spirit.

Thomas Tany's Religious Views

Thomas Tany was a more extreme and systematic dualist than most other Ranters. In clear terms, Tany differentiated between God and the world. "God is good, undeniable by any," he wrote, "but for all his creation to be good in themselves, that is denied."(*Apok.* p. 37) Tany differed from other Ranters, however, in attempting to delineate a full system of aeonian emanation through which he accounted for how a pure and good God might have created a foul and disgusting material world. In a less obscure moment Tany explained that "God, from all eternity did create stages and degrees in creation,"(*Apok.* p. 57) and in a more obscure moment delineated that "distilling from the fountain [i.e., God] is trouble to the same that was one with the fountain in the head or center, by the variety of ascents and descents that it doth encounter with its course."(*Apok.* p. 16) Or, the purity of expression that characterized the center of the fountain was lost through the ascents and descents through the aeonian chain of emanations. From the center of the fountain, each additional emanation was decreasingly divine and increasingly removed from the "fountain of divine light" for light "can not be light *as it was in the fountain* for descents must be from ascents."(*Apok.* p. 17)

Tany explained that creation was initially divine because God provided the initial impulse when "a command came from that essence, that is to say, from the Lord creator to his first, second, third descents, etc." (*Apok.* p. 32) From the divine perspective, the idea of creation involved "infolding, infolding, infolding in itself, unfolding (the world) is created by and from the unfoldings" (*Apok.* p. 7) and elsewhere "the whole creation is but the unfoldings of himself in his varieties and his clothing himself in the creative, in their creatived estate."(Apok. p. 33)

The constant unfolding involved in creation where pure ideas were trundled from aeon to aeon and would lead, in turn, to other ideas thereby creating the plenitude or fullness of ideas characterizing the beautiful world of God's fullness. "Now know if God should cease from varieties, he must cease from being God," (*Tany2*, p. 57) Tany explained, but also that "God is love, he let down his loveliness in created appearances."(*Tany2*, p. 85) Thus, the idea of creation and the ideas involved in creation were beautiful and good and demonstrated God's outward expanding love. Unfortunately, these beautiful ideas soon became enmeshed with matter.

Before the encasing of man within a fleshly exterior, he existed as another of the pure ideas found within the mind of God. At this point, "When we were not created and uncome forth, we were as he is, that is, in perfection." (*Apok.* p. 12) This condition changed drastically in creation when man became physical, a process referred to by Tany as "the first fall."(*Apok.* p. 17) Explaining that "the body earthly is clay and dung," (*Apok.* p. 3) Tany noted that "he fell by coming forth, he no sooner was but he was not." (*Apok.* p. 17)

Tany rejected the Scriptural story which accounted for evil and sin by blaming humanity for some failure of will or character flaw in original sin. Rather than presenting man as the perpetrator of the crime, Tany, like other Ranters, saw Adam as the victim of the crime. He wrote about creation in matter: "Thus he fell, how? Not by eating an apple."(*Apok.* p. 9) Rather, Tany taught that "his very being in flesh was his fall and he became like a beast that perisheth."(*Apok.* p. 57)

In one sense only did man differ from animals of the field. Man possessed a soul which is "not of the body, but enclosed within the circumference of the body."(*Apok.* p. 3) Unlike the body, the soul "is no created substance for this is the divine breath of God."(*Apok.* p. 3) At first, the soul did not realize that it was enclosed in matter and isolated from God. Tany compared man to "vegetables, yet again we were in innocence, then being so, but the spirit of the great world took us into it and so we became one with that."(*Apok.* p. 12)

Tany's "spirit of the great world" was essentially the same force referred to by others as Satan. He rejected the simplistic Bible story where mankind was beguiled by a talking reptile and similarly, Tany also rejected the simplistic Bible story that accounted for Eve's creation from Adam's rib. "God made man and woman, not as the story saith," Tany wrote, "of a rib of the man, I deny that."(*Apok.* p. 23) Rather, Eve was made from pure matter without a soul and hence "this subtle beast of the field, in Genesis, was the lustful desire that hold within the woman."(*Apok.* p. 51) Never actually explaining Eve as the devil, but as the reptile and chief agent of the devil, Tany continually envisioned Eve as man's opposite much as Satan was God's opposite. He wrote, "As the Lord liveth, the woman is man's weakness," (*Apok.* p. 56) and it was Eve who turned "the mind of man to lust." (*Apok.* p. 55) It was Eve who represented the "spirit of the great world" and Eve who brought about the second fall of poor Adam. "The woman is weakness to strength," Tany explained, "for it doth like a foil set off the luster of the diamental perfection."(*Apok.* p. 55) The result of Eve's innate lustfulness was "polluted man, [where] the divine and evangelical light in its species is so far vilified that the luster [i.e., soul] is buried in the grave of man's carnality."(*Apok.* p. 6) In forcing Adam to live according to the "spirit of the great world" he no longer sought God but the devil. "Everything loves his own," Tany explained of Adam's latent carnality, "so man must by that rule love the earth he was made of." (*Tany2*, p. 89) Human consciousness and awareness were carnal and not holy, fleshly and not spiritual and thus "the body is acted upon by the spirit in man and not by the soul."(*Tany2*, p. 37) There was one great service woman provided for mankind. Though she led Adam into sin, Eve's descendants could be of value to man. Should a man wish to be spiritual but find himself plagued by female sexual thoughts and fantasies, "the woman taketh away that lust, that desire [and] in this state the woman was good. You men and women understand what I mean."(*Apok.* p. 55)

This very demeaning and sexist view of women and femininity is repugnant to both classical Christianity and twentieth-century social ideals, if for different reasons. Though Tany believed Eve did not possess a soul, his views reflected the traditional understanding that women were of little value in themselves, and the source of temptation and cause of evil in the world. And yet, woman might be enjoyed sexually for it was Eve who first led poor Adam into sin by seducing him. From the dualist's vantage point Eve was an easy target. Earlier Gnostics held femininity responsible for the creation of matter in the world and we have observed how Salmon and Foster, too, accounted for evil in the world by pointing to feminine complicity. Salmon identified evil with femininity and described femininity in terms of evil. Tany was even more crass for he denied Eve a soul and held her accountable for evil by turning man's heart to sex. And yet, he also maintained that man might indulge in sex "to lower the desire for lust." Thus, between God's inability to create ideas without use of matter and female culpability for polluting the male's beautiful, clean and spiritual soul, poor Adam was doomed from the start with almost no hope at all. As a result, "The Devil is within, that is, the deceiving heart in man is always hatching his own deformity."(*Apok.* p. 25)

The redemption from an evil carnal world followed usual Ranter ideas. Over and again Tany wrote that no righteousness was possible until the material body was destroyed. "Until the tincture of evil be cast forth, righteousness can not be acted,"(*Epitah* p. 9) Tany wrote, or "alas, this hell is your body . . . you are prisoned here and your resurrection is at going out of this hell."(*Apok.* p. 57) When the body is destroyed "the life returns to the fountain from whence it had its origin, the gross material body beastial returning to the influences."(*Apok.* p. 3) In short, "the human tastes death that the spirit may take life."(*Apok.* p. 4)

Man's soul is redeemed through God's efforts much as it was first lost because of God's creation. Hence, much as original sin was not the result of human effort, "Salvation, tis not to be obtained by man neither is it lost by man."(*Apok.* p. 4) Other Ranters emphasized the value of human suffering as the process through which the believer might extricate the soul from the body and most envisioned the mortal Jesus Christ providing the pattern of suffering to be emulated by man. Christ's humanity was an essential feature in Ranter soteriology for there was little hope for any person if a mortal Christ could not overcome the material force of the world.

Tany's soteriology differed from typical Ranter fare in two significant ways. First, it is God and not man who affects human redemption. Other Ranters provided for an initial divine calling to enable man to find his soul, but Tany has God provide the entire process of salvation. "His work now is to unwork this Adam and unbury this buried truth" Tany wrote. "Tis God his work in restoring him and giving him his that was at first."(*Apok.* p. 6)

Tany also differed from other Ranters regarding Christology. Because his dualism was more extreme than that of most others, Tany could envision no possibility for man to overcome his own corporality on the basis of his own efforts. Hence, Jesus was not mortal and provided no pattern of behavior for others to emulate because no mortal could transcend the body.

Over and again Tany explained, "God is a spirit, Jesus is the same. 'I and my Father are one.' "(*Epitah* p. 3) Elsewhere he emphasized the essential point of Christ's celestiality. "I beseech you, mind, Christ as he is stated in your testament, *could not be born,* I say it is blasphemy to hold it forth. " (*Tany2.* p. 3) In clear terms Tany stated, "God could not be a man for a man is a created thing and made and that can not be God."(*Tany2.* p. 3) Certainly the thought that a divine Jesus was born as a mortal was also illogical. "For thus man to confine God his maker into his own thing made is to undeify God and deify man himself . . . to ungod God and make man God," (*Tany2.* p. 4) and he rejected any argument which implied or maintained a human Jesus for "humanity to be very God in the earthly form is absolute blasphemy." Concerning the Scriptural text *"the word was made flesh,* that text is false,"(*Tany2.* p. 69) Tany flatly stated, adding "You can not deny this."

Tany also rejected any possible relationship between Jesus and Mary. The thought that God might have been generated from a soulless beast was repugnant and absurd to Tany. "I beseech you, remember," he reminded the reader, "she, Mary I mean, was but flesh,"(*Epitah* p. 3) adding on the same page "what is born of the flesh is flesh . . . and flesh and blood can not inherit eternal life."(*Epitah* p. 3) It was logical that "he must be celestial for no less will be security unto any."(*Epitah* p. 11) Had Christ been a man, his promise would have been a hoax for no man could be God. The worst offender of this teaching was "the Church of Rome [which] hath built their church upon that body which is not Christ's body but upon man's dung and not Christ, *for true Christ hath not nor can have any true corporeal body for he is a spirit and a spirit is free from flesh."(Tany2.* p. 83)

Tany's early writings opposed the concept that Christ might have suffered for mankind, and even the Ranter idea that he suffered for his own benefit. Since Christ was celestial, he could not suffer. "Now let me speak the truth," Tany confided, "He died not, he suffered not, he sinned not, he saved not by any act that was done."(*Apok.* p. 27) Indeed, Tany had little patience with accounts of Christ's having suffered at all. In language sure to offend almost everyone Tany wrote, "Now let me tell you, many men suffer more than he did. I beseech you, mind, I speak the truth. Let not the received opinion delude you."(*Apok.* p. 33)

Christ's celestiality guaranteed human salvation for it was because of his divine efforts that he was "the transcendent pipe in which the deity passed through."(*Apok.* p. 30) Advancing a notion of grace not far removed from that taught by the Catholic Church he criticized, Tany taught that Christ's celestiality passed to the believer through a "transcendent pipe," "causing a resurrection of itself to arise in you and by that you are renewed from death to life."(*Apok.* p. 8)

Tany could not predicate his notion of salvation *via exemplum Christi* upon a human Christ and emphasize the importance of suffering or emulating Christ's human life. He was able to build a very acceptable alternate basis for his divine Christology, however, which remained fully dualistic and fully Ranter. By predicating Christ's effectiveness upon an allegorical reading of Christ's descent into hell, Tany could argue that He descended into the hell of each believer's flesh and being to redeem the enclosed soul.

Since the Reformation, orthodox Christianity has had little use for the ancient creedal concept which maintained that Christ descended into hell at his death and remained there for three days. Calvin maintained this was a simple reference to the grave and others taught the more standard view that the *descensus* was Christ's effort to redeem pre-Christ Old Testament worthies from hell, or from the "bosom of Abraham." Sixteenth-century radicals, especially Hutterites, argued that Christ's descent into hell was his life on earth where he suffered at the hands of persecutors and tormentors. Tany combined this notion with Ranter belief that hell was in this world within each person's flesh to argue that "he descended into hell . . . that descent is into us who are hell or devils . . . for his descending into our hell is his own resurrection in us, in him."(*Apok.* p. 29) A throughly celestial Christ appears to our souls held captive in hell, and his power frees the soul from its fleshly confines and illuminates the soul "for to behold Christ is the truth, the turning us into himself and so into the Father . . . and so a union is made, but this is mysterious."(*Apok.* p. 14) When the soul is able to overcome its carnal captor, the believer is able to rise to God. "Till you are in Christ you are woman," Tany taught, "That is weakness. In Christ you are man, that is a strong conqueror."(*Apok.* p. 28) A mortal Christ could bring only weakness to the believer while a divine Christ could free the equally divine soul. Consistent with the death-life, matter-spirit dichotomy of his dualism, Tany concluded, "Be dead to live for thou art crucified to the world through the operation of God's spirit."(*Apok.* p. 59)

Tany's fully divine Christ obviated the need for human activity such as suffering or emulating Christ's life in other senses. Tany's attitude about suffering changed after he was imprisoned for six months in 1651. This ordeal may have proved very difficult for a person with so tenuous a grip on reality and as a result, Tany discovered a way to incorporate suffering into his religious system. Indeed, an emphasis on suffering characterizes all his later writings. In *Theauraujohn Tani His Second Part* of 1653, Tany wrote that "all they that would live up to the *life of Godliness*, they must suffer persecution."(44) Ready to sing the virtue of suffering, his own in particular, Tany now asked, "Now for what cause is this that we suffer? It is to make us perfect through suffering,"(44) and later in the same volume he wrote to the broken in spirit, "Rejoice that you are made partakers in Christ's suffering."(*Tany2*. p. 74) Despite this new found appreciation for the value of suffering, salvation still came only with death for "nothing can be saved until it is destroyed for destruction is absolute salvaltion."(*Tany2*. p. 56)

Thomas Tany's Social Views

Tany's earlier disavowal of Christ's suffering notwithstanding and his vehemence that "he saved not by any act that was done."(*Apok*. p. 30) Tany's social ethics were in fact grounded in the notion that human beings must accept all his social teachings and emulate the good deeds acted by Christ in Scripture. In his early writings Tany noted, "Brethren, till ye be doers, you are a lie and are deceived . . . but love is Jesus acting by a living distributing life to his members."(*Apok*. p. 34) In the later writings he again asked, "Brethren, doth virtue and righteousness dwell in speaking names? No, I say all is lies if not declared in things, that is doing, for the doer shall be justified and the sayer condemned."(*Tany2*. p. 90) The later writings emphasized that social activism is necessary for "God's teachings are always effectings and from them effectings flow forth actings of mercy unto thy poor distressed brethren."(*Tany2*. p. 50)

Tany's definitions of social responsibility were typically Ranter and might have been identified in the writings of every Ranter thinker. In one location he wrote in words very reminiscent of Coppe, "He commmands *do works of mercy, how many starve for want of bread*? He said *clothe*, how many naked?"(*Aurora* p. 13) Again reminiscent of Coppe, Tany requested his readers to "visit the fatherless and widows in their diversity."(*Apok*. p. A3a) His later writings again remind us of Coppe when Tany advises, "Feed the hungry, clothe the naked, oppress none, set free them bounden and if this be not, all your religion is a lie, a vanity, a cheat, deceived and deceiving."(*Tany2*. p. 90)

Tany's sentiments regarding organized religion were also those expressed by other Ranters. Churchmen speaking for a national church were motivated by a desire for power rather than out of love of religion. "Christ hath been the great priests' market, they have bought and sold him"(*Apok*. p. 27) were views expressed by virtually every radical of the age. Bishops and

THOMAS TANY

Presbyters were the same for "having forgotten the living God [they] embraced gods of gold, silver, land and inheritances."(*Apok.* p. 64)

The search for power and authority also motivated the orthodox sense of religious dogma. Doctrine was developed to increase the clergy's grip over commoners. "Though election and reprobation is absolute blasphemy" Tany noted, "and tis false and no original sorts foundation but to bind men in obedient fear, to bring them in and keep them subject."(*Apok.* p. 49) Where religious fear did not suffice, the use of repression was called for. Tany recounted, "I have suffered six months imprisonment . . . [because] I said that hell and damnation were not as ministers held forth." (High Priest p. 6) In short, Tany held the religious establishment in low esteem, and concluded, "Now know, *all* religion is a lie, a cheat, a deceit." (*HighPriest* p. 5)

The abuse of authority was also the major theme of Tany's single political treatise, *Nation's Right in Magna Charta*. Like many others on the radical left and all Ranters, Tany favored a governmental policy which would "distribute all to the poor, release all pawns without advantage, give back to them that were not able to redeem."(*Apok.* p. A2b) His political views applied both to monarchs and to protectors. "Now what is a tyrant?" he asked, "An oppressor, an encroacher, a cojoiner to himself of that that is not his, [and] against that the nation convenanted."(5) All of England's history might be understood as the people's struggle against unjust tyranny. Initially, all England "was made poor through the tyrannical power of the Norman yoke."(*HighPriest* p. 2) This tyranny was compounded century after century until the Stuarts surpassed all others. Tany noted, "I opposed Charles Stuart in ship-money, was committed for [it] in London, my horse taken and sold for ship money in Cambridgeshire."(*Magna Charta* p. 8) The convenant referred to earlier was the civil war which Tany believed was "a new choice . . . according to true election" (3) and he called the execution of Charles "a glorious work." The anticipation of all those who had joined in the convenant was simple. "Then was the time to have made us a free people, as you call us"(3) and "our lands being made free from the Norman subjection, we may lawfully claim our lands and inheritances in the commonwealth."(*HighPriest* p. 8)

The government created by Parliament was no better than the one it replaced. "I pray mind this," Tany asked of his new captors, "can you say you are for us?"(5) The reality of England was disappointing: "Your calling us free, we can not say amen but we may safely affirm that we are worse bound."(3) Tany requested of Cromwell that he live up to the goals of the revolution and "take down your thing set up by you, that thing, nay, named Parliament and let the right descend into the people again and a new choice made."(7) Should this not happen, the revolution must continue for "there must be an account rendered for the invading all our rights in that state."(3) Much as England convenanted against monarchy, the nation must join forces against Parliament, for "the nation is bound by oath to take it down or else they are perjured men and convenant breakers and let all the earth know covenant breakers God will judge."(5)

In 1651 Tany continued to have faith in the army to bring about needed reform. He chided Parliament's treatment of the army that "it is a dishonor to you that the soldier is not paid fully to the penny his due, yea, much hardship have they suffered for nothing."(4) And addressing the commons Tany advised, "Tis not the soldier that wrongs you, love the soldier, none can help you but he, it is he that should pay the soldier that wrongs you."(8) Thomas Tany could think of no reforms that might help bring about the society he and others wished for. But then, how does one reform a society so venal that it confiscates the horse of an itinerant smith?

Little is known about Thomas Tany after 1655 and it is possible that he met his end in that year. In mid-December of 1654 Tany made a great bonfire in Lambeth into which he threw his sword, tent, saddle, pistols and a Bible. Then on December 30 he appeared before the Parliament building brandishing a rusty sword. He had come to deliver a petition and proceeded to attack the doorkeeper. He was imprisoned for several weeks and finally released on February 10, 1655. According to Muggleton, Tany then left England for Holland in a small boat to call Dutch Jews to redemption. He never arrived in Holland and never returned to England.

In his insanity, or despite it, Thomas Tany was the consummate Ranter. In a world of dualist Ranters, he was more extreme than most. He denied ordinances, churches, dogma, and all else. He denied Scripture and learning but created his own intellectual system and his own system of sources and intellectual justification. He was an intellectual anarchist unwilling to use language, method, or sources established by others. Indeed, Tany went further and even denied an established personality. It is easy to dismiss Tany as a lunatic for what else can we think of one claiming to be the Earl of Essex or the proper ruler of Austria, Rome and Reme?

And yet, it would be a mistake to dismiss Tany's views as the intellectual reflections of a madman. It is true he knew no Scriptural languages, but Luther was deficient in Hebrew, and Lefevre compensated for his own deficiencies through numerology. Calvinists knew all Scriptural languages but the Council of Dort succeeded in creating a religious system the primary logic of which was hardly Scriptural. Of course, Galileo would have dis-

190

missed Tany as a madman, but then this age also dimissed Galileo because of the obviously incredible and insane view that the Earth moved around the sun. If Tany believed he possessed a little piece of God within himself, so did George Fox. The Presbyterians knew both were wrong because only they truly understood the totality of God's mind. Tany was mad, but his intellectual positions were a caricature of the time. Surely he was irrational but no more so than the rational authorities solemnly chasing witches all over Europe. Attacking a doorkeeper of Parliament with a rusty sword may seem crazy but Colonel Pride did the same thing and no historian calls this madness. Thomas Tany wrote gibberish and was mad in believing what he wrote true. The rational Isaac Newton filled volume upon upon volume with alchemical notes and believed in every page of it, but is considered a great thinker.

Gentlemen Ranters

13. Captain Francis Freeman

Captains Francis Freeman and Robert Norwood were both gentlemen and Ranters too. Their religious views were consensus Rantism, though neither considered himself principally a religious thinker. Both were primarily interested in explaining the deplorable condition of England after the civil war. Perhaps because these gentlemen came from a different social strata from that of most Ranters, neither proposed the redistribution of property nor entertained apocalyptic solutions to England's woes. Both must be considered moderates within the Ranter household, and yet, like their more radical associates, both were cashiered from the army and suffered legal harassment at the hands of local religious authorities.

Virtually nothing is known about Captain Francis Freeman other than the limited information presented in his treatises. His earliest work, *Eight Problems Propounded to the Cavalliers* (1646), defended Parliament's cause against the crown with Freeman identifying himself as an officer and a gentleman. His next few small works were no more informative or useful for our purposes. They were written while Freeman was a Baptist and before he was a Ranter, and concern such religious questions as the nature of baptism. Freeman's last work, *Light Vanquishing Darkness*, published in 1650, is fully Ranter, as the title indicated, and provides the basis for this short chapter.

Like so many other Ranters, Freeman experienced a varied personal religious past including virtually every orientation found in contemporary England. Freeman tells the reader, "I had been a papist, Protestant, Presbyterian, Antinomian, Independent, Anabaptist, Seeker. But I gave God thanks that I passed through them all and that Scripture was fulfilled in me."(5) Perhaps expressing the hierarchical frame of mind peculiar to an army officer, Freeman explained that "the highest degree of Papists are almost Protestants, and the highest degree of Protestants are almost Presbyterians, the highest degree of Presbyterians are almost Antinomians, the highest degree of Antinomians are almost Independents, the highest degree of Independents are almost Anabaptists and the Anabaptists are almost Seekers and the Seekers are at a stand."(1–2) Without God's intervention in the personality of the Seeker, no additional spiritual progress was possible for "although they are in the uppermost form, yet they know there is something above all these forms which they have not yet found."(2) Freeman, however, was pleased to anounce to the world that he was no longer a Seeker, that light had indeed vanquished darkness and "I had certain evidences and demonstrations of the Spirit of God working in my spirit."(5) Consequently, with great pride Freeman's title page declared, "After that which men call heresy will I worship the God of my fathers." The same title page also indicated, "The spiritual man judgeth all things yet he himself is judged by no man." Captain Freeman considered himself a spiritual man for God's light had vanquished the darkness within him.

Captain Freeman may have admitted to no mortal judges but the experiences recounted in this treatise indicated how many mortals believed they could, should, and must judge him. This treatise concerns Freeman's conflicts with the army and local civil authorities during the years 1646–1647, and his travels through England's countryside during the civil war where he witnessed grinding poverty and unendurable suffering. It was this inhumane treatment of the poor that converted Freeman to Rantism.

Freeman believed that two qualities characterized contemporary England's ills: a corrupt political system and the aggravated abuse of private property. Both conditions, he believed, were the result of the Norman conquest of 1066 and Freeman was one of several Ranters subscribing to the theory of the Norman Yoke. This theory accounted for contemporary class divisions and political abuse as the result of a foreign invasion rather than an indigenous political-economic process. England's many problems originated with William the Conquerer, Freeman explained, "For you know that the people have lived under a kingly power many hundreds of years and have been held in bondage and slavery ever since the conquest, under those laws which were prescribed by a usurper. And have been still kept under the Norman Yoke[35] by reason of an absolute arbitrary power domineering over them, raised up by William the Conquerer when he subdued the nation by the sword."(55) Earlier in his career Freeman defended Parliament against the king but in the interval, like many other Ranters, he came to believe that there was little to distinguish between them. Freeman explained that "all those laws which came in by the Norman Conquest and have continued ever since successively by kings and consequently, by tyrants, till the late king's head was taken off, which laws (for the substance) are still in use as if he were still alive, only the form altered."(57) Expressing the same faith as his more radical Ranter associates, Freeman concluded,

"My counsel is that they may be wholly taken away and wholesome laws prescribed in the room that the people may no longer lie under that Yoke which is an intolerable burden."(57)

Political abuse was only one aspect of a larger problem making reform of the body politic through new laws either very difficult or futile. Like Clarkson who wrote, "We are their tenants, they are our masters," Freeman too believed that the pattern of land ownership made change meaningless. "And truly for my part," Freeman wrote, "I have seen exceedingly unequal distribution of things. Some all and some nothing at all."(56) Hoping to keep his friends in power, William the Conqueror, Freeman explained, distributed all wealth to his friends and supporters. "Those who were his creatures, his favorites, he created them to be Lords of Manors and so divided and distributed the land amongst themselves and the poor to become tenants unto them . . . and hence came in that which we call propriety as derived from the Norman Conquest."(55) The subsequent resulting class system was primarily intended to protect the integrity of the French usurpation. Hence, "These great Lords of Manors, by marriage, matching sons and daughters, joined house to house and land to land and so became greater Lords than ever."(55)

The foreign invaders joined land to land and house to house while the local indigenous English population could only join misery to misery to become increasingly poor. With every generation, Freeman explained, the Lords "exhausted greater rents from their poor tenants by degrees . . . and so the poor people came to be mere slaves to their Lords and Masters, their rents being continually raised and set upon the rack and tenterhooks of their wicked consciences, and are not able to maintain themselves and families though at a pitiful poor low rate in food and raiment, notwithstanding all their labor and painstaking both early and late." (55–56)

Systematic economic abuse of the English commoner was apparent for all to see, in Freeman's opinion. Using the words for which the Brethren of the Free Spirit were known centuries earlier, Freeman asked, "Is there not daily crying out in your streets, 'for bread, bread, for the Lord's sake' not only in this city [i.e., London] but in the country also by many thousands of poor people who are ready to perish with famine?"(56) In one very moving passage Freeman recounted his experience in the poor rural north during the civil war. "I speak from experience of my late travels in the North where I have seen multitudes of poor people go bare footed and bare legged, and scarce a rag of clothes to cover their nakedness or having any bread or any kind of food to put into their bellies to keep them from starving."(56) Discovering the parties responsible for this grinding poverty was no more complicated than simply asking who owned the land. "Ask the poor people whose land they lived in or who was their Lord," Freeman advised. "They would tell us it was either the Earl of Northumberland or the Lord Gray."(56) That is, the supporters of tyranny and heirs to William the Conqueror.

Freeman also condemned the economic concerns of the clergy in terms common to most Ranters and other radicals. He wrote, "This unjust and intolerable burden of tithes may be wholly taken away that those who go under the notion of ministers may live on Gospel maintenance and not by law."(58)

Freeman believed that only when "the laws be taken away, both root and branch" would there be justice. Consequently, addressing Cromwell, Freeman requested "that you wholly take away all the laws in one day and give us such wholesome laws the next . . . most suitable to what they were before the Norman Conquest."(58)

The concept of the Norman Yoke was an admirable vehicle through which to advance the claims of radical social change; it identified both the origin of the problem and its solution as well. Social evil was the result of the foreigner, indeed, the French foreigner, and rectification of the problem could result from eliminating the foreigner's heirs. The same process which identified the foreigner as the source of the problem also guaranteed the moral integrity of the English people. However simplistic such thinking might appear in retrospect, the theory of the Norman Yoke in fact appealed to the age-old sentiment that has always motivated the foreign policies of civilized countries; hatred of the foreigner.

Freeman's problems in the army and with civilian authorities did not result from his maintaining radical social doctrine but from his espousal of religious Rantism. Freeman noted that he often discussed religion with his fellow officers and in one instance shocked his comrades by advancing the view "that I saw God in all things and in everything that had a being in the whole creation, working in the creature according to the several dispensations wherein he had placed them."(3) When a colleague asked if this included candlesticks and table boards, Freeman replied, "Yea, I saw him in both."(3) On another occasion a certain Colonel Okey asked him about the value of ritual and church ordinances. Freeman replied that he did not object to them "and that I liked them well that were zealous in the performance thereof for I did believe that some had comfort in the use of them."(4) More radical were Freeman's opinions regarding the value of Scripture and he noted, "I told them that every Scripture is a mystery until it be made known to us or revealed to us."(4) Freeman's colleagues were disturbed when Freeman testified, "The word of God, which is God in his word, written in me, is more to me than the whole book of Scripture, both the Old and New Testament."(5) Despite these and other religious differences, Freeman wrote that these discussions were pleasant and civil, marked by neither rancor nor malice, "for all the time they were very merry and pleasant with me in so much that I could not conceive they had any prejudice against me."(4)

Either Freeman spoke more freely than he realized or his superiors were in fact very much annoyed with his religious conversation. Freeman received a written summons to appear before his superiors which read, "Thou art accursed and indicted by the name of Captain Francis Freeman for thou has feloniously denied the Scripture and made God the author of sin. Thou hast said thou art Christ and thou hast countenanced Blasphemy."(12) Later, additional charges were added to these: "that I was a base scandalous fellow and I had sung bawdy songs upon my march which was made a grief to all Godly Christians."(18) Freeman explained that he was innocent of these charges and had been purposely misunderstood by evil and malicious people. It was not true, for instance, that he sang bawdy songs but that others in the company did. And he never claimed he was really Christ, only figuratively.

Freeman was separated from his troops and was not given another command. Soon thereafter Captain Freeman became embroiled in an even worse religious conflict with the local civilians. Mr. Cox, a preacher in the town of Taunton in Somerset County, accused Freeman of preaching heresy. The charges were familiar: "that I said I was Christ and that I denied the trinity. My answer was that he accused me falsely." Either way, "the constable and other officers came to me to go before the mayor and the Justice Nicolas."(34–35) He was given the choice of posting sureties or going to jail to await the next assize. "My answer was that for the present I must submit to the power of the Magistrate and so chose rather to go to prison."(35) General Fairfax, Freeman's commanding officer, was informed of Freeman's incarceration and intervened on behalf of the junior officer. Before Freeman was released, however, Judge Nicolas warned him, "Captain Freeman, you delivered strange points and indeed points not disputable, but I am sure they are punishable."(41) For the time being Captain Francis Freeman was free, but barely. He might have been better off in jail.

Freeman's life out of prison was probably more complicated than he desired. General Fairfax made him responsible for the billeting of troops in Taunton but requisitioned neither supplies nor the funds required for this task. Consequently, Freeman, already disliked by his fellow officers and distrusted by the local townsfolk, was forced to request credit from local merchants. As might be expected, this was not popular in Taunton. When Freeman led his troops into town, the population lined up on both sides of the avenue, shouted obscenities, and pelted the soldiers with garbage.

Quite incredibly, Captain Freeman's situation deteriorated. His soldiers got drunk, and a civilian was seriously wounded in one particular unruly brawl. The merchants, religious leaders and townsfolk were in such an uproar that Fairfax was evidently forced to withdraw his troops from Taunton. The next we hear in Freeman's story is his standing trial for blasphemy at the Assize and he was probably reincarcerated until then.

The major accusation against Freeman was that he had claimed to be Christ. Freeman reasoned, "Now if it be so, I had said that I had been Christ, certainly I had spoken blasphemy in the highest degree."(50) He tells us no more about the trial, other charges, his defense or his punishment, stating only that he was purposely and maliciously misunderstood by his adversaries. He probably went to jail, however, for he was dismissed from the army with this treatise written subsequently to clear his good name. In any event, Freeman justified himself by observing that "as the mercies of the wicked are cruelty and oppression, so there are none that live Godly in Christ Jesus but shall suffer persecution either by false accusation, imprisonment, or both."(33) Like other Ranters, Freeman had the satisfaction of knowing that he had suffered for Christ.

14. Captain Robert Norwood

Captain Robert Norwood was one of the most prolific Ranter authors. His writings address a variety of concerns including religious thought, political criticism, analyses of England's religious condition and descriptions of his legal entanglements with both religious and civil authorities. Unlike others, Norwood was not insane, did not advocate bizarre social policy and entertained no peculiar notions of the army's special divine role in English affairs. Similarly, Norwood harbored no illusions about the glory to be had if only England could be burned to the ground, and he never presented himself as a divinely appointed prophet to the English people. In short, Captain Robert Norwood was a respectable gentleman maintaining Ranter views and was horrified when he was treated like a Ranter and thrown into jail.

Norwood's writings fall into two categories. His early works defend his honor against accusations of blasphemy made by the Independent minister Sidrach Simpson. In this category we find Norwood's *Declaration or Testimony, The Form of Excommunication,* and *The Case and Trial of Captain Robert Norwood, Now Prisoner in Newgate,* all published in 1651. In the following year Norwood published *A Brief Discourse.* All of these works treat Norwood's troubled relationship with Simpson and describe the former's trials and incarceration.

Norwood continued to write on a variety of themes after leaving prison. Indeed, the last treatises were Norwood's most thoughtful products and reflect a growing radicalism. His *Proposals for the Propagation of the Gospel* was published in 1652, with *A Pathway Unto England's Perfect Settlement* and finally *An Additional Discourse* appeared a year later.

Norwood was not a systematic thinker in general and was not particularly comfortable writing in a religious idiom. Consequently, his religious ideas are presented in bits and pieces throughout his several treatises against Simpson and the legal authorities. In his first essay, however, *A Declaration or Testimony,* Norwood attempted to outline his religious beliefs.

Norwood used a variety of images in discussing God. In one location he wrote, "He is said to be the light and life of the world"(2) and elsewhere God is described as "one infinite eternal being which only or alone gives a being to all things . . . he alone having life in himself and is the lone life of all things . . . for he *IS* or *I AM*."(1) Essentially, God is the *élan vital* invigorating the universe.

Like other Ranters, Norwood seemed to draw inspiration from classical dualistic thought. He explained, for instance, that "there must be and is a perfect truth to every created creature according to its kind, which is the invisible life and being of it, the visibility being only a representative or figure of the invisible life."(3) In humanity this dualism takes the form of a dichotomy between a divine soul and a crass material body. Regarding this soul Norwood wrote, "I take or believe it to be of divine essence for it is said God breathed into him the breath of life . . . [and] I can not conceive it to be less or other than his own essence or spirit."(2) The body, however, was less a cause for joy, "for the body which is indeed bestial [is] of the same nature and substance with the beasts."(5)

If the soul was divine and the body a dumb beast, the human personality, or "human spirit" as Norwood wrote, owed more to the latter than the former. "The spirit of a man or man's natural spirit," Norwood explained, "is called the Devil or Satan or Anti-Christ or false prophet or Spirit of Darkness or Death or sin or hell."(4) Consequently, human existence was a conflict between the material and the spiritual, and "Scripture everywhere comprehends all under these two states or terms, of light and darkness, the natural man and the spiritual man, children of light and children of death and darkness."(4)

With the exception of Tany, Norwood's friend and associate at this time, few Ranters presented so complete a divorce between the material and spiritual as did Norwood. Indeed, few used the Manichaean terms "children of light and darkness," with the explicit meaning "his servants you are to whom you obey, whether it be of sin unto death or of obedience unto righteousness."(5) Consequently, the righteous and the evil were two warring camps and "he that hath righteousness is righteousness as he is righteous; he that commiteth sin is of the devil."(4) This conflict existed not merely within each individual, between the fleshly and the spiritual, but within the cosmos as a whole. Indeed, Norwood was one of only a few Ranters teaching a total Zoroastrian-like division of existence with "everyone and everything taking its dominion from the property and quality of that spirit which hath the major or most ruling power over and dominion in and over him or it."(4) Thus, when a person acted properly, "it's not I but Christ in me," and when the contrary, "it's not I but sin in me."(4)

Despite his writing of children of light, those who followed Christ in the spirit, Norwood's dualism was so extreme that he had difficulty conceiving of any divine acceptance of the human soul while it resided in a material form. Where other Ranters taught a heaven and a hell within the human mind, and Norwood also cited the proper verses of Scripture to support these views, his truest position appears to have been more extreme. He noted that "in no proper or true sense whatsoever can flesh and blood inherit the kingdom of heaven."(6) Divine acceptance then would come "not until we have laid off our earthly garments."(5) Here too we find a strong similarity between Norwood and Tany.

When discussing the resurrection, Norwood again expressed a more extreme form of spiritualism than that of other Ranters. He wrote, "I conceive the chief if not the only resurrection pointed unto in Scripture is the rising up out of that death and darkness or hell we were held in or kept in or kept under by." (5) Norwood rejected the concept of sainthood within life, preferring to believe instead, "Neither think I this will be in its height and full perfection till the separation by that which we call death."(5) Unlike other Ranters stressing Christ's suffering, Norwood emphasized only his death and "for this purpose the Son of God was made manifest, that he might destroy the world of the devil."(4) Only Tany's views were close to these expressed by Norwood.

Other than stating the essentials of his dualism, Norwood attempted no additional elucidation of any religious ideas in this first treatise and as a result many issues remain vague. As an example, Norwood's Christology is typically Ranter in many respects, yet nowhere did he specifically affirm Christ's humanity. As a true mortal, Jesus could not have attained any spiritual benefit before death and the resurrection of his spirit. This would be true of every individual when he died and hence there was no need for righteousness within this life since none could be had in any event. If this is true, however, Norwood would have to explain how the children of light ceased being children of darkness. In short, Norwood's dualism was so extreme as to make impossible any virtue within this life, even Christ's life. Also, Norwood nowhere explained how he conceived Scripture. Whether it was a mere history, a base for allegory or the actual word of God is nowhere explained. Rituals and observances, always eschewed by Ranters, received no mention in this first treatise.

Most unclarified issues received far greater elucidation in the remainder of Norwood's writings, especially those addressed to Sidrach Simpson. It is also clear that Norwood, like Freeman, was no theologian and both made careless presentations of their religious beliefs. Yet, Norwood was outraged when Sidrach Simpson, the minister of the Independent London congregation to which Norwood had at one time belonged, condemned the former's Ranter views. Referring to Simpson's charges, Norwood wrote, "I further declare whatever man or men report, accuse, or charge me with blasphemy or any error . . . and do not duly prove the same against me, it is in the sight of God and man a slanderer, back-biter, and murderer."(6) Indeed, Norwood challenged Simpson to debate such usual Ranter ideas as who Christ and the devil were, the nature of the anti-Christ and where it resided, and how Eve was tempted.(6) Simpson never took up Norwood's challenge as the former anticipated, and excommunicated Norwood from his church.

The actual excommunication document and Norwood's reply to Simpson were published together in 1651 under the title *The Form of Excommunication*. In a series of letters prefacing the excommunication, Norwood introduced the history of his conflict with Simpson which began with religious harassment and ended with his being imprisoned.

The next letter, the Dedicatory Epistle, was directed to Parliament and defended Norwood's honor as a gentleman and his reputation as an officer in Parliament's army. He wrote, "My sufferings by the late king before this Parliament sat were not inconsiderable, both by imprisonment, seizure of my goods, long and tedious suits and otherwise."(A2) Indeed, it was for these very reasons that Norwood became an officer defending Parliament and he reminded them "You have had the greatest part of my time for six or seven years, you have had my purse and person at your command upon all occasions. My whole estate, which is not inconsiderable, lies with you in your power and command."(A2) Yet, despite his total allegiance to Parliament's cause, Norwood insisted he had never asked for any real compensation. "I have never yet for all my services, for all my pains and excessive charges, monies lent, hazards and hardships, which have not been few for little, neither without the loss of some blood, received by way of place or office, in money or in any other way whatever, so much as 60 shillings."(A2) Despite a record of service and devotion, crude spirits "have made loud cries against me, report the things I never did, nay, which never was so much as in my mind to do."(A3) The only legitimate charge against him, Norwood wrote is "that I have neglected myself, my private and particular friends and engagements, to serve the public."(A2b)

Norwood's gentlemanly honor was also abused by the rough treatment he received from arresting authorities subsequent to his excommunication. This treatment seems about the same as that experienced by other Ranters, but Norwood was shocked and outraged. In great indignation he reported, "I was taken out of my house in a very rude uncivil way and by force and violence carried and put amongst the Thieves and Murderers at the Sessions house by Newgate where was present upon the bench my Lord Justice Rolls, Baron Thorp and others, both of them declaring the illegality thereof. After a while, two articles were read against me, neither whereof were against any act of Parliament whatsoever."(A3)

At the time of writing, Norwood awaited trial at the next sessions. He believed Simpson's hand had motivated his harassment and has his adversary think aloud, "First we will excommunicate them and after turn them over to the secular power to indict them at the Sessions, right or wrong, be it legal or illegal. One of my subjects is Chief Justice there, he will say as I say, do as I bid him, else I will excommunicate him."(37) Warning of the dangers inherent in church-state entanglements, Norwood pleaded, "Gentlemen, be no longer thus ridden by the clergy, break those yokes from off your necks, those iron yokes."(33) Otherwise, Norwood warned, there would be no end to clerical tyranny where "they will excommunicate you, yea, and the Parliament too . . . and then Sir, the next turn we must take is to the Sessions House, and so to Tilburn."(33)

The dedicatory letters addressed to Parliament also took up the issue of religious censorship by the religious establishment. Norwood attempted to explain how "we have at this time the cry of blasphemy and heresy up as loud as ever, the spirit of the persecution in the clergy as high as ever."(3–4, no printed number) Contemporary orthodox authorities, true Pharisees, are never consistent in their definitions of blasphemy or heresy and are an unreliable guide to religious policy. Norwood wrote, "Supposed blasphemy and heresy have within a very little time after been embraced and owned for sound and orthodox truths, as King Edward's, Queen Mary's, and Queen Elizabeth's reigns witness and our own times are full of pregnant proofs."(5–6, no printed number) Noting that "empty tubs make the loudest sounds," Norwood compared his own harassment with that suffered by Jesus at the hands of the Pharisees who also "cried out blasphemy and heresy."(4, no printed number)

Norwood's arguments were typical of those advanced by mechanic preachers against their more educated adversaries. Simpson was a respected minister and master of Pembroke Hall of Cambridge University, but it was Norwood's position that Scripture was "hidden and obscured if not wholly buried by men's inventions, false glosses and absurd translations and traditions."(3, no printed number) Thus, "the highest excellencies have usually risen in and from the deepest obscurities."(3, no printed number) Perhaps claiming himself to be one of the deepest obscurities, Norwood believed his own more Spiritual interpretation of the Bible "imports a higher discovery or manifestation of divine light and knowledge than was ever made known in the apostles' time."(3, no printed number)

Simpson charged Norwood with rejecting heaven and hell and believing that man was God, both accusations covered by the Blasphemy Act. Norwood replied concerning the first, "I say the Scripture testify not of any local place"(18) which was a usual Ranter argument against locations for an afterlife. Objecting to Simpson's very literal interpretation of Scripture to support a literal understanding of heaven, Norwood asked, "Is there no other *ascents* but up a pair of stairs? We are said to be risen with Christ whilst we are here and upon this earth." If indeed, heaven was a definite location somewhere in the sky, "What resurrection and ascension and what heaven is that, think you, there spoken of?"(16) However insufficiently expressed in his first treatise, Norwood's beliefs of heaven and hell were clearly Ranter. It is also clear that Simpson's traditional Protestant literal interpretation of Scripture and Norwood's more allegorical method were at odds and would not be reconciled.

The second issue, whether man was God, again demonstrated how there was little these two antagonists could share. Simpson argued that if every soul were indeed God, as Norwood claimed, there would be as many Gods as there were souls and further that God would then be the author of sin. Norwood thought Simpson's reasoning facetious. Norwood postulated that "no derivative is that from whence it had its derivation no more than the rivers that come from the sea are the sea or the light that comes from the sun is the sun, though of the same essence, nature, property and quality with them and essenced in them."(23) Or, to put the same thought in the condescending tone with which this gentleman treated this preacher, Norwood asked, "If my little toe is of the same nature, essence, and substance with my whole body, therefore the same honor is due unto it as is due unto my head and whole body. O Profound Arguing!"(23) A page later Norwood turned the tables and asked Simpson, "if Christ dwells in every believer, are there therefore so many Christs as there are believers?" Norwood chided, "Are so many drops of water as run from the sea so many seas? Is this an argument to come from the head of a school of learning?"(24)

Norwood had undisguised contempt for Simpson's orthodoxy. He caricatured Simpson's brand of religion where parishioners go to a minister and cry out, "I have sinned wherefore God is angry with me;" and then answer themselves, "Well, I will now to fasting, to prayer, then all is well again."(29) Norwood again chided, "It is a very easy matter to tell of a Christ dying at Jerusalem . . . of repentance from dead works, of faith towards God, of baptism, of laying on of hands and resurrection of the dead and eternal judgment."(13) These views and many others were not from God, "but testimonies human, being written or translated by men and by men of corrupt judgments and practices, as can not be denied by any."(17)

BLASPHEMY, IMMORALITY, AND ANARCHY

The last issue Norwood addressed in his condemnation of Simpson's orthodoxy was the fact of the excommunication itself. Norwood asked the reader, "Did Christ excommunicate his disciples for their being ignorant of the resurrection or Peter for denying him?"(9) Asking the reader to consider the simple views he has expressed, Norwood wrote, "He saith they are errors and blasphemies; what or whom have I blasphemed? Whom have I spoken evil of? Whose fame have I blasted, except his and his fraternity?"(32) In Norwood's mind, the real basis of Simpson's excommunication was that Norwood had dared contradict him. "He proves nothing of error against me and yet excommunicates me," Norwood explained, "He tells you Jesus Christ requires it of them; so doth the Bishop of Rome . . ."(9)

Norwood's open criticism of Simpson and his orthodox religion must lead the reader to wonder why Norwood had ever been a member of Simpson's church, and whether he had not provoked Simpson while still an active parishioner. From Norwood's perspective, it was his very desire to leave Simpson's congregation that in fact first initiated the latter's ire. Claiming to have withdrawn from Simpson's congregation long before the excommunication, Norwood asked, "But have I withdrawn from the people of God because I have withdrawn from you? Are those *you* are withdrawn from all damned?"(10) From Norwood's point of view, Simpson, like the bishop of Rome, was for reasons of power, primarily concerned with maintaining the integrity of his organization. "He tells you you have no grace whosoever and whatsoever you are if you be not admitted into his society or fellowship of those of his way. If your children be not in his way baptised and yourselves receive the Supper, you have no grace for you have not the signs of grace."(36) No more concerned with spiritual matters than the papacy, Norwood explained that Simpson cared more for power and money. "Finding their longtrade and occupation begins to sink, to be called into question," Norwood wrote,"they cry out 'blasphemy, blasphemy, heresy, heresy.' "(11) Simpson's only concern, "and troubled indeed he may be," Norwood added, was "fearing the loss of his fleeces."(10)

Shortly after he completed his response to Simpson's excommunication, Norwood went to court charged with blasphemy. Norwood wrote about his trial in two short treatises. *The Case and Trial of Robert Norwood, Now Prisoner in Newgate* of 1651 presented the outlines of the case against him, and a year later he added material in his *A Brief Discourse*. Both works repeat the accusation that Sidrach Simpson motivated the legal action against him. He noted in the first that the Lord Mayor of London, Thomas Andrews, was a member of Simpson's society.(3) Norwood also maintained that his arrest warrant was illegal because "no fault, crime or misdemeanor being specified in the said warrant, the illegality whereof was then and there declared by the Lord Chief Justice Rolls and Baron Thorp."(3‒4) When he finally appeared before the court in the Old Bailey, the two charges made against him were "that the soul of man is the essence of God and that there is neither heaven nor hell but what is here."(4) When told he must appear at the next Assize and post bail for his release, Norwood noted proudly, "Recorder Steel very civilly replied that I was very well known and my own good word was sufficient."(4)

Norwood believed that the actions against him, from start to end, were illegal and humiliating. He makes no mention of the Blasphemy Act though it is clear that it served as the foundation for his incarceration. His account of his trial does not present much procedural information and Norwood's sole intent in these treatises seemed to have been to condemn the legal process that found him guilty of blasphemy.

When Norwood appeared before Judge Warburton he asked why there were no lawyers present representing the state's case against him. Warburton's answer was that "it is now in this case as it was formerly in the kings time . . . neither was it necessary that he who prosecutes for the state should [appear] for there was only the change in the name. Before it was in the name of the king and now in the name of the state."(5) Norwood attempted to introduce written materials in his own defense, for he believed, "My books and papers attested with my own hand fully speaking and owning and acknowledging both heaven and hell, both salvation and damnation, which I offered to give in evidence, but it would not be received."(10)

Confronting a process obviously intending to imprison him, Norwood took what he believed to be the course of greatest prudence. "I told the court," Norwood explained, "that if I did speak the words in the sense they understood them, I did there unsay them . . . and I did solemnly declare that I held both heaven and hell, both salvation and damnation."(14) These efforts were to no avail. Despite his conciliatory efforts, "All this would not serve turn; I must to Newgate there to be kept for six months without bail or mainprize."(14)

Norwood did not write about his experiences in jail though several very bitter treatises were written at least in part during this incarceration. *A Brief Discourse* argued that he was tried according to the terms of the Blasphemy Act but nothing in his indictment came under the purview of that law. Norwood was incorrect in this unless his blasphemous statements were made in private conversation. Instead Norwood argued that it was unlawful to teach "that the true God or the eternal Majesty dwells in the creature and nowhere else."(4) He taught, however, that the soul was divine but not that divinity resided only in man. To strengthen his case Norwood indicated that the writings of the prominent Puritan member of Parliament, Francis Rous, presented identical ideas. Norwood demonstrated that his own writings were actually less extreme than Rous' by citing long passages from Rous' *Mystical Marriage.*

Norwood also believed his views of heaven and hell were unjustly condemned. He argued that the Blaphemy Act condemned only those denying both heaven and hell, salvation and damnation, whereas he denied only hell and damnation but not heaven and salvation. In any event, Norwood continued, no court in the land would have found him guilty had it not been for the intervention of Sidrach Simpson.(5)

Though he was never a friend of organized religion, in this treatise his venom against Simpson became a passion against clerical institutions, governmental authorities, and lawyers as well. "You see the close combination between the clergy and the other gentlemen of the Long Robe," Norwood commented, "Sidrach Simpson, his called pastor excommunicates me . . . [Lord Mayor] Andrews gets me to the Sessions House."(10) The political combination of priests and lawyers, Norwood explained, must lead to tyranny. Indeed, by arguing both sides of every issue Norwood believed these two groups were the cause of the civil war. "Here gentlemen, you may see who or what hath been next to the clergy the greatest cause of England's miseries. The clergy hath persecuted us into blood and hath brought gospel for justification of each party. And the other long robed gentlemen, they have pleaded and argued us into blood and adjudged each party's actions and proceedings legal. And by them of each party hath the people been condemned by one and the same law. Thus both clergy and Lawyer can make the chamelean show any color."(7) Consequently, despite bloodshed, rioting and the minor alterations involved in changing England from a monarchy to a republic, in fact nothing changed. "The nation hath run so many hazards, spent so much treasure, lost so many precious lives, made so many poor dismembered creatures the land over, only for a change in name only, and . . . very little if anything at all more."(5)

Norwood explained that before the civil war England was at the mercy of arbitrary royal authority expressed through a legal system the lawyers for which justified its every illegal act. After the civil war the citizen was at the mercy of an arbitrary Parliamentary power the lawyers for which, indeed the same lawyers as before, justified that agency's every illegal act with the same laws employed hitherto. The late king's lawyers found his actions against Parliament "so legal and so justifiable" while "those who remained here [in London] and joined with Parliament, they declare and judge their proceedings warrantable and justifiable also; and both these by one and the same law."(6) Both sets of lawyers condemned the arguments of the opposition "and still by one and the same law."(6) Norwood's conclusion was that the rule of law was a great sham through which all breaches of the law might be justified. "Their care and study is, how to make the law speak multiplicities of riddles whereby to confound . . . and so serve their own, their Lord's and Master's turn, what the prince, state, or client's desires, occasions and interests call for."(6) Consequently, despite arguments concerning the legality or illegality of actions taken or opposed, government in fact had no legal basis at all. Norwood asked, "I would ask them all this one single question: Whence, from what or from whom [do] yourselves . . . hold and derive your rights, power, and authority? In, from and by the law or in, from, and by the sword?"(6) A page later Norwood answered his own question and presented what would be the dominant theme of his later writings. "You are completely under the power, dictates and commands of the sword. What use or need is there of any of your sufferings, of your judgments or judicatories."(7) And for the first time this gentleman, military officer in Parliament's cause and erstwhile upholder of all that was good in England, explained that there would be no justice "until those square headed benchers be dismounted and their long tailed retinue thrown over the bars and be turned out of their several cloisters and meeting places."(5)

Other than government and lawyers, the third head of Norwood's hydra or Chimaera, the church, was also severely condemned. "Men have as little reason to trust the clergy now as those in Christ's time had to trust the Scribes and Pharisees."(13) While government "sins by oppression, by injustice, by deceit or by other carnal fleshly sensual and devilish actings," the clergy sells salvation "with some of their bread and wine, perhaps also their all's well, they must to heaven without dispute. O Rome, O Rome, O Rome."(17) Through the tithe, the church "lays all upon the back of a poor weak man like ourselves dying at Jerusalem."(17) Given the state of organized religion in England, "verily, I can not but abhore the doctrines and principles of most Christians,"(17) Norwood wrote. Organized religion was a faith predicated upon convenience and ease. Vicarious atonement made another person, Jesus, responsible for each person's salvation and rituals made true faith unnecessary. "Brethren, be not deceived," Norwood admonished the reader, "it's not suffering, it's not the blood, it's not the death of Christ slain at Jerusalem will save you."(14) Rather, expressing consensus Rantism, Norwood wrote, "The life of the flesh must be totally extinguished before we shall or can live the pure virgin life or in the spirit."(19) Once again we can note that Norwood's rejection of suffering and affirmation of the importance of death approximated Tany's views.

It is obvious that his experience in prison radicalized Norwood the gentleman and officer in Parliament's cause. The three treatises Norwood wrote after being released from prison reflect this very radical tone and attempt to present a conceptual understanding of how England degenerated into its present condition and what it might do to rectify this condition. Taken together, these works present views best described as nostalgic anarchism, hoping to return England to her pure condition before the Norman invasion.

In his *Proposals for the Propagation of the Gospel* . . . (1652), Norwood discussed the proper role of religion in society. Norwood's attitude had undergone even further hardening, for after being released from prison the previous year, Norwood again found himself in trouble with religious authorities. On the very first page of this treatise he wrote, "The occasion of my presentment of these at this time is my being charged with Blasphemy (or being a blasphemer) at the Committee for the Propagation of the Gospel, by M. Scot chairman thereof."(1) The charges against him were familiar, with Norwood explaining, "I do and ever did acknowledge both heaven and hell and these as distinct as light and darkness . . . a certain local limited place being only by me denied. And to say that the soul of man is of a Divine Essence or of the Essence of God is no more (if rightly understood) than to say that the soul is immortal."(1) The outcome of these difficulties is unknown but Norwood nowhere in subsequent writings mentions an additional jail sentence. The remainder of the treatise concerned Norwood's ecclesiastical views, or "how far any man or men are empowered, constituted, ordained, appointed, fitted, furnished, enabled or annointed by Christ here unto."(6) Or, to what extent any human beings are appointed by Christ to investigate the lives of good Christians, like Captain Robert Norwood.

In attempting to discover the true church Norwood distinguished between the ordination of the spirit and the ordination of men. Only the former expressed God's desire and was expressed only within the soul of believers. The latter, Norwood explained, was a formal fiction upon which venal institutions were built and through which power was deployed but which in no way represented God. Additionally, the former comprehended the vanity of ritual and practice while the latter, void of the spirit, emphasized rituals that were built precisely on such a false foundation. Christ's truth, Norwood concluded, "lies not in a few outside preachings, prayings, baptisings, humiliations, thanksgivings and the like. Not in any or all the outward visible forms of administrations whatsoever, that ever were, are, or shall be."(9) Whatever the value of these in the past, "The Temple with all the rites, laws and administrations thereof are [sic] ceased and done away."(13) God's spiritual intentions were made clear by Jesus' life and death. Despite the goodness of his life and his teaching, the apostles could benefit nothing from them and "although they had the promise, yet they were not to stir, they were not to go forth to preach the gospel until they themselves had received the gospel, the promise of the Father."(6) The true spiritual gospel came not in Christ's life but in his death for "Christ himself also, as he was after the flesh, must be crucified, that veil rent away and done away."(13)

Rather than encouraging the spirit, the Christian church historically pursued a far different course hoping to establish power on earth. The best example of this use of religion for political ends lay in the establishment of Parliamentary committees to oversee belief, such as the Committee for the Propagation of the Gospel. "To what end or purpose," asked Norwood, "was it for them to propose anything to Parliament were it not in their power or the power of the Magistrate to make laws in such cases and to punish the breakers of those laws so made?"(8) Speaking in Parliament's voice, Norwood wrote of such committees' desires "to cut all their throats who believe not as we believe, although we can indeed and in truth give no better reason nor show any better commission than our bare say so."(8)

Had these self-proclaimed and self-righteous censors possessed Christian charity or humility, they themselves would see the folly of their ways and methods. Norwood asked, "If his kingdom be spiritual (as it is said to be) what then should carnal weapons do in it or about it?"(10) Norwood noted how "you would have men punished for denying Christ although none can know or acknowledge him without the power, help and assistance of him who is altogether above and beyond his reach and power."(19) Christ himself indicated a different approach when he "did good to sinners, loved sinners and gave his life for sinners, even those who persecuted and blasphemed him."(20) Simple logic should indicate that the blind and ignorant are to be pitied, not punished, and Norwood asked "Will God think you punish a man that's born blind because he can not see, neither is it at all in his power to get himself eyes?"(19)

Norwood noted that the intellectual justification for Parliamentary committees was the safeguarding of public virtue from the immoral influence and teachings of the few blasphemers. Yet, these same orthodox Calvinist ministers believed people were divinely predestined to heaven or hell and hence beyond such influence. "If our righteousness (which is our strength) reaches him not," Norwood asked, "will our unrighteousness or sins (think you) which is our weakness, reach him or extend to him?"(19) If man had free will and might be influenced by evil preachers surely there was need for such committees. But if God predestined the elect and reprobate, such committees would seem to have no function but safeguarding their own power. Moreover, if human beings could not merit salvation but were granted the free gift of grace determined arbitrarily by God, how could such administrative agencies justify their actions in God's name?

Rather than admit to intellectual dishonesty or leave mankind free to pursue their own spirits within God, the church stifles all dissent. "If any man understands not these mysteries as they do, unfold, or open these riddles or parables according to their sense, meaning or interpretation, he must presently without all doubt or peradventure be a heretic or blasphemer."(11) Yet, the church can have no fixed definitions of heresy for in pursuing power, the church must often weave strange doctrine. "What's heresy and blasphemy today, nay this hour, the next day or hour is found orthodox truth. Have not our eyes oft seen this and our ears oft heard this thing?"(18) The only conclusion for Norwood was that those "who have at any time in any age dissented from, disowned or disavowed their preachings or practices, their doctrines or principles have by them been constantly pursued with excommunications, execrations, sword, fire and faggot. And yet, they are all for the gospel."(18)

Norwood's proposals for dealing with the flagrant violation of religious authority were as decisive as the church was evil. Norwood wished to create a totally free religious environment so that truth might emerge of its accord. "Let them alone to stand or fall of their own master," Norwood thought, "And if Christ be their master, what need they fear?"(11) Consequently, Norwood wished to eliminate all religious policy rather than simply to create a wider franchise or a more liberal religious policy. First, Parliament must abolish all religious legislation including "all such statutes, orders, ordinances and acts."(15) Second, the tithe, "that all compulsive and forcible maintenance for such who call themselves the ministers of God be also done away."(15) Third, "that there be no outward compulsions or enforcements of any to receive their or any other men's doctrines or principles. Neither that any mulcts, fines, banishments or any other corporal punishment be inflicted upon those that receive them not or who write, preach or speak against any others so that no affronts, injury or violence be done by the one unto the other."(16) In short, no religious authority at all.

Norwood never identified organized Christianity as the religion of the devil as did Coppin and others. Yet, there can be no doubt that Norwood's views were not far removed from those of earlier Bogomils and Cathari dualists, for like them Norwood envisioned the church as the greatest single source of evil in the world. In one place he asked whether "in all ages, kingdoms and states the clergy have not been the chief if not the only occasioners if not the fomenters, hatchers, plotters and contrivers of all the considerable or eminent treasons, treacheries, conspiracies, wars and bloodshed . . . and that under the name or notion of the kingdom and Gospel of Christ."(18) Essentially, the best church was no church at all.

Norwood's treatises concerning government and England's current state of governance expressed the same antiauthoritarian attitude already encountered. In his two treatises *A Pathway Unto England's Perfect Settlement* of 1653 and its companion piece of the same year entitled *An Additional Discourse*, Norwood, the gentleman, expressed political views hardly removed from the mainstream of Ranter anarchism. The first work was theoretical in nature while the second, far more radical, was a historical exercise on the problem of government.

The central question posed in the *Pathway* was "what ground, basis or foundation shall we then now settle a rule or government upon?"(15) Norwood's answer has a familiar ring. "Verily," Norwood wrote, "I for my part can find no true and certain fixed ground or foundation anywhere."(18) The single constant running through the many ages of human government was simple greed where "laws have been and are so often stretched and tentered, hauled and pulled, rent and torn this way and that way, to serve particular and private uses and ends of some private and particular persons."(39) Hence, "it is a mistake to think that Parliaments are the foundation of law."(38) Indeed, according to our gentleman author, self-interest was the only law known to Parliament. Under the pretense of policy debate where "one saith this, another that, this way it must today, another way and thing tomorrow," the actual meaning of the words was "this party and interest draws this way, another party and interest another way and a third, a third way."(31)

Though Norwood had served in Parliament's army for seven years, he was now thoroughly disillusioned with the entire course of the civil war effort and questioned whether any true reform was possible or had ever been intended. He asked, "What have any of us gotten except wounds and bruises? Have we not been feeding upon husks upon the winds?"(29)

Norwood was no more kind to Cromwell about whom he cynically observed, "He builds up Babylon and confusion (and can not do otherwise) first in himself, in his own imaginations; there he forms laws, statutes and ordinances and these must men be governed by."(20) In the end Cromwell must fail because his rule was not consonant with what Norwood conceived of as the natural state of man and England's early history and native political development. Without distinguishing the various forms of tyranny known as monarchy, Parliament or Protectorates, Norwood asserted that "if one man do exercise Lordship or kingship over another . . . *it was not so in the beginning.*"(10) And a few pages away, Norwood added, "Nor . . . was there any rule given unto him over any man or men, nor, indeed, appears there any need."(15) Human beings were all equal and able to govern themselves equitably though "all have not the like measure of seeing and understanding, have not the like measure of wisdom and knowledge, etc. Yet everyone hath (as may upon good grounds be presumed) enough in himself in reference to himself though perhaps not so much to things without himself, in reference to others."(17)

Later in 1653 Norwood wrote *An Additional Discourse*, the cover page of which informs the reader that this treatise is the second half and further elucidation of *The Pathway*. Its central theme is presented early in the work. "The ruins, deaths and destructions that have so constantly attended and befallen mankind have principally, if not only, been caused and occasioned from the desire of government rule, power and dominion which some man or men do or would assume, usurp and exercise over others, whether in things civil or religious."(2)

Like Clarkson and so many other Ranters, Norwood conceived of organized religion as the ideological cover or umbrella justification for the political machinations of the power hungry where "kings and priests claim a right, power, privilege and prerogative from God there unto, distinct from and above other men, as being better, more excellent or more holy than they."(18) Such pretenses notwithstanding, "you shall always find their kings and priests leading the people into error and all profaneness and wickedness."(19) Such governance by the rich, for the rich and against other men "must be a constant and continual succession of bloodshed, ruin and destruction, even unto all eternity and it can not be otherwise."(13) Each side parades under a succession of names and titles and promises reforms but "names and titles have much undone us all. What are Parliaments, kings or priests?" Norwood asked. "Why nothing and to be esteemed as nothing . . . a lie, a nothing."(46) Those fighting for power, however, are not taken in by names and titles. Hence, while it promised reform, Parliament thus "so much triumphed over the late king, the people's servant, they thought they might do the same over the people also."(43)

Thus far this treatise echoed views expressed by other Ranters and by Norwood himself in the *Pathway*. In this treatise Norwood also devoted his attention to explaining how this lamentable situation first came about and what might be done to rectify matters. The *Pathway* first introduced the idea that tyranny was not the native governance of Englishmen and this treatise further developed the notion that Englishmen originally possessed great personal freedom and enjoyed a democratic government. These rights existed to the time of the Norman Conquest but were eliminated by William the Conqueror. Since that time "many undue, unjust and irregular process and proceedings, judgments and executions have been had, made and done."(12)

According to Norwood, the true indigenous English tradition of free government was very old indeed. Norwood cited Strabo, speaking of the ancient Britons, "saith that for a long time diverse of them abhorred the very name of a king and when they had a king, the crown passed by election."(13) Norwood also cited Caesar that the Britons had no king in time of peace, and Tacitus, that war-time general-kings were elected by the people.(22, 28) The democratic impetus was so deeply imbedded in the English character that even the nobility in Parliament were popularly elected and "the Lords in Parliament or barons were chosen by the people and not chosen or summoned by the king. Their creation or being was anciently and at first from and by the people only and not by the king . . . but by the election and choice of the people only."(31–32)

Unlike other proponents of the Norman Yoke, Norwood even argued that Scripture too attested to the democratic British character. "Nennius confesseth that the British Annales had the descent of their Brute or Britto from Japhet . . . whose geneology through twenty descents to Noah and Adam, he saith, he had from the traditions of those that lived here in the first times of the Brittons."(12–13) Thus, from the very beginning of time and the time of creation, the British were democratic and "had their original from their rise, being and beginning with the purest laws of nature in the spirit . . ."(13) For all these reasons, "King William, before he was crowned and accepted by the people, did solemnly swear to observe and keep their old laws."(24, incorrectly listed as 16)

In his own times, Parliament represented monarchical tyranny and expressed the illegitimate abuses of the Norman Yoke. Thus, Parliament was in fact no different from the institution it replaced, and Norwood concluded, "I pray you, let us be men and no longer children to be frightened with the bug bear, with the name Parliament."(47)

If indeed Parliament was merely a forum for Norman class interests, "to think that acts of Parliament must therefore be observed and performed and executed because they are acts of Parliament, is most ridiculous."(51) On the contrary, Norwood argued in the early pages of the treatise, "All the acts of Parliament whatsoever, having not their foundation plain and visible in our common law, are in themselves null and void."(12) Later the same attitude was expressed when he wrote, "That which hath erected itself without Law may (for ought I know) be so taken away and thrown or cast down."(33)

Unlike other Ranters, Norwood believed England might be redeemed from its deplorable state of tyranny. Indeed, despite his many statements of futility, Norwood continued to believe that reform was really quite simple. "I propose not any new thing, nor would I that any should," Norwood was quick to explain, for like Clarkson and other Ranters we have read, Norwood was cynical about ideologies and platforms and programs of action. Such programs "constantly hath, and necessarily doth, cause and occasion many long and great and hot contentions, ululations, strifes, hatreds and wars, and those not without the effusion of much blood."(8)

Norwood advocated the total local control of all political offices where "every officer and minister of justice who or whatsoever, by the laws of this nation, are to be fully chosen by the neighbors where they are to officiate and administer."(14) Additionally, all such office holders should receive a wage and thereby be obligated to those paying their wages "for to him who appoints me my work and pays me my wages, him who makes me all and whatever I am or possibly can be in reference to that office, place or employment, certainly his I am."(34) Norwood does not argue that such officeholders should be poor commoners though such would be more obligated to the community paying his wage than a wealthier and more independent person. In any event, such a local government would be "bound and obliged by oath duly and truly to observe, keep and maintain the ordinances, customs and constitutions of our Forefathers, the ancient fundamental laws of this Nation inviolable."(41)

The first task of this democratic local government would be to create "a law equally common unto all men or a law in which each and every one hath a like and the same common or right and propriety and from or by which all and everyone is to have a like justice and equity done them without any the least respect to any kind, sort or degree of persons whatsoever." (*Pathway* p. 10) Noting that "the loss or detriment of any part being a loss and detriment to the whole and every part,"(*Pathway* p. 39) Norwood attempted to argue for the harmonious holistic purposes of local government

214

which "carefully and diligently look to the preservation of the whole, so of each particular according to the ordinances thereof in reference to the whole."(*Pathway* p. 39) In plain language, each individual's rights affect those of others of the community and thus government must do nothing to abridge the rights of the individual.

The second task of local government was, in Norwood's view, the abolition of a state church. Expressing a view we have read more than once, Norwood admitted, "Verily, I was never so much afraid of any sort of men as those who come so much clothed with the name of God and religion," he wrote, and "I profess before heaven and earth, they are generally the most dangerous and deceitful men in the whole world and were so from the beginning."(17) Lest "these zealous men undo us all," and because "the true and real service and worship of God lies not in forms but essentialities,"(17) Norwood could see no value in an organized church and believed the free practice of religion without coercion was part of the indigenous English character, for according to Bede, "when the king and diverse great men were converted and baptized, yet there was no force used to compel others to be of that religion."(15–16)

Captain Robert Norwood entertained views that were a blend of sophisticated analysis and simplistic prescriptions. His cynical views of the clergy and the role of organized religion in society were shared by all Ranters but also by many others in 1653. England had experienced the Presbyterian attempt to benefit from governmental authority, and elsewhere in Europe large numbers of people were sighing in relief that the Peace of Westphalia had ended the fighting of the Thirty Years' War in 1648. At the time, only Protestant ministers and Catholic clergy wished the fighting to continue. If few Englishmen knew of the German war, many understood that the fall of the Church of England meant only the rise of a similar institution with the name Presbyterian.

Similarly, Norwood's very cynical views of government were well understood by many in his age. The English civil war may have been fought for higher purposes than the French Fronde of the same years, but in fact both contests witnessed the emergence of special interest groups, which were better understood in their own age than by some of the historians recalling those times. The English civil war pitted Parliament against the king with both willing to make alliance with the Scots who also sought alliances with both, according to their own benefit. The French nobility fought for their interests and in Germany these same noblemen carried the day against central government. Indeed, in 1653 only an incomparable fool would invest government with idealism when throughout the world those who fought for power did so in order to enact the sort of self-interest legislation Norwood so clearly identified.

And yet, it was simplistic to assume that England's woes might be swept away through the election of local officials reestablishing some imaginary English "ancient constitution." Despite its absurdity, the concept of the Norman Yoke was taken seriously by more than one Ranter and a great many others. It is no doubt true that societies in trouble often look back to a less complicated time when justice was "real" and government expressed the goodness all hoped for. Imperial Romans were nostalgic for the simplicity of the Mars Field; Hebrews during Solomon's heavy-handed and expensive reign remembered the time of the tribal confederation when there was no monarchy and each man sat under his fig tree and enjoyed the fruits of his labors. Americans have long yearned for the old West and Germans for their Teutonic roots. In all instances this nostalgia was attractive because error and grievance might be laid at the feet of some foreigner. Captain Freeman blamed the French and the Germans blamed the Jews, and both ignored the fact that the nostalgic past died because of indigenous changes in society. Commercialism, central government and the end of rural communal life were English inventions from which there could be no redemption.

Both Captains Freeman and Norwood were silent on the question of private property. Freeman condemned the concentration of land occasioning Norman power but nowhere demanded the redistribution of property, and Norwood neglected this issue entirely. Other Ranters, as we have seen, were as adamant about property as about government and church but perhaps this attribute was in keeping with the fact that Freeman and Norwood were Ranters, but gentlemen too.

Tales of Two Parsons

15. Thomas Webb

Many of the Ranters we have dealt with thus far were itinerant preachers or lay preachers. Some, like Salmon and Coppin, preached regularly before fairly well-established audiences and certainly Coppe and Clarkson had large followings. In this chapter we will have the opportunity to view two Ranters holding regular and established positions as parsons or rectors. Both held wealthy livings, lived controversial lives, and preached outrageous sermons, as Ranters were likely to do. Both were condemned by their communities but where one was tried before religious authorities, the other appeared before the civil courts of Assize. Despite many differences between them, both lived peculiar lives, indeed, in the case of Thomas Webb, a bizarre life.

Thomas Webb was minister of God in Langley Burial in North Wiltshire. Our information concerning this peculiar gentleman comes from three sources. Foremost is the considerable volume of 1652 entitled *The Wiltshire Rant*, by Judge Edward Stokes. Justice Stokes was the local JP trying Webb, but he did not write this treatise to condemn Webb but to defend himself from Webb's slanderous attack upon himself in Webb's no longer existent treatise *Mass of Malice*. A second source of information is Mr. Thomas Edwards' very hefty volume *Gangraena* (1646) concerning the many heresies and blasphemies Edwards believed a plague in Revolutionary England. The last source is Webb's own treatise, *Mr. Edward's Pen No Slander* of 1646, which also provides much useful information concerning the bizarre events of Webb's peculiar life.

Of these several sources, the most important and informative is the treatise by Edward Stokes. Stokes was not an irate minister making a name for himself by attacking the easy prey of Ranter immorality and belief. Neither was Stokes a crusading justice bent upon destroying every remnant of social-religious radicalism in England. He was a very conscientious local JP who knew Webb intimately from the time the latter first came to Langley until the time Webb was finally deposed from his position. Stokes, the only justice to write a full account of his contact with Rantism, took pen to hand to counter Webb's treatise *Mass of Malice* wherein that author maintained that all his legal troubles resulted from a personal vendetta on Stokes' part which resulted in his being harassed by the legal and religious communities.

Like a good jurist, Stokes argued his case in exemplary legal fashion by presenting the reader with a detailed factual account bolstered by the submission of letters, depositions, court records and transcripts as well as verbatim testimony from local witnesses. Stokes' account is sometimes bitter but never without apology to the reader, and it always attempts to be objective. He never argued beyond what third party sources could corroborate. Moreover, Stokes had no argument with Webb on religious grounds and at no point did he attempt to vindicate conventional religious thought from Ranter radicalism. Stokes' sole concern was to clear his name from Webb's accusations that the judge bore him malice and performed inadequately in a professional sense. In the introductory Epistle to the Reader Stokes wrote that he wished "to clear up the innocense of those in authority and to make it manifest that their proceedings against the said Thomas Webb were neither unjust, illegal, nor malicious." Stokes explained that his account would be as complete as possible but the names of several Ranters and their letters to him would be deleted to guard their privacy and because "the author was unwilling to publish those works and papers which he received from others of the Ranting crew concerning them, in the hopes that they will acquit themselves like men." Additionally, Stokes believed that any information concerning Webb that was not germane to his defense of himself was a violation of Webb's own privacy and would therefore be omitted.

Stokes began his account by telling of when Webb first came to Langley Burial to become a parish minister. He related how Webb was well accepted by both prominent and common members of the community. Webb's popularity soared when he refused to accept his due tithe of £70 per annum and condemned the tithe as an unjust tax.(3) This popularity, however, proved short-lived.

Shortly after Webb first came to Langley, his second wife took ill and died. During the period of illness, however, Webb became involved with several married women and with at least one unmarried woman, with "at least one of his former loves charging him with breach of promise."(4) Webb also became romantically and sexually involved with a certain Mrs. Mary White, a very prominent local lady, and was quoted as having preached from the pulpit "that there is no heaven but women nor no hell save marriage."(4) Perhaps because Webb was quickly acquiring the reputation of a womanizer, when his wife died and he chose a "modest sober young woman" of local background as his next wife, many were upset and

218

he married her "without the consent and to the great grief of her friends."(4)

In March of 1650, Webb and his third wife took up residence in the White family manor house. Mr. and Mrs. White and the parson and his wife all seemed very happy with this arrangement and Stokes agreed that it made sense because the White manor house was very grand with more than enough room for all. At this time, no one realized the extent of the intimate friendship between Pastor Webb and Mrs. White, but Mrs. Webb soon became very suspicious. When she complained to her husband, Webb reacted in a very unusual fashion. Rather than simply allaying her fears, Webb, together with Mary White and two other residents on the estate, William and Edith Lewis, hatched a plot to catch his wife *in flagrento* with a young man from the village.

While Webb preached before the community one Sunday morning, Mrs. Webb was fooled into taking a local young man to bed. Knowing what had been planned, Webb left the pulpit in mid-sentence and returned home to catch his wife and her would-be lover in bed. Rather than scolding her, Webb exclaimed, "Well done wife, well done, pray God bless you"(7) and returned to finish his sermon. Though the extent to which the different husbands and wives living at the White residence were involved with one another was not known at that time, the estate soon became the center of an extensive Ranter social life. As far as Stokes was concerned, all seemed aboveboard, and despite growing gossip, there was no evidence that anything untoward or illicit was occurring at the estate.

At about the same time that this unusual household was becoming a center of gossip throughout the region, Webb became sexually involved with a local "comely young man, and a man of a seeming sober behavior."(8) At a loss to explain the nature of this relationship, Stokes wrote that the young man, referred to as X, was "taken by Thomas Webb as men used to take their wives." Evidently Webb was unconcerned with potential community reaction and he did not hesitate to appear in public with X where, according to Stokes, "this man is honored with the title of 'Webb's wife', for so he calls him, 'My wife X' or 'X owns Webb for a husband.' "(8)

If Webb was little concerned with increasing public curiosity, wonder, consternation and unhappiness with the minister's unconventional bedside manner, his housemates became increasingly jealous. His mistress Mary White was jealous of Webb's relationship with his legal wife, Mrs. Webb, and his other wife, X, and "acts the part of jealosy even to distraction, pretending she would be her own executioner and lay violent hands on herself."(10) Mrs. Webb, jealous of Webb's public wife X, and his house mistress, Mrs. Mary White, was also threatening suicide, and "seems willing to choose death at any hand rather than her husband should continue in the tenets of wickedness."(9) As the Webb-White-Lewis-X household exhibited more and more inner tension, Webb became "the common table talk of the county." The members of this unusual household increasingly expressed their anger and jealous feelings in public, and the common opinion was "the pitiful parson is in a pack of troubles."(10)

Fortunately for Webb, X, his male "mistress," quit the area leaving Webb to contend with his legal wife and Mary White. Disputes in public between members of this triangle increased to the point where Mary White took the decisive step of bringing legal action against Webb, charging him with sexual and religious irregularity, even though it was partially with her that such irregularity had occurred. On September 2, 1650, court was convened at Chippenham before Justices Shutte and Stokes. This court meeting was the latter's formal introduction into all these events.

Stokes understood that Mary White's suit resulted from her jealousy of Webb's relationships and that she took this legal action to damage Webb's public image. Through the sworn testimony of her maid servant, Elizabeth Briscoe, Mary White alleged that she heard Webb state that "Moses was a conjurer and Christ was a deceiver of the people, and that preaching and lying were both alike unto him."(12) and that Webb "drank to the confounding of Parliament." Even worse, both women testified that Webb boasted "he could lay with any woman except his own mother"(12) and recounted his laying with six women, including the wives of two Captains in Bristol, Mistress R of Bath, a wife of a Captain M, and his Aunt D at Batheston and the wife of a Major in London. According to the testimony of Mary White and Elizabeth Briscoe, Webb was not always happy with his sexual exploits. He was sorry "he had lain with one S.C. of Slaughtenford and that she had given him the French Pox and he gave it to his wife."(12) Mary White did not indicate whether she, too, had the French Pox.

Mary White additionally charged that Webb had attempted to rape her and that he had made sexual advances to her maid servants. Finally, Mary White claimed Webb was a secret Ranter and produced two letters from Joseph Salmon to Webb, both of which were placed into evidence and published by Stokes.(13) Stokes, later vilified by Webb as the malicious source of all his troubles, was careful to point out to the reader, "You see what the charge is and by whom laid against this profane parson. Not by the justices, nor by such as were his enemies by profession but by his own converts, his endeared lovers and fellow creatures."(14)

Webb's defense was as charitable to his erstwhile lover as her charges had been to him. He maintained that however indiscreet, he was innocent of the charges and was "so exceedingly beset by a pernicious woman and her perfidious bloody company, that did you know the particulars you (would) take her to be the only monster of that sex."(11) Webb then threw himself on the mercy of the court and successfully convinced the jury that he was a changed man.

This strategy was wise for several reasons. First it was unlikely that he would have been found guilty of the charges since all knew they had been lovers and guilt depended upon believing her word rather than his. Second, had Webb been found guilty of adultery, a capital offense at this time, the jury would have had to condemn one lover but not the other for only one was so charged. The real danger for Webb was that even if found innocent he might be forced out of his living. Consequently, begging the court's indulgence and mercy would guarantee his being found innocent of the charges and make it difficult for the community to dismiss him. But there was more to Webb's strategy.

According to Justice Stokes, Webb's plea for mercy was convincing for several reasons. First, Stokes explained, Webb seemed truly contrite. When presented with the charges against him, "he smote himself upon the breast and threw himself upon the ground before so many witnesses."(15) Second, he confessed all his sins. Webb cried before the court and explained "that ever since the death of his second wife that he had committed the detestable sin of uncleanness"(15) from feelings of desolation. Webb insisted that he had never attempted to rape Mary White, "neither needed he to do so but that always she tempted him to commit the sin of uncleanness with her." In fact, Webb claimed that Mary White was sexually insatiable and that she forced him "to commit the detestable sin of uncleanness so often in one day that he was glad when he could take the air."(15)

Webb's contrite courtroom behavior and his open admission of guilt were further strengthened by a series of letters Webb wrote to Stokes during the trial which were then made public and were included in the volume. In one letter Webb wrote, "I profess to you my heart is smitten within me for my sin is great and lies very heavy and sore upon me . . . God hath called me home from the ways of an adulterous woman . . . I know the way of an insatiable woman is ruin and to have the life of one whom they can not mold to their lusts. And for my part, if she doth ruin me, as that is her intention, I shall glory in it for greater would my misery have been if I should have contrived in the ways of her uncleanness . . . But oh, let me be accursed, and oh, that the earth might swallow me up alive rather than I should harken to her again."(16–17)

In another letter Webb explained how terrible he had felt trapped in the snares of sin. "We have both committed a great evil of which it pleased God to make me sensible; whereupon I began to forsake . . . and estrange myself from Mistress White while she, perceiving and having attempted all ways and means to keep me, but finding it was all in vain, she now proceeds in this way against me."(17) Webb resigned himself to receive punishment. "Much more might be said to prove that it proceeds to be from malice . . . and if it be the will of God that through the malice of a strange woman I must suffer, I dare not question my God for it, it is the wages of sin . . . I can testify to the whole world that my present sufferings are because I will no longer serve the filthy lusts and desires of the flesh." (18) Stokes noted that the packed courtroom was in total sympathy with their evidently contrite minister, and it was at this point that Webb detonated a bombshell. Webb then shocked the court and Mary White as well when he confessed that the child Mary White was then carrying was in fact his child and he gave the date of conception and further noted that Mary White had wanted them to run off together and even put money aside for that purpose.(16) Indeed, Webb cried that she took legal action against him because he had refused to run off with her.

Having transformed himself from perpetrator and sinner to victim and object of another's malicious criminal intent, Webb still found it possible to express pity for Mary White. "Oh pity that woman," Webb begged Stokes, "for there is a most fearful coming of the Lord's vengeance and judgment upon her."(19) All were very much impressed with the obvious change in Parson Webb's behavior and character. Consequently, no legal action was taken against him and the case was dismissed. Indeed, the community was entirely delighted with the return of their pastor. After his release, Webb was received back into the community's heart and love, for "he was real and so truly sensible and sorrowful for his evil and unclean life and therefore he was received again into favor amongst many good people who exceedingly rejoiced in his returning . . ."(20)

Stokes, too, confessed to having mused that justice had truly been done, for Mary White's action had had the effect of bringing a good man to his senses. As Stokes himself explained his feelings at the time, "Was not this man as a silly bird to wander from his place? From his lawful calling? From the wife of his bosom?"(20)

It is easy to rejoice with Langley Burial. If one aspect of the minister's role in the community was to teach the truth of morality, surely Webb was an exceptional representative of God's way. Not content to preach the way of truth, Webb was a walking-talking-living example and expression of the miraculous curing power of God's love of the sinner. Who better than Webb demonstrated every individual's need for the church as a chastising rod? Who better than Webb could represent God and his truth to this community of good Christians struggling with the temptations of life? Webb's esteem in the community had never been greater.

We might pause to consider who won and who lost in this lovers' quarrel and legal tournament held in public. If Mary White had hoped to hurt Webb by denouncing him in public, bringing him to court, and conceivably, making it impossible for the community to retain him as a pastor, she failed. Instead Mary White succeeded in providing Webb with a vehicle through which he might set himself straight with the community by denouncing her as the source of evil, as an insatiable woman, and, most shocking of all, as the soon to be mother of his child. Seventeenth-century society may well have condemned adultery in both sexes, but certainly Webb, as a male and as a pastor, was better able to turn the situation to his own advantage. Mary White went to court to demand justice, but she received none because the community understood her to be at least as guilty as Webb. When Webb went to court begging the community's forgiveness, he demonstrated that he was better than she, and certainly Puritan society could well appreciate the powerful lure of the devil in the form of an insatiable woman.

Webb may have miscalculated on one major issue: the effect of his defense on Mary White's husband. Webb had told an unhappy tale about Mary White's personality and he confessed that she now carried his child. Rather than divorce his wife and thereby attempt to salvage his pride and reputation, Mr. White sued Webb on the same grounds as had his wife, if only to clear his name and vindicate his wife's reputation and what looked like his untenable social position as a cuckolded husband. In bringing a suit against Webb, Mr. White demonstrated his faith in his wife's account of events, her innocence, and his own paternity of the soon to be born child.

Webb was able to turn this suit to his own advantage as well. Once again Webb explained that it was the malicious intent of others that hurt him. He wrote to Stokes, "I have sent Mr. White word more than once or twice but he can not leave his old ways of contention. And therefore, out of a malicious spirit he troubles your worship, seeking thereby to make you an instrument to execute the base and wicked desires of his wife and her wicked confederacy."(19) Mr. White's suit, like that of his wife Mary, had the effect of strengthening Thomas Webb's position in Langley Burial.

How edifying it must have been to the community that their minister could preach repentance with the honesty and candor of one recently con-

verted from the path of sin! How upsetting it must have been when, after
the space of a few months, Webb not only returned to all his old ways but
became even worse than before. "The old lascivious dress and garb is now
taken up again," Stokes complained, "and the humble parson acts afresh
the part of the most proud and insolent phantastic, and appears like unto a
profane stage-player than parish priest or sober Christian. His long shaggy
hair, which has lately hung like a forgotten excrement, is now taken into
consideration and furbished up with so much frizell and powder."(21)
Even his sermons were impossible as "his study of the Scriptures must give
place to a study more noble in the esteem if illiterate Ranters, called astron-
omy."(22) Worst of all, however, was the continuing inability of the White-
Webb-Lewis household to air their differences in private and reconcile
their problems among themselves. The same community that had so willingly accepted Webb into its heart, was "lately grieving for his Ranting and
wickedness."(20)

It is a little difficult to piece together the exact flow of events but it appears that once the trials were over, Webb and Mary White took up with
each other again to the chagrin of both Mr. White, who had demonstrated
his faith in his wife's claim against Webb, and William Lewis, Webb's
replacement lover while Webb and Mrs. White were in contention. The
result was that once again this curious assembly used the public square as
an open forum to vent their grievances and strike at each other. This time,
however, the relationship was the opposite of what it had been before. Earlier, Mrs. Webb, Mary White, X, and others competed for the attentions of
Thomas Webb. Now, Thomas Webb, Henry White and William Lewis
competed for Mary White's attention. Stokes could never quite explain, or
perhaps understand, the relationship that had subsequently developed
among Webb, Mr. White, and William Lewis since the ending of the trial
several months before. Their public displays were increasingly rowdy,
however, and Stokes came to fear that matters would again be brought before the bench, and worse, before his bench. In a word, "What if one or two
fellow creatures be fallen off from and out with these choice lovers and tell
tales out of school and swear in public what was acted more private?"(36)
This is precisely what occurred and in the middle of the night, William and
Edith Lewis, fearing for their lives, woke Justice Stokes from his sleep to
lodge a complaint against Thomas Webb. Writing about himself in the
third person, Stokes described his reaction. "Wherefore Mr. Stokes demands of them why they trouble him about such complaints. Why at that
time of night. Why they did not rather get the assistance of some of their
friends to reconcile them or, if not, [he] wished them to repair to some other

justice of the peace."(24) Unfortunately, Stokes would not be left to a decent night's sleep, for what followed this nocturnal visit was a series of court hearings even more bizarre (and humorous, if from the distance of centuries) than those we have already recorded.

Before he had the opportunity to learn what had caused this latest series of charges and countercharges, his worst fears were realized for on November 26, Mr. Henry White, out of jealousy of William Lewis' relationship with his wife, Mary, brought charges against the Lewises accusing them of having stolen some property while living under his roof. The Lewises defended their innocence by bringing Mary White, Henry White's wife, to testify on their behalf and the case was quickly dismissed.(28) Then, two weeks later on December 9, the Lewises brought a suit against Henry and Mary White and Thomas Webb alleging adultery. Edith Lewis swore that "she saw the said Thomas Webb lying on the body of the said Mistress White and being in the very act of adultery with her, upon the bed there."(29–30) To compound matters further, "she, this informant saith, that there was in the same room at the same time one John Morris . . . and that afterwards they together with said Morris fell to dancing, using in the said dancing much filthy and unclean language."(29–30) Adding to the damaging testimony, William Lewis swore that "her servant, Elizabeth Briscoe, was as good as herself [i.e., Mary White] for she lay with John Morris and Young Organ of Castlecomb."(31)

Stokes included letters in the text from both Webb and Mary White, each accusing the other of engineering conspiracies against himself, herself, themselves and each other.(34–40) In short, this legal battle was a total free-for-all, for while the Lewises had fallen out with the Webbs and Whites, the latter two evidently each blamed the other for all that was happening. As a result of these charges and countercharges, the three justices involved in this case—Stokes, Shutte and Nichols—took action against all those involved. Webb, and both Whites were thrown into jail without bail to wait for the next Assize. This decision, in turn, brought another flurry of letters from all the defendants concerning bail, criminal rights, and anything else the author of the letter could think of. The judges were totally confused and unable to unwind the knot of charges and accusations but were aware that a great deal more was happening than was immediately apparent. Expressing the common frustration of all three justices, Stokes observed, "They know well enough how to manage the business, they can produce witnesses enough to outswear whatsoever shall be sworn against them."(36)

If by remanding Webb and the Whites to jail without bail Stokes had hoped for some peace and quiet, he was to be sadly disappointed. All parties concerned continued to bombard him with letters damning and blaming the other for his/her sad condition. Webb wrote that it was extremely important to detain Mary White in jail but that he should be released immediately. According to Stokes, Webb wrote that "he was exceedingly wearied and tired out with Mistress White's company in jail, that she by her flatteries and frowns still endeavored to keep him in his evil and unclean course with her, whose provocations and temptations gave him no rest."(41) As an example, Webb noted that he "had no rest unless he were sucking at her breasts which was his work amongst others . . . or merry and frolick with her according to the accustomed manner."(41)

Mary White also wrote to Stokes to solicit his favor. She wrote "I am very sensible of your realities and endeavored friendship towards us, you shall find us as truly yours in whatever lieth within our powers when opportunity shall honor us with some ample expressions whereby we may express in deed rather than word what we would be."(42)

Stokes presents the reader with few details about the course of these trials "because all things acted there were in the face of the whole country . . . [and] it's so famously known in Wiltshire."(43) Sorting out all the claims and counterclaims is very difficult. Previously Elizabeth Briscoe charged Webb with boasting of immorality with six women and Mary White charged Webb with attempting to rape her maidservant, but now Edith Lewis swore she saw Mary White and Webb having sexual intercourse and her husband, William Lewis, testified that Elizabeth Briscoe had sex with John Morris and that the latter, John Morris, together with Mary White and Webb, danced and sang bawdy songs. In between, Mr. White had charged the Lewises with theft of his property but Mary White's testimony exonerated them of this charge. All of this came on the heels of Webb's claiming that the pregnant Mary White carried his child while Mr. White sued Webb for defaming Mary White's and his own honor.

Had anybody's testimony been accepted, both Mary White and Pastor Webb, as well as Elizabeth Briscoe and William and Edith Lewis as well as John Morris and Young Organ of Castlecomb, would have been convicted of adultery, a capital offense in England at this time. Stokes merely noted, "The Grand Jury finds the Bill of Indictment, the jury, for life and death, finds him not guilty, whereupon he is freed."(43) Presumably, Mary White and all the others were also released at this time.

Without a transcript it is impossible to be certain why the defendants were found innocent. It is possible the jury had little patience with any of those involved or that they believed Webb and White guilty as charged, but may have been hesitant to condemn to death either Webb or Mary White. Even in this age of faith, execution may have seemed too severe a penalty for adultery. For Webb, however, his acquittal merely reinforced him in his unfortunate ways. According to Stokes, "He continues the same as before, nay, he becomes more proud, imperious and impudent than ever."(43)

Two weeks after this last trial, during the Christmas season of 1651, Webb decided that he could not happily live in this community. After celebrating Christmas with Ranters in Sarum, Webb returned home where "he publicly owns his relation to his fellow creatures [i.e., Ranters] to above and more binding to him than his relation to his own wife which was but formal, but the other was real."(43) When Webb finally addressed the community from the pulpit, "he breathes out no less than ruin and destruction against all opposers, amongst which Mr. Stokes must have a large share."(44)

The next few months must have been incredible, for Webb was hardly out of the public eye, as later testimony indicated. Matters took a different turn several months later in May of 1651, when Webb was called to London to appear before the Committee of Plundered Ministers to answer various issues coming to their attention. This Parliamentary committee had broad powers and could remove an incumbent minister from his post for a variety of reasons ranging from religious irregularity to questions of personal competence. Stokes does not explain how Webb came to Parliament's attention, but, as we shall learn later, Webb had been known to Parliament for several years. Unfortunately for both Webb and Stokes, the latter was commissioned by the Committee to act in their behalf and gather testimony and depositions from local residents concerning Webb's fitness as a minister. After he had compiled this material, copies were to be sent to London for the committee's perusal where a decision concerning Webb would be made. Other than the committee's deliberations, to which Stokes was not privy, all other materials, evidence, depositions and sworn testimony sent to London were included by Stokes in his volume.

Most of the early charges against Webb from his innumerable trials were raised again at this time. His alleged adultery, unfortunate comments about Parliament, and irreligious statements concerning marriage, Moses and Jesus were obtained for the record. Because the reader is already familiar with Webb's relationship with Mary White and how he came to contract the French Pox, as well as other aspects of his eccentric behavior, such issues will not be dealt with again at this time. One must note, however, that Stokes was able to compile more evidence concerning these charges than had originally been presented in court. Of these old charges, only

BLASPHEMY, IMMORALITY, AND ANARCHY

Webb's anti-Parliamentary statements attracted attention in London in part because Webb aggravated his earlier drinking "to the confounding of Parliament" with additional complaints that Parliament was unjust, took too much money in taxes and stated that "God would appear for and in behalf of the Cavalliers once more."(50) Even worse, Webb attempted to persuade the sentry guarding him to desert his post.

Two new charges of a serious nature were more important than those already dealt with. First, Webb was accused of abusing church property by cutting down trees from church lands, selling the lumber and pocketing the proceeds. Also, he was charged with dismantling two church outbuildings and selling the wood for his own benefit. Evidently, it was through such activity that Webb was able to forego accepting the tithe. The second important charge was that Webb preached "false and unprofitable doctrine" a catchall charge used against all radical or obnoxious preachers.(48)

The abuse of church property was a very serious charge. Webb's rejection of the tithe when first coming to Langley Burial may have made him popular but his outright condemnation of the tax probably made him suspect to Parliamentary clergy in whose eyes it was more than just. If the committee wondered how Webb supported himself, the answer was found in the testimony of several witnesses who claimed, "When the said Mr. Webb came and entered Rectory or Parsonage of Langley aforesaid, the glebe lands there unto belonging was very well stored and replenished with timber trees and other under woods and that since that time the said Mr. Webb hath cut down, burned and sold all or the greatest part of the same trees and underwood. And hath also pulled down two substantial outhouses belonging to the said rectory or parsonage house and sold away the materials thereof."(51) Additional testimony maintained that Webb "mored and grubbed up about one half part of the copice ground belonging to the said rectory. And that in summer last . . . the said Mr. Webb did hire workmen who did by his appointment pull down a handsome barn belonging to the said rectory and sold away the materials thereof."(54)

No less serious than the abuse of church property was the abuse of religious authority. In the absence of mass education, the local minister's sermons and lectures interpreted and explained the meaning of Scripture to the community. The pastor's sermon was also a main source of ideas and news about reforms in Parliament. From Parliament's point of view, the pastor was also a most important bulwark against widespread confusion regarding what religious observances were proper and which sects were not. Hence, the local minister could play a role for continuity or cause widespread dissension. We have noted in earlier chapters how ministers and local JPs often worked together to keep the religious and social peace and how Ranters often found that arguing with the one led to charges and jail sentences by the other.

According to Webb's parishioners, the pastor preached "that the works of Jesus Christ and his apostles were dead works and carnal and ended when they died and served for their time only and that people might live unto God without Jesus Christ."(54) In a similar vein, "that the baptism of water was only John's ministry . . . that God's teaching his people is not by any outward ordinance or ministry or means but by the inward unction and anointing."(65) Webb told his flock "that preaching and praying [should] cease for the Lord hath no ears to hear,"(55) and more radical still, "that all preaching . . . is but mere declaring to each other what we are taught and not any ministry [and hence] he knew not whether Paul's epistles do concern us or no."(56) In short, neither Scripture nor ministry was of value. Concerning his own role, Webb had explained "that he was no minister of God and wished them not to look upon him as a minister, for (saith he) God had put an end to all ministers and ministrations."(51) More outrageous still, "that he hoped to live so long, and that it was now in working, that there should be no such thing as a parsonage or ministry in England."(56) All religious authority should be done away with, and Webb "persuaded the people not to conform themselves to any visible ministrations either for church or state . . . and that they should not obey any ecclesiastical or civil authority . . . [because] God requires no obedience to any Scripture commands."(51)

Even more outrageous than the above were Webb's sermons concerning sexual morality. He preached "that he did live above the ordinances and that it was lawful for him to lay with any woman."(53) Another time, "the said Mr. Webb, observing a great cock pigeon to tread diverse of the hen pigeons, there said . . . that it was lawful for every man and woman and that they ought to take that liberty and freedom one with the other, as those pigeons did, although they were not married one to the other."(53)

One is hesitant to accept this local testimony yet the same points were made repeatedly by many witnesses over and over again. The contents of these sermons may have been unusual for Langley Burial but were espoused by most Ranters we have encountered. In any event, Webb had ample opportunity to cross-examine these witnesses or question their testimony and chose not to. Indeed, there was so much testimony against Webb and he sat listening so quietly that the judges repeatedly prodded and encouraged Webb to question those giving evidence against him. In no instance did Webb question a single witness.(56) It is unfortunate that Stokes was not privy to dicussions in London or could not secure a transcript of the Committee's deliberations. In any event, the outcome was fairly predictable; Webb was ejected from his living.

Had the story of Thomas Webb ended here and had Webb simply melted into English or London countryside, Edward Stokes would have been a very happy man. This was not the case, for in fact the most outrageous part of the story actually began precisely at this point.

Webb's reaction to his ejection was typical of many radicals forced from their living or prosecuted in a court of law; he moved to London and wrote a treatise attacking his former adversaries, Stokes in particular. Though this treatise, *A Mass of Malice Against Thomas Webb*, is no longer extant, Stokes devoted a great deal of space to describing it, its arguments, and included lengthy citations in his own treatise so that he might defend himself against the author's accusations. Indeed, Stokes devoted seven closely printed pages merely to listing what he considered to be Webb's 130 untruths.(60–66)

Together, the 130 untruths listed by Stokes concerned Webb's evaluation of his earlier trials, presented many *ad hominem* attacks upon Stokes himself, and arrived at the conclusion that he had suffered because of the malice of Edward Stokes and others who bore him ill will. Despite Stokes' conscientious work, it is difficult to do justice to Webb's treatise through his adversary's eyes. Yet, Stokes' list contains so many bizarre and outrageous claims made by Webb, which are in turn supported by so many citations from Webb's *Mass of Malice*, that it is difficult to believe that this work could have been very different from Stokes' presentation of it. As examples, Webb argued that Stokes thirsted for Webb's blood and attempted to have him killed (items 44, 111, 142); also, that the Lewises were behind the whole conspiracy against him (item 5); additionally, that Stokes was a very irreligious man (items 73–79) and a sexual pervert. (items 80–83) We are informed that Stokes stole church money (items 90, 91) and Mary White's property as well. (items 125, 126) If any one issue raised by Webb clearly seems the most slanderous, and hence perhaps the leaven in the entire loaf, it is Webb's charge that Stokes was a sexual pervert.

According to Webb, he and Stokes travelled together to Salisbury where they shared accommodations at the Boer's Head Inn. One morning Stokes allegedly filled a bottle with his urine and set it next to his excrement and asked Webb to kneel and partake of communion. Webb asserted that Stokes said, "pointing to his dung, 'Here is the Body of Christ'. Pointing to his urine, saith he, 'Here is the blood of Christ.' "(page 64, items 80–83) In his own defense, Stokes rejected the story in its entirety. Writing in the third person he noted, "Mr. Stokes affirms that he was not with said Webb at Salisbury at that time nor at any time since, except when we were upon his trial for adultery at Lent Assizes in 1650. Mr. Stokes affirms that he never lay at the Boer's Head in Salisbury by himself, with the said person, nor with any other person and that he knoweth no such sign. Moreover, he affirms that if he can be disproved in either of these answers, he is contented to be branded with the blackest mark of infamy that ever was due to a blasphemer. Mr. Stokes believes that were himself (or any) guilty of so horrid and accursed actions, God is so just and jealous of his own glory that as great plagues and furies pursue the offender . . . Mr. Stokes affirms the whole story of the blasphemy, as penned and published by Webb, is of the libeller's own invention and never had a being but in Thomas Webb's brain or practice till it come from thence to fill up his *Mass of Malice* against Mr. Stokes."(70)

Stokes was not content merely to deny the charge but asked "is a man of his coat and calling to conceal a blasphemy without check to the blasphemer or complaint to the magistrate for two years together?"(71) And addressing Webb's other charges regarding his theft of money from both the church and Mary White, Stokes demonstrated that the amounts Webb mentioned were in fact public funds raised by Stokes for public use and presented documents as evidence.(77−79) Moreover, Stokes asked the reader, "If Mr. Stokes were guilty of such foul crimes, how comes it to pass that Webb in all his angry and reproachful letters never mentioned a word to Mr. Stokes in any one of them?"(80)

Were such stories true, Webb might have blackmailed Stokes at any point during his many trials and might have mentioned the Salisbury incident in any of the letters Webb wrote to Stokes while he sat in jail. Most convincing was Stokes' inclusion of a letter from Webb to himself dating from the period after Webb's ejection from Langley but before the *Mass of Malice* was written. The letter's tone is friendly and respectful with Webb indicating that "while you were in London, I longed for your coming home because to you I would unbosom myself, but I was cast off by you to my great grief and sorrow."(80) Additionally, Webb wrote that he considered Stokes "a cordial and true friend to the saints and truth of Christ."(80)

Stokes was unable, or perhaps unwilling, to account for Webb's peculiar behavior while minister at Langley. He does note that "the ridiculous author of the *Mass of Malice* . . . having made himself drunk with the much bibing at the Ranter Cup, behaves himself like a mad Bedlam, striking those that are next to him."(81) But if Stokes was unable to explain Webb's accusations and charges, he was able to demonstrate that Webb's writing of the *Mass of Malice* and the sort of arguments therein contained was typical of his behavior for much longer than he was minister at Langley Burial.

The information Stokes presented concerns Webb's life before he became minister at Langley and hence before Stokes knew of him. Consequently, at the very moment that the reader anticipates finally being finished with Thomas Webb, Edward Stokes begins an enlightening new story of an earlier Thomas Webb. Though he did not know Webb at that time, public records support Stokes' statements.

It seems that in 1644 Webb stood charged with blasphemy before the House of Lords. He was committed to prison but finally won his release by claiming "repentance of those errors, subscribing a form of Recantation with his own hand and afterwards gave thanks to a minister of the assembly for being a means to draw him off from those errors."(82) In other words, in 1644 Webb did what many Ranters did and apologized for maintaining their horrible views. He was to do this again in 1651 when he thanked Stokes for showing him the straight and narrow path and the folly of his ways. Stokes was not concerned with Webb's religious views of 1644 any more than he was concerned about his views several years later when Webb stood trial in Stokes' court. Stokes was disturbed by Webb's character which he believed clearly expressed the same qualities throughout his life.

Webb was also known to others. In 1646 Thomas Edwards, no great liberal or tolerant person, wrote about Webb in the first edition of his mammoth catalogue of contemporary heresies, blasphemies, schismatics and heretics called by the colorful title *Grangraena*. This stalwart defender of Protestant orthodoxy reported receiving a letter from a minister describing Webb's religious views. The unnamed minister made no attempt to quarrel with Webb but felt it his duty to report the existence of so serious a blasphemer. He wrote as follows: "Not long since [Mr. Webb's release from prison] I had some conference with one Mr. Webb, a man that pretends a New Light, who said unto me . . . That he blessed God he never trusted in a crucified Christ nor did he believe him to be the Son of God, nor the Scriptures divine but human invention and not fit for the rule of life . . . there was no more resurrection of a man than of a beast nor had he any more soul than the body yet he granted a spirit in both wicked and godly which he says goes again to him that gave it . . . he denies any local hell or Devil more than men are Devils in themselves" and finally that "many follow him in city and country."(54) Clearly, the Mr. Webb reported by Edwards was a fully committed Ranter subscribing to cardinal Ranter tenets. Moreover, this description of Webb in 1646 would indicate that he was an early Ranter.

232

Many of Webb's other views also corresponded to those maintained by other Ranters. Edwards was told about Webb that "he loves not the Scottish nation but terms them the Babylonish Beast and the Presbyterian government, the Priest's Monopoly."(55) Like other Ranters, Webb disliked organized religion as well as the state and did not differentiate between them or distinguish which was worse. Edwards' source indicated that Webb told him that organized religion "set at variance King and Parliament, the King against the Kingdom, and things would never be well until the Golden Calf [i.e., the Church] and the Brazen Serpent [i.e., the state] were beated to pieces."(54)

Some pages later Edwards reported that he, too, knew of Webb's brush with the law in 1644. "There is one Thomas Webb in and about London, a young man about twenty or twenty-one years of age," Edwards wrote. "This Webb was complained of to the Assembly and the Assembly sent up articles to the House of Lords; he was by that honorable House committed and stood so some time. But upon recantation of all those errors, by word of mouth and with his hand subscribing to a form of recantation drawn up, he was freed from imprisonment. But since the time of his release, he hath both in city and country vented many of his strange opinions."(74) Among the cities where Webb was well known, according to Edwards, were London, Suffolk, Essex, Kent, Colchester and Milton. Edwards gives no more complete description of Webb's views. Though the first Ranter treatises date from 1646, Ranter opinion clearly existed before this time. Nothing in Webb's views, as reported by Edwards, indicated sexual libertinism, but this might have developed later. The use of a recantation to gain release from prison was evidently a common practice.

Webb was evidently stung to the core by what Edwards had written of him and consequently responded to Edwards' description of himself in his little treatise of 1646 entitled *Mr. Edwards' Pen, No Slander.* Though separated by several years and circumstance, Webb's response to Edwards may shed light upon his subsequent response to Stokes in his *Mass of Malice.*

Webb argued that Edwards treated him unfairly. While conceding that he had been called before the House of Lords, Webb contended, "I wonder, and it's something strange, that I should recant of those blasphemous doctrines when indeed, as unto me they were read, I did not own them. It is true there were many doctrines read over me by the Clerk of the House of Lords which would admit of dangerous and blasphemous constructions and were of dangerous consequences, indeed, quite contrary unto my judgment or opinion . . . now if this were a recantation, I refer it to wise judicious considerations."(1) From Webb's memory and account, he was fully able to satisfy the House of Lords that they had apprehended the wrong Thomas Webb. Indeed, Webb wrote that he was not really sure why the Lords had called him. "The Justices' reason was I know not," Webb explained. "He [i.e., Edwards] himself did endeavor to give a false interpretation of my words, saying, that I spake as Mr. Edwards did indeed write. But before we parted I did clear myself before them."(12) The reason he was retained in jail, if indeed the Lords were satisfied, Webb explained, concerned "a little money matter."(1)

Having denied ever maintaining the erroneous views ascribed to him in Edwards' tome, Webb turned the tables and argued that Edwards was a very poor Christian. He wrote, "I am a stranger to him and him to me yet not so strange but we believe each other to be Christians, Now if he had any love towards me, or Christianity, it would have carried him forth to have acted the acts of Christianity."(3) Elucidating upon this theme, Webb explained why any criticism of him was necessarily unChristian. "I never from him did receive any brotherly or friendly admonition and the Scripture saith that if thy Brother trespass, thou should not presently tell it [to] the Church till after twice or thrice admonishment."(4) Consequently, when Edwards criticized Webb for maintaining antinomian views, Webb contended "that I am ignorant of, but I humbly desire Mr. Edwards that if he writes again, he would be willing to explain what he means by antinomianism . . . and if there be man or woman that can charge me with delivering antinomian doctrines, I, in a brotherly manner desire to be informed."(5) Similarly, rather than standing condemned for teaching wrong doctrines of Scripture, Webb was horrified at the thought. "I speak the truth," he cried. "I do with an unfeigned detestation utterly detest it or any opinion that shall lead me to the questioning of Scripture . . . [and] I am willing to lay down my life for the truth of it."(9) Additionally, Webb announced that he "desires to be overcome by truth in everything though it comes from the hands of the poorest creature under heaven, whose scholar I am ready to be whenever God shall teach me anything by him."(7)

Other than responding to Edwards' slander of himself, Webb saw further dangers in Edwards' work. "He mightily wrongs the cause wherein those that are truly cordial to Parliament are deeply engaged. First, in giving the common enemy . . . an advantage against us and this he doth by divulging abroad to the world the differences that are amongst us."(13) Indeed, the very outcome of the civil war may well hinge on Edwards' criticism of himself. We are informed, "me thinks if he had not been altogether for himself but had altogether aimed and fought after the Kingdom's good he would willingly have lost honor rather than his kingdom and its Parlia-

ment should die."(14) This thought truly saddened Webb. "It's a sad thing
that a Kingdom should die, Parliament die, and all because we can not pass
by honor . . . Oh who would not but pass all for this Kingdom's
good?"(14) Webb ended the treatise but he might have gone on to lament
the fall of all creation and possibly the rise of the anti-Christ as well because
of Edwards' attack upon him.

From his earliest days Webb was able to stir controversy but was consistently unwilling to live with the results of holding the views he did. Webb
viewed any criticism of himself a malicious slander. Edwards was a selfish
man wishing to destroy the kingdom, Mary White was an insatiable nym-
phomaniac unable to take responsibility for herself and Edward Stokes was
a sexual and religious pervert. Though more information about Webb
would have been desirable but was not available, the information we do
have indicates that Thomas Webb was both a Ranter and a rotter.

16. John Pordage

Both John Pordage and Thomas Webb were Ranter parish priests ejected from their livings, yet it is hard to imagine two more different cases. John Pordage (1607–1681) was the son of a London grocer, but nothing is known about his education or childhood. He was curate of St. Lawrence Reading and seems to have been a thoroughly responsible, if unusual, local clergyman when he was appointed rector of Bradfield in Berkshire. By 1649 there is evidence that Pordage entertained Ranter views. In that year Abiezer Coppe was his house guest and Pordage appeared before Reading authorities on Coppe's behalf. Later, Thomas Tany, the strangest Ranter of them all, would also take refuge in the Pordage household and it seems the Bradfield rector offered hospitality to other radicals on other occasions.

Pordage's first encounter with the authorities came in 1649 or 1650 when the Committee of Plundered Ministers charged him with preaching heresy and blasphemy. He was acquitted of these charges in March of 1651 but in 1654 Pordage was again tried for heresy, this time by the Berkshire County Commissioners on behalf of the Committee for the Ejecting of Scandalous Ministers, a Parliamentary committee which succeeded the Committee for Plundered Ministers. This second series of trials and hearings led to Pordage's dismissal from his rectorship. Though no records of the earlier troubles of 1650 exist, Pordage faced the same charges in 1654 and his two treatises tell us much about the earlier trial as well as the later one which led to his dismissal.

Pordage's first treatise, *Truth Appearing Through the Clouds of Undeserved Scandal* of December 1654, was a brief account of his several ordeals. Three months later in March of 1655, Pordage published the more nearly complete *Innocency Appearing Through the Dark Mists of Pretended Guilt*. Pordage's travails were also the subject of Christopher Fowler's treatise, *Daemonium Meridianum, Satan At Noon*, also of 1655, written to answer Pordage's first treatise. Fowler, a local minister, aided the prosecution at both of Pordage's trials and presented a somewhat different viewpoint regarding these events. This work, together with the two by Pordage, presents us with a fairly complete account of Pordage's ejection from Berkshire.

Because he wrote after his ejection from his living and in defense of his good name and reputation, Pordage's second treatise was introduced by

236

three dedicatory letters. The first of these, the "Dedicatory Epistle Addressed to the Lord Protector," complained about restrictive religious legislation in general and the power of examining committees in particular. Pordage asked, "Will not the establishment of such laws, left to the arbitrary use of such judges without any further appeal, destroy that due liberty, both civil and religious, which is the best interest of states and nations?"(3) Pordage requested of Cromwell, "Be like Cyrus, God's anointed cherub, stretching your wings of tenderness and protection over all good people."(1)

A different tone pervades Pordage's letter to his judges. He condemned the commissioners for "doing the same work with those who killed the prophets,"(5) and he looked to a time "when the saints who have been judged and condemned for their testimony to truth as heretics and evil doers shall judge the world and possess the kingdom."(5) Comparing himself to an earlier martyr to truth, Pordage asked, "Was not Christ thus judged an evil doer though he never committed any crime?"(6)

Pordage's identification with Christ's suffering is also the theme of his third letter, addressed to his friends and acquaintances. He soothed his followers, "It is enough to remember that thus, even thus, must all Christ's eminent witnesses be civilly killed in their honor, names and reputations, thus cast condemned, thus cast out of the synogogues and thus injured in their estates."(8) His own ordeal, Pordage indicated, was his own personal fulfillment "of the saint's suffering as preparatory to his second coming in power and glory."(8)

Pordage recounted how his difficulties first began when he received a summons to appear before the local county commissioner meeting as the Committee for the Ejecting of Scandalous Ministers. The committee, consisting of local JPs and ministers, summoned Pordage to appear before the court in Bradfield in Berkshire on September 18, 1654, although the first session actually convened on October 5. From the very outset, Pordage and his inquisitors differed regarding proper procedure. Though it was an open hearing, neither of Pordage's two witnesses was permitted to enter the courtroom to testify.(1) Even more grievous, the nine charges against Pordage were the very same from which he had been exonerated in 1650. According to the accusations, Pordage allegedly preached "that the fiery deity of Christ mingles and mixes itself with our flesh"; "that Christ is a type and but a type"; and "that Christ is not God and not Jehova." Additionally, he preached that Christ's efforts on man's behalf, his imputed righteousness, was "sapless" and "flashy and fleshly discoveries" compared with the freedom "of the fiery deity of Christ in the center of our souls." Last, when

Genesis 1 referred to male and female, Pordage was alleged to have preached that the text meant the creation of mankind from a distinctly divine male element and a carnal female element.(2)

The charges did not include the usual accusations of disregard for church ordinances and rituals, but they struck at the heart of Pordage's Ranter soteriology from an orthodox Calvinist orientation. As we shall see later, Pordage believed man was composed of separate divine and human elements and possessed the freedom to amplify the powers of the divine soul to weaken the carnal flesh. Like other Ranters, Pordage rejected Christ's divinity in favor of adoptionism and hence he also rejected vicarious atonement and any special role for Mary. Christ was a role model for the remainder of mankind and man, like Christ, might be adopted too would he but eschew his carnal nature.

Rather than using Ranter explanations, Pordage couched his answers in orthodox terms and expressions. This same approach had been used in 1650 and resulted in his acquittal and Pordage believed the same method might be used once again with similar results. When Pordage informed the court that he had been acquitted of these charges once before, the court requested that he produce a document to that effect at its next session.

On October 19, Pordage produced his charter of acquittal, dated March 27, 1651, but the court proceeded against him nonetheless. When requested to respond to the charges against him, Pordage objected on both procedural and substantive grounds. He pointed out that none of the charges against him fell under the terms of the Blasphemy Act.(4) Moreover, according to that legislation, charges must be made within six months of the offense and not after a space of five years. Additionally, since these were the same charges from which he had been acquitted earlier, they originated from before the promulgation of the Blasphemy Act and, therefore, before a general pardon was issued by Parliament on February 24, 1651 for all punishable offenses subsequently covered by that act. Last of all, he had already produced documentary evidence of his earlier acquittal and must not be tried for the same offenses a second time.(5)

Having protested the hearings, Pordage geared his substantive answers to an orthodox audience. He conceded that in a private conversation in 1649, and not in a sermon or in published material, he had said that Christ was not Jehova, but that these words had been taken out of context. In any event, he now accepted that Christ was God.(7) Pordage explained that the expression "deity mixed with humanity" was a metaphor to describe Christ's relationship with his church. Similarly, the expression "Christ was a type" said no more than "his life and conversation was a type, that is, a pattern and example for us Christians."(7)

These answers were orthodox sounding and Pordage was asked to present witnesses willing to swear that these interpretations constituted the intent of his sermons. Before adjourning for the day, the court brought several new questions for Pordage to answer. The court wished to know about a certain Everard, probably John Everard, who had lived with Pordage for a while and about a "Tawny," actually Thomas Tany, who had also lived under Pordage's roof. Additionally, Pordage was asked why he had attempted to discourage a certain couple from having children.

On November 2, Pordage explained to the court that discouraging an unfit couple from having children had little to do with the Blasphemy Act. Everard, lately a known conjurer, had worked for him during a single harvest season four years earlier before the latter took to conjuring. As for Tany, Pordage noted that as a minister it was his practice to receive all who were in need, were hungry and without means of a livelihood.

The next several sessions were very frustrating for Pordage. As he would explain away one set of charges, the committee would bring in new ones, often including rephrased versions of old ones. Thus in mid-November Mr. Christopher Fowler, minister of St. Mary's in Reading, brought in a list of fourteen charges. Among these, that Pordage taught that Jesus' efforts on man's behalf were sapless, that Pordage denied the separate persons of the trinity, that he kept a mistress in London and held conversations with angels in his home.(14) Also, depositions from local parishioners attesting to Pordage's having preached a variety of peculiar sermons were entered into evidence. Pordage wished to make clear that such evidence was not to be taken seriously. In his account of the trial Pordage wrote in the margins that many of the depositions were "perjured testimony" while others were "unsubstantiated" and others yet allegedly made by non-existing persons. Whenever possible, Pordage answered the court in orthodox language, hoping thereby to explain what he considered the unfortunate wording of his sermons.

By the end of November the commission hearings had become a contest. As the prosecution raised new charges, Pordage explained them away. Nonetheless, the commissioners were not convinced that Pordage's orthodox-sounding answers constituted his true beliefs. Hence at the November 30 session, John Tickell, a local minister, asked Pordage for the third time, why he "delivered from the pulpit that the fiery deity of Christ mingleth with our flesh."(36) Once again Pordage answered in orthodox fashion only to be asked, yet again, why he preached a dualistic interpretation of Genesis 1.(44) When Pordage responded, he was then asked by Tickel why he had referred to Christ as a type.(46) Once again Pordage responded, "I never owned or stood to that of Christ's being *but* a type,"(46) and "Christ was a complete redeemer."(47) No sooner had Pordage answered this query than Tickell asked him why he denied that Christ was Jehova or God.(49) During the next several sessions newer charges were introduced with the same old ones demanded of Pordage yet again. Eventually, the minister of Bradfield was charged with approximately sixty-five charges of blasphemy and heresy. As one reads the proceedings, it becomes increasingly clear that the commissioners did not believe anything John Pordage said.

It may seem peculiar that Pordage would be forced to answer the same charges over and over again. Part of the explanation was that John Tickell and Christopher Fowler were part of the 1650 commission which tried and exonerated Pordage only to learn thereafter that in fact he did indeed preach what they believed he did and had been tried for. Pordage used the same orthodox-sounding explanations used previously but the commission members, who may have believed themselves hoodwinked previously, continued to pressure Pordage until they got answers they were prepared to accept.

Also contributing to the negative attitude of the commission was the fact that many of them did not understand much of what Pordage said. He would often launch into long philosophical explanations which either bored the court or antagonized them. Fowler's account of the trial deletes these digressions altogether but we might look into them to discover what it was that Pordage believed and what his audience had no interest in discussing.

Like all dualists, Pordage conceived of existence in terms of separate material and ideal planes of reality. He wrote, "There are two invisible internal principles opened and discovered to us which may be called the *mundus idealis*, being two spiritual worlds extending and penetrating throughout his whole visible creation."(73) The first of these, the *mundus luminosus*, consists of the plethora of platonic possibilities and expressed itself through "the multiplicity variety, and beauty of these . . . various wonders and objects of the world, clothed in the purest tincture of light and color."(75) The second world, the *mundus tenebrosus*, was the demon-dominated world of physical realities void of spiritual content. This dichotomy of idea and matter was also the basis of other dichotomies such as God and the Devil, good and evil, light and darkness.

The realms of light and darkness were each represented by angels or emissaries reflecting this same dichotomy within the universe. Pordage explained that "there are two angels or spirits, good and evil, light and darkness, holy and wicked, who are continually tending upon men in this world; the evil to tempt and draw men into the same condition with themselves, the good to guard and preserve them from evil influences and malicious designs of the other."(66)

After the fall, man lost the ability to distinguish the difference between the two poles and hence the importance of divine revelation as a beacon of light cutting through the fog of human ignorance. Pordage believed that God had granted him a special dispensation and extraordinary vision to see and comprehend what others failed to see, the very forms and ideas of the spiritual world. Pordage modestly explained, "Now these could not have been seen had not that inward spiritual eye, which hath been locked up and shut by the fall, been opened in an extraordinary way in us."(73)

Hoping to make his special gift available to others, Pordage met with a circle of followers "for the space of three weeks or a month where we exercised the inwardly and outwardly vision through that great conflict which was betwixt those two worlds and their inhabitants."(76) When members of his circle experienced strange occurrences and heard peculiar music, Pordage became convinced that he and his associates were witnessing the conflict between good and evil tearing at the fabric of the universe. At one meeting there was "the appearance of one in the form of a giant with a great sword in his hand without a scabbard which he seemed to flourish against me."(73) Also visible was "the shape of a great dragon which seemed to take up most part of a large room, appearing with great teeth and open jaws whence he oft ejected fire at me."(73) Others saw visions "appearing in the shapes of lions, elephants, tigers, bears" while others conceived of shapes "monstrously misshapen as with ears like those of cats, cloven feet, ugly legs and bodies and eyes, fiery-shaped and piercing."(74)

These visions of the evil world of darkness may have been frightening, but, Pordage reasoned, "Surely it rather argues that he hath blessed me with a strong faith in that he permitted such great trials and made me instrumental to overcome them by prayer and fasting."(26) Pordage explained that he was able to overcome these evil apparitions through the aid of angels with whom he regularly conversed.(67ff) These good angels enabled Pordage to interpret Scripture properly and create a pattern of morality leading to salvation emphasizing the soul's triumph over the flesh. From Pordage's vantage point, God's very special treatment of him and his circle could have only one real meaning: "God's end in permitting it was very good, even to bring us nearer to himself in a stronger dependence upon his eternal power."(74) For the Berkshire commissioners, these visions had an altogether different meaning. Either Pordage was absolutely crazy or he was absolutely in league with the devil and was a witch. Either way, Pordage's bizarre experiences were ill befitting a parish minister.

Pordage taught a social morality more ascetic than that of Bauthumley or Coppin. Oddly, Pordage was condemned for this no less rigorously than Clarkson or Coppe were castigated for holding the very opposite views. We have already noted that Pordage was criticized for discouraging a married couple from having children, Pordage found no difficulty in expressing what he believed to be the proper sexual relationship. "I must therefore acknowledge that I prefer virginity before matrimony, the single state before the conjunct, and that persons though in a married state yet assured by grace of the gift of continency, may by consent abstain from the enjoyment of that state . . . as though they were not in it, living as single though in unified form."(57) In this sense, Christ was a type for all humanity and Pordage referred to Jesus as the "eternal virgin."

Spiritual virginity involved the total abnegation of sexual communication and "to abstain from the concupiscible lustings of venus under the spirit of this great world is but the life of outward chastity."(77) Additionally, the individual must reach the higher plane of consciousness where all physical stimuli are rejected. Pordage referred to this as "the way of total self denial and forsaking all" and "the way of annihilation and conformity to Christ's death."(77)

Despite encouraging words about potential human purity, Pordage, like other dualists, was of two minds concerning the human ability to reach a true spiritual state within this life. On the one hand he wrote, "The virgin life is not attained till the will of the soul is brought through death to be so passive . . . for till then the soul can not be a pure virgin nor live without all desire, lust and imagination which must all cease."(77) Yet, on the other hand, his court testimony indicated that Pordage believed his circle of associates to have liberated themselves from the world and they gave themselves new names to indicate a new spiritual birth. Pordage was Father Abraham and his wife Deborah, with others assuming yet other Old Testament names to indicate their new status. When writing about this shared spiritual existence Pordage explained, "We were shown that the way which led up the virgin essence, the New Jerusalem, was straight and narrow . . . without lust, with our eyes fixed upon the Being of love pressing forward after fixation in the eternal house of God . . . there always to be

242

the name of God and the name of the city of God which is the New Jerusalem."(77)

From Pordage's perspective, he was unfairly harassed, for nothing he taught came under the terms of the Blasphemy Act. His views would not lead others to sin and there were no indications that his followers were an immoral or irreligious lot. Thus, when all testimony was completed but before the committee began its deliberations, Mr. Starkey, Pordage's attorney, was given liberty to speak. He "recited all the evidence . . . showing that if they squared their proceedings by the rules of law they were to act by, they could have no ground to give sentence against me."(92) The commissioners were of another mind. In their official verdict the justices explained that "although many of the proofs brought against the Doctor were not proofs according to the law, yet to the commissioners who are a court of equity and of an ecclesiastical jurisdiction and so are not obliged to judge according to the positive laws and statutes, they were and might be esteemed sufficient proofs."(92) In short, this court would not determine guilt or innocence in a criminal sense and their decision would not result in subsequent punitive action by the state. As an administrative agency charged only with determining competence, they were not bound by the standard legal procedure of the commonwealth. On this basis, Pordage was condemned for denying Christ's divinity, for maintaining that Christ was but a type, and for general ignorance. Pordage was found unfit for his position and was ejected from his living.

It is difficult to determine the scope of the commission's authority, rules of evidence and the nature of proper procedure. It is true that the commission did not recommend subsequent legal action against Pordage and nowhere gave evidence of desiring to imprison him. But if the Blasphemy Act would not serve as a basis for determining Pordage's fitness for office, other standards were even less sure in law. In the case of Thomas Webb another such committee had little difficulty defending their actions. A libertine way of life and the selling of church property for personal gain added to the evident ill will of the community and his peculiar sermons clearly made Webb a poor candidate for religious office. Pordage, however, represented a very different set of circumstances. His morality, perhaps overly ascetic, was beyond reproach and there was no evidence of community resentment against its rector. Pordage claimed to have visions and in general seemed a little weird, but these deviations did not seem to lead his followers into sin. There was no evidence that Pordage performed poorly in his capacity.

Pordage had good reason to believe his judges had determined his guilt before the hearings convened. Regarding these judges, Pordage wrote of a

Mr. Dunck that even before any testimony had been presented this judge said I was "worse than a felon and asked me passionately how I durst deny the Godhead of Christ the first time of my appearing before them."(103) Dunck swore "that at the next Parliament he would throw me out of my living."(103) Another judge, Mr. Trapham, said three times during the proceedings that "he could as willingly run his sword into the bowels of such as I as into the bowels of a common enemy."(104) Mr. Nutkins, like Mr. Trapham, sat on the previous court of inquiry looking into Pordage's life. At that time, Pordage recounted, "I had vindicated myself . . . he gave me his vote to clear me of that imputation, confessing that he was satisfied . . . who now, not withstanding this, hath condemned me for the same thing he then voted to clear me of."(104)

Two other judges, Christopher Fowler and John Tickell, were local clergymen who conducted most of the questioning because of their assumed expertise in religious matters. They too, according to Pordage, were predisposed toward finding him insufficient for his post. Concerning Tickell, he "was fit to be both judge assistant, witness, and as far as I know, accuser, I never seeing any other name to his articles."(102) The other minister, Mr. Fowler, attempted both before and during the proceedings "to persuade all he meets that I am a familist, a conjurer, one that practices uncleanness."(102) Like Tickell, Fowler played more than one role. "It is a sad thing," Pordage sighed, "that a man of this spirit should be one of the assistants, acting the part of the judge at the trial . . . and be also witness and accuser together."(102)

Pordage's long account of his trial, though detailed, is unsatisfying in some senses. Nowhere does he attempt to explain how he was found guilty, other than by assuming malevolence on the part of the commission. Pordage did not appreciate that the Blasphemy Act was not the point of contention and dismissed all the evidence against him. He claimed much was hearsay or was perjured yet Pordage brought few witnesses on his own behalf and only rarely challenged depositions entered by the prosecution. His philosophical explanations were probably difficult for the judges to understand and discussions of visions of pirates brandishing swords, dragons and the like would raise eyebrows. If Pordage's account does not clarify how the judges understood the evidence against him or his own defense, another account of these hearings can help fill in the gaps.

Christopher Fowler was very much upset by Pordage's account of the commission's hearings and consequently took pen in hand to describe what he believed had transpired. His treatise *Daemonium Meridianum,*

JOHN PORDAGE

Satan at Noon, was published in 1655 and tells us a great deal about the committee's attitude. Fowler described the trial in full, added some information about Pordage himself and the bases upon which the Bradfield minister was ejected.

Fowler defended the magistrate's right to determine the nature and quality of local religious life. In his opening letter to Oliver Cromwell, Fowler expressed traditional orthodox disapproval of heterodoxy with the usual contemporary hyperbole. He noted, "We had rather 10,000 times that we and our dearest relations should die stark mad in chains in Bedlam then to live and die in such execrable opinions against our Lord Jesus." The next letter addressed to the reader also defended the right to eject blaspheming ministers such as Pordage, calling such efforts "the noblest work that can be undertaken." Fowler returned to this theme in the closing pages of his treatise. In one instance he wrote that "the civil sword was appointed as a remedy against blasphemy . . . and therefore it is not true that the Lord Christ never appointed the civil sword as a remedy in the case of blasphemy for he did expressly appoint it in the Old Testament and he never did abrogate it in the New."(166) He added a page later how "we are well acquainted with it, the cryers up of a toleration, the whore of Babylon's back door."(167)

The issue of religious toleration must be underscored, for Fowler, like many other Englishmen, was disconcerted by the *de facto* religious toleration existing in contemporary England. The Blasphemy Act was not conceived by its authors as the criterion of orthodoxy but as the fundamental religious standard beyond which lay not merely heresy but views dangerous to the commonwealth. Using this document as a standard, the vast majority of Englishmen would be well within this consensus, for the law was intended only to weed out the most extreme of Ranters. The unsettled politics after Charles' death, and the lack of any consensus other than in condemning Ranters, left the Blasphemy Act on the books but made impossible any other legislation concerning views less extreme than those espoused by Ranters. Consequently, the parliamentary commissions discussed in this and the previous chapter faced a difficult task. They could not stop people from publishing radical treatises but they could attempt to remove ministers preaching views unseemly from an orthodox perspective. Hence, much as the law, or lack of law, left a condition of *de facto* toleration, Parliamentary commissions consisting of orthodox ministers and JPs attempted to keep this perceived cancer from contaminating the priesthood. If these commissions did not act according to the letter of law and

245

legal procedure, neither did those who published radical treatises. Both, in fact, were the result of the religious free-for-all characterizing the interregnum, a condition Thomas Edwards called gangrene.

When Christopher Fowler, and presumably Tickell and the other judges as well, sat in judgment of John Pordage, they willfully chose to neglect the Blasphemy Act as the basis of their legal deliberations. Clearly, use of this law as a standard would have left Pordage in his living. Thus, in answer to Pordage's claim that the Blasphemy Act should have been used, Fowler responded, "Now if this defense of the Doctor's be true, we express our unfeigned sorrow from our most innermost hearts that the blessed glory of our dear Lord Jesus Christ was no more consulted if there be no provision made for stopping of the mouth of blasphemy against the Lord Jesus Christ by the civil magistrate."(16–17) In his capacity as inquisitor, Fowler claimed he "will never suffer any to be preachers of the Gospel who are blasphemers of the Lord Jesus."(18)

Fowler's account of the trial demonstrates that none of the commissioners believed anything Pordage said in his own behalf and may even have been angered by his attempt to defend himself. Fowler was annoyed with Pordage on almost every issue where he diverged from Calvinist orthodoxy. Concerning the oft-debated issue of how deity and humanity mixed within man, Pordage's answers about "the fiery deity of Christ with flesh," were condemned as Ranter and worse, as pelagian. It was heresy to preach that neither God nor grace relieved man of sin in favor of "the fiery deity burning in the center of the soul" that was responsible for "consuming and destroying sin there."(17) Consequently, the resulting liberty of the individual common to all people, even non-Christian peoples, denied the veracity of original sin and Christ's vicarious atonement. Fowler summarized what he found offensive in Pordage's views as "a glorious liberty which liberty (saith the Doctor) is not . . . purchased by the blood of another and applied to the cleaving of the soul, but to the fiery deity burning up our lusts and corruptions in the center of the soul."(9) Hence, Pordage's soteriology and Christology were unacceptable.

Though pelagianism was not condemned by the Blasphemy Act, Pordage compounded his radical views with even more radical ideas. His belief that Christ was but a type meant that he was not God and that there was no vicarious atonement. In disbelief that any could accept such views, Fowler observed, "We do not see these figure makers and makers of types, which God never made, which never came into his heart."(45) Worse, the "sin" from which humanity required redemption was for Pordage the physical condition of life either created by God, or existing despite God. In either event, Pordage expounded views that were clearly blasphemous.

To appreciate how onerous such views must have seemed to Fowler we need only recall that the issue of the individual's role in his own salvation and spiritual satisfaction was the issue debated by Erasmus and Luther in 1524 and a central theme separating Protestantism from Catholicism. The emphasis of the Calvinist tradition upon predestination especially stressed human incompetence. From the time of Theodore Beza through the Belgian Confession of 1561 to the TULIP Formula of the Council of Dort, major Calvinist confessions espoused predestination and even double supralapsarian predestination. From this perspective, pelagianism and the erroneous Christology involved in its soteriology was the single most serious error possible short of the denial that God's creation was good. Pordage held the wrong views on both issues.

Fowler also believed that John Pordage was a liar. It was obvious to him that God did not grant visions to a humanity laboring under the burden of sin; consequently, when Pordage claimed to have had special visions from God, Fowler could envision only two possible explanations. Either these visions were from the devil, which meant Pordage was a witch, or else Pordage was an outright liar and made them up in his head. Thus Fowler wrote, "The commissioners did not look upon him as a conjurer but as an imposter who made use of apparitions and visions in a ministerial way, viz., to confirm his blasphemies."(18) In short, Pordage was a blasphemer and worse yet, a minister using lies and deceit to advance his blasphemous ideas.

Fowler's treatise is filled with guilt-by-association slurs of Pordage's character. In one instance Fowler wrote of Pordage's views, "Is not all this and the rest taken out of the evangel of Henry Nicholas and Jacob Bohm?"(34) Pordage's other intellectual friends were no better. In response to Pordage's claim that he received Tany as an act of Christian good will, Fowler wrote, "We profess we do not know, neither can we learn of any that he hath entertained but Abiezer Coppe, notorious for blasphemy and Rantism, in whose behalf this Doctor appeared before the committee at Reading . . . or Coppin to whose book that *crawls* with blasphemy, the Doctor gave his approbation."(60–61) In fact, Coppe's name nowhere appears in either transcript of the trial, but Fowler's mention of Coppe and Coppin indicates that the commission was aware of Pordage's Ranter connections and believed such associates evil people.

Much as Pordage was contaminated by others, Fowler believed all having contact with Pordage were as evil as he was. Thus, witnesses for the defense were condemned as birds of a feather. As an example, Pordage called a Mr. Higgs to testify on his behalf. From Higgs' favorable testimony about Pordage, Fowler was able to see and find what he wished. Fowler wrote that Higgs' presence annoyed the commission and he was "scurrilous, against universities, ministers, learning and maintenance."(11) Even worse were Higgs' responses to questions regarding Scripture. Fowler wrote, "This deponent was infected with the pernicious and now spreading heresy of anti-Scripturism, he denied the Bible to be the word of God . . . that if we had the spirit we might made as good Scriptures as these."(13) In short, Higgs was a Ranter. Fowler, and evidently the rest of the commission as well, believed Pordage responsible for Higgs' views, for "from whence he should have this venom we can not imagine but from Bradfield visions, we are also satisfied that this is one of the Doctor's opinions."(13)

So great was Fowler's distrust of everything Pordage said and thought that the latter's views of virginity were suspect. Fowler wrote, "You say in your book that you do not dissuade people from marriage but you propose even to the married the virgin life as most perfect."(118) Fowler observed that such abstention "tends to destroy the bond of marriage" and consequently, such a policy would "introduce a more heathenish community."(104)

Fowler's book introduced at least one issue altogether unmentioned by Pordage. There was testimony to the effect that Pordage conducted financial and business arrangements unbecoming a parish minister. Fowler asked Pordage, "Why did you hire out your teams of horses to carry bark and this to the great hindrance of your neighbors who did use to earn money that way? Why did you then when your poor neighbors had agreed to carry at such a price, agree at an under price for less to get employment out of their hands?"(121) Unfortunately, Pordage, by his silence, gives credibility to Fowler's charge.

Christopher Fowler was convinced that John Pordage was an evil man, a blaspheming heretic and a dangerous minister. Pordage's views, his followers and associates, insane visions, all presented the commissioners with adequate reason to eject him from a position of public responsibility. The commission believed it had adequate reason to relieve Pordage of his living and Bradfield of its minister.

Fowler's religious bias was evident throughout the treatise for the author, convinced of his righteousness, felt little reason to hide his feelings. Pordage's assertion that his judges were predisposed to find him guilty was probably very true and yet Fowler pointed out that "the Doctor had his liberty to propose and question and produce any witnesses."(33) Pordage did produce Higgs as a witness though one must wonder what Pordage believed this Ranter could say in the minister's support. Perhaps Pordage could call none other than Ranters. Fowler may have been prejudiced against Higgs and Pordage, yet he was very sensitive to the latter's charges that he had not received a fair hearing. Over and again Fowler noted that "the commissioners did several times offer the Doctor and all his friends that if anyone could say anything to evidence the Doctor's answers to be true . . . he should be heard with all freedom and willingness."(30) Pordage, no doubt, might have presented a more energetic defense. It probably would not have made any difference.

However one evaluates Pordage's experience, a world of difference separated him from Thomas Webb. One is tempted to wonder what might have happened had Webb been tried by Fowler and Tickell and had Pordage faced Stokes in a court of law. No doubt Webb would have been thrown out of his living much sooner and Stokes would not have been awakened in the middle of the night by Pordage's friends and would not have had to defend himself against slander. It is likely that greater justice might have resulted, and also, that there might have been fewer treatises dealing with Ranters.

Part Two: The Anti-Ranters

17. The Anti-Ranter Offensive

During the very years that Ranter leaders such as Coppin and Clarkson were able to attract large crowds and incite local unrest, there was a powerful anti-Ranter offensive under way. Yet, despite vehement sentiment against everything the Ranters represented, society's best efforts against the Ranters met with ambivalent results. Part of this was because of the state of anarchy characterizing the interregnum in general but it was also because of the inability of the Blasphemy Act to curb Ranter activity.

It may seem strange that so carefully written a law as the Blasphemy Act should have been unable to close Ranter mouths. The provisions were clear and concise; in fact almost every Ranter discussed in these pages faced prosecution according to its terms. John Tickell, the orthodox minister from Abingdon and great prosecutor of the Ranters, was happy there was a Blasphemy Act because "before the late act against the Ranters they spoke boldly, now they dare not."[36] Tickell would seem accurate and we have had the opportunity to observe how many Ranter leaders went to jail for the required six-month jail sentence. But we also saw that Ranters such as Coppin soon learned to navigate around the terms of the Blasphemy Act and avoid condemnation. The attempt at subterfuge is evident in many Ranter writings and in almost all legal proceedings. Coppin wrote of the need "to appear in the clouds and speak sometimes darkly and under parables"[37] and other Ranters also openly discussed their linguistic subterfuges to avoid the strict wording of the Blasphemy Act. One could claim to be God but not necessarily THE God, a distinction made by many Ranters. It was strictly forbidden to deny the existence of heaven and hell, but since they were difficult to describe, it was often possible to reject the common teaching while still subscribing to some other view. One could deny a commonly taught heaven and hell but assert that souls, like water from a stream, joined God in some great beyond. It was forbidden to deny the importance of moral behavior or deny the difference between immoral and moral actions but one could write about that glorious state of the saint where all such moral and legal restrictions were useless and meaningless. Consequently, Ranters often found that the very precise wording of the Blasphemy Act provided their best defense. So effective were Ranters at

251

hiding their true meaning that Pastor Tickell complained that Ranters learned "to speak one thing and mean another." From considerable personal experience he conceded "It seems to me, from what I have known of them, they will put themselves on all expressions, ways and windings, to keep themselves from being known but to their own. You shall not know where to find them so as to fasten on them, but their own shall know their meaning." Faced with Ranter deceit, subterfuges, and just plain double-talk, judges and juries often experienced great difficulty in determining what Ranters were actually saying or writing and what they meant by it. Knowing their best defense lay in obfuscation, vagueness and outright lying, Ranters often turned legal proceedings into circuses.

Parliamentary committees such as those for the Ejecting of Scandalous Ministers had greater latitude because they were administrative agencies rather than courts of law. Indeed Ministers Webb and Pordage were evicted from their livings by such agencies. Most Ranters were itinerant "mechanic preachers," however, and therefore not subject to such Parliamentary bodies. Unlike Quakers and others forming gathered churches, the Ranters were too amorphous to fall prey to institutions of government and too willing to lie to fall prey to courts of law.

Even had the Blasphemy Act ensnared every Ranter leader and Parliamentary bodies removed every Ranter minister, such efforts would have had little effect upon the mass of followers surrounding Ranter leadership. When those claiming to be God appeared in court, as in the case of John and Mary Robins, the cases were treated with amusement. Even William Franklin and Mary Gadbury received little more than a slap on the wrist. Despite their prosecution and renunciations of divinity, both found loyal followers in and out of jail.

Ranters similarly learned to temper their social criticism. Like others on the left, they lamented a property relationship which created and tolerated terrible poverty. None were foolish enough to preach armed robbery, though a few came close. Coppe kept reminding the reader that he was no "sword leveller" while he described the iniquities of the day. Only Salmon was disciplined—and then by the army—for maintaining an active revolutionary view. One could preach and write what one chose and avoid prosecution.

If society's institutions could not deal with the amorphous Ranter fog, it is not surprising to find individual orthodox ministers taking whatever specific action they believed available to them. Sidrach Simpson excommunicated Captain Norwood and Walter Rosewell challenged Coppin to a debate in Rochester Cathedral. Here again, the results were not impressive. Norwood certainly remained excommunicated from Simpson's congregation, a church so orthodox that it is hard to understand why he chose to belong in the first place other than to cause trouble. In any event, he repeatedly attacked Simpson in print, and it is possible that he received the attention he desired. Minister Rosewell should not have challenged an effective street speaker like Coppin. The debates only discredited the local orthodox ministry and further popularized Ranter thinking.

Orthodox ministers concerned about the Ranter curse could and did write treatises against Rantism and thereby hoped to inoculate their own community against it. Whether such ministers believed in freedom of conscience or deplored it; whether they opposed the *de facto* freedom of publication that existed or supported it, their only recourse was to court decent folks' opinion by attempting to convince them of the danger posed by Rantism. A free press may have been conceived as an open sewer letting loose a stream of poison into the population but it was also the only viable means available to attack radicalism. Thomas Edwards' *Gangraena* deplored freedom of expression, the same freedom he used to denounce the radicals that so frightened him. If one uses the four-volume index of the Thomason Collection as a guide, it would appear that almost everyone took pen in hand to present what he thought of the state of society. At no time in previous human history had so many people expressed so many thoughts about so many social options available to a society in transition. Some, therefore, took pen in hand and wrote interesting polemics demonstrating their concern with this horrid Ranter curse which seemed to exist all over England. Because few strictures limited publication, everyone and anyone wishing to write about the Ranters could, and seemingly, did. Unless one evaluates the polemics written against the Ranters, one may not appreciate how the age perceived the danger posed by this group of "mechanic preachers" and theologians.

Anti-Ranter writings took two general forms; scandalous tracts and serious criticism. Most serious treatises were written by orthodox churchmen concerned about the rapid growth of Rantism. Some treatises were better than others but most were honest and sincere in their belief that Rantism was the logical result of the freedom of conscience and free press burden England was forced to endure.

Competition was another motive for writing against the Ranters. Many Ranters such as Coppin and Salmon reported the success of their doctrine of free universal grace which attracted followers from ministers preaching predestination, limited grace and limited atonement. But the Ranters were not the only radicals attracting large crowds. Other competitors included such radical sects as the Muggletonians and the Quakers whose ideas were similar to those of the Ranters and other Antinomians on the extreme left. These groups attacked each other with a ferocity one might have anticipated more from orthodox opponents than kindred spirits. Such radical competitors also wrote against the Ranters to distance themselves from them in the popular mind. It is both amusing and sad when they mimic orthodox attitudes toward Ranters at the same time they express shock at orthodox attitudes toward themselves. Quakers in particular were concerned lest they be identified with Ranters in the popular mind. This may have been of more concern to George Fox than James Naylor, however. It is interesting to note that while all groups attacked and counterattacked one another in print, only Coppin and Norwood felt it important to respond to criticism made against themselves. Evidently other Ranters did not care. Perhaps this indifference, too, contributed to the difficulty in circumscribing Rantism.

Quite different were the scandalous writings. These tracts, often only a few pages in length and of anonymous authorship, were usually serious, sometimes outrageous and on occasion extremely humorous. Most appeared between 1650 and 1653 and almost all were concerned with alleged Ranter immorality and libertine sexuality. For all of these anonymous scandalous authors, the Ranters were hell bent upon the destruction of the commonwealth, true religion and civil society. One is tempted to dismiss such writings as sensational and titillating yellow journalism yet their great number attests to their popularity and the credence given them. Today, similar opinion appears in the *National Enquirer* and in many Rupert Murdock publications. Such journals are usually dismissed with contempt but we should keep in mind that the *National Enquirer* has the largest readership of all the newspapers in the United States, and the Murdock household grows primarily because readers find his variety of reporting credible and worthy of purchase.

While we must accept the importance of scandalous literature, we must also appreciate the classic qualities present. These treatises reflected the traditional horror unconventional religion and morality have always evoked among the more psychologically rigid in society. Indeed, the attacks upon the Ranters are reminiscent of the attacks upon sectarians in all ages, even upon Christians in the Roman Empire. In the end, the anti-Ranter literary/polemical attacks, like the legal offensive, failed because most Ranters, after abjuring their faith, eventually became Quakers and people hated them almost as much as they hated Ranters.

18. Orthodox Critics

If one had asked orthodox contemporaries what they disliked most about Ranters, he would have encountered a variety of very morbid answers. Richard Baxter, the orthodox Presbyterian divine, wrote that "Ranters cry down Church, the Scriptures, the present ministry and our worship and ordinances, and call men to hearken to Christ within them."[38] Unlike other antinomian groups, Ranters "conjoined a cursed doctrine of libertinism which brought them to all filthiness of life," and, Baxter noted, "I have seen myself letters written from Abbington, where, among soldiers and [city] people, this contagion did then prevail, full of horrid oaths and curses and blasphemy, not fit to be repeated by the tongue or pen of man."

Baxter's words may seem the harsh appraisal of one Presbyterian but others vehemently agreed. Ephraim Pagitt, the student of heresy and all that troubled England during the difficult years of the interregnum, had little patience with the Ranters. "The Ranter is an unclean beast, much in the make of our Quaker, of the same puddle and may keep pace with him. Their infidelities, villainies and debauchments are the same, only the Ranter is more open and less sour."[39] While it was certainly true Ranters were more open and less sour than the Quakers, the inclusion of both into one category might, for some, make Pagitt a prejudiced observer and unreliable. In any event, Pagitt went on to describe some Ranter beliefs. "He denies that there are God or Devil, heaven or hell . . . (and) it is a maxim with them that there is nothing sinful but what man thinks it so. They are above ordinances, hence it is that nothing is to be forbidden them, nothing can be unlawful."

Given the dimensions of their sin, it is not surprising that there was no lack of orthodox critics of Rantism, though not all granted them the same time and effort. Some, like Thomas Edwards, wrote massive tomes haranguing the reader about the terrible nature of contemporary radicalism in general and included some information about Ranters coming to his attention. Others wrote entire treatises against the Ranting curse. We are fortunate to have a few writings, presented in this section, though it is possible that other treatises, possibly a fair number, have been lost during the past few centuries.

Three of the five authors concerning us in this section are known to the reader. John Tickell was a local minister in Abingdon and served as a committee member in Reading investigating John Pordage in his capacity as rector of Bradfield. As the reader will recall, the committee ejected Pordage from his living. Walter Rosewell was the orthodox minister debating Richard Coppin in Rochester Cathedral. Coppin believed these debates were a setup and led to his incarceration by local authorities. Humphrey Ellis was the faithful and objective reporter investigating and informing us about Mary Gadbury and William Franklin, pretenders to deity. Edward Garland is unknown to the reader and suffice it to say that he was, like his orthodox colleagues, both frightened of Rantism and disgusted by it. Not much more is known about him. Gentle John Holland was also frightened by the Ranting menace and also tried to help his friends understand Ranters by discovering the nature of their views.

These five authors wrote against the Ranters for somewhat different reasons and from different orientations. While uniformly anti-Ranter, they present us with a fascinating view of what orthodox leaders feared and hated most about these particular radicals.

John Tickell, minister of Abingdon in Berkshire, wrote his treatise, *The Bottomless Pit Smoaking in Familisme* in 1652. If the title itself did not adequately reflect Tickell's antipathy to all things Ranter, surely his closing prayer to God that "from Sin, Satan, and Ranters deliver us"(88) certainly did. We have already encountered Tickell who, along with Christopher Fowler, provided the religious expertise for the Committee for the Ejecting of Scandalous Ministers which tried and ejected John Pordage in 1654.

Tickell had also served on the Berkshire County Commissioners' Committee which investigated Pordage in 1651 and exonerated him from the same charges for which he would later be ejected. During the earlier hearings in 1651 Pordage had defended Coppe who happened to have been visiting him at the time. Coppe, we recall, had been released from jail after writing a formal recantation and abdicating his earlier Ranter principles. Tickell was upset with Pordage for being a Ranter, angry with Coppe for being a Ranter, frustrated that both Pordage and Coppe had been in court and been released, and convinced that both Coppe and Pordage were liars, still maintained their Rantism, and in general were up to no good.

Tickell took pen in hand to inform the world that Ranters were double-faced liars who would say anything at all to gain their freedom for neither they nor their followers had any integrity at all. While John Tickell gave every indication of being narrow-minded, he could in fact write about Ranter duplicity from good experience. Indeed, Pordage himself indicated that he used the same orthodox phrases in 1654 that he had skillfully employed in 1651 to win his release. Other Ranters, too, made no secret of their willingness to hide their truest opinions, and even the sober and upright Richard Coppin used verbal duplicity to protect himself. Quite simply, what John Tickell knew and was terribly afraid that others did not sufficiently appreciate, was that "familists used to speak one thing and mean another."(37)

Tickell's familiarity with Rantism was not limited to his contact with Pordage and he was able to ascertain that Ranters were of several types. They "have their several strains; the Lascivious Familist, he turns all that way, the Speculative [or] the Sceptical Familist, he strikes another way, will go as far as hell in principle, though not in practice."(44) Both types, however, were of one mind concerning deception and duplicity.

Tickell explained that "Parliament's act concerning Ranters hath done, blessed be God for it, much good."(intro. letter) This legislation meant that Ranters could no longer preach freely and Tickell explained how "before the late act against the Ranters, they spake boldly, now they dare not."(37) Unfortunately, Ranters were very skilled and used care in their public expressions in order to circumvent the Blasphemy Act. Tickell observed that "familists have *double tongues* and can sometimes use both at once for their advantage."(intro. letter) Later in the treatise Tickell elaborated upon this duplicity. "Familists are grown extremely cunning," he warned, "to order their words so that, 1-they may be in a sense true; 2-[they may] defend themselves from the hands of the Magistrate; 3-and yet, let their own know their devilish and blasphemous meaning."(88)

Tickell was convinced that Ranters used an allegorical method of interpreting Scripture for the sole purpose of hiding their lying. Noting Coppe's views on the subject, Tickell wrote, "He said that the whole Scripture was to be understood allegorically, This, I am sure, is the sense of all the Familists." Through the manipulation of the text, it is "no wonder then that such doctrines are drawn from Scripture."(80) As an example, he noted common Ranter interpretation of the crucifixion. "They will tell you that Christ was crucified at Jerusalem, a sound expression . . . but in what sense? Abominably corrupt, as a type and figure of the true death of Christ in them."(38) This example met all three of Tickell's criteria. It sounded orthodox, would fool the magistrate and yet the radical meaning would be clear to other Ranters. "They will put themselves on all expressions, ways and windings to keep themselves from being known but to their own," Tickell taught, and as a result, "You shall not know where to find them so as to fasten on them, but their own shall know their meaning."(39)

Where Ranters could not bend the words of Scripture to their own pur-

257

poses, confuse outsiders through their "ways and windings," they would simply lie. Possibly referring to John Pordage or to Abiezer Coppe, Tickell wrote how "a familist before a committee at Reading could say Christ was not God and yet at Ildesly could say that the fiery deity of Christ . . . was in the center of our souls, burning and consuming, and yet at the same time in Reading could call in all which lament not so."(intro. letter) Later in the treatise Tickell again referred to events in Reading and asked the reader, "What do you think now readers, of Mr. Coppe's Recantation?" and he concluded, "A familist repentance is a devil-trick."(88)

It is unlikely that Tickell thought better of other radicals than he did of Ranters though the latter were certainly more dishonest and more difficult to deal with. From Tickell's perspective, a "good" radical was one who openly and honestly stated his disgusting views so that the magistrate might then punish him to the edification of the true church and its followers. A "bad" radical was one who did not openly state his views and therefore made his prosecution much more difficult. Indeed, it was even possible that some radicals might state their terrible views but in such a fashion that they might avoid prosecution. This indeed was the Ranter. Tickell did not doubt the magistrates' authority to punish religious dissenters any more than that magistrates should hesitate to punish other forms of social deviants. The minister's job in this process was to draw the radical out, to make him express his views and then publish them far and wide so that other ministers and judges might be warned to seek the same radicals within their own community. John Tickell exonerated his ministerial responsibility with this treatise.

Walter Rosewell's experience with Richard Coppin was almost a case study in the application of Tickell's anti-Ranter principles. Rosewell, attempting to draw Coppin out, debated with him in Rochester Cathedral in 1655. Coppin believed that his subsequent incarceration resulted from Rosewell's efforts and criticized that orthodox divine for encouraging an open debate which then served as a basis for his imprisonment. When dealing with this debate earlier, we noted that Major Kelsey, the mayor, and many other city dignitaries were present and at various times Major Harrison threatened Coppin with legal action, especially as it became more and more apparent that Coppin was winning the debate and the hearts and minds of the townsfolk. Major Kelsey was also of this opinion, and he wrote to Cromwell that both his troops and the townsfolk were infected with Coppin's Ranter radicalism. Was the debate merely a ruse to draw Coppin out so that he would condemn himself with his own words spoken in public? Like Tickell, Rosewell was convinced that Ranters would never speak

ORTHODOX CRITICS

openly; hence the significance of Rosewell's title *The Serpent's Subtlety Discovered* . . . published in 1656. In this treatise, Rosewell explained how he ensnared Coppin into the open forum.

For Rosewell, the story did not begin with Coppin, but several years earlier. He wrote that about 1650 Joseph Salmon first came to Rochester and began preaching to increasingly large audiences twice each Sunday.(1) His sermons, which Rosewell conceded were very effective, concentrated upon the allegorization of Scripture and decrying all religious forms and rituals. During the summer of 1655, Salmon was replaced by Richard Coppin, whom Rosewell described as "being exactly of the same principles with his brother in evil that preceded him . . . venting the same errors, but more openly and with less artifice of words than the other had done."(2)

To his chagrin, Coppin was an even more effective preacher than Salmon, and Rosewell soon found his own parishioners infected with "doctrines so gross from Sabbath to Sabbath, they were in the mouths of many that heard him."(2) Fearing for the souls of his parishioners, and the dwindling number at his own service too, no doubt, Rosewell believed it his responsibility to take action, "whereupon . . . I went to hear him." Whatever he had anticipated, Rosewell wrote that he was absolutely shocked. In one single sermon Coppin taught "that Christ the redeemer was a sinner in respect of his human nature . . . [and] that Job in that place nor St. Paul in 1 Corinthians 15 did speak of the resurrection of the body, with many more pestilent errors."(2)

Coppin's local influence grew and Rosewell and his colleagues were increasingly forced to devote their midweek services to countering Coppin's ideas. Coppin's influence covered a wide range of topics, but Rosewell was very much upset when "he railed against the priests that told people of their sins and would make them believe that God was angry with any of them for their sins."(3)

Rosewell decided to take action against Coppin and described his method as follows. He explained that Coppin would end each religious meeting with a general request that anyone finding fault with his sermon should challenge him. Rosewell decided this should be his course of action, challenged Coppin, and eventually a date was set for a public debate. Rosewell was able to select the opening topic of discussion, which, he described as "he that persuades the people to believe that Jesus Christ was a sinner and that the human nature of Jesus Christ was polluted with sin, he is a perverter of Scriptures, a blasphemer of Jesus Christ and a venter of damnable heresy."(4)

As we recall, Coppin's account of the four sessions of the debate indicated

259

that Rosewell took a beating, with the audience increasingly supporting Coppin's own positions. It is not surprising, therefore, that Rosewell does not concentrate upon the actual flow of the conversation, content to point out that Coppin proved himself to be a very, very evil man. Rather than conceding that he took an intellectual walloping, Rosewell observed, "I am afraid he is but too deeply guilty, he doth so desperately contradict and blaspheme the clearest truths of the blessed gospel of Jesus Christ."(9) And since he could not convert Coppin to reason, "and being wearied myself to hear the word of God so wretchedly and wickedly abused," Rosewell announced, "I resolved never more to have to do with him, unless I should be called to it by such as had authority and required it to vindicate the truth against him."(10) In short, Rosewell would not have further dealings with Coppin other than if required by a court of law or perhaps by a marshal of the realm such as Major General Kelsey.

Rosewell understood the contention between himself and Coppin in the simple terms of right and wrong, good and evil, and never doubted his own responsibility to inhibit Coppin's actions. In Rosewell's own words, "Richard Coppin is a false prophet and prophesies lies in the name of the Lord. Ergo, Richard Coppin is an enemy of the State."(10) As an enemy of the state, Coppin was entitled to no consideration, and certainly no action Rosewell might take against a religious felon might be considered wrong in any sense. Though he admitted framing the thirteen-point list of charges brought against Coppin, Rosewell continued to deny that he had actually fooled Coppin in any way or had had "the least hand in informing or engaging the Major General [Kelsey] against him [Coppin]. What was done in that kind was done by others (I know not whom) without my persuasion and privity. Yet, I confess, when it was done, I could not but approve it."(15) Either Walter Rosewell was a very naive person or he was a liar.

One can not expect total candor from Rosewell regarding his own complicity in Coppin's entrapment. Even an orthodox minister would understand the difference between honest debate and a disguised attempt to entrap an opponent, and how miserable his own actions must have seemed not only to Coppin but to the large audience that attended the debate and evidently sympathized with Coppin. In order to exonerate himself from the idea that he had done something immoral to an honest fellow Christian, Rosewell devoted the remainder of his treatise to a smear campaign which would attempt to prove that Richard Coppin was in fact a . . . . JESUIT!

It may seem incredible that Richard Coppin could be a Jesuit but Jesuits were indeed hated and feared and perhaps some of the laity would not notice that the charge made no sense. Rosewell called Coppin "A Jesuited

Familist, tutored by Jesuits, prompted by the Devil, he and his older brother Joseph Salmon should be sent for a present to their Holy Father, the Pope of Rome."(16) Rosewell believed that all opponents of the Presbyterian Church, whether from the left or from the right, were in fact the same for all were in league with the devil and with one another, bent upon the destruction of God's true kingdom in England. Hence, both Salmon and Coppin were the same as the Jesuits for all in question were guilty of "undermining the very foundation of the Protestant religion and persuading Protestants to believe that there is no Anti-Christ in the world but what is to be found in the most zealous Protestant ministers nor any other whore of Babylon but the Reformed and Reforming Protestant Churches of England. Consequently, the Pope of Rome is not the Anti-Christ."(16) Rosewell was convinced that Salmon and Coppin were "sent forth *tanquam legatos a latere*, [i.e., like Papal messengers or agents] to propagate the faith of Rome whose faith is faction, whose religion is rebellion."(16) Hence Coppin was not simply a dissenting minister but a true danger to the commonwealth. As Rosewell explained, and no doubt believed, "I am of the opinion that the prevalency of Anti-Christ will not be so much in a way of fraudulent seduction as in a way of violence and bloody persecution."(intro. letter). In short, it was not he that persecuted Coppin but in fact, he Rosewell, was the one persecuted by Coppin.

Humphrey Ellis believed Ranters a deceitful lot and considered their views dangerous to the commonwealth. He did not, however, consider them Jesuits advancing the cause of Rome. Ellis' treatment of Mary Gadbury and William Franklin in his 1650 treatise *Pseudo-Christus* was fair, objective and serious. He explained what he knew of their lives, their deeds, and the outcome of their trial. He spoke to their neighbors to understand what may have caused seemingly sober and well-considered persons to present themselves as Jesus and Mary.

Despite his cool objectivity in recounting the main story of the treatise, in his last section Ellis permitted himself full freedom in condemning Ranters. Despite his objectivity, Ellis concluded that "the blasphemous opinions, speeches and practices of John of Leyden and the Münsterian Anabaptists is nothing in comparison of the things I have here related concerning these persons. David George, Thomas Munster, William Hacket come very short in their blasphemy and wickedness to what hath thus been by these acted."(54)

Ellis' main objective was in explaining "how it could be that any persons should be so grossly deceived for anyone so to renounce Christ as to set up himself in his stead. Or for any others to hearken to such manifest deceits

261

and to give up themselves and their faith to such a deceiver . . ."(55) We noted earlier that Ellis considered Mary Gadbury a thoughtful and intelligent person capable of preaching in an "austere and eerie" fashion. Ellis also noted that Gadbury, among many others, claimed to have had visions and these, too, had proven very influential. Expressing care when dealing with this subject, Ellis explained, "I deny not but such things may have been seen and heard by them which they have related." Yet, he reasoned, "The manner and matter of them was so unlike to any of the dealings of God with his servants, yea, even then, when by visions and such like ways he made himself and his will known to them."(56) Ellis' conclusion was that these visions were "only by themselves devised, to deceive the better by them."(56)

Ellis was also concerned about the easy abuse of millenarian expectation. Here again, the gullible would be deceived by the same people presenting themselves as God or by those having visions. Ellis could only hope they would think carefully before committing themselves, "but let them also consider how easily they lay themselves open to such deceit, how easy a thing it may be for them to be deceived by any such deceiver, that taking the advantage of this expectation of theirs, [he] shall pretend himself to be such a one as is expected by them."(61)

There was but one such safeguard against such false claims and deceits: the Bible. Writing as a minister, Ellis observed, "What a warning may this be to many in these times with whom the Scriptures are so much in contempt, that they look on them as low things, themselves above them, and set up a *teaching of the spirit within themselves.*"(56) Leaving the certainty of Scripture for the variability of the spirit would result in being "settled in nothing, carried up and down with every wind of doctrine, constant and certain in nothing but inconstancy and uncertainty."(57) As a result, "once such persons are come to such a slighting of the Scripture, then they are, if not *past hope of recovery, yet certainly . . . in the roadway to error.*"(56)

Ellis' observation was both insightful and historically true. From an orthodox perspective, only a sure footing in Scripture might save rudderless souls from the Ranters and only a sure belief in the authenticity of Scripture might act as an antidote to inconstancy and uncertainty. It is unfortunate Ellis did not write a full rebuttal of Rantism for he seems to have possessed insight, intelligence and patience, the very virtues required to write a thoughtful polemic.

A far more interesting picture of Ranter belief emerges from the pen of John Holland. Indeed, his treatise, *The Smoke of the Bottomless Pit . . . or, The Mad Crew*, of 1651, described some of the most radical Ranters we know anything about. From his introduction it would appear that Holland was a preacher curious about the Ranters and that he published his treatise after seeking them out in London. Holland does not indicate his city of residence, church affiliation or religious orientation but stated that he was writing "at the earnest request of diverse of my friends"(1) which must indicate a following of some type. His purpose, Holland wrote, was "to publish to the world the more and worse than atheistical blasphemies of these men, not with any intent (the Lord knoweth) to make their persons odious unto any, much less to stir up any to persecute them basely for their judgements."(1) Despite the hostile tone of the title *The Smoke of the Bottomless Pit . . . or the Mad Crew*,(1651) the conciliatory postscript indicated Holland's true objective tone expressed throughout the treatise. "Reader," Holland noted, "I have not followed that orderly method I might have done but I have written the judgements of these men in a confused manner, and I do profess in the presence of the Lord . . . I have done them no wrong in the manner of their judgment except it be in forebearing to repeat their bloody swearing and cursing and for this offence I hope that those that truly fear God will excuse me."(6) In fact, Holland created a rather special document. Without ever haranguing the reader, Holland catalogued Ranter responses and statements on some fourteen issues. Unfortunately, Holland did not organize his material and may have been terribly confused by his subjects. It is also unfortunate that Holland omitted any information through which the group he encountered might be identified. Names and locations are omitted, perhaps out of some prior agreement or from Holland's unwillingness to bring harm to these Ranters with whom he disagreed so vehemently. From the views expressed, however, the group would appear to be followers of Abiezer Coppe's Libertine Rantism.

Regarding God, Holland reported "the titles they give God are these: They call him the *Being*, the *Fullness*, the *Great Motion, Reason*, the *Immensity*,"(2) terms to be found among most Ranter groups. Holland was confused by Ranter ideas of creation. Because material creation falls short of God and yet still reflects God in some sense, the Ranters entertained what seemed to Holland a very confusing ambivalence to matter. Citing Isaiah 45.7, one Ranter attempted to explain God's complicated relationship with the world of creation. "I *form* the light and *create* darkness," the Ranter explained, "I make peace and *create* evil."(5)

Like others we have encountered, these London Ranters believed the universal dichotomy of matter and spirit was best expressed within the human microcosm. Man, we are told, "differeth in nothing from the brute beast" as a physical entity, and "man lives and feeds on nothing but his own excrement for thus they reason, that man's excrement, dung, the ground, which causeth the ground to bring forth corn and grass and the beasts eat the grass and we eat the corn and the beast."(5) Like the rest of material creation, man is alienated from God and "man can not know God or believe in God or pray to God."(2) Unlike the rest of nature, every person possessed a small amount of divinity in the soul and thus "it is God in man that knoweth himself" and "man ought to pray to no other God but what was in them."(2) Thus, a befuddled Holland observed that the Ranters conceived of humanity as both a dung eating beast and God at the same time. Much as they affirmed human dungness, Holland reported that "I heard a man swear that if there was any God at all, he was one . . . another made answer, he was not *the* God, but he was God because God was in him."(2)

For as long as the divine soul was trapped in a beastly body there was little point in anticipating human righteousness. At best, each individual would know the God within himself and no more. For better or worse, depending upon the dictates of the soul, every person was a total but separate universe subject to his own definition of spirituality about which there could be no general rules or definitions.

Ranter ideas of the devil seemed no less confusing to Holland than their ideas about God. On the one hand, "they say the devil is the left hand of God or back part of God or the dark side of God."(5) The relationship of God to the devil was completely confusing to Holland. "They say the Devil could do no evil at all if God did not give him a power to do it[i.e., create in matter] and therefore, the devil is not so much in the fault as men believe he is."(5) This schizophrenic description of God's relationhip with evil, the fundamental thesis of Bauthumley's important treatise *The Light and Dark Sides of God* (1650), was predicated upon the dualists' traditional love of God's purity and despair when confronting the world of corrupted material creation. But if God was not altogether good nor the Devil altogether evil, the terms *piety* and *sin* would seem to have no meaning. Indeed, the Ranters told Holland "there is no such thing as that which men call sin" and "that sin and holiness are all one to God and that God delights as much in the one as in the other."(5) After citing the examples of Abraham, Saul, David, and others who were commanded by God to kill and plunder their enemies, Holland's Ranters asserted that "sometimes he commands men to kill, to steal and to lie, and at times he commands the contrary" and consequently "if it be a sin to kill, to steal or to lie, God is the author."(5)

Holland was shocked and upset by the seeming indifference of these Ranters to the moral distinctions others took for granted. Even more upsetting was the Ranters' belief that God too was indifferent to wickedness. "God seemeth to complain much of evil and wicked men," they observed, "then why doth not God take away that power he hath given them and then there would be nobody to trouble him?"(5) There was no sin, no reward or punishment and hence "they teach there is neither heaven nor hell but what is in man and that those that do see God to be in all things . . . these men are in heaven and heaven in them. But those that can not see and believe these things are in hell and hell in them."(6) Additionally, "there is no such thing as a day of judgment but that it is only an invented thing to serve as a bugbear to keep men in awe."(6)

Equally radical and troubling to Holland was the Christology taught by these London Ranters. Eschewing Jesus' divine personality and his place within the trinity, Ranters also rejected vicarious atonement. Jesus was a mere mortal arbitrarily adopted by God to demonstrate to mankind the subjugation of the flesh and the pathway back to God. "What Christ did in his own person," they told Holland, "was only a figure or *type* of what should be done and acted in every man and that every man must do and suffer as much as Christ did."(3) Emphasizing that Christ's life in no way held profound significance for the life of any other person, the Ranters taught "what he did in way of suffering was for himself, for none had or even should have benefit by his suffering but himself."(2) As we have seen in previous chapters, emulating Christ was somewhat easier for Ranters than for other Christians if only because Ranters were persecuted and thrown into jail and suffered from poverty and sickness.

The illuminated state of the saint is so exalted that rituals, church ordinances and practices could add little to so spiritual a status. After explaining to Holland "that ordinances are made for weak Christians such as those under the teaching of the letter, meaning the Scriptures," the Ranters continued, "that ordinances are ceased to them."(5) Even the demands of the New Testament are nothing for "the ministry of Christ himself or by his apostles as it is held forth in Scriptures, is ceased, as well as the ministry of Aaron."(2) Indeed, even the legacy of Adam and original sin is meaningless. "All the commandments of God, both in the Old and New Testaments are fruits of the curse," the Ranters explained, "and that all men being freed from the curse are also freed from the commandments."(4) Hence, conventional morality, too, was meaningless for those who lived within the spirit and Holland was shocked to learn "that for one man to be tied to one woman or one woman to be tied to one man is a fruit of the curse, but they say we are freed from the curse and therefore it is our liberty to make use of whom we please."(4)

The condition of sainthood, like that of the curse, is also temporary.

Eventually the body dies and "when men die their spirits go into God as small rivers go into the sea."(6) Even this is not necessarily the final rest of the soul, however, for "as the sea sends back the same water again, sometimes into one spring, sometimes into another, so doth the spirits of men after they are gone into God, they return and appear sometimes in one form or shape and sometimes in another."(6) Reincarnation may have provided solace for the serious but one Ranter told Holland he hoped never to return as a horse "for, saith he, a horse hath the most toilsome life of any creature that is."(6)

Holland's London Ranters were skeptical of Scripture. "The best they say of the Scriptures" Holland reported, "is that it is a tale, a history, a letter and a dead letter and more, the fleshly history, they call it a bundle of contradictions."(3) Some of the Londoners were openly hostile to Scripture, teaching "the Bible hath been the cause of all our misery and divisions, both in religion and civil affairs, and hath been the cause of all the blood that hath been shed in the world and that there would never be peace in the world till all the Bibles in the world were burned."(4)

The Londoners presented various reasons for holding the Bible in low regard. They noted conceptual inconsistencies as "when Cain fled from the presence of the Lord, he went to the Land of Nod and there he built a city. He could not have built a city by himself and it was needless for him to build a city for his own household."(4) The Bible made no more sense against the background of natural history. They said, "The world had been created many thousands of millions of years before we read of creation," Holland was told, "and that it shall continue many millions longer than we expect."(6)

Yet a third objection concerned the human inspiration through which Scripture was written. These Ranters asked, "if Paul had the spirit of God by which he wrote Scripture, saith he, I have the same spirit, why may not I write the Scriptures as well as Paul?"(4) All things considered, the Bible was of very little value and regarding its teachings, "neither are they any rule for us to walk by or live after."(4) Holland, unlike Rosewell and Tickell, believed that simple description of Ranter error would be sufficient to ensure that others would remain free of contamination. Others believed it necessary to counter Rantism point by point, on every belief and idea.

At least one serious and complete orthodox appraisal of Ranter thought exists. In 1657–1658 Edward Garland wrote against Richard Coppin in a long volume entitled *An Answer to a Printed Book Falsely Entitled A Blow at the Serpent, It Being Truly a Blow of the Serpent.* Unfortunately, very little about Garland himself is known. He described himself as an "M.A.

266

and minister of God's Word at Hartclip in Kent" which meant that he had probably attended Coppin's trials brought by the ministers from Kent and was familiar with Coppin himself. This treatise demonstrated that Garland was indeed well educated and could argue against the Ranter position with intelligence and clarity.

Garland found much about Rantism grievous, but fundamental to his criticism of Coppin was the latter's use of allegory. Attempting to avoid the snares and pitfalls of vague thought that caught Coppin's previous opponents, Garland stipulated that "an allegory is when one thing is spoken and another understood," adding pointedly "but in the history of the Bible, the very same thing which is spoken is to be understood."(4) Use of allegory then can "overthrow the whole history of the Bible, the creation, redemption and salvation of man."(3–4) These ideas were quite conventional and sit at the heart of Protestant belief that Scripture was a sure and easily understood guide to righteousness. Coppin's previous opponents had been unable to respond to his arguments that Scripture must be understood allegorically especially when he used Paul's allegorical interpretation of Abraham's two wives, Sarah and Hagar, to bolster his own extensive use of this method. Picking up on the argument that Rosewell had handled so badly, Garland asked, "What? Because St. Paul made an allegory of Abraham's having Sarah and Hagar, doth it follow that all the Scriptures are allegories? Or, because that was an allegory, may we believe there was no such history?"(4) It was vital for Garland to bolster this cardinal point of method without which subsequent arguments could not be made. Garland asked how the allegorical method helped in areas of Scripture obviously meant to be interpreted literally. "What is the history of the creation of the world? The history of the Kings? The history of the Acts of the Apostles? And of our redemption by Christ?"(28) Hence, Garland proposed the axiom, "allegories do not therefore overthrow the history, but confirm it."(4) Additional use of this method was undue and "therefore your allegorizing is absurd and erroneous, most repugnant . . ."(81)

In point of fact Garland was inconsistent in his condemnation of allegory. He criticized Coppin's extensive use of this method but his own use of allegory contradicted this criticism. Garland disapproved of Coppin's interpretation of *Revelation* 12:7 concerning the battle of Archangel Michael against the Dragon. Coppin's understanding of this text would limit God's power and authority for he believed that it was from this time that Satan controlled the universe. Hence, it is surprising when it is Garland who rejected Coppin's allegorical interpretation and then offered instead that "first, for the Dragon and also for his angels and instruments [are understood] as persecutors, heretics and all profane and ungodly persons that live in sin without repentance, who are therefore called the seed of the devil."(44) Elsewhere, too, Garland was willing to defend his use of allegory while severely attacking Coppin's use of this method. Indeed, Garland was distressed by Coppin's use of literalism too. Coppin, for instance, cited *John* 2:19–22 when the Pharisees ask Jesus for a miracle and Jesus tells them to destroy the temple and in three days' time he will raise it up again. Coppin believed this must be interpreted literally to indicate how Jesus, too, was against material structures and religions. Garland, however, argued, "When he saith unto the Jews, destroy this temple and in three days I will raise it up again, he spake of the temple of his body,"(34) to which Garland added, "Can anything be more plain?"

In another instance Garland discussed the interpretation of the book of Job. Coppin and other Ranters liked this volume which opened with a contest between God and the Devil and has Job suffering the torments of life on earth at the hands of the Devil, thereby indicating that physical life itself was hell. In this instance, Coppin wished to accept Job in its literal interpretation. Garland's response was, "Oh horrible that you have the impudence to say or infer that."(32) Garland would not accept the idea that God delivered Job into the Devil's hands and instead wrote that "Job was then in darkness" to explain his suffering. Garland added, "Therefore he comforts himself with a spiritual estate, with the resurrection."(32) Unfortunately, the physical resurrection is not a concept found anywhere in the Old Testament and possibly not in subsequent writings either. In short, both Garland and Coppin were willing to use various methods to deliver the results they desired. Coppin defended allegory but used literalism. Garland defended literalism but used allegory. The differences between Coppin and Garland were real but not in terms of method. They differed in their overall systematic presentation of Christianity and each would defend the totality of his system with any method available.

In almost every instance where Garland attacked Coppin's views, he used words and expressions that Coppin himself might have used in a slightly different context. As an example, Garland was terribly upset by Coppin's belief in universal salvation, yet how it was necessary for God to come to the soul as a thief in the night to liberate it from a material body. Such views upset Rosewell and Garland, too, wrote, "You say now so long as man is without this manifestation of God which is Christ in him, he is reprobate. This is false." (36) Yet, this was precisely the condition of the soul in Garland's orthodox system where God predestined some to election and others to damnation. Yet, on the very same page Garland wrote that "reprobation is a part of God's eternal decree whereby God hath purposed to pass by some that were in the state of corruption as well as to elect others unto eternal election." Thus, both thinkers postulated that there were some elect and some reprobate and that the elect and the damned were so designated by God's action, either by divine predestination or by God appearing as a thief in the night. Yet, neither would accept this same action by God in the other thinker's system.

This comedy of words became absurd when Garland attempted to support *his* view of divine election against Coppin's view of the same. Garland argued that "it can not be denied that he loveth some of mankind more than the rest . . . in that he hath elected them, effectually called them, justified and glorified them, so that the love he bears to others, whom he hath not elected, called, etc. compared to this may in a manner be called hatred, agreeable to that of *Romans* 9:13; 'Jacob have I loved but Esau have I hated.' "(63) Surely Garland must have known that Coppin, too, used the very same verse of Scripture to demonstrate that there were two forces in the universe each of which had devotees within this world who were called saints and sinners. In short, here was an instance where both thinkers actually shared the same view, used Scripture through the same allegorical method, came to the same result and should, therefore, have agreed on this point however much they have disagreed on everything else. Yet, Garland wrote about Coppin's version of things and his use of this Scriptural verse, "but here you fall to your old shift of allegorizing the Scriptures, but very unhandsomely . . . [for] here God threatens to destroy the house of Esau and to establish his church, the house of Jacob . . . ,"(80) which was also Coppin's belief that the saints would triumph over the sinners.

In at least one instance Garland was aware that in fact he and Coppin were running along parallel lines of thought and method. When discussing *1 Corinthian* 15:22, "as in Adam all die, so in Christ shall all be made alive," Garland realized that "what the apostle brings here to prove the resurrection of the body, you urge to prove the resurrection of the soul; a goodly argument."(67) Yet, Garland was not a dualist and believed in the physical resurrection while Coppin denied the resurrection because he rejected the flesh. Hence Garland was forced to argue "as Satan slays both [i.e., both flesh and soul] so Christ doth raise up both in his members"(33) where Coppin would have argued that Adam [i.e. flesh] slew all while Christ [i.e., spirit] redeemed all.

Garland was far more perceptive than most anti-Ranter authors and more intelligent than those who had previously challenged Coppin. He understood that other than the basic philosophical difference between them, Christology was perhaps the fundamental conceptual difference separating them. In one instance Garland observed, "Now I hope you will not be so graceless as to say that Christ ever died the death of sin and therefore it [i.e., Christ's death] must be understood as a death of the body which he voluntarily suffered that he might destroy him that had the power of death, which was the devil."(51) In fact, that was the essence of Coppin's Christology which he had the gracelessness to teach in all his works. Garland understood the drift of such views and while his own ideas of vicarious atonement were diametrically opposed to Coppin's adoptionism, he could write, "To make the second person in the trinity a sinner [i.e., as Coppin taught] and thereby (as much as in you lies) raise the very foundation of religion for if he had been [totally mortal], he could not have been a sacrifice to take away sin but would have needed himself to be purged,"(3) which in fact was the very essence of Coppin's adoptionism.

Garland also understood the essence and implications of Coppin's views on Christian liberty. Garland taught that "the liberty which the Scriptures speak of is a liberty from ceremonial law, from the power and domination of sin, from the rigor and curse of the Law."(54) This orthodox view of gospel liberty was opposed to Ranter views and was "not an exemption from ecclesiastical and civil government . . . [and] those under the color of Christian liberty who go about to take away ecclesiastical and civil government and abuse the Scriptures and as much as in them lies, endeavor to destroy both church and state."(53) Admitting that "it is a great curse to have evil magistrats or evil ministers and yet it is far greater evil to have none at all, for then every man doth what he will,"(53) Garland taught a reasonable position. In the end, however, interpretation depended upon whose ox was gored. Garland could live with evil Protestant ministers but would not have been so charitable about Catholic princes in places of authority. Coppin might argue on a more radical tack and oppose all government in the name of Christian liberty because there was little chance of a Ranter commonwealth.

Whose ox was being gored was also the operating principle in their approach to other social-religious issues. Coppin and other Ranters attacked the tithe as an unjust tax to support an unrepresentative clergy. There was logic to this position for Ranters were almost always excluded from the tithe and were therefore unable to depend upon a regular living. Garland, living on the tithe, credited Coppin's opinions noting, "You charge me with preaching for hire, saying the priests divine for money."(55) Garland, however, was wise enough to turn the tables and charged, "It is you and such as you are that preach for reward, that live by gifts and bribes wherefore you devise false doctrine such as will please foolish and corrupt men's fancies . . . [and] sow pillows under men's elbows that they may sleep at ease in sin, that tell the wicked they shall live though God hath said they shall surely die . . ."(55) Indeed, Ranter thought must have seemed this way to an orthodox minister preaching an unpopular double supralapsarian predestination which frightened his parishioners, while Coppin preached a popular universal salvation, the end of all sin and total Christian liberty. Surely without the tithe few would have supported the dour message Garland taught, and in open competition with Coppin he might have suffered the same fate his colleague Walter Rosewell faced. As the reader will recall, the audience rejected predestination and welcomed universal salvation.

Whatever the differences between these two theologians, the men were well matched. Garland was an able and competent opponent and it is unfortunate that it was not these two that had not met in Rochester Cathedral or that Coppin never responded to Garland. For the first and only time, Coppin had an orthodox opponent worthy of himself.

19. Sectarian Critics

More unkind than the scandalous treatises and less objective than the criticism from orthodox sources were the anti-Ranter writings emanating from sectarian origins. Despite strong similarities among many radical sects, wrangling between their spokesmen was tragic, pathetic, and sometimes funny. None from the radical left could condemn Ranter demands for freedom of conscience, and opposition to the tithe was also shared by all dissenters since all found themselves disenfranchised from such financial arrangements. All Quakers, Ranters and Muggletonians shared similar ideas concerning the essentials of dualism, the conflict of spirit and flesh, and God and the Devil. They also shared the same views of the inner light and expressed very similar ideas about the pathway to liberate the soul from the corrupt world of matter. All opposed ritual and hierarchy. Many, perhaps most, radicals shared the same political and social views. Like the Diggers, Ranters called for the abolition of private property but all called for some measure of economic reform favoring the interests of the poor. All shared the same misgivings about Parliament and the course of events under Cromwell. In short, Muggletonians, Ranters and Quakers shared more than separated them and even much of their membership floated from one group to another. Indeed, it was this very sense of competition which provided the impetus for the absolute hatred and animus other radicals held for Ranters. As there is no hatred to rival that of brothers, so too were the anti-Ranter treastises from the radical left the most viciously anti-Ranter of them all.

Though the modern Quaker is too sober to share much with the Ranters, Quaker ancestors were indeed close to the Ranters in many ways. James Naylor's views and demeanor approximated Rantism and the "Proud Quakers" were in fact Quakers with a decided Ranter bent because many had previously been Ranters.[40] Unfortunately, most Quakers had little good to say about them. Indeed, Quakers were often their harshest critics and wrote some of the most deeply vicious polemical tracts against them. George Fox, the charismatic leader of the Seeker branch of the early Quakers had dealings with Ranters since he, like them, spent much time in jail for mantaining controversial religious views. In his journal Fox wrote about a chance encounter with Joseph Salmon and a band of Ranters in the Coventry jail. "They said they were God but I asked them whether it would rain tomorrow and they could not tell. I told them God could tell."[41] Another time he met with them to discuss religion "and they were rude, and sung and whistled and danced," and later still, in 1654 at another such meeting, "they began to call for drink and tobacco."

If indeed the Ranters were but "unclean beasts and sung, whistled and danced," it is difficult to understand why Quakers were obsessed with them. On the other hand, the Friend Samuel Fisher gave us a picture of Rantism close enough to Quaker thought when he wrote, "They considered that the present dispensation, which is that of the spirit, since Christ had come again spiritually, they had no longer any need of lower helps and outward administrations, carnal ordinances, visible representations of Christ, and mere bodily exercises as baptism, and fellowing together in breaking of bread . . . all these shadowy dispensations had their day."[42] Like their sectarian cousins, Ranters believed there was a new dispensation and told Fisher that they alone had been born into this new age and additionally told him about "his coming into men by the spirit or in such full measures and manifestations of his spirit into men's hearts, that they may be able to live up with him in spirit." Since most Ranters believed themselves reborn in this fashion, they did indeed teach that they were part of God. This sentiment may account for Fox's discussions with Salmon while both sat in jail, and may also explain why Ranters sang, whistled and danced. If Quakers did not care for dancing, certainly they were as happy as Ranters about their own proximity to God.

One treatise demonstrating the sense of competition dividing these groups is Richard Farnsworth's *The Ranter's Principle and Deceits Discovered . . .* , published in 1655. More than any other single author, Farnsworth, a Quaker, expressed the ambivalent love-hate relationship anti-Ranter radicals experienced when dealing with Ranters. One part of the treatise was an outright and total condemnation of all things Ranter while the second part was an explanation of the Quaker principles Farnsworth hoped Ranters might accept. Before dealing with Farnsworth's condemnation of Rantism, we might first see what principles Farnsworth hoped Ranters might accept. This will enable us to understand in what ways these two groups differed and, hence, the source of Farnsworth's criticism.

Farnsworth's definition of God might have come from Coppin, Bauthumley or others we have dealt with. Farnsworth taught that "God is light and in him is no darkness at all and that every good and perfect gift is from above that cometh from the Father of Lights, within whom is no variableness."(12) Moreover, this definition of God is placed within a stridently dualistic conceptual framework. "Here are two seeds acted by two powers and receiveth strength from two roots," Farnsworth explained, and that "good and evil are from two roots, distinct and two powers."(9) Indeed, not only Quakers and Ranters but Muggletonians too accepted a strong notion of dualism, for both Quakers and Muggletonians made use of Coppin's ideas of the two seeds to account for those who are saintly and those who remain corrupt. Also similar to Ranter positions was Farnsworth's definition of man's relationship with the world in both a spiritual and social sense. He wrote, "Consider O Man, that thou art mortal and must return to dust and be cast into torment and burning if thou wilt not give ear to the cry of the poor, that which is pure in thee, that it may work thee into charity . . . and cut oppression and tyranny."(10)

Farnsworth also shared typical Ranter antipathy to universities and book learning. He wrote that a university education "is a borrowed or false light that leads them [i.e., the scholars] to books and studies to find out the truth by their carnal wisdom, which is gathered up from the Serpent," and hence, he that seeks "to gather up knowledge out of old authors or books without [i.e., about] them, he knows not the true light."(13)

Like Ranters, Farnsworth taught that the soul was divine and would provide the proper spiritual path. "This light is within thee," Farnsworth explained, "it is not without, in Books nor Scripture. The Scriptures do declare of it, but they are not the light."(17) If Farnsworth did not condemn the Bible as mere history, his low opinion of it was shared by more than one Ranter who would also have agreed with Farnsworth when he wrote about rituals and observances that "this light will tell thee that all thy prayers are an abomination to the Lord."(16)

Ranters and Quakers shared other ideas as well. Farnsworth taught that "he that is born of God the Father and the Son, they are all one," and he that follows Christ's example and suffering, "he is made clean in and by the power of righteousness."(6) Clearly, the reason so many Ranters would filter into the Quaker movement was that they held a great many ideas in common.

Yet, despite these similarities, Ranters and Quakers differed concerning the reality of hell and evil. Ranters, we have noted, rejected the existence of a local hell and the reality of sin. Quakers stood with more conventional Christians in affirming the existence of both. Rather than writing how the kingdom of God is within, Farnsworth emphasized that "there is a devil and a hell and a root whence all evil doth proceed."(7) And rather than taking a tolerant view of the needs and deeds of the flesh, as Clarkson and Coppe taught, Farnsworth was closer to Bauthumley, Coppin, and even Salmon when he observed that sexuality was "under the Dominion of the

Prince of Darkness and such poisons [were] from the corrupt root and so feeds [*sic*] the flesh and wallows [*sic*] in the mire and lust of their own conceivings, inventions, and fleshly imaginations."(6)

Perhaps out of some recognition that Ranters and Quakers ran along parallel conceptual lines, before beginning his condemnation, Farnsworth observed, "You did run well but you have lost the right way and are turned into the paths of darkness again and you act in darkness."(1) Farnsworth might have ended his treatise on this note of conciliation and fraternity with kindred, if erring, Ranter spirits; he did not.

The first page of Farnsworth's treatise observed that "you have turned the grace of God into wantonness" and on the last page, after writing "you Ranters stink," Farnsworth concluded his tirade with the statement, "the serpent thou art, and you Ranters, scorpions, serpents, you shall not escape the damnation of hell."(20) The pages in between were somewhat less conciliatory.

The object of Farnsworth's anger was a Ranter named Robert Wilkinson, unknown but for this treatise. According to the author, Wilkinson came from Coates in Leicestershire where local Quakers considered him a horrible radical. "He said he was born of God and can not commit sin and said he was both God and the Devil, and he said there was no God but him nor no devil but him, and he said whom he blessed was blessed and whom he cursed was cursed . . . he said the apostles were lying deceivers . . . and he said the Bible was a pack of lies and there was neither heaven nor hell but here, and yet he was in both heaven and in hell."(19) In a word, Wilkinson said a lot of things that upset Farnsworth.

If Farnsworth was accurate, Wilkinson represented the more radical Ranter fringe, though none of his views were in themselves truly unusual. Most disturbing yet were Wilkinson's moral views, which Farnsworth found deplorable and about which he wrote, "Thou art a whore-master, as thou saidest, and art in the mystery of Babylon, committing fornication and art full of the filthiness thereof."(20) We will recall that the only Ranter proudly calling both himself and God a whore-master was the London Anonymous dealt with in chapter 10.

Hoping to bring Wilkinson to his senses, Farnesworth devoted several pages to explaining why Ranter concepts of Christian liberty were erroneous. He explained that "the liberty which Christ purchaseth to and for his, is a liberty and freedom from sin, and he that saith he is in Christ ought to walk as he also walked."(4) Of course, Quakers defined sin differently from the way the Ranters did and hence freedom from sin also had a different meaning. Farnsworth was aware of this and attempted to preclude Ranter opposition by observing, "You may object and say, 'Did not the apostle say stand fast in that liberty where with Christ hath set you free.?' *Gal.* 5;1. And he saith all things are lawful for me."(4) Farnsworth's explanation was identical to that of other Christians in arguing that "when he said all things were lawful to him, he was speaking of meats and such like but he did not use any liberty to the flesh."(5) Similarly, Farnsworth explained, "When he saith . . . that there is nothing unclean of itself but to him that esteemeth it to be unclean, it is so, but he is not speaking of sin nor fleshly liberty but to tender consciences in that place . . . about the unlawfulness of eating all meats and such like."(5)

There was little reason to believe that Wilkinson or any other Ranter would find Farnsworth's explanations of Christian liberty any more convincing than they had found the same explanation coming from other religious authorities. Yet, because Farnsworth too was a dualist of sorts, he believed he might better understand the pitfalls of Ranter libertinism. Thus he wrote about Wilkinson's Ranter orientation, "Now thou mayest see it was but the weak and low apprehensions in those things, there is neither hell nor devil nor any such thing but what is in thee and thou hast got through those conceits, now rejoice and be merry and take thy pleasure, use thy freedom."(3) If indeed such be true then "Rejoice, let thy heart be merry, use all things in righteousness and there is no sin in them."(3) "But," Farnsworth asked, "is it so because thou sayest so, will not the very natural man [in thee] . . . tell thee thou art a liar and speak only thy conceits?"(7)

In the end Richard Farnsworth was never certain how to deal with Wilkinson and his type. On the one hand, he concluded with the warning, "Woe unto thee Ranters, this book is as a testimony against you from us whom the world called Quakers, and you and your wicked principles we deny and hold them and you accursed."(19) On the other hand, it was precisely the Quaker dualist who best understood Rantism and could also observe, "I know many were once tender and simple hearted and did make conscience of your ways and were zealous for the truth and did practice what was made known in some measure."(2) It is likely that Ranters were equally ambivalent about Quakers.

There were some Quakers for whom Rantism was the most horrible expression of false religion they had encountered. Certainly George Fox thought so and so did Richard Hickock whose treatise *A Testimony Against the People Called Ranters*(1659) expressed only shock and horror at Rantism and had nothing at all conciliatory to offer. Ranters are "swearers, cursers, liars, drunkards, adulterous, proud, convetous and all manner

276

of evil workers [who] are in darkness, degeneration, alienation and transgression."(2) Moreover, Ranters are also "children of darkness . . . whose seed, birth and state is accursed."(2) Even worse, Ranters practice their filth and then "lay it upon the Lord as him to be the mover and the leader thereunto."(2) Such practices could not come to a good end for "you are turned into that way that leads to hell and destruction."(1) Worst of all, "you are become like a sow that was washed, which is again wallowing in the mire, and to the dog which is swallowing down his vomit which he once had vomited up."(1) Friend Hickock was not favorably disposed to Rantism.

Other sectarian leaders were no more favorably disposed to Ranters than Mr. Hickock. Even Gerard Winstanley, the leader of the equally detestable Diggers, had only contempt for Ranters. Indeed, Winstanley feared that ignorant people would mistakenly identify Diggers as Ranters and, as a result, wrote his eight-page 1649 treatise entitled *A Vindication of those . . . Called Diggers.* Early in the treatise Winstanley explained, "This I was moved to write as a vindication of the Diggers who are slandered with the Ranting action."(7, pages unnumbered)

Should the reader wonder what reasons Winstanley might have had for attacking Ranters, other than to disassociate the good name of the sect he represented from Rantism, the author of the treatise explained that "my end is only to advance the Kingdom of Peace in and among mankind, which is and will be torn to pieces by the Ranting power if reason do not kill this . . . beast."(7) The Ranting power was so dangerous in fact, that Winstanley warned even the removed but curious reader of impending danger for "all you that are merely civil, you are the people that are like to be tempted and set upon and torn into pieces by this devouring Beast; the Ranting power."(7)

Not one to leave the reader wondering what great evils lay in the Ranting Power, this treatise was a full explanation of the nature of Ranting evil and the social and biological implications as well. Winstanley explained that the Ranting power expressed itself "in the abundant eating and drinking and actual community with variety of women . . . is the life of the Beast or living flesh."(2) Such sensualism was not merely morally and religiously repugnant, but Winstanley wished the world to appreciate the dire biological results of such a lifestyle as well. Sensualism "brings vexation to the mind, or man within, when you want your delight in the excessive copulation with women . . ."(3) The physical result of such behavior is that "anger, rage and variety of vexations possesses [sic] the mind and inflames [sic] their hearts to quarreling, killing, burning houses or corn or to such

277

like destructiveness."(3) Moreover, sexuality "bring diseases, infirmness, weakness and rottenness upon the body . . . [and] diseases of the body causes [sic] sorrow of mind."(2)

Other than disease, Winstanley believed it a poor idea for men to spend too much time in the company of women. For one thing, "this excess of feminine society hinders the pure and natural generation of man and spills the seed in vain and instead of a healthful growth of mankind, it produces weakness and much infirmness through immoderate heat."(4) This in turn affects not merely the male but the female as well for in seed-spilling "the mother hath much more pain in child bearing" or, "it [the child] proves a burden to the mother or nurse."(4) Worse yet, the child of seed-spilling parents "proves either not long lived or a fool or else a sickly weakly thing that is a burden to himself."(4) The logic may be illusive but contemporaries probably understood him.

Immoderate heat also brings about other problems for society. It is for this reason that "the Ranting practice is the support of idleness . . . [for Ranters] neither can nor will work but live idle lives like wandering busy-bodies."(4) The social result is "that by seeking their own freedom, they enbondage others."(4) In short, the Ranting power is guilty of "bringing forth nothing but misery to the inhabitants thereof."(2) Should the Ranting Power be permitted to flourish, the social results could be disastrous for England, for "the whole body, whole families, nay, whole nations are thus distempered."(2) No man is a prophet in his own land and Winstanley's early warning of 1649 went largely unheeded. One can only speculate what England's prosperity and physical health might have been had his warning been heeded.

Our last anti-Ranter author was himself a prime stimulus causing others to attack Ranters. Probably none more than Lawrence Clarkson captivated the imagination of Englishmen and expressed the essence of what they feared and hated in Rantism and against whom the Blasphemy Act was promulgated.

Clarkson left Rantism in the middle of the decade to become a follower of John Reeves and Ludwig Muggleton. Indeed, he attempted to wrest power from Muggleton and establish himself as the sect's leader much as he had been Captain of the Rant earlier. He could not dislodge Muggleton's authority, however, and finally agreed to cease from publication and accept a secondary position.

Clarkson's spiritual development during his post-Ranter years paralleled that of Abiezer Coppe who abjured Libertinism for a Rantism not far removed from Coppinism. Clarkson's later writings include *A Paradisical*

Dialogue Between Reason and Faith (1660), *The Quaker's Downfall* (1659) and *The Right Devil Discovered* (1659), also published under the colorful title *Look Around You For the Devil That You Fear Is in You*. These treatises, especially the first, can be categorized as Coppinist or Philosophical Rantist. There is a strong dualist thrust to these works as well as a very strong moralistic tone. Of these writings, only *The Right Devil Discovered* is of interest to us here for it was in this treatise that Clarkson attacked Rantism. Indeed, this treatise condemned virtually everyone in England not sharing Clarkson's views, especially Ranters and Quakers. It would appear that in abjuring his libertinist positions, Clarkson adopted the more objectionable guise of an intolerant bigot.

After roundly condemning Quakerism for every possible religious perfidy, Clarkson wrote that "the next sort of this cursed seed [of Satan] . . . is the White Ranting Devil [who] doth approve of all his wickedness to be righteousness."(100) Ranting Devils believe the Bible "is a history of man's invention for they say the Scripture is a meer map of contradiction."(98) Ranters, we are informed, quite incredibly reject divine reward and punishment "for hell and damnation, it is all here, so if they can but escape prison, sickness and want of money, they fear no other hell or torment hereafter whatsoever."(98–99) Indeed, despite a morally atrocious lifestyle, Ranters believe there is no afterlife that "when we die we shall be swallowed up into that infinite spirit as a drop into the ocean and so be as we were and if ever we be raised again, we shall be as a horse, a cow, a root, a flower and such like."(96)

Because Clarkson had been Captain of the Rant, though nothing of the sort is ever hinted at in this manuscript, he was able to provide indepth information concerning the nature of Ranter immorality. He noted for instance that Ranters enjoyed cursing and listed several examples, including "God damn me, I will have my will," or "the Devil take thee." Worse yet was "the Devil confound me body and soul if I be not revenged on thee" and the worst of all was "the pox of God take thee for a pocky devilish whore."(104)

Worse than cursing was Ranter sexual immorality. Ranters believe "the Scripture commands us to love our neighbors as ourselves and therefore we are to love our neighbors' wives and how can our love be more expressed than in kissing, sporting and laying one with another?"(95) Because Ranters claim they "know none lawfully married in this world" the logical result is that "they say to lie with a maid, a widow, or our neighbor's wife is no more than to lie with that woman you call my wife."(95) In an obvious reference to Coppe, Clarkson chided that "some in London said it is no more for a man to lie with any woman than a cock to tread a hen or a bull to serve a cow."(92) And in a reference to his own earlier views, which he did not mention ever having owned, Clarkson presented an even worse Ranter view, "saying, till a man can act as in no sin, he can not be free from sin" with the result being "for thinking this, it is impossible for any man to be free from these sins unless he can steal, murder and commit adultery as no sin, and not till then, they say, thou hast no power over sin."(93) Yet another Ranter position was "that nothing is unclean of itself but to him that esteemeth it so . . . [and] from hence including all manner of filthy acts whatsoever."(93) And still others asked, "If I lie with twenty, they are all but one to me and these being of a free consent, what sin can be in this?"(92) In fact, Clarkson himself had offered all these as explanations for his earlier ideas of redemption through evil.

The results of these many immoral excuses to justify even more immoral behavior were pitiable. "Witness the tears of many a poor virgin-wife and the sad misery many an innocent virgin hath undergone," Clarkson moaned, "the defilement of her own body and eternal hazard of her soul."(94) Ranters, however, had no sympathy for such unfortunate souls, as "all this is justifiable in thy reprobate mind if thou canst but satisfy thy lust and spend her money."(94)

One can almost sense the anger of Clarkson's righteous indignation when he asked, "When this pretty deluded creature comes and tells thee how the case is with her, 'I am with child by thee and thou hast spent all my money, what wilt thou do with me? Wilt thou according to thy promise make me thy wife and do thy best endeavor to satisfy me for this wrong thou hast done me?' "(94) As a Muggletonian minister, Clarkson had, no doubt, met many unfortunate victims of Ranter immorality and was thus in a position to ask, "What is the answer you think?" and then answer "Even this he will reply 'Alas, what can I do for thee? Marry thee I can not in that I have a wife and to maintain thee I can not in that I have it not for my-self.' "(94) And when the poor soul realizes that she is now lost and re-sponds in horror, "Thou toldest me thou wasn't single . . . so I did con-descend to lie with thee thinking thou woulds't make me thy wife by which I have not only brought myself to shame and beggary, but for ought I know, have damned my soul."(95) The Ranter, however, always evil and incapa-ble of responding to human need, will only respond, "A pox take you for a whore, you are a dark devil indeed to say thou shalt be damned for thy love."(95)

From Clarkson's perspective, Ranters were far more heinous and disgust-ing than other sinners. Unlike others, Ranters believed that God loved their every immoral action, arguing, "There is nothing that I can think, speak or do but God is the author of it."(92) Consequently, when pressed by outsiders or by a court of law, the Ranting Devil merely shrugs and says, "It is not me but the Lord in me, of myself I can do nothing . . . thou thought it was I that committed adultery, that did cozen and lie with the innocent, thou thoughtest it was I in thee that moved thee to swear, whore, cheat thy fellow mortals, but thou shalt know that I am a God . . . and so worship me as a God filled with all unrighteousness, fornication, wretchedness, covetousness, maliciousness, envy, murder, debate, deceit, an inventer of all evil things."(96—97)

Clarkson was willing to concede that not all Ranters were quite so evil as the hypothetical picture he provided the reader. Some were not openly immoral and "will speak against these cursed actions and that because he doth not only know them to be evil, but he is afraid his wife, husband, children or parents should know of it and not only that but he is afraid the law will take hold of him and so punish him if not put him to death for it."(100) Hence, not morality but cowardice and fear and "such like are the motives inducing him to speak against that with his tongue which his heart burneth and lusteth after."(100)

For the mature Lawrence Clarkson, the Ranter was the totally immoral and evil person the young Lawrence Clarkson in fact was. The deeds he described in this treatise were the very actions he justified earlier as Captain of the Rant, and the dialogue he presented between a Ranter and the mother of his illegitimate child was in fact the very relationship that Clarkson personally experienced and wrote about in exactly the same words in his treatise *Lost Sheep Found*. Perhaps Clarkson wished to atone for sowing wild oats in his youth, or perhaps he was still an opportunist looking to be dramatic in his political joust with Ludwig Muggleton.

20. Scandalous Tracts

Of all religious groups subject to popular condemnation, surely the most vulnerable were antinomian sects. Those who would scrap Scripture and other commonly held guidelines for human behavior in favor of the vagaries of the ethereal spirit were easily condemned as dangerous libertines if only because of the perceived potential for abuse. It is not surprising, therefore, that all Ranters were condemned as immoral libertines because all rejected the certainty of law and tradition as guides to human behavior. Even before the Ranters, however, previous antinomians and libertines had been condemned. To appreciate and understand these scandalous writings and to provide some sort of background for this unusual form of literature, we will first analyze a few similar pieces written against Familists and Adamites and dating from 1641, before the Ranters appeared. Such works will illuminate later anti-Ranter writings.

There is little evidence to suggest that Henry Niclaes and his Familist followers were anything but the most ascetic of spiritualists. Their denials of objective written codes of behavior and their espousal of the free spirit meant, for their critics at least, that the Familists were necessarily both immoral and evil. One treatise of 1641, entitled *The Plot Discovered and Counter Plotted*, was typical in the danger to the commonwealth it saw in the Familists. The antinomian libertines would undermine civil society. According to this author, "The libertines, such as I understand, to be the swearer, drunkard, whore-master, prophaner of the Sabbath, scorner and despiser of others, following no calling but their sinful lusts, harsh and cruel in their dealings as though God had granted them a charter to do what they list . . ."(10) In short, the libertine was a composite of all the morally offensive qualities to be found in the human species. The plot referred to in the title is not made clear and the counter plot is never mentioned, but the author no doubt felt much better having warned Englishmen of the true state of things.

More ambitious, but no more coherent, was another treatise of the same year entitled *A Description of 29 Sects Here in London*. The anonymous author lamented the deplorable state of affairs where sects increasingly dominated English religious life. His list of dangerous sects included such groups as Puritans, Calvinists, Lutherans and Papists, and the Family of Love is described as follows: "Here's a loving sect presented to you, they think a man may gain salvation by showing himself loving, especially to his neighbor's wife. For by their law it is allowed for one man to lie with another man's wife while she sleepeth."(4) Equally illuminating was this author's conception of Adamites. "Here is a shameless sect, they ground their religion from our father Adam (and yet they go naked when they hear prayers or prophesying) when he hid himself from the presence of God because he was naked."(4) The Socinians too were included in this compendium of error and we are informed that "Socinus, the wrangling disputant was the father of the sect. They hold no true point at all with the Protestants but wrangle in every article."(5)

Authors of anonymous treatises are often confused about who Adamites really are. One treatise entitled *A Nest Of Serpents Discovered . . . called Adamites* (1641) noted that they "of late sprung up in this Nation to the wonderment of all that hear of it."(2) This author is not sure who "Adam" actually was. There was "one called Adam the Patriarch"(2) but on the next page he observed that "by the subtlety of the devil it was again set up by one called Adam Pastor . . . from whom they that were his disciples were called Adamites."(3) More recently, we soon learn, "they had their main champion in one Pickardus."(4)

In fact, Adam Pastor was a sixteenth-century antitrinitarian with no Adamite sympathies at all. Pickardus was not a person but a reference to Picardy, the alleged point of origin of some Bogomil and Free Spirit influence according to Inquisitional authorities. Indeed, Pickard may also have been the origin of the more familiar term "beghard." Holland, too, was important in this connection. "In the year 1535," the author informs us, "there was a knot of them gathered at Amsterdam . . . they climbed naked to the tops of trees and there would sit naked expecting bread from heaven."(5)

Other than sitting naked in the trees and waiting for manna, Adamites were involved in other forms of strange behavior. Other than being "seen to go naked in Holland," the author reported, "They had wont usually to meet in hot houses or stoves or in such places where they might have the convenience of artificial heat to set their natural heat on fire. They put off their clothes at their entrance . . . sit all naked, mixed as they entered, men and women."(4) In point of fact, this description of the common mixed sauna, still the rule in northern Europe, was not sexual at all, yet this author believed that they "allowed promiscuous copulation, any man with any woman whom he liked best,"(4) which was certainly logical if not true.

With one exception, "Adamite" religious rituals were usual enough. "They hear their lectures naked, pray naked, receive the sacrament naked."(5) In short, the Adamites were so called because they did every-thing naked. The author concluded that "they will be caught in the midst of their lewd and abominable exercise which is so scandalous, blasphem-ous and abominable."(6) When the author added, "At their discovery more shall be written," it is clear that in fact none yet had been apprehended and that the author's fund of information was more folklore than fact.

The reading audience may have been willing to believe anything at all about promiscuous and dangerous radicals. Indeed, the more outrageous the story, the more often it was repeated by subsequent authors. Yet, these authors lacked credibility because, as the last treatise demonstrated, few could actually boast first-hand contact with the dangerous and promiscu-ous radicals discussed. To compensate for the lack of hard factual informa-tion, some authors used a different format more like the "I was there" or alleged "eye-witness account" journalism that would develop in later cen-turies. One treatise of this type is *A Description of a Sect Called Family of Love* (1641), which purported to present an unbiased account of one per-son's experiences with that group.

According to the subtitle, this was the true story of Mistress Susan Snow of Surry County, "who was vainly led away for a time through their [i.e., Familists] base allurements and at length fell mad till by a great miracle shown from God, she was delivered." The following six pages tell the sort of religiously edifying tale one might currently hear on any Christian broadcasting network.

A gentleman named Snow had a wonderful and dutiful daughter named Susan in whom the devil sought to "subvert and eradicate this well planted virtue."(1) One day, as Susan conversed with her father's workmen about the profusion of sects then appearing, one gardener reported the existence of a group of 100 Familists in a forest not six miles away. Excited and unable to sleep, Susan rose early the next morning, saddled a horse, and "vowing not to return till she had seen some of their behavior"(2) set out to find some Familists. She rode to Bagshot and found the Familists in the Forest of Birchwood there. At this meeting, the spiritual leader read sexual poetry by Ovid, Virgil and others and afterwards presided over a dinner of "exceeding delicacies."(3) After dining, the leader succeeded in seducing Susan and she stayed with them in the forest for one week during which time she witnessed their many rituals and observances. Surely this was the high point of the treatise where the author would inform the eager reader about what the strange Familists did. Unfortunately, the author, presum-ably either Susan or her confidant, indicated that to do so "will be too long for this little pamphlet to bear."(4) In fact, no details at all were given the reader.

Susan eventually found her way home and lied to her father concerning her whereabouts of the previous week. It was soon obvious to all, however, that Susan was a very changed person. She began spending much time alone and for a period of two weeks became increasingly melancholy. Susan became so unruly and disobedient that "she would break glasses and earthenware and throw anything at the heads of the servants, and was incontinent till she fell stark mad."(4) Seeing his daughter in so poor a state, Mr. Snow called for Master Yoder, "a very honest man and a most reverend divine living in Oxford."(4) When the good master came to interview Susan she screamed 'the Devil, the Devil, I am damned, I am damned, I am damned,' with many such like horrible exclamations."(5) After half an hour's discussion Master Yoder called for wine but Susan, still under the influence of the devil, threw the glass at the minister and cried out that she was not a simple material object that she might be so easily fixed. Miraculously, the pieces of the glass came flying back together and Susan was so overwhelmed by this sign from God that she became sane and was again an obedient daughter to her father, and, presumably, no longer smashed her father's property.(6)

This account of what might be understood as usual adolescent travails consisting of sexual awakening, disregard for authority and moodiness, served several functions in 1641. The treatise assured the reader that unruly behavior by women came from the devil and that the Familists were the expression of evil in the world. Poor behavior led to madness and reading the ancient poets would lead to licentious behavior. God, working through the efforts of a good minister [i.e., Oxford, not local], would provide for the righteous. God might not cure the ill or feed the hungry but he would certainly look after the daughter of an upstanding man of property. In this seventeenth-century version of "God as cosmic bell hop" the Familists, like subsequent motor-bikers, rock and rollers and denizens of pool halls, were structurally integrated into contemporary life to account for the unfortunate behavior of an otherwise very virtuous [i.e. well brought up] young lady.

Like other treatises, this one was a product of the author's imagination and had no bearing on the reality of the Familists. They did not read Ovid as a religious devotion, eat sumptuous meals and enjoy one another sexually in the forests. Indeed, the treatise reads more like a country bumpkin's account of the questionable deeds and lifestyle of well educated urban sloths who, according to many accounts, read poetry, eat gourmet food and have sex all the time. This description also reads much like a traditional account of Pan's followers. It was also fairly classical in presenting what Romans believed early Christians were all about. Like the Familists, the subversive early followers of Christ met in forests, read esoteric literature [Bible], enjoyed a special meal [eucharist], followed by communal love acts [agape charity]. Additionally, the Romans also thought Christians were cannibals because they consumed Jesus' very body and blood. Familists limited themselves to delicacies. Similarly, it is not coincidental that the first newspaper accounts of the mass suicide in Jonestown, New Guinea involved lurid descriptions of bizarre sexual behavior although, as subsequent reporting made clear, there was no foundation in fact for such ideas. And again, many people believe that contemporary cult practices include use of drugs and promiscuous sex although in fact there is no evidence at all that Moonies or Hare Krishna are interesting enough for either. In short, the anonymous anti-cult treatise believing strange sexuality was the core of irregular religiosity, conforms to a type of opinion current from the time of the emperors to the Moral Majority.

We will deal with more than a dozen scandalous anti-Ranter treatises of various types ranging from true accounts of Rantism to those that are total fabrications of an author's fertile imagination. Of these different types, the most objective and honest was the 'court-statement' account which used an individual's own words against himself. Thus, *The Ranter's Creed* of 1651, consisted of a compilation of court statements made by John and Joan Robins, Joshua Garment and others appearing before Judge Thomas Hubbert of the Middlesex County Court of Assize. This form of treatise is neutral because the anonymous author-compiler, possibly an officer of the court or a local minister, simply presented the most damning of the defendant's statements without adding any personal commentary, testimony or sense of outrage. The defendant's statements are often taken out of context or presented in the worst possible light but no false statements were put into Robins' or Garment's mouths. If we recall, Robins taught that he was God but believed the course of prudence demanded abjuring his faith rather than going to jail. His followers were less enthusiastic about his choice. The author-compiler of this treatise had little need to falsify Robins' statements and could well let this would-be God speak for himself.

Similar in format is the treatise *Strange News From Newgate and the Old Bailey* published in 1650. This treatise reported the statements of two Ranters, I. Collins and T. Reeve, who appeared before court at the Old Bailey on January 20, 1650. Unfortunately we possess no additional accounts of this trial but the testimony this anonymous compiler puts into their mouths has the ring of truth and does represent the sort of statements that London Ranters of the Coppe or Clarkson variety might make. Without indicating how much of their testimony was not being cited, we are told "that this Collins, Reeve and others were sitting at table eating a piece of beef, one of them took it in his hand, tearing it asunder, said to the other, this is the flesh of Christ, take and eat it. The other took a cup of ale and threw it into the chimney corner saying, 'This is the blood of Christ' . . . and blowing through two pieces of tobacco pipes, he said that was the breath of God."(2–3)

Such accounts provided the reading audience with scandalous statements made by Ranters but deleted the main substance of the hearings. Nothing, for instance, was written about any charges or accusations coming under the purview of the Blasphemy Act. This type of court statement proved very popular because many other subsequent treatises repeated these same words, sometimes alleging they were spoken by other Ranter leaders.

A different type of treatise was one generally upset by the confusion of the times with Ranters presented as the very worst manifestation of sectarian dissension. Thus, *The Black and Terrible Warning Piece* of 1653, was subtitled "a scourge to England's rebellion" and expressed disgust with everything, but especially "the dangerous proceedings of the Ranters and the holdings of no resurrection by the Shakers in Yorkshire and elsewhere."(1) The anonymous author continued, pointing out many other dangerous ideas espoused by Ranters "who hold themselves to be above ordinances and that they have walked through all dispensations, denying the sacred Scriptures, the Resurrection of the saints, and like the sons of perdition condemn all gospel promises and Christian privileges, saying there is no God, no Devil, no heaven, no hell, and that the soul is mortal."(1) The author was also upset with Parliament, Cromwell, and everyone else as well and no doubt felt much better for having got if from off his chest.

Similarly, *Hell Broke Loose* of 1646 was concerned with the religious pollution evident in England and is subtitled "a catalogue of the many Spreading Errors, Heresies and Blasphemies of these times." In seven pages, the anonymous author succeeded in listing the most grievous errors and beliefs associated with the Ranters in general and Lawrence Clarkson in particular. Among other views condemned were that Scripture "is but human and not able to discover a divine God,"(3) that "the called of God have no sin in their consciences,"(4) the permissibility, indeed, desirability of adultery,(5) and that many Ranters believe they are Jesus Christ(6) and "that all ordinances as ministry, baptism etc., that have a given end are carnal ordinances and from the devil."(7) Most anonymous authors were unsure what might be done about the deplorable state of affairs but that, too, no doubt, was part of the scandal of the times.

The overwhelming number of anti-Ranter treatises were alleged descriptions of Ranter sexual belief and practice. These scandalous works were based on some degree of fact for some Libertine Ranters were indeed free livers, but most were the product of the author's imagination and were often quite humorous. *The Routing of the Ranters*, of 1650, claimed to be "a full relation of their uncivil carriages and blasphemous words and actions at their made meetings."(Title page) We are informed that Ranters "delight not only in gluttony and drunkenness, chambering and wantonness and the like, but deride the Holy Scripture, deny Christ, and blaspheming, and, as it were, spit in the face of God himself."(2) The very worst offender was Abiezer Coppe, "being lately brought before a committee to be examined, feigned himself mad, used strange kinds of uncouth behavior, throwing nutshells and other things about the room and talked to himself when questions were put to him."(2) One humorous line was the response one Ranter, probably Coppe, gave when asked "what he thought of the Devil, he answered that it was an old woman stuffed with parsley."(2)

Our author informs us that he was present when a large group of Ranters congregated and indulged in uncivil, immoral, and illegal behavior. In one instance, "when a competent number of them were gotten together, they began to sing filthy bawdy songs to the tune of David's Psalms, after which they drank a health . . . this being over, one of them lets fall his breeches and turning his shirt aside another of the company runs and kisses, saying they must all do the like."(4) In another instance the author assured the reader, "this time the meeting began about four of the clock in the afternoon and was continued by some until nine or ten of the clock of the next day, which time was spent in drunkenness, uncleanness, blasphemous words, filthy songs and mixed dances of men and women stark naked."(2)

Several treatises attempted to demonstrate that Ranter sexual license was an integral and necessary aspect of their religious doctrine. Thus, the author of *The Ranter's Recantation* of 1650, tells us of a Ranter leader named Arthingworth who on one occasion preached to his flock "I will do and require you to subscribe unto these ensuing commandments in manner and form as followeth: 1. That you shall not acknowledge nor yield obedience to any other gods but me. 2. That it is lawful to drink, swear, revel and lay with any woman whatsoever. 3. That there is no sabbath, no heaven, no hell, no resurrection and that soul and body die together."(2) If fact, we know of no Ranter leader named Arthingworth, though an Elizabethan radical by that name was condemned. Another treatise, *The Ranter's Bible*, of 1650, divided Ranters into various sects of libertines including Clements, Athians, Seleutian Donatists and several others.(3—4)

The Ranter's Religion, of 1650, tells us that Ranters "affirm that god is so far away from being offended at the crying sins of drunkeness, swearing, blasphemy, adultery etc., that he is well pleased therewith and that (O' Strange and Horrid Impiety!) it is the only way to serve him aright."(4) The sexual ethic common to all Ranters highlighted by this author is that "they affirm that all women ought to be in common and when they are assembled together (this is a known truth!) they first entertain one another, the men those of their own sex and the woman their fellow females, with horrid oaths and execrations, then they fall to boozing and drink deep healths . . . then being full heated with liquor . . . they fall to their lascivious embraces with a joint motion."(5)

One feature common to most treatises is the active sexual role taken by women at the Ranter meetings, perhaps in fulfillment of deep-seated male sexual fantasies. This is a major theme of *The Ranter's Last Sermon*, of 1654, "written by J. M. (a deluded Brother) lately escaped out of their snare."(title page) In the most sexually explicit of anti-Ranter writings, J. M. tells us that Ranters "taught that they could neither see EVIL, know EVIL, nor act EVIL and that whatever they did was good and not EVIL, there being no such thing as sin in the world."(3) As an example, he told of Mistress E. B. who "coming to one of the men, she offers to unbutton his cod-piece, who, demanding of her what she sought for, she answered FOR SIN, whereupon he blows out her candle and leads her to the bed where in the sight of all the rest they commit fornication."(4) Some Ranters were real perverts and J. M. related how "the sister who can make 'the beast with two backs' the most strenuously, viz., entertain the most men longest and oftenest, hath a sufficient canonization for a saint triumphant."(6) Men too were appreciated for their piety and we are told that "that man who tipples deepest, swears the frequentest, commits adultery, incest or buggery the oftenest, blasphemes the impudentest, and perpetrates the most notorious crimes with the highest hand and rigidest resolution, is the dearest darling to heaven."(5)

Many treatises repeat each other and other than by date of publication, it is impossible to determine which treatise was the initial source. *The Ranter's Religion*, for instance, repeated the story about Collins tearing meat apart and saying "this is my body."(8) The same treatise presents a sexual story also found in several other treatises. The anonymous authors all attest to having witnessed when "a she Ranter said openly in the hearing of many (a friend of mine accidentally one of them) that she should think herself a happy woman and should esteem herself a superlative servant of God if any would accompany her carnally in the open market place."(8) Both this story and the one preceding can also be found in slightly modified form in the 1650 treatise *The Arraignment and Trial of the Ranters, with a Declaration.*(3)

Several types of Ranter perversion appealed to audiences of these anonymous treatises which may account for their inclusion into so many of them. One treatise informs us "one of these roysters sitting over his cups (with the rest of his companions) *evacuating wind backwards* used this blasphemous expression, 'Let everything that hath breath praise the Lord.' "(8) Almost all treatises tell of Ranter meetings where hundreds upon hundreds of Ranters engaged in immoral behavior. Thus we read of Ranters "dissembling together (where) they exercise themselves in nothing else but lascivious and unparalleled vices, accounting it no sin for hundreds of men and women (savage like) to lay with each other, publicly all together, either in houses, fields or streets . . ."(5 of *Ranters' Bible*). Another treatise tells us about a couple fornicating in public "after which he was to set her on her head to go about the room on her hands with her coats about her ears . . . and in the presence of about sixty persons entered into venial exercises."(2 of *Ranters' Recantation*).

If anonymous accounts lacked credibility, one could read Gilbert Roulston's account of his life as a Ranter. He described himself as "a late fellow Ranter," and his *Ranter's Bible*, of 1650, affirmed much that anonymous authors wrote. On his own good authority he recounted that "on the 16th of November, 1650, a great company of this new generation of vipers called Ranters gathered together near Soho in Westminster where they exercised themselves in many riotous and uncivil actions. And after some actions spent in feasting and the like, they stripped themselves quite naked and dancing the *Adamites' Curranto*, which was, that after two or three familist gigs, hand in hand, each man should embrace his fellow female in the flesh for the acting of that inhumane theater of carnal copulation." Other authors tell us of additional Ranter sports, including a seventeenth-century version of sado-masochistic activity. "After the satisfying of their carnal and beastly lust," one author wrote, "some have a sport that they call whipping the whore."(4 of *Strange News*) Unfortunately, no illustrations were included though the imagination needs little more to reconstruct what occurred.

John Reading also signed his name to his anti-Ranter treatise of 1650

entitled *The Ranter's Ranting*. Unlike others, Reading could report only
on what his friend's friend experienced with Ranters. We are told of "a
gentleman of quality (as I am credibly informed)"(5) whose intimate dealing with a Ranter were strangely well known to him. He met her in a tavern
and "after a little familiar discourse, he told her he was in indifferent well
health but "wanted a stomach," whereupon she replied that if he pleased to
come to her lodging the next day she doubted not but she should find something to which he had appetite." The next day this gentleman visited the
lady at her lodgings "and appearing in nothing but her smock, [she] asked
him how he liked her and whether his stomach would not come to him
. . . and immediately presented herself to him naked, saying, 'Fellow
Creature, what sayest thou to a plump leg of mutton (striking her hand
upon her thigh) with the eats that are now in view.' "(5) Our gentleman of
quality was so shocked that he ran out of her lodgings and only later did he
"discover her to be a proselyte of Coppe and Clarkson and the rest of their
infernal gang which have been dispersers of a diabolical opinion that there
is neither heaven nor hell, for otherwise she could not be so audacious."(5)
One must wonder what brought this gentleman of quality into the tavern
in the first instance and how he thought her to be other than a working girl.
In any event, Reading's message is very clear indeed; those who deny
heaven and hell are doomed to eat mutton.

Other than sexual activity, anonymous authors were outraged by Ranter
political thought, especially their alleged disregard for legitimate political
authority. The author of *Hell Broke Loose*, of 1646, was horrified that Ranters taught "that the civil magistrate hath no power at all to meddle in matters of religion."(6) Such views may have been scandalous in 1646 but other
Ranter opinions would have disturbed some Englishmen at any time: first,
that government representatives "may go no further in anything, nor sit no
longer, nor dispose of anything but according to their commission and
power received from the represented."(7) Even worse than any notion of
representative government were Ranter views of popular sovereignty. "The
body of the common people is the earthly sovereign," Ranters believed,
"and the king, parliament, etc., are their own mere creatures to be accountable to them and disposed of by them at their pleasure; the people may
recall and reassume their power, question them and set others in their
place."(7) Democratic sympathies have always seemed shocking.

In 1650 M. Stubbs also wrote about the shocking nature of Ranter social
thought in his tract *The Ranter's Declaration*. Like Roulston, Stubbs
claimed to be "a late fellow Ranter" and reported that at one meeting, many
Ranters complained about the hard financial times, "Desiring to know

how they should be maintained," Stubbs reported, "answer was made that they should borrow money and never pay it again and that they should not only make use of a man's wife but of his estates, goods, chattels also for all things were in common."(6) No less serious was alleged Ranter support for monarchy. Samuel Tilbury's tract *Bloody News from the North*(1650), observed that "Ranters seem to be for monarchy and declared that they held themselves bound to yield all due obedience and loyalty to Charles II." Tilbury's credibility must be questioned, however, for he also noted that Ranters "say there is no God but Pluto."

When Ranters were not drinking, swearing, whoring, stealing people's property or overthrowing the government, John Reading would have us believe they were attempting to murder their opponents. He wrote of one Ranter named Evan Bean, "born of good parentage near Bishop's Castle in the county of Salop, was for many years a constant hearer of the Word, yet afterward fell into strange opinions and would admit no sacrament, no baptism, no duty, no obedience, no devil, no hell etc. In a short time after his fall into these grand errors (the Devil growing short within him) that for no other cause but that they were conscientious and finding an opportunity, he cut off the heads of his mother and brother for which he was hanged in chains in Shrewsbury."(6 of *Ranters' Ranting*).

Samuel Tilbury also told of bloody Ranter doings. He wrote of "a bloody plot discovered concerning their resolution to murder all those that will not turn Ranter." (cover of *Bloody News*) This keen social observer claimed to be present at a large meeting "at the sign of the star in Stonegate." After much discussion, "at last they came to their diabolical resolution. That each man's wife or woman's husband that denied their just and lawful principles of Ranting for the holding of all things in common, should be massacred."(1) By way of substantiation, Tilbury offered how "one Mr. Smart, living at Fowforth, a mile from the city, repairing home to his house did come to his wife and asked her whether she would turn Ranter. She replied no . . . whereupon he immediately stabbed her to the heart with his knife and presently fled."(1) If this was not convincing enough, Tilbury told of "another of these bloody villains coming from one of their infernal meetings hath also killed his wife and wee children at Pontefract."(1)

One treatise of the "Susan Snow young woman of virtue," variety treated earlier was the strange case of Mary Adams whose regrettable life was retold in the treatise *The Ranter's Monster*, of 1652. This treatise combines many elements from other anti-Ranter tracts and added a few novel touches as well. Like Susan Snow, Mary Adams came from a good and religious home, in Tillingham in Essex County. She became an Anabaptist and then a Familist, "and immediately turned Ranter, holding an opinion that there was no God, no heaven, no hell, but that creation came by Providence [and] that woman was made to be a helper for man and that it was no sin to lay with any man whether bachelor, widower or married but a thing lawful and adjured thereunto by nature."(5)

Despite the author's claim that Mary lost all faith in God and religion, we are also told that Mary "said she was the virgin Mary and that she was conceived with child by the Holy Ghost and how all the gospel that had been taught heretofore was false and that which was within her she said was the true messiah."(3) Because of Mary's strange views, her erstwhile minister, a Mr. Hadley, had Mary incarcerated where after eight days of difficult labor Mary gave birth to a monster. "It had neither hands nor feet," we are told, "but claws like a toad in the place where the hands should have been and every part was odious to behold."(4). Since she had given birth to a devil, Mary met a sad fate. "She rotted and was consumed as she lay, being from head to foot as full of botches, blains, boils and stinking scabs as ever one could stand by another."(4) Unlike Susan Snow, Mary did not come to a good end but then again, Rantism was worse than Familism.

In these many treatises, there was only one instance of divine intervention. *The Ranter's Recantation* tells of fifty-nine souls won back to Christ when a Ranter leader "went to the chamber door and called for a Turk's Head, in plain English a piss-pot, and in an instant, upon a great flash of fire, vanished and never was seen more to the great admiration of the spectators."(5)

These popular and funny anti-Ranter treatises had little to offer in the war against blasphemy. A few described more general Ranter opinions but most seem more interested in telling a good dirty story and used the Ranters as their subjects much as earlier treatises used Familists to express many of the same things. While it is doubtful whether much in these treatises was genuine or truthful, London Ranters at least did have a loose and colorful lifestyle. Clarkson lived as a Ranter during these very years and both he and Coppe attracted much attention. As such, one can not entirely dismiss these anonymous treatises.

21. Anti-Ranter Fun:
Poems, Pictures and a Play

Judging from the poems and pictures authors used to adorn their otherwise serious condemnations of Rantism, the Ranters were a great deal of fun. Even in the midst of serious concern about the shocking Ranters, funny little pictures adorned the texts and many authors incorporated into their text funny poems of alleged Ranter authorship. Other authors, it is true, incorporated serious poems, filled with righteous indignation about the Ranters. These were not intended to be humorous reading and yet one must wonder what motivated an author, allegedly truly upset with Rantism, to put his anger to verse.

All of the poems and pictures included in this chapter were taken from the scandalous treatises of chapter 20. Hence, even those poems allegedly written by Ranters were written by the anti-Ranter authors themselves. There is no evidence of any indigenous Ranter poetry presented in any of the treatises we have studied and like the pictures adorning these pages, the poems were meant to amuse the reader and belittle the Ranter.

An example of a poem about Ranters was presented by Samuel Tilbury. He does not claim authorship of the poem but published the following among others. (*Bloody News From the North*)

> A sect of Ranters of late revived
> Who seem more innocent than ever Adam lived,
> Such as will naked go and think it a sin,
> To wear a garment, they're so hot within,
> With lust, that they all clothing do disdain.
>
> . . .
>
> Thus marching naked sisters with a brother
> For want of clothes they cover one another
> In some dark grove thus meet they, where tis fit
> That they the deeds of darkness should commit.
> . . . All must go naked, 'cause they say,
> Truth itself naked goes and so should they.

ANTI-RANTER FUN: POEMS, PICTURES AND A PLAY

This poem poked fun at Ranter tastes for prayer in the nude, a practice to which Abiezer Coppe seems to have been habituated. Even if such practices were rare and limited only to London Libertine Ranters, the image was bound to evoke a public reaction. If the poem did not state much about who the Ranters were or what they actually believed, it stated what the author, and probably the reader, thought most interesting about them.

John Reading also included a song in his treatise but insisted it was of Ranter authorship, was to be sung "to the tune of David's Psalms,"(3–4) and was sung at all Ranter meetings. This was clearly meant to be humorous. The most outrageous stanzas are presented below. (*Ranters' Ranting*)

> If Adam was deceived by Eve
> It was because he knew
> Not how to exercise the gifts
> Which Nature did imbue.
>
> The Fellow Creature which sits next
> Is more delight to me,
> Than any that I else can find
> For that she's always free.
>
> Yet whilst I speak of loving one
> Let no mistaking come.
> For we that know our liberty
> In loving all love none.
>
> Then let us rant it to the fill
> And let our love too range
> For it hath wings and they are free'st
> That in their loves do change.

Whether this poem was actually sung to the tune of David's Psalms must remain a mystery, as must the steps to the *Adamites Curranto*. The poem is more cute than licentious and probably provided good fun. The greatest virtue of this poem and of the one preceding is that both rhyme consistently, more or less.

The Ranters Ranting

The apprehending, examinations, and confession of *Iohn Collins*, *I. Shakespear*, *Tho. Wiberton*, and five more which are to answer the next Sessions. And severall songs, or catches, which were sung at their meetings. Also their severall kinds of mirth, and dancing. Their blasphemous opinions. Their belief concerning heaven and hell. And the reason why one of the same opinion cut off the heads of his own mother and brother. Set forth for the further discovery of this ungodly crew.

Printed by B. Alsop, 1650

ANTI-RANTER FUN: POEMS, PICTURES AND A PLAY

Far less serious but far more salacious was J. M.'s poem in the *The Ranter's Last Sermon* published in 1654. This poem was clearly in the poorest taste of all the literary efforts of those who found the Ranters in such poor taste. According to the author, this hymn was a permanent feature of all Ranter ceremonies.

> Oh hug them hard and suck them in
> Until they even burst your skin,
> Spread forth the crannies of those rocks
> That lie beneath your Holland smocks.
> Stretch out your limbs, sigh, heave and strain,
> Till you have opened every vein.
> That so, love's gentle juice that flows
> Like divine nectar out of those
> That press you down may run a tilt
> Into your womb and not be spilt.(5)

There was also proved many other blasphemous words and uncivil behaviour, as the kissing of one another's Breeches, more lively represented by this figure:

A somewhat different and much more serious effort can be found in the five-page poem by "J. F." entitled *A New Proclamation* (1653). This long lamentation-poem presented no new information about Ranters, but it tells us much about the author's anti-Ranter orientation and his understanding of Ranter perversity.

> O' Land! How doth thy Church to ruine run,
> By schisms broken and sects undone!
> O' how they swarm! No age could ever tell
> A brood too monstrous for their parallel.(3)

This good Anglican had good reason for shock, for by 1653 England was hip deep in sects of various types. Rather than conceiving of this latitude and religious liberty as a positive development, the author argued that contemporary anarchy had no historical precedent. Scripture, however, could provide an apt allusion to England's dissension.

> Speak out ye Jews what loss your land befell
> By suffering of one such Jezebel,
> . . . We have a hundred such
> Who act her sons.(4)

Jezebel was a curious image unless the author meant to attack Cromwell as partially responsible for England's woes. The Jews lost their land because of their sacrilege; how much worse for England with a hundred such who are described as

> O' Woeful England! Whoever thought to see
> Such wretches born and monsters bred in thee!
> But are there any such? Yea, such as these
> Ranters or Rake-hells, call them what you please.
> A Ranter! What is he? One that lives in
> All wickedness and saith he can not sin.(5)

The remainder of the poem lists all the horrid things that Ranters did.

> Oh that a man should curse, swear, whore and cry
> 'tis a delight to heaven's Majesty.

and even worse.

> He'll swear and curse and drink and hath the face
> To boast of these as characters of Grace.(5)

Even when observing their religious rituals, Ranters betrayed a true inner perversity.

> . . . they do not fail
> To call for wine, tobacco, beer and ale,
> These being the spirits they're inspired by
> Half drunk, half mad, each hath his prophecy.(6)

J. F. also wrote about Ranter social views, usually of little concern to anti-Ranter rhymesters. J. F. was no more happy about this aspect of Rantism.

> He's one that would all civil right destroy
> and turn all to a strange community.
> With each man's interest he'll have to do,
> his goods, wife, his maid and daughter too!(5)

And to summarize:

> No God, no good, no sin, no hell, no bliss,
> O' Tremble heaven and hell and earth at this!(7)

The Adamite's Curranto

THE
RANTERS
MONSTER:

Being a true Relation of one MARY ADAMS,
living at *Tillingham* in *Essex*, who named her self the Virgin
Mary, blasphemously affirming, That she was conceived with
child by the Holy Ghost; that from her should spring forth
the Savior of the world; and that all those that did not believe
in him were damn'd: With the manner how she was deliver'd
of the ugliest ill-shapen *Monster* that ever eyes beheld, and afterwards rotted away in prison: *To the great admiration of all*
those that shall read the ensuing subject; the like never before heard of.

London, Printed for *George Horton*, 1652. *May* 30

The Ranters Religion.

OR,

A faithfull and infallible Narrative of their damnable and
diabolical opinions, with their deteſtable lives & actions.

With a true diſcovery of ſome of their late prodigious
pranks, and unparalleld deportments, with a paper of
moſt blaſphemous Verſes found in one of their pockets,
againſt the Majeſty of Almighty God, and the moſt ſa-
cred Scriptures, rendred *verbatim*.

Publiſhed by Authority.

Behold theſe
are Ranters.

London, Printed for *R. H.* 1650.

Scandalous treatises, alleged eye-witness humorous accounts, funny pictures, and dirty poems do not exhaust the literary talent expended upon Ranters. The most ambitious effort was Samuel Sheppard's 1651 five-act play about Ranters entitled *The Jovial Crew, or, The Devil Turned Ranter*. Despite its limitations, which included difficulties with plot development, characterization, dramatic action, and language, this play poked good fun at the Ranters and demonstrates how much this group had caught the contemporary English imagination. The title page tells us this comedy contains the "cursed conversations, prodigious pranks, monstrous meetings, private performances, rude revellings, garrulous greetings, impious and incorrigible deportments" of the Ranters, all of which sounded like great fun.

The play covers most of the themes we have encountered in other anti-Ranter writings. There is little emphasis on conceptual matters such as Ranter religious or political ideas, and the author seemed content to treat the Ranters exclusively as sexual libertines. In keeping with the other anti-Ranter literature we have seen, women are the worse sexual offenders and are given the most lascivious lines. Indeed, with some slight modification, the play might be about flappers in the 1920s or coeds during the 1960s sexual revolution. Unfortunately, the music for the enclosed lyrics is unknown because the author did not include a score.

The first act opens with a discussion between Dose, an apothecary, and Apostasus, described as "a sometimes Episcopalian and scholar." Dose, wearing a bandage over his bloodied head enters and says, "This cap you see covers a cruel wound. I was yesternight with a crew of those who talk of heaven and of a place of torment, to whom, when I began to preach our doctrine, one of the company with a pewter pot struck me upon the head with all his might."(1) Apostasus is sympathetic and gives an indication of the Ranter beliefs they espouse and for which Dose was beaten. "By our only sacred laws, every man's wife must be at his friend's use" and he complains about Mr. Pigwidgen, a fellow Ranter who "is content to rant with other women but to expose his own spouse he denies."(2) Dose agrees, adding his own distaste for marriage vows and "that men should be such fools to pinion their own arms and tie their own legs and propose such strange nothings to themselves on purpose, to keep themselves in awe when they could but perceive their happiness . . . is solely theirs."(1) The two Ranters head for their favorite tavern called "Sychophantio's" where Dose is planning to drug Mr. Pigwidgen "so while he sleeps, I'll use his wife before him and 'twill be rare sport."(2) Dose considers this "a meritorious work" and sagely observes "we must sometimes save souls against their wills."(2)

302

To emphasize how dastardly Ranters were, the author introduces the Devil and his helper Pandorses to testify on their behalf. The Devil, certainly an authority on evil, says, "I have surveyed the universe, as France, Spain, and Italy, yet can not parallel the Ranters of this our English climate. I've blinded them with pleasure of this world by putting on a mask of religion to make it no sin, that makes my proselytes run head long down to the infernal lake . . . into the infernal flames at length they're cast."(2)

After it has been established that Ranters are immoral and in league with the Devil, the next scene takes place in the Ranter tavern where we are presented with the full cast of female Ranter characters, all holding hands and dancing and singing. Other than Dose and Apostasus, whom we have already encountered, there are the Ranter wives Mrs. Minks, Wriggle, Fulsome, Crave-Drink, Dissimulatio, All-Prate, and Incorrigible. As they dance, they sing the following song:

> Come my boys, receive your joys
> And take your fill of pleasure.
> Shoot for shoot, away let's do'it
> But we must have our measure.
>
> All lie down as in a swoon
> To have a pleasing vision
> And then rise with bared thighs
> Who'd fear such sweet incision?
>
> No hell we dread when we are dead
> No gorgon nor no fury.
> And while we live, we'll drink and——
> In spite of judge or jury.

Between each of the stanzas all sing the chorus of

> Come away, make no delay,
> Of mirth we are no scanters.
> Dance and sing all in a ring,
> For we are the Jovial Ranters.(3)

The second act introduces two new actors, Mrs. Idlesby and Mrs. Do-Little, both of whom wish to join the Ranters without their husbands' knowledge. One says to the other, "Gossip, if I am not on fire to be acquainted with some of this new sect." The other replies, "Without doubt,

The Prologue.

Bedlam broke loose? yes, *Hell* is open'd too:
Mad-men, & *Fiends*, & *Harpies* to your view
We do present: but who shall cure the *Tumor*?
All the world now is in the *Ranting Humor*.

THE
JOVIALL CREVV, 7

OR,

The Devill turn'd *RANTER*:

Being a Character of
The roaring Ranters *of these Times.*

Reprefented in a

COMEDIE,

CONTAINING

A true Difcovery of the curfed Con-
verfations, prodigious Pranks, monftrous
Meetings, private Performances, rude Revellings,
garrulous Greetings, impious and incorrigible
Deporements of a Sect (lately fprung up a-
mongft us) called *Ranters*.

Their Names forted to their feverall Natures,
and both lively prefented in Action.

London: Printed for *W. Ley.* 1651.

1650

they are a rare society, lead heavenly lives, nothing but acting good for one another, drinking love-healths and amorous deportments." Other comments passing between these ladies include, "I am resolved to be of their religion and go to heaven the nearest way" and both agree that such should be their goal, despite "what our impotent husbands will allow."(4) Clearly, the plot is thickening.

The next scene takes us back to Sychophantio's Tavern where all the chamber pots, vessels and jars have been filled with wine. All the Ranters are drinking and sporting with the women becoming sexually agitated while the men just get drunk. Mrs. Wriggle says to several males, "I thank you fellow creatures, I'll serve either of you, soul and body." Not wishing to be neglected, Mrs. Crave-Drink adds, "Have I a dog's face that I'm so neglected?"(6) Everyone continues to drink with the men engaging in much loose talk and with the women indicating their desire for less talk and more sex. Among the stanzas the women sing are the following:

> Come some man or other
> And make me a mother,
> Let no man fear for to board me.
> Come as many as will
> I will give' em their fill
> And thank' em for what they afford me.
>
> . . .
>
> Come any strong rogue
> That would fain disimbogue
> Let's mingle and try who's the strongest
> I fain would comply.
> With him that dare vie
> To stand to his tackling the longest.(7)

The men too sing a song, but a far less bawdy one. Finally Mr. Asnego says, "Sweet Mrs. All-Prate, I grow proud beneath a navel and must need crave your aid."(8) Apostasus adds, "Here's a health to all our friends in Kent, let her pledge me that dares make a 'Beast-with-two Backs' before the whole society."(8)

Act Three sees the two new members introduced to the Ranter assembly where they are welcomed with wine and kisses. Tobacco, too, is passed

ANTI-RANTER FUN: POEMS, PICTURES AND A PLAY

about the group with Mrs. Pigwidgen saying, "Let the stream of the strong Indian weed involve us as we sit in the clouds"(10) which reminds one less of English Ovals than Mary Jane. When all the Ranters feel the wine and smokes, they gather in a circle and sing:

> By goats' desires and monkeys' heat
> Spanish flies and stirring meat,
> By the vigor of a horse
> By all things of strength and force
>
> We adopt this happy pair
> Of our liberties to share
> Arise, arise, blessed souls and know
> Now you may rant, *cum priviligio.*

Unfortunately for the two new Ranters, their initiation night would be dull. Spolario, the Bar Keep, pours the wine containing Dose's drugs, and the entire assembly fall asleep on the floor. Spolario then calls a constable and a lorry takes all the Ranters to Finsbury Prison.

Act Four finds all our Ranters in jail, slowly coming out of their drunken sleep. They laugh when they learn how they were apprehended. The husbands of the two new members are brought into the men's cell and inquire about the assembly's religious beliefs. Apostasus speaks for the community and explains that in being a Ranter "you believe you are the best servants to heaven when you roar the loudest, drink deepest, swear profoundest, whore the oftenest, swear the execrablest, and rant the highest."(13) In addition, "you acknowledge yourselves obliged to prostrate each man his wife to the use of his fellow creatures" and last "that you have taken an oath . . . to be drunk at least five times a week and so use your utmost endeavor to convert all out of their faith to our manner of life and worship."(13) The husbands are so enraged by what they hear that they proceed to beat all the Ranters.

The fifth and final act presents a confrontation between the two new Ranter members and their non-Ranter husbands. Mrs. Idlesby says, "For heaven's sake husband, pardon me,"(14) with her husband replying, "Thou are beyond the bounds of absolution." Mrs. Do-Little also asks forgiveness but her husband replies, "I'll get me a new mate." The husbands turn to the prison beadle and request, "Lash my wife well prithee, I'll pay thee for it."(15) And so ends our play.

BLASPHEMY, IMMORALITY, AND ANARCHY

While this was not first class literature, the author succeeded in writing a humorous play. There were jokes, puns, songs, sexual innuendo, outraged husbands, devils and drugs. Not everyone took the Ranters so seriously as did Messers Tickell and Rosewell.

To conclude this chapter, we will include one last poem entitled *A Total Rout, or a Brave Discovery of a Pack of Knaves and Drabs. . . .* written in 1653. As in many other poems, the author was half serious and half humorous when he asked the Ranters to buck up and walk right. Though quite long, the following stanzas well express the mood of the author, who did not add his name to his creation. Once again, unfortunately, we must make do without the music, for the author did not include his score.

Come leave your 'God-Dammees' and hearken to me,
O' tis pity that fuel for Hell you should be.
Your spirits heroic will quickly be quelled,
When once the General Sessions are held.

Chorus: But hark my poor Ranter, I'll tell thee a tale
      Thy cursings and bannings will buy thee no ale.

You stole 'way their smocks and petticoats all,
Besides did not pay 'um for what you did call.
Fie, Fie, my base Ranter, this is but poor,
A shabbed come off to plunder a whore.

Chorus: But hang't my poor Ranter, thou can'st not devise,
      To daube up the constables mouth with thy lies.

Now off goes the silver lace from the coat,
The buttons, so needless, and the points too to boot.
Two shirts are too many and rather than fail
One must be changed for tobacco and ale.

Chorus: Then hang't call a Broker, and let him brink chink,
      We'll sell him our hats, yea, our heads, for good drink.

But oh my poor Ranter, thus tattered and torn,
And almost as naked as ere you were born.
what means't thou to live so damnably base,
And die in a jail 'tis a desperate case.
Damnation and hell comes posting together,

And without repentence thou shalt suffer either,
Thy cursed 'God-Dammees' and damnable cheats,
Ungodly endeavors and horrible feats,
Are all cable ropes to draw thee to hell,
But yet, prithee, Ranter Serpent, so farewell!

Conclusion

The Ranters were the latest expression of a two-thousand-year tradition of religious dualism which divided existence between the material and the spiritual, the dark and the light, the rich and the poor, the Satanic and the divine. They were, however, also a product of the seventeenth-century civil war conflict and interregnum confusion which occasioned the destruction of England's most fundamental institutions and witnessed the inability of England's established classes to create new ones. In terms of both the past and the present, the Ranters were the children of anarchy.

Contemporaries dismissed the Ranters as cranks, madmen and lunatics because they would not accept the logic of current political, economic and religious institutions, and they soon became the very image of all that was personally, morally and socially unacceptable. Not content to focus their dissent on any one specific religious, political or social issue, Ranters rejected the premises upon which rational ideas might be accepted at all. No single policy was ever at fault: the existence of policy-making institutions was the essential problem. Hence, authoritarian Presbyterians certainly considered the Ranters dangerous radicals, but they were equally disliked by almost everyone else seeking to play at the game of public governance in the name of some greater good. Ranters made Cromwell fume and Hobbes shake, and other sectarians attempted to salvage their own reputations by attacking them. Englishmen may have agreed on little else, but all were of one mind when it came to the Blasphemy Act and what should be done with people so reprehensible as to deny the validity of the social process in its entirety.

Ranters had no respect for God's true church, and even less regard for the government of the Christian prince. Worse than that, from the Presbyterian perspective, the Ranters did not believe in the sanctity of property, perhaps the most obvious sign of God's pleasure with his true saints. But the very worst offense was that Ranters behaved like animals; they sang, whistled and danced, drank, smoked, hooted and whored. Sexual Libertine Ranters were even worse. Even seemingly moral individuals like Coppin taught the inflammatory concept of universal grace, that great spiritualist battering ram against social and religious privilege. In an age where divine sanction provided the right to rule and the possession of property was a tangible sign of God's predestined good pleasure with his true saints while poverty was proof of sin and damnation, the idea that God loved all equally and would eventually save all was too radical, disgusting, and obviously unacceptable. Even worse, such ideas might undermine property.

From almost every perspective, the Ranters were terrible indeed. And yet, those making this harsh judgment had only just executed a king, split the country into two and turned class against class, religion against religion, and purged and hobbled Parliament once, twice and three times to create a virtual caricature of governance. And if that were not sufficient, one need only mention the glorious role played by Puritan divines and local JPs against another real danger to the commonwealth, England's witches. The Ranters were disreputable, but, strange to say, they were also representative of a large segment of the English population whose voice, that of experienced apathy or disgust, is not often heard.

Historians have often told us about the concerns and issues dividing the established classes. More recently, scholars have written about those radicals accepting the premise of legitimate government but wishing a wider franchise for greater commoner participation in that system. Historians have been less successful describing that largest part of the population remaining on the sidelines, convinced they would play no role and reap no benefit from transpiring events. This part of the population remained, as always, silent, but the Ranters come closest to expressing their sentiments. If the Levellers were the bridge connecting the lower class radicals in the army with Parliamentary and governmental legitimacy, the Ranters were the bridge between that frustrated and defeated Leveller radicalism, which increasingly expressed itself in sectarianism, and the large number of people who would simply watch events, knowing nothing good for them would come of it all. If the Levellers provided the religious-conceptual ideology of hope seeking a greater role within the world's institutions, Rantism was the frustrated cry of despair which hated the world it could not inherit and erected a dualistic conceptual edifice to explain God and the Devil, good and evil, the haves and the have-nots.

The Ranters tell us about the sentiments of the poor in this age of other people's social idealism and others people's political reform and they come closest to representing the common man normally abused both by institutions of power and then by those who overthrow those institutions. We have observed how most Ranters simply did not differentiate between the claims of Parliament and those of monarchy. Both were considered property-class institutions primarily existing from their exploitation of the poor. The king stole Tany's horse and deprived him of his living, and Parliament's actions did not encourage hope it would be returned. The horse was gone, Parliament invented new taxes and while Tany was mad, he did not delude himself with the utopian foolishness of social programs. Sentiments of loyalty for the army were quickly abused by Cromwell. Bauthumley, Freeman, Norwood and Salmon were all thrown out of the army in the general purge of radicals of 1650–1651. Any small measure of idealism that might have survived was frustrated by the outrage of increasingly severe economic inequality. Freeman vividly described those who had neither food to eat nor clothing with which to cover their broken and bloated bodies, and Clarkson, Coppe and Foster wrote of the need for economic relief. George Foster could conceive of no programs of reform to ameliorate the condition of the poor. His best effort was a vision in which a strong general-king literally threw money at the poor from the window of the treasury building. Coppe was more direct and wrote about cutting the throats of the rich and taking their wealth. Clarkson was so cynical about the possibility of reform that he ridiculed every socially acceptable view and argument to demonstrate how society would use the very call for reform as the basis for delivering even greater tyranny and abuse. Perhaps Clarkson's "What can we do? Nothing" is too pessimistic for a modern generation of scholars raised with a political ethic of beneficial change. In fact, Clarkson was correct, for nothing did come of the interregnum; even those reforms coming a generation later in 1688 did not benefit Freeman's naked and starving poor and would not have gotten Tany a horse.

It may have been despair that led some Ranters to envision change in apocalyptic terms. In this universal battle of saints against the rest of the world, Foster would have everyone die or become soulless dogs and chickens, while the early Salmon dreamed of a class war in which the common soldiers rebelled against officers, a war which in turn led to a universal conflict against all others. Unlike the Fifth Monarchists and other millenarians conceiving of the battle of Gog and Magog as part of God's unfolding plan for the world, Ranter apocalypticians were bitter, impotent social observers knowing in their bones that nothing short of the hate-filled wrath of a vengeful God could bring about the justice they sought. They could speak for this angry God because they, like him, had been alienated by the forces of Satan.

The Ranters' writings tell us much about the classic qualities of life and what concerned people during the interregnum. Franklin and Gadbury assure us that every age possesses charlatans who use their social charm to attract and then bilk humbler folk of their money and their pride. John and Mary Robins indicate how these charlatans may actually believe in their own divinity. John Pordage reminds us that intellectual abuse is not the

CONCLUSION

province of the ignorant and illiterate alone. The ignorant Robins believed he could raise the dead, but the educated Pordage believed he fought spiritual dragons and pirates brandishing swords and was the associate of friendly spirits everywhere. The credulity of their followers, then as now, attracted the professional handwringers such as Thomas Edwards, John Tickell and Sidrach Simpson, and led to the creation of governmental committees such as those which ejected Pordage. But it was no more possible for society then to protect the innocent from religious chicanery than it is for today's governments to protect the common man from cults, the claims of diet pill manufacturers and salesmen of aluminum siding. Thomas Webb reminds us of all the tasteless people we have known who abuse the public's patience.

The most important spiritual message found in the writings of these simple "mechanic preachers" is the unadorned religiosity finding no contemporary institutional expression. Like many others, Ranters found the fetish of religious ritual spiritually withering and believed that without social morality there was no true religiosity and no spirituality. Ranters attacked the tithe, censorship and other ecclesiastical restraints that defended corrupt institutions solely bent upon the aggrandizement of those in power. If Ranters went further than others and also rejected conventional concepts of heaven and hell, they did so because religious teaching had converted these concepts into Pavlovian rewards for adhering to human institutions carrying out policies of greed in God's name. If Ranters rejected prayer, they did so out of shame for humanity's lack of shame in calling upon the cosmic bellhop every time some new refreshment was desired. If Ranters removed God from the world it was because they believed God could have found a better representative than Bishop Laud, or the Presbyterians, and could not possibly have ordained Parliament to represent his best interests. And if some Ranters practiced a personal immorality predicated upon the deification of the self, what was this, in Clarkson's or Coppe's words, compared to organized religion's tacit ordination of private property and gleeful acceptance of a double supralapsarian predestination-based starvation of obvious sinners as an expression of God's love? Because of the cynicism, the legal harassment and abuse, the economic privation and distrust of all government, Ranters believed that the social system did not reflect God's desires and that wisdom lay in knowing the way back to his purity and goodness.

Despite all that has been written about the legislated godliness of the 'Puritan Revolution' and the attempt to create a society of saints, Ranter writings indicate that many seventeenth-century Englishmen took the social possibilities of religion no more seriously than have any other people at any other time. The anti-Ranter writings confirm the openly sexual Ranter boisterousness and fun that even non-Ranters might experience, if only vicariously. The Ranters demonstrated that churches are important but that taverns are too and that there is probably as much abuse and spirituality found in the one as in the other. Most of the anonymous treatises make clear that the Ranters were in fact terrific fun and there can be no doubting that Samuel Sheppard, the author of that silly play about Ranters, *The Jovial Crew*, thought them a better subject than Puritans or Quakers. Many sectarian and orthodox anti-Ranters authors may have been shocked by the Ranters but the anonymous tracts do not give evidence so much of Puritan disapproval as of jealousy or just plain fun. It is reasonable to assume that most Puritans such as Edwards were as unhappy with salacious anti-Ranter writings as they were with the Ranters themselves.

By 1660 Cromwell was dead, the New Model Army was gone and the Levellers were just a memory. Coppe no longer preached in the nude, Clarkson had become a boring and sanctimonious Muggletonian, Anonymous was over his midlife crisis and was probably married again, and Tany had died attempting to reach Holland in a rowboat. Thomas Webb was a Fifth Monarchist, Pordage a follower of Boehm, but worse yet, Salmon was depressed, and Bauthumley was a librarian. By this time the Ranter rank and file were all Quakers, who, in turn, were becoming more sedate. Rantism could not last because it proved too difficult to sustain for long the paranoia of the dualist's hatred of the world, the alienated person's fear of powerful institutions, the hope that God exists, somewhere, and the sensualism born out of fear that nothing else does exist. In the end, the Quakers took what was spiritually best and discarded most of what made the Ranters so radical and so interesting. Indeed, with the restoration of monarchy and restrictive religious legislation the sectarian moment was over. But even if radical sectarianism diminished, England would not be without amusing troublemakers in the future. By 1660 Charles II was back, Parliament was in session once again, the Church of England was the official religion of the realm and the social problems originally contributing to the civil wars would soon be apparent once more.

Notes

1. *Encyclopaedia Britannica*, 11 ed. (New York, 1910–1911), vol. 22, p. 895.

2. Rufus M. Jones, *Studies in Mystical Religion* (London, 1923) p. 467.

3. George Fox, *Journals* (London, 1902), vol. 1, p. 47, and following citations are vol. 1., p. 199 and p. 95.

4. Concerning these ancient and medieval heresies, the reader might consult the following: T. Whittaker, *The Neoplatonists*, 2nd ed. (Cambridge, England, 1918); S. Pétrement, *Le dualisme chez Platon, les gnostiques et les manichéens* (Paris, 1947); E. R. Goodenough, *By Light, By Light; the Mystic Gospel of Hellenistic Judaism* (Oxford, 1935); R. McL. Wilson, *The Gnostic Problem: A Study of the Relations Between Hellenistic Judaism and the Gnostic Heresy* (London, 1958); J. Duchesne-Guillemin, *Zoroastre* (Paris, 1948) and, *The Western Response to Zoroastre* (Oxford, 1958).

Gnosticism: Robert M. Grant, *Gnosticism and Early Christianity* (New York, 1959) and *Gnosticism: A Sourcebook of Heretical Writings* (New York, 1961); G. Quispel, *Gnosis als Weltreligion* (Zurich, 1951); Hans Jonas, *The Gnostic Religion*, 2nd. ed. (Boston, 1963); E. de Faye, *Gnostiques et Gnosticisme* 2nd. ed. (Paris, 1925); H. Leisegang, *Die Gnosis*, 4th ed. (Stuttgart, 1955); L. G. Ryland, *The Beginning of Gnostic Christianity* (London, 1940).

Manichaeism; F. C. Burkitt, *The Religion of the Manichees* (Cambridge, England, 1925); H. C. Puech, *Le Manichéisme, son fondatuer, sa doctrine* (Paris, 1949); G. Windengren, *The Great Vohu Manah and the Apostle of God: Studies in Iranian and Manichaean Religion* (Uppsala, 1945) and, *Mesopotamian Elements in Manichaeism: Studies in Manichaean, Mandaean, and Syrian-Gnostic Religion* (Uppsala-Leipzig, 1946) and *Mani and Manichaeism* (London, 1965; New York, 1966).

Messalians, Paulicians, Bogomils and Cathari: Steven Runciman, *The Medieval Manichee: A Study of the Christian Dualist Heresy* (Cambridge, England, 1947) and, *History of the First Bulgarian Empire* (London, 1930); M. Spinka, *A History of Christianity in the Balkans* (Chicago, 1933); V. N. Sharenkoff, *A Study of Manichaeanism in Bulgaria* (New York, 1927); H. Söderberg, *La religion des Cathares* (Uppsala, 1949); Joseph R. Stayer, *The*

NOTES

Albigensian Crusade (New York, 1971); Savino Savini, *Il Catarismo itali-ano ed i suovi vescovi nei seculo xiii e xiv* (Florence, 1958); Walter l. Wake-field, *Heresy, Crusade and Inquisition in Southern France* (Berkeley, 1974); M. D. Lambert, *Medieval Heresy: Popular Movements from Bogomil to Hus* (London, 1977).

Joachimism and Brethren of the Free Spirit: Margerie Reeves, *The In-fluence of Prophecy in the Later Middle Ages: A Study of Joachimism* (Ox-ford, 1969); C. T. Berkhout and J. B. Russell, *Medieval Heresies: A Bibliog-raphy* (Toronto, 1981); and by Russell, *Religious Dissent in the Middle Ages* (New York/London, 1971). Edward Peters, *Heresy and Authority in Medieval Europe* (Philadelphia, 1980); Ernest W. McDonnell, *The Be-guines and Beghards in Medieval Culture* (New Brunswick, 1954); Raoul Manselli, *Spirituali e Beghini in Provenza* (Rome, 1959); Dayton Philips, *Beguines in Medieval Strasbourg* (Stanford, 1941); Robert E. Lerner, *The Heresy of the Free Spirit in the Middle Ages* (Berkeley, 1972); Gordon Leff, *Heresy in the Later Middle Ages*, 2 vol., (Manchester, 1967); Romana Guar-nieri, "Il movimento del Libero Spirito," *Archivo Italiano per la storia della pietà* 4 (1965) 351–708; W. Miller and Jared W. Scudder, *Wessel Gans-fort: Life and Writings (New York/London, 1917);* Jerome Friedman, *Mi-chael Servetus: A Case Study in Total Heresy* (Geneva, 1978); Claudio Man-zoni, *Umanesimo ed eresia: Michele Serveto* (Naples, 1974).

Libertines: for Loy Pruystinck, see Julius Frederich's *De Secte der Loisten of Antwerpsche Libertijnen (1525–1545); Eligius Pruystinck (Loy de Schaliedekker) en zijne aanhangers* (Gent, 1891); John Calvin, *Contre la secte phantastique et furieuse des libertines qui se nomment spirituelz* and, *Epistre contre un certain Cordelier suppost de la secte des Libertines*, both in his *Opera Omina*, ed. Baum et al. (Brunswick, 1864–1900) vol 35. Cal-vin's works have been translated by Benjamin Wirt Farley, *John Calvin: Treatises Against the Anabaptists and Against the Libertines* (Grand Rap-ids, 1982). See Farley's good introductory essay, pages 161–186, for an eval-uation of the secondary literature concerning sixteenth century.

5. See for instance Robert Barclay, *The Inner Life of the Religious Societies of the Commonwealth* (London, 1876); W. C. Braithwaite, *The Beginnings of Quakerism*, 2nd ed. (Cambridge, England, 1955) and, *The Second Period of Quakerism*, 2nd ed. (Cambridge, England, 1961); Rufus Jones, *Studies in Mystical Religion* (New York, 1923); *Spiritual Reformers in the 16th and 17th Centuries* (London, 1914, 1923 etc.); *The Quakers in the American Colonies* (New York, London, 1923); *The Later Periods of Quakerism*, (London, 1921). And more recently, Hugh Barbour, *The Quakers in Puritan England* (New Haven, 1964) and Barry Raey, *The*

Quakers and the English Revolution (London, 1985). See the bibliography for additional listings.

6. Unitarians: See the many articles written by Alexander Gordon in the DNB, and his *Heads of English Unitarian History* (London, 1895). Most important are the works by Earl Morse Wilbur, *A History of Unitarianism*, 2 vols. (Cambridge, Mass. 1945) and *The Socinian-Unitarian Movement: A Bibliography* (Rome, 1950). The most recent work is by H. J. McLackland, *Socinianism in 17th-Century England* (Oxford, 1951). The reader might also consult the *Transactions of the Unitarian-Universalist Society*.

Baptists: L. F. Brown, *The Political Activities of the Baptists and the Monarchy Men in England during the Interregnum* (Washington D.C., 1912); A. Taylor, *The History of English General Baptists*, vol. 1. (London, 1818); E. A. Payne, *The Baptists of Berkshire* (London, 1951). Also, consult the many articles on this period in the *Transaction of the Baptist Historical Society*.

7. The literature on the Levellers is large indeed. The reader might consult the following by William Haller: *Liberty and Reformation in the Puritan Revolution* (New York, 1955); with Godfrey Davies, ed. *The Leveller Tracts* (New York, 1944); *Tracts on Liberty in the Puritan Revolution*, 3 vols. (New York, 1934); *The Rise of Puritanism* (New York, 1938). Also, A. Gibb, *John Lilburne, the Leveller* (London, 1947); D. Wolfe, *Leveller Manifestos of the Puritan Revolution* (New York, 1944); A. S. P. Woodhouse, *Puritanism and Liberty* (London, 1938); Perez Zagorin, *A History of Political Thought in the English Revolution* (London, 1954); David Petegorsky, *Leftwing Democracy in the English Civil War* (London, 1940); T. C. Pease, *The Leveller Movement* (Washington, 1916); David Petegorsky, *Leftwing Democracy in the English Civil War* (London, 1940); Howard C. Shaw, *The Levellers* (London, 1968); Henry N. Brailsford, *The Levellers and the English Revolution* (Stanford, 1971). A volume with a particularly large annotated bibliography is Michael Mullett, *Radical Religious Movements in Early Modern Europe* (London, 1980).

The Diggers, while receiving some attention in many of the above, have also been studied by the following: L. H. Berens, *The Digger Movement in the Days of the Commonwealth* (London, 1906); T. Wilson Hayes, *Winstanley the Digger* (Cambridge, Mass. 1979); W. H. G. Armytage, *Heavens Below: Utopian Experiments in England, 1560–1960* (Toronto, 1961); Christopher Hill, *The Religion of Gerrard Winstanley* (Past and Present Supplement, vol. 5, Oxford, 1978). Further, the reader should consult the bibliography in this volume and those of the above as well.

8. The reader might consult the following regarding the Fifth Monarchists and the English apocalyptic tradition: Philip K. Christianson, *Reformers in Babylon: Apocalyptic Visions from the Reformation to the Eve of the Civil War* (Toronto, 1978); Bryan W. Ball, *A Great Expectation, Eschatological Thought in English Protestantism to 1660* (Leiden, 1975); L. F. Brown, *The Political Activities of the Baptists and Fifth Monarchy Men in England during the Interregnum* (Washington, D.C., 1912); B. S. Capp, *The Fifth Monarchy Men: a Study in 17th Century Millenarianism* (London, 1972); Katharine R. Firth, *The Apocalyptic Tradition in Reformation Britian, 1530–1645* (Oxford, 1979); W. M. Lamont, *Godly Rule: Politics and Religion 1603–1660* (Cambridge, England, 1969); Philip G. Rogers, *The Fifth Monarchy Men* (Oxford, 1966); Peter Toon, ed. *Puritans, the Millenium, and the Future of Israel: Puritan Eschatology 1600–1660* (Cambridge, 1970). For the relationship between millenarianism and secular futuristic movements, see Norman Cohn, *The Pursuit of the Millenium* (New York, 1961).

9. Familists: The two most recent studies are Jean D. Moss, *"Godded with God": Hendrik Niclaes and His Family of Love* (Philadelphia, 1981); Alastair Hamilton, *The Family of Love* (Cambridge, England, 1981); concerning the Ranters, see A. L. Morton, *The World of the Ranters* (London, 1970). Additional references to other literature about the Ranters can be found in notes number 21, 22 and 25. Concerning the Muggletonians, first cousins to the above, see Christopher Hill; Barry Reay and William Lamont, *The World of the Muggletonians* (London, 1983). Since publication, two of these authors have disagreed concerning the primacy of Reeve and/or Muggleton. See Lamont's "The Muggletonians, 1652–1979: A Vertical Approach." *Past and Present*, n. 99 (May, 1983) pages 22–40. Hill's rejoinder and Lamont's subsequent rebuttal are: Hill, "The Muggletonians," *Past and Present*, n. 104 (August, 1984) pages 153–158; W. Lamont, "A Rejoinder," *Past and Present*, n. 104 (August, 1984) pages 159–163.

10. Rufus M. Jones, *Mystical Religion*, p. 467; following citations from pages 467–81.

11. Christopher Hill, *The World Turned Upside Down* (London, 1972). The Ranters do not seem to find their own feet in this otherwise excellent volume. Chapter 9 tells us about "Seekers and Ranters" and chap. 10 (—) about "Ranters and Quakers." But are two half loaves of different breads the same as one whole loaf?

12. George Williams, *The Radical Reformation* (Philadelphia, 1962).

13. G. F. S. Ellens, "The Ranters Ranting: Reflections on a Ranting Counter Culture," *Church History*, vol. 40, n. 3 (1971) p. 91–107.

NOTES

14. Frank J. McGregor, *The Ranters*, Oxford B. Litt. Degree Thesis. Dated November 1968, n. 1434; And also, "Seekers and Ranters," *Radical Religion in the English Revolution*, edited by J. F. McGregor and B. Raey. (Oxford, 1984).

15. A. L. Morton, *The World of the Ranters* (London, 1970). More of a collection of general essays than a true analysis of Rantism, this volume has one general chapter on Ranters, one on Clarkson with the remaining five chapters devoted to aspects of Leveller democratic thought. Nonetheless, it is very useful.

16. Norman Cohn, *The Pursuit of the Millenium* (New York, 1961).

17. Nigel Smith, ed. *A Collection of Ranter Writings* (London, 1983). Selections by Coppe, Clarkson, Salmon and Bauthumley and a good introduction by Smith.

18. The literature concerning the civil wars and the interregnum is very great indeed. A good general account and good bibliography of the standard literature in a variety of diverse areas from economics to music to ecclesiastical and legal affairs is Godfrey Davies' *The Early Stuarts, 1603–1660*, 2nd. ed. (Oxford, 1959), expecially pages 416–443 for the bibliography. C. Hill, from note 11 is the best source for radical ideas.

19. Concerning the army, see C. H. Firth, *Cromwell's Army: A History of the English Soldier During the Civil Wars, the Commonwealth and the Protectorate*. 4th ed. (Oxford, 1962) and also L. F. Solt, *Saints in Arms: Puritanism and Democracy in Cromwell's Army* (Stanford, 1959).

20. The standard history of agricultural prices is James E. Thorold Rogers, *History of Agriculture and Prices* (1866–1902) vol. 5, p. 205. Also, see Margaret James, *Social Problems and Policy during the Puritan Revolution, 1640–1660* (London, 1930) p. 278.

21. See George W. Daniels, *The Early English Cotton Industry* (Manchester, 1920); Also, Ephraim Lipson, *The History of the Woolen and Worsted Industries* (London, 1921).

22. See E. M. Leonard, *The Early History of English Poor Relief* (Cambridge, England, 1900), (1965). More recently, A. L. Beier, "Poor Relief in Warwickshire," *Past and Present*, n. 35 (December, 1966) pages 77–100.

23. See H. Scobell, *A Collection of Acts and Ordinances. . . .* (London, 1658) part 2, p. 124126. Also see Jones, 478ff and Cohn, 331ff. For information concerning courts at this time, the reader might consult Sir James Stephen, *A History of the Criminal Law of England* 3 volumes (London, 1883) and the introduction to James Tait's *Lancashire Quarter Session Records* (London, Manchester, 1917). Concerning the criminal system in general, the reader might consult Cynthia B. Herrup, "Law and

NOTES

Morality in Seventeenth-Century England," *Past and Present*, n. 106, pages 102–123. The footnotes to this article are complete and will provide the active reader with a great many works dealing with almost every aspect of the social function of law and the court system. For additional sources, in this matter as well as others, the reader is directed to Godfrey Davies, *The Early Stuarts, 1603–1660*, 2nd ed. (Oxford, 1959).

24. John Thurloe, *The State Papers of John Thurloe*, ed. Birch. (1742) vol. 3, III, 468.

25. *Records of the Borough of Leicester*, ed. Helen Stockes (1923) p. 236 and Joan Simon, *The Two John Angels*, Transactions of the Leicester Arch. and Historical Society. n. 41, p. 39ff.

26. *Perfect Diurnal*, March 11–18, 1650; *Whitlock Memorials*, March 14, 1650.

27. *The Man in the Moon*, March 13–20, 1650.

28. G. Fox, *Journals* p. 182–83.

29. Concerning Jewish Messianic expectation and the year 1656, see Gershom Scholem, *Sabbatai Sevi, The Mystical Messiah* (Princeton, 1973); Abba H. Silver, *A History of Messianic Speculation in Israel* (New York, 1927; Boston, 1959). See also Peter Toon, *Puritans, the Millenium and the Future of Israel* (Cambridge, England, 1970). The reader might also consult Lucien Wolf's standard work, *Menasseh ben Israel's Mission to Oliver Cromwell* (London, 1901), and more recently, David S. Katz, *Philosemitism and the Re-Admission of the Jews to England* (Oxford, 1982).

30. *Mercurious Fumigosus*, n. 32, January 3–10, 1655, p. 252.

31. The reader might consult the following about the nature of medieval exegesis; B. Smalley, *The Study of the Bible in the Middle Ages*, 2nd. ed. (London, 1952); Henri de Lubac, *Exegese Médiéval; Les Quatre Sens de l'Ecriture*, 4 vols. (Paris, 1959+); C. Spicq, *Escuisse d'une histoire de l'exégèse latine au Moyen Age* (Paris, 1944); J. S. Preus, *From Shadow to Promise; Old Testament Interpretation from Augustine to the Young Luther* (Cambridge, Mass., 1969).

32. The following volumes should help the reader concerning Reformation age and Protestant exegesis; S. L. Greenslade, ed., *The Cambridge History of the Bible: The Reformation to the Present Day* (Cambridge, 1963); E. G. Kraeling, *The Old Testament Since the Reformation* (London, 1955); David Daitches, *The King James Version of the English Bible* (Chicago, 1941); Jerome Friedman, *The Most Ancient Testimony; Sixteenth Century Christian Hebraica in the Age of Renaissance Nostalgia* (Athens, Ohio, 1983). Part Three, "Scripture and the Myth of the Past," pages 120–78.

NOTES

33. Further information about Lefevre method can be found in Friedman, *Ancient Testimony*, pages 81 and 132. Also, see Heiko Oberman, *Forerunners of the Reformation* (New York, Chicago, San Francisco, 1966).

34. Luther's general ignorance of Hebrew has been largely overlooked by historians far more interested in demonstrating the widsom of his translations from the Hebrew Old Testament Scripture than in asking how he managed to do it. Most scholars gloss over the issue by subscribing to the old excuse that he knew a little Hebrew and had use of resident Hebraists' skills. Luther himself tells us that he saw little need for grammar or philology when translating the Hebrew text. He was not in the least defensive about his ignorance of Hebrew, how rules of grammar and other "formalities" were of little value and how he was able to teach his Hebraists the real meaning of the words. Luther has been the subject of the work of a great many scholars but the following should help the reader appreciate his linguistic skills: Friedman, *Ancient Testimony*; W. Schwarz, *Principles and Problems of Biblical Translation*, (Cambridge England, 1955); H. Bornkamm, *Luther and the Old Testament* (Philadelphia, 1969).

Bucer knew Hebrew well and was well aware of the difference between translating the text and forcing the text to bear a preconceived interpretation. He was completely at home with, and praised, such Jewish literalists as Ibn Ezra, David Kimchi, and others as well. It was his exceptional understanding of the theoretical problems involved with translation as well as the languages themselves that led him to refer to himself as a "paraprast" rather than a translator though his Scriptural studies were, in fact, more accurate and of better quality than those of others claiming to be translators. The same is true for Zwingli. He too appreciated the difference between translation and interpretation. For more infomation, see Friedman, *Ancient Testimony*, p. 126ff and notes 10 and 11 of pages 8–9.

English students of Scripture in the sixteenth century were no more equipped to translate the Old Testament than was Luther. Though it was not G. Lloyd Jones' intention to prove that Tyndale, Coverdale, and many others usually considered fundamental to English Reformation Biblical scholarship, knew no Hebrew or knew too little for their knowledge to be of any true value, this is the negative result of his volume. Indeed, it would appear that few early English students of Hebrew had more than a passing familiarity with this language of Scripture. G. Lloyd Jones, *The Discovery of Hebrew in Tudor England: a third language* (Manchester, 1983) chap. 5, pages 115–43.

35. The importance of the theory of the Norman Yoke and its signifi-

cance to the political thought of this period is far greater than this short treatment of Gentlemen Ranters would indicate. The reader should see J. G. A. Pocock, *The Ancient Constitution and the Feudal Law: A Study of English Historical Thought in the Seventeenth Century* (Cambridge, England, 1957). Also, Christopher Hill, *Puritanism and Revolution*, chap. 3, pages 50–123.

36. John Tickell, *The Bottomless Pit Smoaking in Familisme. . . .* (London, 1651) p. 37–40.

37. Richard Coppin, *Truth's Testimony* (London, 1655) p. 18.

38. Richard Baxter, *Narrative of His Life and Times* (London, 1696) pt. I, p. 26, and the next citation is p. 76–77.

39. Ephraim Pagitt, *Heresiography* (London, 1645) p. 143.

40. Concerning the Proud Quakers, the reader might consult the following: Robert Barclay, *The Inner Life of the Religious Societies of the Commonwealth* (London, 1876); W. C. Braithwaite, *The Beginnings of Quakerism*, 2nd. ed. (Cambridge, England, 1955). Though not of Ranter origins and not usually associated with the Proud Quakers, James Naylor was one of the more colorful Quakers. See *DNB*.

41. George Fox, *Journals* (London, 1902) vol. 1, p. 47, and following citations are vol. 1, p. 199 and p. 95.

42. Samuel Fisher, *Baby Baptism Mere Baptism* (London, 1653) p. 511–12.

Bibliography

Primary Sources

A (anonymous). *The Plot Discovered and Counter Plotted.* 1641.

A. *A Description of 29 Sects Here in London.* 1641.

A. *A Nest of Serpents Discovered . . . Called Adamites.* 1641.

A. *A Description of a Sect Called Family of Love,* 1641.

A. *Hell Broke Loose.* 1646.

A. [J. F.] *John The Divine's Divinity.* 1649. (Pro Ranter).

A. [J. F.] *A Justification of the Mad Crew in their Ways and Principles.* 1650. (Pro-Ranter).

A. *Strange News From Newgate and the Old Bailey.* 1650.

A. *A Blow at the Root.* 1650.

A. *The Ranter's Recantation.* 1650.

A. *The Routing of the Ranters.* 1650.

A. *The Ranter's Religion.* 1650.

A. *The Arraignment and Trial of the Ranters, with a Declaration.* 1650.

A. [G. H.] *The Declaration of John Robins.* 1651.

A. *The Ranter's Creed.* 1651.

A. *Hell Broke Loose, or, The Notorious Design of the Wicked Ranters.* 1651.

A. *The Character of a Time Serving Saint.* 1652.

A. *The Ranter's Monster.* 1652.

A. *The Black and Terrible Warning Piece.* 1653.

A. [J. F.] *A New Proclamation.* 1653. (Anti-Ranter).

A. *A Total Rout, or a Brave Discovery of a Pack of Knaves and Drabs . . .* 1653.

A. [J. M.] *The Ranter's Last Sermon.* 1654.

A. *A list of Some of the Grand Blasphemers.* 1654.

A. *The Ranting Whore's Resolution.* 1663.

A. *The Ranting Rambler.* 1670.

Bauthumley, Jacob. *The Light and the Dark Sides of God.* 1650.

Baxter, Richard. *Reliquae Baxterianae.* London, 1896.

Calvin, John. *Omnia Opera.* Edited by Baum, et al. Brunswick, 1864–1900.

_____. *Treatises Against The Anabaptists and Against the Libertines.* Edited by Benjamin Wirt Farley. Grand Rapids, 1982.

BIBLIOGRAPHY

Clarkson (Claxton), Lawrence. *A Pilgrimage of Saints by Church Cast Out*. 1646. (No longer extant).

———. *Truth Released From Prison to its Former Liberty*. 1647.

———. *A General Charge of Impeachment of High Treason*. 1647.

———. *A Single Eye All Light, No Darkness*. 1650.

———. *The Right Devil Discovered*. 1659.

———. *Look About You For the Devil You Fear Is In You*. 1659. (Identical to above).

———. *The Quaker's Downfall*. 1659.

———. *The Lost Sheep Found*. 1660.

———. *A Paradisical Dialogue Between Reason and Faith*. 1660.

———. *A Wonder of Wonders*. 1660. (No longer extant).

Coppe, Abiezer. *Some Sweet Sips of Spiritual Wine*. 1649.

———. Preface to Coppin's *Divine Teachings*. 1649.

———. Preface to Anonymous, *A Justification* . . . 1650.

———. *The Fiery Flying Roll (and Roule,) Part I and II*. 1650.

———. *A Remonstrance*. 1651.

———. *Coppe's Return to the Ways of Truth*. 1651.

———. *A Character of a True Christian*. 1680.

Coppin, Richard. *Divine Teachings*. 1649

———. *Anti-Christ in Man*. 1649. (No longer extant).

———. *The Exaltation of all Things in Christ*. 1649. (Part of *Divine Teachings*).

———. *Man's Righteousness Examined*. 1652.

———. *Saul Smitten for Not Smiting Amalek*. 1653.

———. *A Man Child Born*. 1654.

———. *Truth's Testimony*. 1655.

———. *The Threefold State of a Christian*. 1655. (No longer extant).

———. *A Blow at the Serpent*. 1656.

———. *The Twenty Five Articles*. 1656. (Published along with *Michael Opposing* . . .)

———. *Crux Christi*. 1657.

———. *Michael Opposing the Dragon*. 1659.

Edwards, Thomas. *Gangraena* . . . 1646.

Ellis, Humphrey. *Pseudo-Christus*. 1651.

Farnsworth, Richard. *The Ranter's Principle and Deceits Discovered*. . . . 1655.

Fisher, Samuel. *Baby Baptism Mere Baptism*. 1653.

Foster, George. *The Sounding of the Last Trumpet*. 1650.

———. *The Pouring Fourth of the Last Vial*. 1650.

324

BIBLIOGRAPHY

Fowler, Christopher. *Daemonium Meridianum, Satan at Noon.* 1655.

Fox, George. *Journals.* London, 1902.

———. *Journals,* edited by J. L. Nickolls, Cambridge England, 1952.

Freeman, Captain Francis. *Eight Problems Propounded to the Cavalliers.* 1646.

———. *Light Vanquishing Darkness.* 1650.

Garland, Edward. *An Answer to a Printed Book Falsely Entitled A Blow at the Serpent. It being Truly a Blow of the Serpent.* 1656–7.

Garment, Joshua. *The Hebrews' Deliverance at Hand.* 1651.

Grant, Robert M. *Gnosticism: A Sourcebook of Heretical Writings.* New York, 1961.

Hickock, Richard. *A Testimony Against the People Called Ranters.* 1659.

Hippolytus. *Refutatio.* Edited by P. Wendland. Leipzig, 1916.

Holland, John. *The Smoke of the Bottomless Pit . . . or the Mad Crew.* 1651.

Hyde, Edward Jr. *A Wonder and Yet No Wonder.* 1650.

Man in the Moon. March 13–20, 1650.

Norwood, Captain Robert. *A Declaration or Testimony.* 1651.

———. *The Form of Excommunication.* 1651.

———. *The Case and Trial of Captain Robert Norwood, Now Prisoner in Newgate.* 1651.

———. *A Brief Discourse.* 1652.

———. *Proposals For the Propagation of the Faith.* 1652.

———. *A Pathway Unto England's Perfect Settlement.* 1653.

———. *An Additional Discourse.* 1653.

Pagitt, Ephraim. *Heresiography.* 1645, 1661.

Perfect Diurnall. March 11–18, 1650.

Pordage, John. *Truth Appearing Through the Clouds of Undeserved Scandal.* 1654

———. *Innocency Appearing Through the Dark Mists of Pretended Guilt.* 1655.

Reading, John. *The Ranter's Ranting.* 1650.

Rosewell, Walter. *The Serpent's Subtlety Discovered . . .* 1656.

Roulston, Gilbert. *The Ranter's Bible.* 1650.

Salmon, Joseph. *Anti-Christ in Man.* 1647.

———. *A Rout, A Rout.* 1649.

———. *Heights in Depths.* 1651.

Scobell, H. *A Collection of Acts and Ordinances . . .* London, 1658.

Sheppard, Samuel. *The Jovial Crew, or, The Devil Turned Ranter.* 1652.

Smith, Nigel, ed. *A Collection of Ranter Writings.* London, 1982.

BIBLIOGRAPHY

Stockes, Helen, ed. *Records of the Borough of Leicester*. 1923.

Stokes, Edward. *The Wiltshire Rant*. 1652.

Stubbs, M. *The Ranter's Declaration*. 1650.

Tany, Thomas. *I Proclaim . . . The Return of the Jews*. 1650.

––––––. *Theauraujohn His Theous-Ori Apokoliptical*. 1651.

––––––. *Theauraujohn His Aurora in Tranlogorum in Salem Gloria*. 1651.

––––––. *Nation's Right in Magna Charta*. 1651.

––––––. *Theauraujohn, High Priest to the Jews*. 1652.

––––––. *Theauraujohn Tani, His Second Part*. 1653.

––––––. *Theauraujohn, His Epitah*. 1653.

––––––. *Hear O'Earth*. 1654.

––––––. *Thau Ram Tonjah*. 1654.

Taylor, John. *Ranters of Both Sexes*. 1651.

Tickell, John. *The Bottomless Pit Smoaking in Familisme*. 1652.

Tilbury, Samuel. *Bloody News From the North*. 1650.

Thurloe, John. *The State Papers of John Thurloe*, edited by Birch. London, 1742.

Webb, Thomas. *Mr. Edward's Pen, No Slander*. 1646.

––––––. *A Mass of Malice Against Thomas Webb*. 1652. (No longer extant).

Whitlock Memorials, March 14, 1650.

Winstanley, Gerard. *A Vindication of those . . . Called Diggers*. 1649.

––––––. *A Testimony Against a People Called Ranters*. 1659.

––––––. *The Works of Gerrard Winstanley*. G. H. Sabine, ed. Ithica, New York, 1941.

Secondary Sources:

General Works of Reference:

Fortescue, G. K. ed., *Catalogue of the Pamphlets, Books, Newspapers, and Manuscripts Relating to the Civil War, the Commonwealth, and the Restoration, Collected by George Thomason, 1640–1661*. 2 vols. London, 1908.

Gillett, C. R. ed. *Catalogue of the McAlpine Collection of British History and Theology*, 5 vols. New York, 1927–1930.

Kennedy, J, W. A. Smith, A. L. Johnson, eds. *Dictionary of Anonymous and Pseudonymous English Literature*, 7 vols. Edinburgh, 1926–1934.

Pollard, A. W. and G. R. Redgrave, eds. *A Short Title Catalogue of Books Printed in England, Scotland, and Ireland . . . 1475–1640*, New York and London, 1906.

BIBLIOGRAPHY

Wing, Donald, ed. *A Short Title Catalogue of Books Printed in England, Scotland, and Ireland. . . . . 1641–1700.* 3 vols. New York, 1945–1951.

General Works:

Armytage, W. H. G. *Heavens Below: Utopian Experiments in England, 1560–1960.* Toronto, 1961.

Ball, Bryan W. *A Great Expectation, Eschatological Thought in English Protestantism to 1660.* Leiden, 1975.

Barbour, Hugh. *The Quakers in Puritan England.* New Haven, 1964.

Barclay, Robert. *The Inner Life of the Religious Societies of the Commonwealth.* London, 1876.

Beier, A. L. "Poor Relief in Warwickshire." *Past and Present,* n. 35 (December, 1966) pages 77–100.

Berens, L. H. *The Digger Movement in the Days of the Commonwealth.* London, 1906.

Bornkamm, H. *Luther and the Old Testament.* Philadelphia, 1969.

Brailsford, Henry N. *The Levellers and the English Revolution.* Stanford, 1971.

Braithwaite, W. C. *The Beginnings of Quakerism.* 2nd. ed. Cambridge, England, 1955

––––––. *The Second Period of Quakerism.* 2nd ed. Cambridge, England, 1961.

Brown, L. F. *The Political Activities of the Baptists and Fifth Monarchy Men in England During the Interregnum.* Washington, D.C., 1912.

Burkitt, F. C. *The Religion of the Manichees.* Cambridge, England, 1925.

Burrage, C. *The Early English Dissenters.* Cambridge, England, 1912.

Capp, B. S. *The Fifth Monarchy Men: a Study in 17th Century Millenarianism.* London, 1972.

Christianson, Philip K. *Reformers and Babylon: Apocalyptic Visions from the Reformation to the Eve of the Civil War.* Toronto, 1978.

Cohn, Norman. *The Pursuit of the Millenium.* New York, 1961.

Cole, Alan. "The Quakers and the English Revolution." *Crisis in Europe, 1560–1660,* p. 341–358. Trevor Astin, ed. London, 1980.

Cole, R. C. and M. E. Moody, *The Dissenting Tradition: Essays for Leland H. Carlson.* Columbus, Ohio, 1975.

Collinson, Patrick. *The Elizabethan Puritan Movement.* 1967.

BIBLIOGRAPHY

———. *Godly People. Essays on English Puritanism.* London, 1983.

Daitches, David. *The King James Version of the English Bible.* Chicago, 1941.

Daniels, George W. *The Early English Cotton Industry.* Manchester, 1920.

Davies, Godfrey. *The Early English Stuarts, 1603–1660.* Oxford, 1959.

Dickens, A. G. *Lollards and Protestants in the Diocese of York, 1509–1559.* Oxford, 1959.

Duchesne-Guillemin, J. *Zoroastre.* Paris, 1948.

———. *The Western Response to Zoroastre.* Oxford, 1958.

de Faye, E. *Gnostiques et Gnosticism.* 2nd ed. Paris, 1925.

Figgis, J. N. *Studies of Political Thought from Gerson to Grotius, 1414–1625.* 2nd ed. Cambridge, England, 1925.

Firth, C. H. *Cromwell's Army: A History of the English Soldier during the Civil Wars, the Commonwealth and the Protectorate.* 4th ed. Oxford, 1962.

Firth, Katharine R. *The Apocalyptic Tradition in Reformation Britain, 1530–1645.* Oxford, 1979.

Frank, J. *The Levellers.* Cambridge, Mass., 1955.

Frederichs, Julius. *De Secte der Loisten of Antwerpsche Libertijnen. (1525–1545): Eligius Pruystinck (Loy de Schaliedekker) en zijne aanhangers.* Ghent, 1891.

Friedman, Jerome. *Michael Servetus: A Case Study in Total Heresy,* Geneva. 1978.

———. *The Most Ancient Testimony: Sixteenth Century Christian Hebraica in the Age of Renaissance Nostalgia.* Athens, Ohio, 1983.

Gibb, A. *John Lilburne, the Leveller.* London, 1947.

Goodenough, E. R. *By Light, By Light. The Mystic Gospel of Hellenistic Judaism.* Oxford, 1935.

Gordon, Alexander. *Heads of English Unitarian History.* London, 1895.

Grant, Robert M. *Gnosticism and Early Christianity.* New York, 1959.

Greaves, Richard L. *Saints and Rebels: Seven Nonconformists in Stuart England.* Macon, Ga. 1985.

———. with Zaller, R. L. eds., *A Biographical Dictionary of British Radicals in the Seventeenth Century.* 3 vols. Brighton, 1982–1984.

Greenslade, S. L. ed. *The Cambridge History of the Bible: The Reformation to the Present Day.* London, 1963.

Guarnieri, Romana. "Il movimento del Libero Spirito," *Archivo Italiano per la storia della pietà.* 4 (1965).

Haller, William. *Liberty and Reformation in the Puritan Revolution.* New York, 1955.

328

———. with Godfrey Davies, ed. *The Leveller Tracts.* New York, 1944.

———. *Tracts on Liberty in the Puritan Revolution.* 3 vols. New York, 1934.

———. *The Rise of Puritanism.* New York, 1938.

Hamilton, Alastair. *The Family of Love.* Cambridge, England, 1981.

Hayes, T. Wilson. *Winstanley the Digger.* Cambridge, Mass. 1979.

Herrup, Cynthia B. "Law and Morality in Seventeenth-Century England," *Past and Present,* n. 106, p. 102–123.

Hill, Christopher. *The World Turned Upside Down. Radical Ideas During the English Revolution.* London, 1972; 1975.

———, with Barry Raey and William Lamont. *The World of the Muggletonians.* London, 1983.

———. *The Religion of Gerrard Winstanley.* Past and Present Supplement n. 5. Oxford, 1978.

———. *Puritanism and Revolution.* New York, 1974.

———. *Society and Puritanism in Pre-Revolutionary England.* New York, 1964.

———. *Antichrist in Seventeeth Century England.* London, 1971.

———. "The Muggletonians." *Past and Present.* n. 104 (August, 1984) p. 153–158.

Hirst, M. E. *The Quakers in Peace and War.* London, 1923.

Huehns, Gertrude. *Antinomianism in English History with Special Reference to the Period, 1640–1660.* London, 1951.

Hutin, Serge. *Les disciples Anglais de Jacob Boehme aux XVIIe e XvIIIe siecles.* Paris, 1960.

James, Margaret. *Social Problems and Policy During the Puritan Revolution, 1640–1660.* London, 1930.

Jonas, Hans. *The Gnostic Religion.* 2nd ed. Boston, 1960.

Jones, G. Lloyd. *The Discovery of Hebrew in Tudor England: a third language.* Manchester, 1983.

Jones, Rufus M. *George Fox: an Autobiography.* Philadelphia, 1903.

———. *Studies in Mystical Religion.* New York, 1923.

———. *Spiritual Reformers in the 16th and 17th Centuries.* London, 1914.

———. *The Quakers in the American Colonies.* New York, London, 1923.

———. *The Later Periods of Quakerism.* London, 1921.

———. *Mysticism and Democracy in the English Commonwealth.* Cambridge, Mass., 1932.

Katz, David S. *Philosemitism and the Re-Admission of Jews to England.* Oxford, 1982.

Kraeling, E. G. *The Old Testament Since the Reformation.* London, 1955.

BIBLIOGRAPHY

Lambert, M. D. *Medieval Heresy, Popular Movements from Bogomil to Hus.* London, 1977.

Lamont, W. M. *Godly Rule: Politics and Religion 1603–1660,* Cambridge, England, 1969.

———. "The Muggletonians, 1652–1979. A Vertical Approach." *Past and Present,* n. 99 (May, 1983) p. 22–40.

———. "A Rejoinder." *Past and Present.* n. 104 (August, 1984) p. 159–163.

Leff, Gordon. *Heresy in the Later Middle Ages.* 2 vols. Manchester, 1967.

Leisegang, H. *Die Gnosis.* 4th ed. Stuttgart, 1955.

Leonard, E. M. *The Early History of English Poor Relief.* Cambridge, England, 1900; 1965.

Lipson, Ephraim. *The History of the Woolens and Worsted Industries.* London, 1921.

Lerner, Robert E. *The Heresy of the Free Spirit in the Middle Ages.* Berkeley, 1972.

Lloyd, Arnold. *Quaker Social History; 1669–1738,* London, 1950.

Lubac, Henri de. *Exegese Mèdièval; Les Quatre Sens de l'Ecriture.* 4 vols. Paris, 1959.

MacPherson, C. B. *The Political Theory of Possessive Individualism.* Oxford, 1962.

Manning, Brian. *The English People & the English Revolution.* 1976.

Manseli, Raoul. *Spirituali e Beghini in Provenza.* Rome, 1959.

McDonnell, Ernest W. *The Beguines and Beghards in Medieval Culture.* New Brunswick, 1954.

McGregor, Frank J. *The Ranters.* Oxford University B. Litt. Degree Thesis. November 1968, n. 1434.

———, with B. Raey. *Radical Religion in the English Revolution.* Oxford, 1984.

McLacklan, H. J. *Socinianism in 17th Century England.* Oxford, 1951.

Miller, W. and Jared W. Scudder. *Wessel Gansfort: His Life and Writings.* New York/London, 1917.

Morley, Iris. *A Thousand Lives: An Account of the English Revolutionary Movement, 1660–1685.* London, 1954.

Morton, A. L. *The World of the Ranters.* London, 1970.

Moss, Jean D. *"Godded with God": Hendrik Niclaes and His Family of Love.* Philadelphia, 1981.

Mullett, Michael. *Radical Religious Movements in Early Modern Europe.* London, 1980.

New, John F. H. *Anglican and Puritan: The Basis of Their Opposition, 1558–1640.* Stanford, 1964.

BIBLIOGRAPHY

Nuttal, G. F. *The Holy Spirit in Puritan Faith and Experience.* Oxford, 1946.

————. *Studies in Christian Enthusiasm: Illustrations from Early Quakerism.* Pendle Hill, 1948.

Oberman, Heiko. *Forerunners of the Reformation.* New York/Chicago, 1966.

Obolensky, D. *The Bogomils.* Cambridge England, 1948.

Oldenburg, Zoe. *Massacre at Montségur:A History of the Albigensian Crusade.* Translated by Peter Green. New York, 1962.

Payne, E. A. *The Baptists of Berkshire Through Three Centuries.* London, 1951.

Pease, T. C. *The Leveller Movement.* Washington, 1916.

Petegorsky, David. *Leftwing Democracy in the English Civil War.* London, 1940.

Peters, Edward. *Heresy and Authority in Medieval Europe.* Philadelphia, 1980.

Pétrement, S. *Le dualism chez Platon, les gnostiques et les manichées,* Paris, 1947.

Philips, Dayton. *Beguines in Medieval Strasbourg.* Stanford, 1941.

Pocock, J. G. A. *The Ancient Constitution and the Feudal Law: A Study of English Historical Thought in the Seventeenth Century.* Cambridge, England, 1957.

Preus, J. S. *From Shadow to Promise; Old Testament Interpretation of Scripture from Augustine to the Young Luther.* Cambridge, Mass., 1969.

Puech, H. C. *Le Manichéisme, son fondatuer, sa doctrine.* Paris, 1949.

Quispel, G. *Gnosis als Weltreligion.* Zurich, 1951.

Reay, Barry. *The Quakers and the English Revolution.* London, 1985.

Reeves, Margerie. *The Influence of Prophecy in the Late Middle Ages.* Oxford, 1969.

Rhijn, Maarten van. *Wessel Gansfort.* The Hague, 1917.

Rogers, James E. Thorold. *History of Agricultures and prices in England.* 7 vols. Oxford, 1866-1902.

Rogers, Philip G. *The Fifth Monarchy Men.* Oxford, 1966.

Runciman, Steven. *The Medieval Manichee, A Study of the Christian Dualist Heresy.* Cambridge, England, 1947.

————. *History of the First Bulgarian Empire.* London, 1930.

Russel, Jeffrey B. *Dissent and Reform in the Early Middle Ages.* Berkeley, 1965.

————. *Religious Dissent in the Middle Ages.* New York/London, 1971.

Ryland, L. G. *The Beginning of Gnostic Christianity.* London, 1940.

BIBLIOGRAPHY

Savini, Savino. *Il Catarismo italiano ed i suovi vescovi nei seculo xiii e xiv.* Florence, 1958.

Schenck, William. *The Concern for Social Justice in the Puritan Revolution.* London/New York/Toronto, 1948.

Schlatter, R. B. *The Social Ideas of Religious Leaders, 1660–1688.* London, 1940.

Scholem, Gershom. *Sabbetai Sevi, The Mystical Messiah.* Princeton, 1973.

Schwarz, W. *Principles and Problems of Biblical Translation.* Cambridge, England, 1955.

Sharenkoff, V. N. *A Study Of Manichaeanism in Bulgaria.* New York, 1927.

Shaw, Howard C. *The Levellers.* London, 1968.

Silver, Abba H. *A History of Messianic Speculation in Israel.* New York, 1927; Boston, 1959.

Smalley, B. *The Study of the Bible in the Middle Ages.* 2nd ed. London, 1952.

Söderberg, H. *La Religion des Cathares.* Uppsala, 1949.

Solt, L. F. *Saints in Ams: Puritanism and Democracy in Cromwell's Army.* Stanford, 1959.

Spicq, C. *Escuisse d'une histoire de l'exégèse latine au Moyen Age.* Paris, 1944.

Spinka, Matthew. *A History of the Christian Balkans.* Chicago, 1933.

Stephen, Sir James. *A History of the Criminal Law in England.* 3 vols. London, 1883.

Stephens, Sir Leslie, and Sir Sidney Lee, eds. *The Dictionary of National Biography.* 21 vols, plus supplements. Oxford, 1917+

Strayer, Joseph R. *The Albigensian Crusade.* New York, 1971.

Tait, Sir James. *Lancashire Quarter Session Records.* London, Manchester, 1917.

Taylor, A. *The History of the English General Baptists.* 2 vols. London, 1818.

Thomas, Keith. *Religion and the Decline of Magic.* London, 1971.

———. "Women and the Civil War Sects." *Crisis in Europe, 1560–1660,* p. 317–340. Trevor Astin, ed. London, 1980. First published 1965.

Tindall, W. Y. *John Bunyan, Mechanic Preacher.* New York, 1934.

Toon, Peter ed. *Puritans, the Millenium, and the Future of Israel: Puritan Eschatology 1600–1660.* Cambridge, 1970.

Wakefield, Walter L. *Heresy, Crusade, and Inquisition in Southern France.* Berkeley, 1974.

Walzer, M. *The Revolution of the Saints: A Study in the Origins of Radical Politics.* Cambridge, Mass., 1965; London, 1966.

BIBLIOGRAPHY

Whittaker, T. *The Neoplatonists*. 2nd ed. Cambridge, England, 1918.

Wilbur, Earl Morse. *A History of Unitarianism*. 2 vols. Cambridge, Mass. 1945.

_____. *The Socinian-Unitarian Movement: A Bibliography*. Rome, 1950.

Wilson, J. F. *Pulpit in Parliament: Puritanism During the English Civil Wars 1640–1648*. Princeton, 1969.

Wilson, R. McL. *The Gnostic Problem: A Study of the Relations Between Hellenistic Judaism and the Gnostic Heresy*. London, 1958.

Windengren, G. *The Great Vohu Manah and the Apostle of God. Studies in Manichaean and Iranian Religion*. Uppsala, 1945.

_____. *Mesopotamian Elements in Manichaeism. Studies in Manichaean, Mandean, and Syrian-Gnostic Religion*. Uppsala–Leipzig, 1946.

_____. *Mani and Manichaeism*. London, 1965; New York, 1966.

Wolf, Lucien. *Menasseh ben Israel's Mission to Oliver Cromwell*. London, 1901.

Wolfe, D. *Leveller Manifestos of the Puritan Revolution*. New York, 1944.

Woodhouse, A. S. P. *Puritanism and Liberty*. London, 1938.

Zagorin, Perez. *A History of Political Thought in the English Revolution*. London. 1954.

Index

INDEX